A Conspiracy
of Optimism

Paul W. Hirt

A Conspiracy of Optimism

Management of the National Forests since World War Two

University of Nebraska Press

Lincoln and London

Publication of
this book was aided by a
grant from the
Andrew W. Mellon Foundation.
Library of Congress
Cataloging in Publication Data. Hirt, Paul W., 1954–
A conspiracy of
optimism: management of the national forests since
World War Two /
Paul W. Hirt.   p.   cm. – (Our sustainable future; v.6)
Includes bibliographical
references (p.   ) and index. ISBN 0-8032-2375-7 (cl.)
ISBN 0-8032-7288-x (pa.)
1. Forest reserves – United
States – Management – History – 20th century.
2. Forest policy – United
States – History – 20th century. 3. United States.
Forest Service –
History – 20th century. I. Title. II. Series.
SD426.H57   1994
333.75'0973'09045 – dc20
94-3858 CIP

For Linda
and for my parents

Contents

Illustrations

Figures

Maps

ix

Tables

Photographs

Acknowledgments

As with any project of this size, one's debts add up. My greatest debt is to my wife, Linda, who shares with me a love of the national forests and a commitment to preserving their beauty and biological wealth for future generations. Too numerous to name but too important not to mention are all my friends who over the years have bounced down primitive roads with me to national forest trailheads, launched canoes with me into clear, cold mountain lakes, scrambled up ridges to join me in viewing the lay of the land, and helped me pore over maps and management plans in an attempt to grasp and maybe help direct the future of these priceless national forestlands. You know who you are. This book is also for you.

I began formal research for this book in 1988 as a graduate student in the Department of History at the University of Arizona. My debts to my scholarly mentors at the University of Arizona are deep and my gratitude profound. My advisers for this project in the History Department, Douglas Weiner and Paul Carter, provided not only unerring guidance but also a long leash, for which I am grateful. Professors Helen Ingram and Frank Gregg in political science and natural resources administration initiated me into the academic world of environmental policy and management, adding valuable interdisciplinary dimension to my understanding of public forestry. Their continuous support — moral, intellectual, and even financial — has been invaluable. Other mentors in the History Department who helped sharpen my analytical skills and supported me in various ways over the years include Roger Nichols, Donna Guy, Karen Anderson, Leonard Dinnerstein, and Michael Schaller. A significant debt also goes to my peers who shared with me the intellectual trial-by-fire hazing ritual known as graduate school. They critiqued my early papers, cheering me on while challenging my analysis. I couldn't have had better friends and colleagues. My thanks especially to Allen Broussard, Leigh Pruneau, Penny Waterstone, Gingie Scharff, Renee Obrecht-Como, and Mark Dyreson.

The historical records necessary for recounting the tale of national forest management this century are voluminous and widely scattered but generally accessible to scholars. Without question, the most valuable archive for this project was the Forest History Society (FHS) holdings in Durham, North Carolina. The FHS manages an incredible collection of primary source documents and regular scholarly monographs. It is also the most "user friendly" archive I have worked in. I am grateful to Harold Steen, Executive Director of the Forest History Society, for his support and for the Bell Research Fellowship the Society granted me to help defray the costs of travel to the archive. I am also grateful to Cheryl Oakes, the FHS archivist, for her generous and enthusiastic cooperation during the month I spent there.

The Denver Public Library holds an invaluable collection of primary source documents in the history of conservation of natural resources in the West, including collections of Wilderness Society files, which were especially useful to this study. Various offices of the U.S. Forest Service hold valuable documents too. I am especially grateful to Terry West, historian at the Washington Office of the Forest Service, for allowing me unrestricted access to his collection of historical materials. (He also suggested to me the apt and provocative title for this book.) Gerald Williams, Forest Service historian in the Northwest, gave me access to historical collections under his care at the Regional Office in Portland, and a small army of helpful employees at other regional offices, forest supervisors' offices, and district rangers' offices opened their filing cabinets and their hearts to me. To all of them I am grateful. The Forest Service is going through troubling times, yet agency employees have been remarkably open and welcoming of scholarly scrutiny. This is a good sign.

While in the form of a finished doctoral dissertation, this manuscript was read and commented on by John Davis and Dale Turner (two perspicacious conservationists and editors — and good friends to boot), by Arnold Bolle (dean emeritus of the University of Montana School of Forestry — a long-time reformer, scholar, and humanitarian), by Bob Zahner (a retired professor of forest ecology and now a full-time conservation activist), and by my mother, Mitzi Hirt (who made valuable criticisms and editorial suggestions despite her bias toward the author). Any clarity in the prose is due in great measure to the especially close reading John Davis and Dale Turner gave the manuscript. A second incarnation of the manuscript was then read by historian William G. Robbins at Oregon State University, historian Donald Worster at the University of Kansas, and Professor Richard Behan of Northern Arizona University's School of Forestry. The comments and criticisms of all three aided me immeasurably. Ecology Professor Steven Hamburg and historian John G. Clark at the University of Kansas also commented on portions of the manuscript, and I am grateful to them and many others who have offered suggestions on bits and pieces of this study. Ann Waters skillfully edited the final manuscript with a fine-tooth comb, untangling remaining snarls.

The technical language of forestry reduces the practice of forestry to simple, abstract concepts like "harvest," thereby obscuring the complexity and emotive dimensions of physical events like large-scale clearcutting. Photographic images provide an important grounding for such abstractions. To that end, I thank Trygve Steen, professor of biology at Portland State University, and Dale A. Burk, former newspaperman for the *Missoulian* (now a publisher in Stevensville, Montana) for their excellent and evocative images that provide a needed grounding for discussions of forestry.

I especially want to thank the Rockefeller Foundation and the Program in Nature, Culture, and Technology at the University of Kansas for providing me an uninterrupted year of research and writing amid a stimulating intellectual community. Every scholar/writer should have such an opportunity. My thanks especially to Donald Worster, director of the Program in Nature, Culture, and Technology, for keeping moral questions at the forefront of humanistic inquiry. Last but not least, my gratitude to James Pritchard, Diane Debinski, Brian and Chris Black, Leos Jelecek, Liz Barnhill, and Janet Crow for their support and friendship in the Land of Oz.

Introduction: An Overview of the Issues

An unprecedented controversy currently rages over the U.S. Forest Service's management of America's national forests. While leaders in the Forest Service claim to be responsible caretakers of the land and servants of the people, interest groups of every stripe concerned about national forest management paint another picture. The timber industry accuses the agency of gross inefficiency. Ranchers complain that the agency is on a campaign to put them out of business. Wildlife advocates and state fish and game agencies charge that Forest Service management practices are destroying the nation's best wildlife habitat and forcing dozens of species to the brink of extinction. Cities bemoan the agency's failure to protect their municipal water supplies from degradation due to logging and grazing in the high mountain watersheds of national forests. Conservationists accuse the agency of failing to manage its resources sustainably or to equitably balance the various "multiple uses" of the national forests. Wilderness advocates say the Forest Service is nothing but a logging agent obsessed with commodifying nature and subjugating all wild land to commercial management. Economists characterize the Forest Service as a bloated bureaucracy motivated mainly by self-aggrandizement.[1] Most significant of all, many agency officers, including forest supervisors and district rangers, have recently announced that they feel the Forest Service is not meeting its land stewardship mandate and has become an agency "out of control."[2] In fact, employee dissatisfaction with agency practices became so widespread in the 1980s that for the first time in the history of the Forest Service large portions of the staff openly rebelled.[3]

This atmosphere of external vilification and internal dissention is a world apart from that of forty years ago when the Forest Service enjoyed a high degree of public accolade and organizational cohesion. Then, scholars cited the agency as a model of public-spirited bureaucratic efficiency.[4] Today, the typical view of the Forest Service might be exemplified by the following quote from a March 1990 article in the London *Economist:* "today the service finds itself assailed from all sides and losing its leadership role in the 191 [million] acres of forests it professes to know best. . . . Compounding the problem, is a stultifying, almost Stalinesque bureaucracy, demoralised by the service's changing reputation. There are signs of internal revolt. One forestry professor says his former students call up to say 'we're raping the woods.' "[5] How and why did this sense of near universal dissatisfaction with the Forest Service evolve? What are the bases of these various complaints, which at times seem so contradictory? Has the Forest Service been a good land steward? These are the issues this book seeks to illuminate.

• • •

America's national forests represent a grand experiment in the public ownership of land and natural resources. The national forest system now comprises 191 million acres — one-tenth of the surface area of the United States. Although the bulk of them are located in the West, they extend from the hilly, deciduous forests of New England to the rainforests of Puerto Rico, from the deep canyons and rocky cliffs of the Southwestern basin and range country to the living glaciers of the Olympic Mountains of Washington, from white-faced, cloud-shrouded Denali to the tropical tangles of the Hawaiian Islands. Spectacular river systems such as the Colorado, Rio Grande, Snake, Missouri, and Allegheny emerge from national forest lands. Approximately 50 percent of the water that falls as rain or snow in the West falls on national forest land. Those waters quench the thirst and support the industry and agriculture of thousands of communities and tens of millions of people. The national forests are home to many kinds of wildlife, including grizzly bears, mountain lions, elk, salmon, bald eagles, and spotted owls. They provide important habitat for two-thirds of the big game in the West and for hundreds of species of plants and animals currently at risk of extinction: The federal government in 1990 listed over 560 U.S. species as threatened or endangered; another 1,000 "candidate" species awaited listing or were categorized as sensitive. More than a third of all those depended on national forests for food and shelter.[6]

The national forests touch the lives of just about everyone in America, although in often unrecognized ways. In 1988 the Forest Service calculated that the lands under its jurisdiction supported 260 million "visitor-days" of recreational use that year, including picnickers, hikers, backpackers, hunters, boaters, anglers, bird-watchers, and sightseers — more visitor use than any other federal land system in the United States. National forests also play a significant role in rural economies. Hundreds of timber-based communities, especially in the West, depend significantly on the national forests for a supply of logs. Similarly, many rural towns in the Great Basin and in the Southwest cater to a livestock industry that makes widespread use of the public rangelands, including the national forests, for a supply of forage. Decisions about how to manage this vast domain profoundly affect millions of people and other species of life, making forest management one of the most significant environmental policy issues facing the nation.

The origins of the national forests go back a century, to 1891, when the United States Congress authorized the president to set aside portions of America's vast federal land holdings in the West as forest reserves. What stood out as significant in the 1891 act was the decision to retain some federal lands in public ownership. Such a policy attracted strong opposition at that time. The prevailing governmental policy was "disposal" — getting federal lands into private ownership as quickly as feasible.[7] This disposal policy had its genesis at America's birth. Political philosophers like Thomas Jefferson envisioned private land ownership as a bulwark against tyranny. In a largely agrarian society, owning one's own farm — one's means of livelihood — would help assure personal liberty, dignity, and economic security. This idea made sense at the time, but circumstances changed.

A century of unswerving government dedication to the principle of private ownership following America's revolution did not eliminate the problems of economic insecurity and concentration of wealth. In a relatively unrestrained market economy, nineteenth-century captains of industry like John D. Rockefeller and Frederick Weyerhaeuser could and did curtail the opportunities, independence, and economic security of others while pursuing their own visions of life, liberty, and happiness. In addition, the unrestrained use of private property by wealthy elites often led to severe environmental deterioration, such as denuded landscapes and polluted rivers, that affected whole communities and sometimes whole regions. This in turn led to a land-use reform movement. Land-use reformers in the mid- to late-nineteenth century focused their criticisms on (1) the concentration of land ownership in the hands of powerful corporations; (2) the depletion of natural resources; (3) the damaging effects of exploitive logging, mining, grazing, and agriculture on soil and water and on the productive capacity of the land; (4) rural instability caused by migratory industries that would exploit a resource and then move on; and (5) waste and inefficiency in natural resource use. Scientists, civic organizations, intellectuals, and others appealed to the federal government to take an active role in addressing some of these issues. Slowly, with a great deal of hedging and controversy, Congress endorsed the idea that some of the nation's lands should be retained in "public ownership" and managed in the "public interest" as a buffer against complete privatization of all land.

Eventually, Congress authorized the president to establish forest reserves in 1891. Congress later dubbed the reserves "national forests" and established the U.S. Forest Service to manage them. This experiment in public forest ownership began, in general, with marginally productive or largely inaccessible forest lands that states, private industries, and settlers had passed over. Even though road construction, new technology, and changed market conditions have rendered increasing amounts of the national forests commercially accessible over the intervening years, the national forests, with a few regional exceptions, remain on the margins of commercial viability. Less than one-third of the national forest lands today are considered suitable for commercial logging — 59 million acres out of a total of 191 million.[8] Even in the early 1970s when the Forest Service was still grandly optimistic about which of its lands could (and should) support commercial logging activities, it identified only 87 million acres suitable for timber production. That translated into only 17 percent of the total commercial forest land base in the United States — and not the best 17 percent in terms of biological productivity. For example, almost a third of the "commercial" timberland managed by the Forest Service was rated in the poorest productivity class. Out of 13.4 million acres nationwide in the most productive class, only 2.9 million were in national forests.[9] Even in the peak years of production, the national forests have never contributed more than a fifth of the nation's total domestic timber production — usually less than that.[10] Because these lands are for the most part marginally productive, some form of federal subsidy has usually been required to maintain commercial timber harvesting.[11]

Despite their second-class economic status, the national forests are extremely valuable as watersheds, especially for the major rivers in the West, and as wildlife habitat for most of the big game in the nation, as natural buffers against environmental exploitation, and as a reserve supply of natural resources in the event that private land owners fail to produce on a sustainable (or adequate) basis. Whether economically productive or marginal, the fundamental purposes of the national forests have remained largely unchanged since the turn of the century: to establish a permanent system of publicly owned forests managed by scientific experts trained to protect the forests from destruction while providing a sustained yield of renewable products and services, including wood, clean water, livestock forage, wildlife habitat, and recreation opportunities. This is a fine idealistic vision — and a tall order. But the prominent forest management controversies of today suggest that these laudable goals may not have been fulfilled.

How did the Forest Service image as a crusading defender of the public interest evolve into a reputation for bureaucratic mismanagement? One reason is that the policy structure for the Forest Service essentially guarantees controversy because it embodies contradictory mandates: first, the agency is directed to provide the public with such products and services as timber, forage, water, fish and game, and recreational opportunities, many of which come into conflict with each other. Second, the agency is supposed to regulate public uses so that they do not impair forest health and productivity for future generations or degrade nonmarket values and cultural amenities such as soil, nongame wildlife, wilderness, scenic beauty, and historical/archeological sites. This dual charge to harmonize a mix of uses while preserving the biological integrity and esthetics of the forest has been difficult to implement. Historically the agency has received no clear guidance for how to reconcile competing demands or how to set priorities when production and preservation come into conflict. Perhaps ironically, this lack of guidance is largely due to the lobbying of agency leaders themselves, who have consistently opposed attempts by Congress to circumscribe their management discretion. Agency leaders since the turn of the century have insisted that "scientific management" by enlightened professional foresters would be able to determine the public interest and to resolve conflicts appropriately. This attitude contributed to an insular, self-confident bureaucratic culture that to user groups appeared inflexible and patronizing.[12]

Another major reason for the declining reputation of the Forest Service has been its domination by professionals trained to harvest timber and its enthusiastic dedication to that activity after World War Two. Prior to the war, private forests supplied about 95 percent of total national wood products needs, so the Forest Service sat at the periphery of the timber market. Its functions primarily involved custodial activities on the national forests: cooperative fire, insect, and disease protection, reforestation, and the promotion of the idea that forests were a "crop." By the 1940s, the gradual exhaustion of private supplies of timber in the last great lumber frontier, the Pacific Northwest, created a growing market for timber from the national forests, as logging companies increasingly turned to public lands to supplement their dwindling supplies.[13] Material production for the war accelerated this trend. Then, after the war, a number of simultaneous social developments contributed to an explosion in lumber demand. Millions of soldiers returned home from Europe and the Pacific in search of jobs and housing, and their growing families caused a postwar baby boom and the rapid spread of suburbanization. The demand for housing skyrocketed, fueled by increasing economic prosperity and the release of consumer pressures that had been restrained for years by the Depression of the 1930s and by wartime rationing. The federal government declared a national housing emergency and sought diligently to increase lumber production on both private lands and the national forests. The Forest Service, with a staff trained to manage forests for wood production ("silviculture"), accepted the challenge gratefully and with zeal, rapidly accelerating sales of timber to private industry. Timber sale purchasers — who actually perform the logging and pay the Forest Service for what they remove — were never quite satisfied with agency logging stipulations or the quantity or timing of national forest timber sales. Thus, the Forest Service's most immediate constituency remained disgruntled and often became antagonistic. At the same time, other user groups became increasingly disappointed with the effects of logging on fish and wildlife, water, recreation, and other values.

As timber demands accelerated in the 1950s, the simultaneous burgeoning of an outdoor recreation movement led to growing conflicts. Rather than making the difficult but necessary decision to regulate uses to moderate levels, the Forest Service tried to maximize production to meet every group's demands, especially the timber industry's. When facing conflicts among users or situations that called for a choice between production and preservation, managers adopted instead the optimistic view that choices did not really have to be made yet if foresters simply applied more intensive management. "Intensive management" was a special phrase adopted by foresters in the agency and in the timber industry that signified the lavish application of capital, labor, and technology to increase the commercial productivity of forests. It reflected a growing enthusiasm for reordering nature on a massive scale to maximize its social utility. Intensive management was essentially a defensive maneuver by the agency, a flexible collection of "techno-fix" theories and practices that allowed foresters to continually say yes to ever-increasing demands for commodities like timber while simultaneously promising to protect soil, water, wildlife, esthetics, and wilderness. Ultimately and tragically, pursuing intensive management allowed the Forest Service to avoid making tough choices and to dodge responsibility for the accumulating deterioration of forest ecosystems. In time, the unrealistic promises and overextended commitment to intensive management would become the agency's Achilles' heel.

World War Two thus represents a major transition period in the history of the Forest Service. The move to intensive management and rapidly expanded production that began with the war and peaked in the 1960s is crucial to understanding the foundation of current national forest management controversies. This study therefore concentrates on the period 1945–60. Subsequent events of the 1960s to 1980s reiterated patterns established in the 1940s and 1950s; and the milieu of reform gripping the agency today can be interpreted as a rejection of the ideologies and practices that became dominant after World War Two. In terms of political culture, this fifteen-year postwar period was dominated by Cold War concerns that strongly influenced federal natural resources policy. As America attempted to rearm and rebuild its allies and bolster its own armaments to contain communism, the importance of maintaining a rising gross national product took on added significance. Ultimate victory in the Cold War, it seemed, would go to the nations with the strongest economies. Policymakers and influential opinion molders constantly reiterated that America *needed* to develop its resources at the quickest pace possible in order for freedom to survive. Additionally, Americans thought that communism only flourished where grinding poverty and social inequities prevailed; therefore, prosperity widely distributed (a home in the suburb for every American family that wanted one) would help preserve democracy. Maximum material production thus became a national duty and a moral imperative. Perhaps the greatest expression of this ideology is found in the voluminous *Resources for Freedom* publication of the President's Materials Policy Commission established by Harry Truman. The following passage from volume I, *Foundations for Growth and Security,* is indicative:

> The United States, once criticized as the creator of a crassly materialistic order of things, is today throwing its might into the task of keeping alive the spirit of Man and helping beat back from the frontiers of the free world everywhere the threats of force and of a new Dark Age which rise from the Communist nations. In defeating this barbarian violence moral values will count most, but they must be supported by an ample materials base. Indeed, the interdependence of moral and material values has never been so completely demonstrated as today.[14]

The authors of *Resources for Freedom* then advocated maximum production of lumber and pulpwood (as well as all other natural resources) in the interests of national security.

As the Forest Service strove to increase material production, its relative importance in the federal bureaucracy grew, as did its work force and budget. All this growth was based on promises to increase outputs and services. Foresters came to believe that their overriding purpose was not so much to protect the national forests but rather to develop their resources to meet the material needs of the American public. They saw their mission as one of overcoming limits, not establishing them. A consciously disseminated "can-do" technocratic optimism imbued the Forest Service with a sense of mission and excitement. This ideological buoyancy found resonance and encouragement in popular American attitudes at that time celebrating prosperity and progress. In a sense, Americans became self-delusive in their enthusiasm for unending economic growth and technological manipulation of natural systems in pursuit of wealth and national power. The Forest Service was equally an advocate and a victim of this ideology.[15]

The scale and pace of changes in national forest management after the war was truly remarkable. Road construction and logging accelerated at breakneck speed. Under continuous pressure to increase timber harvests, the Forest Service engaged in an unprecedented road-building program to open up more and more backcountry. In this fifteen-year period, approximately 65,000 miles of additional roads were bulldozed into the national forests, including new federal, state, and county roads. More than half were specifically timber access roads. (Incredibly, there are 342,000 miles of roads in the national forests today; many forests average more than a mile of road for every square mile of forest. The entire interstate highway system, in contrast, boasts only about 50,000 miles. The Forest Service has been called "the world's largest socialized road-building company.")[16]

But even this did not satiate demand. Other ways of achieving and justifying higher timber harvests were required in order to keep apace with market demands. Each time the agency reached or exceeded its annual allowable cut for a "working circle" (based on sustained yield considerations), it would reevaluate the assumptions used to determine that allowable cut and usually raise the harvest ceiling. Assumptions most often subject to revision included the number of years thought to be necessary to regenerate a mature forest after logging, the number of acres the agency could successfully protect from fire, insects, and disease, the amount of forestland considered "suitable" for timber production, and the estimated amount of wood fiber volume in the suitable timber base.[17] Another method for increasing allowable harvest levels was to replace selective cutting with clearcutting as the dominant harvest technique, although the Forest Service found silvicultural rationales for doing so. It is illuminating to trace over time the rise and fall of allowable cut determinations. Portrayed as an objective, technical calculation tied to sustainability considerations, allowable cut levels and the assumptions that back them up are actually exceedingly flexible and wholly responsive to organizational and political pressures. One might rationally assume that these technical determinations come prior to and thus constrain production goals, but in the real world timber sale goals drive the technical determinations.

A history of the rise of the annual allowable cut (now called allowable sale quantity — ASQ) for the Lolo National Forest in western Montana exemplifies the flexibility and responsiveness of these calculations. The postwar allowable cut was 52 million board feet (mmbf) per year. (A "board foot" equals a plank of wood one foot long, one foot wide, and one inch deep. "Board feet" and "cubic feet" are the standard measures in the United States of wood volume in trees.) Timber production on the Lolo *greatly* accelerated in the early 1950s, exceeding the established 52 mmbf allowable cut ceiling by 1952. In 1955, the Lolo National Forest annual report exclaimed enthusiastically that timber harvests had reached a new record high of 108 mmbf that year — twice the allowable cut.[18] This obviously posed a technical if not ethical problem for the forest managers, so their report further announced that "the allowable cut for the Lolo may be raised somewhat as a result of revision of timber management plans now in progress." This proved to be a vast understatement, as the Lolo managers raised the ceiling on the allowable cut not once but three times in the next eight years, and not slightly but dramatically — always as if trying to stay ahead of the swelling harvests. The allowable cut nearly quadrupled from 52 million board feet in 1955 to 187 mmbf by 1963, and stayed at that level until 1980. The record of actual harvests followed a similar trajectory, jumping from 8 million board feet in 1950 to a high of 167 million in 1970.[19]

Upper echelon leaders of the agency strongly encouraged this trend in the 1950s and 1960s. For example, the Northern Regional Office overseeing the Lolo and other national forests in Montana and northern Idaho produced a regionwide plan in 1959, indicatively titled *Full Use and Development of Montana's Timber Resources,* that proposed to radically increase allowable harvest levels by converting all accessible national forests lands in the region to commercial wood fiber plantations through intensive management. Developed at the request of Montana's congressional delegation, the report was proudly published as a Senate Document and touted as a model for other regions of the country to emulate.[20] Commendations, promotions, and salary bonuses rewarded forest managers who achieved or exceeded production targets. Dissenting — or at least cautionary — voices accompanied every increase of the allowable cut, but political support for economic growth, bureaucratic incentive structures, professional biases favoring an agricultural model of forest management, and congressional funding priorities set in motion an irrepressible march toward maximizing harvests.

Conservation organizations that had been allies of the Forest Service before World War Two grew increasingly alarmed over the changes in national forest management after the war. Some of them, like the American Forestry Association, took the same path as the Forest Service in promoting maximum timber production, but most others became critics decrying the effects of intensive logging on other resources and forest values. These groups would become the Forest Service's alter ego. An outdoor recreation boom after 1945 led to spectacular growth in the memberships of the National Wildlife Federation, Sierra Club, Wilderness Society, Federation of Western Outdoor Clubs, and others. The consequent increase in public visibility and financial resources of these groups enhanced their effectiveness in lobbying for greater attention from the federal government for recreation and wildlife habitat protection.

The promotion of wilderness preservation accompanied this advocacy for recreation and wildlife. The Forest Service had been administratively designating "primitive" and "wilderness" areas since the 1920s, but as the agency moved aggressively toward maximizing timber production after World War Two it increasingly encroached upon previously designated and "de facto" wilderness areas. Skeptical of the silviculturist's vision of a fully managed forest, wilderness advocates pressed for permanent establishment of a collection of wildlands protected from all development. Wilderness advocates reminded policymakers that intact forests were not "idle" but rather provided many nonmarket functions and values. They also pointed to the economic benefits associated with tourism, arguing that scenic vistas, campgrounds, and outdoor recreation were not only beneficial for the human body and spirit but were good for business, too. But as the American public grew more enamored of wilderness, the Forest Service seemed to grow less committed to protecting it.

Interestingly, the newly energized postwar conservation movement did not just advocate more attention to recreation, wildlife, and wilderness; it also supported a total program of rational, balanced, sustained yield development similar to that preached by the Forest Service. Increasingly, conservationists raised their voices about the importance of catching up on backlogged reforestation needs, cracking down on rangeland overgrazing, and protecting soil and water resources that had suffered from commercial resource development. The Forest Service's own promotion of multiple use and its defense of soil, water, and wildlife conservation helped inform and sustain a well-armed body of critics who attacked the growing imbalance between high levels of timber harvesting on the forests and correspondingly low levels of resource protection and rehabilitation activities. Conservationists demanded effective implementation of Forest Service multiple use and sustained yield policies.[21] But as the Forest Service greatly accelerated its timber sales in the 1950s, and as national forest management increasingly resembled industrial forestry practices, conservation groups turned decisively against the agency. Michael McCloskey, who went to work for the Sierra Club in 1961 and eventually rose to the position of national chairman, recently reflected on the past forty years:

> Environmentalists feel a massive sense of betrayal with respect to America's national forests. They were supposed to be the people's forests. Instead they have come to be managed almost as if they were the timber industry's forests. They were supposed to stand in contrast to the industry's own ravaged lands but instead have become adjuncts of their lands — their reserve source of supply. As recreationists and local activists saw this change taking place in the decade from the mid-1950s to the mid-1960s, they reacted with consternation and outrage.[22]

Forest Service propaganda had profoundly shaped public expectations, and beginning in the 1950s the agency found it increasingly difficult to meet those high expectations.

In response to growing criticism of its accelerated timber harvest program in the 1960s, the Forest Service defensively asserted its expertise and insisted that its management conformed to sound principles of forestry. Sound forestry was supposed to work something like this: Trained foresters would stake out a potential timber sale area, design an access road, and mark the mature, dead, or diseased trees to be cut out selectively by the timber purchaser. They would appraise the value of the marked trees, subtract the estimated cost of the harvesting operation plus a margin for profit for the logger, establish a minimum price, and put out for bids. The highest bidder would receive a contract to cut the trees, with the contract containing detailed regulations designed to minimize soil disturbance and other deleterious effects on the environment. After the harvest the agency would ensure

Efforts to maximize timber production on the national forests after World War Two led to the adoption of large-scale clearcutting in lieu of selective tree harvesting. Ironically, for most of the first half of the twentieth century, the Forest Service had criticized clearcutting and advocated selective harvesting. Clearcutting produced the extensive forest fragmentation seen in this photo and has been the dominant logging method on national forest lands from the 1950s into the 1990s. *Photo: Headwaters of the North Fork of Asotin Creek, Umatilla National Forest, Washington. © 1993 Trygve Steen.*

The drive to sustain high timber production quotas led to industrial-style clearcutting even on extremely steep, unstable slopes. The resultant damage to soil, water, wildlife, and esthetics could be irreversible. Ironically, this cut is on the Shelton "sustained yield unit" of the Olympic National Forest in Washington. Such logging practices are anything but sustainable. *Photo: Tryg-Sky/Lighthawk, © 1990 Trygve Steen.*

Road construction is generally considered the most environmentally damaging aspect of logging because functioning roads remain biologically sterile and also cause the greatest amount of soil erosion. Lost topsoil cannot be recovered. The sediment that ends up in streams kills fish and ruins spawning habitat. Here a road has washed out into Canyon Creek, Olympic National Forest, Washington. *Photo © 1992 Trygve Steen.*

Reforestation after logging, an essential component of sustained yield forestry, is often difficult, especially on drier south-facing slopes and in areas with shallow soils. Despite technical
and biological obstacles, Forest Service optimists often incautiously promoted logging in
areas they knew would be difficult to reforest. This photo shows a typical reforestation failure
on Mount Elijah in the Siskiyou National Forest, Oregon. Clearcut in 1969, the Forest Service
has replanted the deforested area three times, most recently in 1983. *Photo: Mt. Elijah, Siskiyou National Forest, Oregon,* © *1990 Trygve Steen.*

Right. Foresters have traditionally judged public complaints about clearcutting to be simply
an esthetic objection. Under that reductionist assessment, foresters in the 1960s and 1970s responded by designing clearcuts to be less visible to tourists and travelers. The photo here depicts the policy of leaving strips of trees intact along major public routes of travel — called
"beauty strips" — to cloak logging activities from public view. *Photo: Route 26 east of Mt.
Hood, Mt. Hood National Forest, Oregon. Tryg-Sky/Lighthawk,* © *1993 Trygve Steen.*

xxx

prompt reforestation. Timber sales would occur only in defined areas ("working circles" in the early days) with long-term harvest plans, and the annual allowable cut would be limited to a level that could be sustained in perpetuity. But this rational, theoretically defensible forestry vision faced tremendous obstacles: contract stipulations were difficult to enforce; large-scale clearcutting mostly replaced smaller-scale selective cutting on the national forests by the 1960s, with increasingly damaging effects on soil, water, wildlife, and esthetics; reforestation efforts often failed; and roads in steep, unstable soils often washed out in storms, clogging streams with sediment and ruining fisheries.[23] Yet, pressure from the timber industry and optimism about progress from new technology led the agency to repeatedly raise the allowable cut, eventually above levels that were sustainable even under optimistic assumptions. Many of the effects of harvesting on the environment and other forest values could not be successfully mitigated. Failures were explained away by the cornucopian enthusiasts as resulting from shortcomings in knowledge, in application, or in funding. They prescribed more technology, better training, and larger budgets as the solution. Although scientists and forest managers could see that nature and human technologies were not faithfully conforming to theoretical assumptions, the ideology of optimism remained so imbued in the profession that it overshadowed persistent rumblings of doubt.

Although in one sense the Forest Service cannot be faulted for having shared in this cultural milieu of techno-optimism, in another sense it must be held accountable for adhering dogmatically to it even in the face of obvious failures. Throughout the post–World War Two era, plenty of physical evidence indicated limits to the effectiveness *and the desirability* of intensive management for maximum production, such as the infamous early 1960s landslides from timber roads in the unstable soils of the Salmon River watershed in Idaho that nearly wiped out the salmon runs. Agency decision makers could have easily justified decisions to promote more conservative management, but they chose to maintain the faith. Thus, a "conspiracy of optimism" developed. This was not a conscious, manipulative conspiracy of self-servers. Most foresters were well-meaning, public-spirited individuals doing what they were trained to do. Most, no doubt, felt that any failures of management were due to uncontrollable natural contingencies or to shortcomings in knowledge or to a lack of institutional support. But blaming external forces for management failures simply obscured the agency's own contribution to the problem. After all, foresters developed the theories of technological control and made the promises that politicians and constituents then expected them to deliver.

Besides, Forest Service leaders had practical reasons for sustaining the faith in technological control over nature. Since the agency's budget and employee base had significantly expanded in response to promises to produce more goods and services, admitting an inability to achieve production targets would weaken Forest Service clout in budget negotiations and threaten job security for hundreds, maybe thousands, of employees. And since intensive management was a means for *increasing* forest productivity to meet escalating demands, abandoning the faith would have meant establishing limits to production, saying no instead of yes to constituents and congressmen, and rationing rather than simply stepping up outputs. This is an unenviable position for a federal bureaucracy to be in, because it entails an adversarial rather than supportive relationship with powerful pressure groups and their advocates in Washington, D.C. Moreover, rationing leads to intensified competition for resources, more calls for political intervention, and hence an increasing threat to agency autonomy. Sociologists have long recognized that a central aim of large organizations, including government agencies, is to maintain self-determination. The Forest Service aggressively fought to retain its management discretion throughout this century and only began to lose it incrementally since the 1960s. Promoting intensive management served the dual purpose of rebuffing the threatening specter of political intervention while establishing a special role for the service as a group of technical experts with privileged knowledge whose decisions deserved deference. Organizational considerations such as these are very influential in agency decision making, especially at the upper echelons of the hierarchy.

In addition to these organizational motivations to promote intensive management were a number of powerful economic incentives built into the Forest Service's logging program that financially rewarded the agency for selling timber. Ten percent of gross Forest Service receipts automatically return to the agency for road construction (authorized by an act of March 4, 1913). Twenty-five percent of receipts are distributed to the local counties where the timber was harvested "in lieu of taxes" (authorized by an act of May 23, 1908), thereby establishing a direct economic relationship between forest managers and county governments. Most important, a nearly unlimited portion of remaining timber receipts can be retained by the agency for "timber sale area betterment" (under authority of the Knutson-Vandenberg Act of 1930 and expanded by the National Forest Management Act of 1976), thus providing a powerful tool for local managers to enhance their budget by selling timber. In one recent example, the Caribou National Forest in southern Idaho spent $400,000 of taxpayer money building timber access roads and preparing timber sales in 1990, from which they collected $814,000 in timber sale receipts. But only $757 of that amount made it back into the federal Treasury. A majority of the balance was retained by the Caribou National Forest, largely under the auspices of the Knutson-Vandenberg Act. Thus, the forest managers were able to greatly enhance their budget by selling timber at a net loss to the Treasury.[24] Resource economist Randal O'Toole, who has analyzed these economic incentives more thoroughly than anyone, makes a credible argument that most of the Forest Service's actions — especially those that seem irrational on the surface — can be explained as rational "budget maximization" behavior.[25]

With these powerful institutional, economic, and political incentives in place, the Forest Service, from the 1950s through the 1970s, dedicated itself to market-oriented production and the conversion of natural forest ecosystems into timber plantations. The silviculturists who dominated the agency generally approved of this approach, but other professionals trained in ecology, wildlife management, soil science, and other fields questioned both the desirability and sustainability of intensive forestry. Ecologists pointed out that the intensive manipulations involved in tree-farming harmed the stability and resilience of ecosystems. Wildlife managers complained that timber plantations benefited only deer while other species such as elk, bear, salmon, and trout declined dramatically under such management regimes. Soil scientists warned that many logging activities, especially road building, destroyed soil permeability, altered soil chemistry, and led to unacceptable rates of erosion, all of which would lead to a significant decline in biological productivity over the long term. In addition to these scientific concerns were social ones, too. Tree-farming preempted many other kinds of forest uses, or at least degraded the value of the forest for other purposes. On a purely esthetic level, landscapes full of large clearcuts with stumps and burning debris offended many people's sensibilities. The public has certainly not been convinced that its national forests should be dedicated to industrial style wood fiber farming—something that foresters were slow to acknowledge in the postwar decades and even into the 1970s.

A greater obstacle to achieving the Forest Service cornucopian dreams loomed in the political arena. Even if the agency had not had to face any technical, environmental, or social obstacles to its intensive management plans, its capacity to successfully achieve sustained yield and balanced multiple-use management remained severely constrained by its budget allocations. The Forest Service does not control its budget. Those in higher levels of the executive branch and in Congress who do determine federal spending have only sporadically supported the long-term, integrated, multiple-use resource management plans developed by the agency. Administrative and congressional budgeters have usually viewed resource conservation activities such as soil erosion control and reforestation as an expense on one side of the fiscal ledger, while viewing timber sales as revenue on the other side of the ledger. Maximizing the timber sales and road building budgets of the Forest Service to generate revenue and stimulate economic development, while neglecting resource conservation and rehabilitation in order to minimize costs, has been common practice. The larger Forest Service vision of rational, integrated scientific management for sustained yield and multiple use has been subordinated to this reality.[26]

Perhaps most disturbing, this disjunction between management plans and agency budgets has been widely recognized by political insiders for at least half a century, yet the problem remains unresolved—partly by design. Budget negotiations are too inaccessible, too technically complex, and too tedious to be of interest to the general public or the media. Thus, the process offers government a large opportunity for discretion. This is where the conspiracy of optimism has caused the greatest damage; where rhetorical endorsements of multiple use and sustained yield gloss over the realities of short-term economic decision-making. This shadowy corner of government operations is central to understanding national forest controversies today as well as in the past. Where public lands and resources are concerned, the federal government has joined in a partnership with private corporations (cemented during World War Two) to convert forests into capital to sustain the accumulation of wealth for organized business interests under the assumption that national greatness is thereby preserved and the public welfare advanced. Pouring tax dollars into uneconomic and unsustainable timber harvests on marginal national forest lands has been viewed as justifiable if the sales keep mills running and unemployment down in rural communities — if only for a few additional years. Historian Clayton Koppes has described this blend of political economy as "corporate liberalism."[27] Whenever public controversy over forestry practices has grown to irrepressible proportions, Congress and the agency have made slight concessions, usually in the form of new policies that could later be ignored or blunted during implementation or budgeting. The public, only superficially informed and sporadically attentive to implementation, has generally believed that environmental policies are faithfully executed. In most cases, however, when an environmental policy has come into conflict with corporate welfare, the former gave way. This cooperative coalition of federal bureaucrats, congressional financiers, and corporate beneficiaries have used the cornucopian pronouncements of the technological optimists as a tool to preserve and defend the flow of timber wealth from the national forests with only token regard for its ecological costs or its economic rationality. Too often, national forest managers either supported the conspiracy of optimism or offered only token protests against the unbalanced implementation of multiple use–sustained yield forestry.

Some members of this coalition dedicated to extracting wealth from the national forests have displayed a decidedly cavalier attitude toward sustained yield. For example, in a keynote address to a conference on the future of the wood products industry in Missoula, Montana, in September 1991, William Galligan of the Forest Products Research Society said that arguments about jobs and the impact on communities may sometimes be helpful in dealing with politicians, but community stability "is not why we're here. We are here because our role in society is to provide a renewable resource that the global economy needs."[28] He suggested that forest industries beleaguered by criticism for "overcutting" should adopt a global perspective on timber supply rather than a local one, and should defend themselves against critics by citing "public demand for wood products" as the rationale for their production strategies. While Galligan's attitude may appear callous, it is in fact a rational viewpoint for a business investor concerned about the year-end bottom line. That is why Congress established the national forests — so that a certain portion of America's lands and natural resources are not dominated by this market mentality.

The disjunction between planning and funding, between promises and reality, caused growing dissatisfaction among the Forest Service's constituents in the 1960s and 1970s. Dodging criticism from all sides, the agency turned inward and defensive.[29] While it continued to promise maximization and harmonization of all uses, it focused almost exclusively on timber production, partly due to its own professional bias and partly due to the lopsided budget assigned to it by Congress year after year. Entirely dominated by silviculturists and road engineers (even in 1990–91 these two occupations made up two-thirds of all professional staff in the agency),[30] the Forest Service advocated logging as the key to all aspects of forest management. Agency public information selectively and enthusiastically touted the benefits of logging on wildlife habitat (increased deer browse), on recreation (more roads for tourists to drive on), and even on water flows (more runoff for downstream users). Often these justifications bordered on the absurd, such as claims that a patchy landscape of clearcuts in various stages of regeneration would offer a more pleasing view to visitors than a "monotonous" landscape of unbroken forest. These arguments were integral to the credibility of the agency's touted commitment to multiple use and helped defend the timber program against critics who argued that the overwhelming emphasis on timber production was shortchanging and degrading other resources.[31]

In the 1960s, Forest Service leaders made a fateful decision: in the tug-of-war over national forest management priorities they decided their fortunes lay with the resource development interests rather than the "new wave" of conservationists who came to be known as environmentalists in the 1970s.[32] A reversal of alliances occurred. Many groups friendly to the agency prior to the 1960s became antagonists, and many corporate antagonists became defenders of the agency's timber program. Environmentalists subsequently viewed the Forest Service not as a protector of the national forests, but as something to protect the national forests against. This distrust led to a flood of initiatives by environmental groups and their growing cadre of congressional allies to restrict agency management discretion and legislatively alter management emphases. The Wilderness Act of 1964 established a procedure whereby certain lands would be congressionally zoned off-limits to development. The National Environmental Policy Act of 1969 required public disclosure of environmental impacts and public participation in planning. The Endangered Species Act of 1973 required the identification and protection of declining populations of wildlife and their habitats on federal lands. The National Forest Management Act of 1976 instituted more restrictive criteria for determining what lands were "suitable" for timber production; it required prompt, successful reforestation after logging, defined sustained yield in very conservative terms, and mandated the maintenance of minimum viable populations of native wildlife and natural vegetation diversity on national forests (a challenge to Forest Service promotion of one-crop commercial monocultures).[33]

These and other environmental protection laws essentially challenged the whole intensive management regime. But implementation of these new policies depended upon support from Congress and the Executive, and upon the skills, cooperation, and organizational resources of the Forest Service. While the Forest Service resisted these attempts to curb their management discretion, it nevertheless took halting steps toward understanding and accommodating the new environmental values. Its approach, however, was to treat environmentalists as just another constituency of users demanding certain goods and services that the agency could supply by applying more intensive management. The more important environmentalist critique of intensive management largely fell on deaf ears. Forest managers continued to place inordinate faith in forestry science, technology, and expanded funding as a panacea for resource conflict. Not until the late 1980s did foresters as a profession finally begin to critically evaluate their own instrumentalist forestry paradigm.

Corporate beneficiaries of the old management style reacted strongly against this revolution in environmental values and policies. The Reagan Administration represented an aggressive and somewhat successful — if temporary — backlash to the environmental protection trends of the 1960s and 1970s. During Reagan's tenure, Assistant Secretary of Agriculture John Crowell ordered the Forest Service to plan for a doubling of its timber harvests over the next few decades. Before his appointment to the Department of Agriculture, Crowell worked as chief legal counsel for Louisiana Pacific, one of the nation's largest industrial purchasers of federal timber. Another Reagan appointee with jurisdiction over the Forest Service was Douglas MacCleery, formerly a lobbyist for the National Forest Products Association, the nation's leading lumber lobby. Crowell and MacCleery initiated changes in forest planning regulations that required national, regional, and local plans to emphasize timber production.[34] Senior members of Congress friendly to the timber industry, such as Senators James McClure of Idaho and Mark Hatfield of Oregon, began attaching amendments to Forest Service appropriations bills (budget legislation) in the 1980s containing specific timber harvest quotas to keep production high.

All these political efforts to focus the Forest Service on logging resulted in a temporary jump in timber production that lasted through the end of the Reagan Administration. But it was an artificial boost to production, like deficit spending, that could not be sustained and that entailed significant environmental and economic costs. The Clearwater National Forest in Idaho provides an example of this. Resource specialists on that forest determined in 1992 that 71 percent of the streams were in violation of the forest plan's water quality standards due to logging-related activities. Of 102 streams on the forest, 63 were at or below 50 percent of their biological potential. Chinook salmon populations were "on the threshold of extinction." Old-growth forest remained on less than 10 percent of the land base.[35] To add insult to injury, the environmentally damaging timber production program on this forest ran a deficit of approximately a million dollars a year in the 1980s.[36]

Although below-cost sales such as those on the Clearwater have been common since World War Two, the losses have accelerated over the years as forest managers increasingly turned to the lower valued and more inaccessible timber in the remote high country to fulfill their logging quotas. According to the Forest Service's own highly defensive economic analysis, two-thirds of the national forests lost money on their timber programs in 1987 and 1988. These below-cost sales amounted to a loss of approximately $350 million per year in those two years. Furthermore, the magnitude of the problem was greater than the agency admitted because the accounting system it used understated costs and exaggerated revenues. For example, the Nez Perce National Forest, next door to the Clearwater mentioned above, spent $10.7 million on timber production related activities in 1988 but took in receipts of only $4.5 million. In its cost accounting, however, it showed a net *revenue* of $293,000 by counting *less than one-third of 1 percent* of the costs of road construction and reforestation against its receipts. It amortized these costs over 302 years, even though the design lifespan of logging roads is about twenty years.[37]

The timber industry has insisted that unnecessary environmental constraints are a major cause of poor timber sale economics and that bureaucratic inefficiency exacerbates the problem. The Forest Service defends
itself by arguing that its multiple use, sustained yield mandate supersedes
considerations of economic efficiency and revenue generation. And while it
agrees that economic losses from timber sales could be reduced by eliminating cumbersome requirements for environmental impact analysis and public
participation, it says below-cost sales are justified in any case because the
subsidies go to sustain dependent industries and rehabilitate cutover lands.
Environmental critics have countered that environmental analysis is not a
luxury but a necessary step in resource management planning and that
public participation is a democratic prerogative. Furthermore, they claim
that the agency could save money *and* provide higher net public benefits by
not logging low-value forest lands, and they see the agency's insistence on
logging marginal lands at a loss as proof of timber bias and an inappropriate
incentive system. In the 1980s, critics of the Forest Service timber program
began a campaign to reduce or eliminate below-cost sales as a specific
reform strategy. And it paid off by the 1990s as the Clinton administration
cautiously promoted a policy of gradually phasing out timber sales on
chronically below-cost forests. The full effect of this policy change — if it is
implemented — will not be apparent until the end of the decade, but it may
reduce timber sales nationwide by as much as one-half from 1992 levels.[38]

The Reagan era push to harvest more timber off the national forests also
led to casualties in scientific integrity and agency credibility as timber planners, under pressure to "get out the cut," adopted unreliable assumptions
and used flawed data to justify the harvest quotas. On many forests, reforestation accomplishments and suitable timber base calculations were
exaggerated, existing timber volumes and "yield" (annual growth) assess-
ments were inflated, while assumptions regarding environmental damage
were underestimated. These flaws often became obvious in subsequent
years during monitoring, as in the Bighorn National Forest in Wyoming, for
example, which had determined in 1985 that it could sustain in perpetuity an
annual harvest of 15 million board feet without violating environmental
standards. Just a few years later, however, a forestwide review found that an
environmentally acceptable harvest level was probably closer to 2.7 million
board feet. A great number of these miscalculations, some of which appear

to be deliberate and hidden deep in the recesses of technical planning documents, eventually came out in the wash, aired publicly by dissidents within the Forest Service and by conservation-minded economists, foresters, congressional researchers, and others.[39]

In the late 1980s, Forest Service employees fed up with political manipulation, unbalanced management, public criticism, and the disappointments engendered by the defunct ideology of technological optimism began to talk openly of reform. A group of agency dissidents organized themselves in 1989 under the banner of the Association of Forest Service Employees for Environmental Ethics (AFSEEE). Their newsletter, the *Inner Voice,* quickly became a major national forum for advocates of a new forest management paradigm. In a separate development, a national convention of forest supervisors in 1989 composed an open letter to the chief of the Forest Service complaining, "Our timber program has been 35 percent of the National Forest System (NFS) budget for the last 20 years while recreation, fish and wildlife, and soil and water have been 2 to 3 percent each. . . . Past and present forest practices do not meet the high quality land management expectations of the public and our employees. For example — clearcutting, riparian management, water quality, and a large percent of western rangelands are in poor condition after 80 years of management."[40] Wildlife management provides a case in point. Congress asked the United States General Accounting Office in 1991 to report on Forest Service progress in meeting wildlife management goals. The GAO concluded that while wildlife needs were uniformly included in planning efforts, actual projects intended to benefit wildlife frequently were not performed. At the same time, they added, most land uses that did take place harmed wildlife. Lack of staffing and funding partly explained the situation, but the GAO also cited "traditional agency deference to consumptive uses" as a significant aspect of the problem: "Agency land use priorities, budgets, and staffing have often reflected the pattern of meeting grazing, logging, and mining objectives first and providing for wildlife as circumstances permitted."[41]

Besides this failure to equitably balance multiple uses and protect ecosystems, the Forest Service also seemed unable to achieve what is arguably its pivotal management goal — "sustained yield" — the commitment to a biologically sustainable, dependable flow of products and services to avoid the booms and busts typical of natural resource economies. As early as the

1960s, the Forest Service predicted that its harvesting levels in the Pacific Northwest, the timber "mother lode" of America, were unsustainable. The agency's *Douglas-fir Supply Study* of 1969 predicted that timber production would inevitably fall off after the liquidation of old-growth forests. The date at which this liquidation would occur depended on future harvest levels and the intensity of management. At the levels of production that subsequently ensued in the 1970s, harvest fall-offs were predicted to begin at the turn of the century and to decline dramatically after 2030 — under the most optimistic assumptions![42] This supply prediction was based on a number of doomed assumptions that exemplify the conspiracy of optimism: The authors of the report — who reflected the prevailing wisdom in the forestry profession at the time — assumed that virtually all marketable timber in the national forests would be available for harvest; that the public would accept conversion of natural forests into fully regulated timber-crops; that no obstacles would prevent the widespread application of insecticides, pesticides, fertilizers, and other chemicals used in intensive silviculture; that genetic improvements would create "supertrees" and improve future yields; that armies of foresters would be available to prune, weed, and thin the timber plantations to maximize annual growth; that impacts on soil, water, wildlife, and esthetics would be acceptable; and that all the government subsidies necessary to achieve this would be forever available.

With many of the agency's assumptions proving overoptimistic, the decline in harvests was destined to come earlier than expected. National forest logging in the Pacific Northwest fell off precipitously from 5.2 billion board feet in 1989 to 2.1 billion board feet in 1992, boosted by the spotted owl litigation in which a federal judge temporarily closed down timber sales in much of the remaining old-growth forests in the region after accusing the Forest Service of deliberately and systematically violating wildlife protection laws.[43] Defenders of higher timber harvest levels and much of the popular press have characterized this problem of declining harvests as a conflict between jobs and endangered species. This is facile and misleading. Even without the endangered species controversy, harvest levels would be falling — albeit less suddenly. The handwriting was on the wall. The executive director of an economic development council for Lewis County in southwest Washington remarked in 1992, "We knew we would have long-term challenges to deal with. But it's coming very, very quickly."[44] *High*

Country News quoted a logger from the Northwest that same year saying, "We knew for years and years that it wouldn't last. In 1979, we were talking, 'Hey, there's only a few more years left of old growth.' You knew eventually the well would run dry."[45] The well ran dry so suddenly and unexpectedly because the illusions promulgated by the conspiracy of optimism masked real conditions. Political and organizational pressures to maximize production led to fantastically optimistic technical assumptions and to a subsequent "overshoot" of capabilities. As Tim Foss, a timber sale planner for the Wenatchee National Forest in Washington and a reform advocate, bluntly stated in 1993: "Timber harvest levels nearly everywhere were based on overly optimistic FORPLAN models [forest planning computer models]. Field personnel knew all along they were ridiculous. And it's finally catching up with the agency."[46]

The decline in timber production is not confined to the Northwest either. National forest supervisors all over the country began announcing in the late 1980s that their timber harvest targets established during the Reagan era were "unrealistic even with full funding," and that timber sales would have to be reduced significantly in coming years.[47] On virtually all the national forests of the Northern Rockies, for example (an area where the spotted owl is not an issue), logging peaked in the late 1960s, then declined until the mid-Reagan years, when it went up temporarily, and then dropped like a rock in the late 1980s and early 1990s. Despite all the rhetoric about commitment to sustained yield, the boom and bust pattern was repeated (see figs. 1 and 2). Many timber-based communities are going bottom-up as a result, with a great deal of suffering and social dislocation attendant.[48]

Conclusion

Great promise has led to great disappointment in the management of the national forests. Why? The Forest Service too often substituted theory for wisdom and expediency for courage; politicians in command of the agency's resources called for responsible management but then failed to enable the agency to act responsibly; Americans demanded illusions of abundance in order to avoid accepting limits to production and consumption. But now the bill has come due. The "Great Barbecue" is over. We can no longer borrow from the future or ignore the repercussions of our actions. Since World War Two, economic interests with the aid of the government have

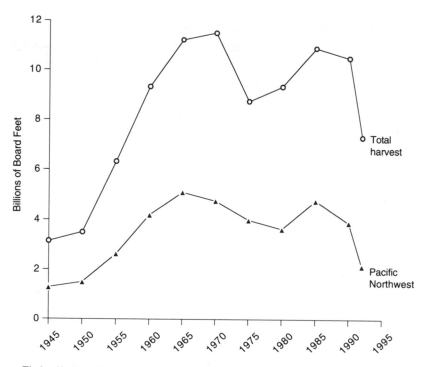

1. Timber Harvests, 1945–1992: National Forest System and Pacific Northwest. Source: U.S. Forest Service, Washington Office, *Reports of the Chief of the Forest Service, 1945–70;* "Volume and Value of Sawtimber Stumpage Sold from National Forests," 1975–85; *Report of the Forest Service, 1990–92;* also, U.S. Forest Service, Pacific Northwest Regional Office, "Timber Cut and Sold" reports.

made substantial profits liquidating the natural, unearned capital (old-growth timber) that matured on the national forests over centuries, some-times millennia; and they left behind a degraded landscape for taxpayers and well-meaning bureaucrats to try to rehabilitate. Old-growth liquidation pro-ceeded at an unsustainable rate following the self-interested logic of the marketplace rather than the logic of conservation. But the illusions and assumptions that lent a facade of respectability to this activity began to unravel in the 1980s. In *Rivers of Empire,* historian Donald Worster ob-served that the oligarchy that built its fortunes on state-subsidized develop-ment of water resources in the American West was beginning to disintegrate in the 1980s. His observation seems equally applicable to the western timber oligarchy. Empires falter, Worster said, as the "illusions on which they are

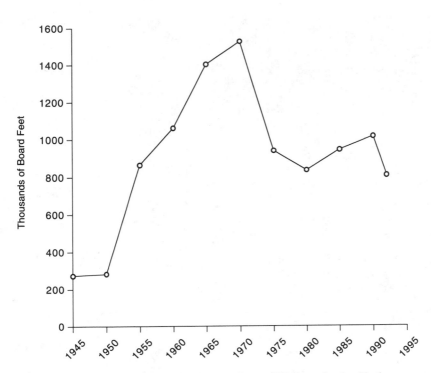

2. Timber Harvests, 1945–1992: Northern Region. Source: U.S. Forest Service, Northern Regional Office, "Timber Cut and Sold" reports.

constructed eventually begin to lose their hold over the minds of people. The promises they have made are simply too grand to be delivered. Contradictions begin to mount, legitimacy to crack and flake away."[49]

The full extent of the artifice of optimism used to promote the rapid liquidation of timber on the national forests is only recently being revealed due to several key historical developments that came into play mainly in the past two decades: the development of federal administrative procedures requiring disclosure of environmental impacts, public access to decision information, and public participation in planning. These three factors have informed and empowered a broader segment of the American public about forest management issues and led to increased federal agency accountability. Greater diversity in forestry research has led to a better understanding of forest ecosystems, while greater diversity in the Forest Service employee pool, along with new requirements for interdisciplinary planning, have begun to break down the hegemony of the old Forest Service elite of silvi-

Logger in a clearcut posed next to an 8½-foot-diameter stump of a 900-year-old Douglas-fir tree. Harvesting such old-growth trees allowed industry to reap a one-time boon from "unearned" wealth that nature had created over centuries. The timber booms fueled by rapid liquidation of old growth have always been followed by timber busts. *Photo: North Roaring Devil Timber Sale, Willamette National Forest, Oregon. © 1991 Trygve Steen.*

culturists and engineers.[50] Computers, remote sensing, and better resource inventories have improved the forest planning database and increased the ability of managers and the public to check old data and assumptions against reality. Expanding professional expertise within conservation groups has allowed them to effectively debate industry lobbyists and national forest managers on their own turf and to challenge their science. The advent of AFSEEE provided a forum for an internal reform movement and enhanced protection for whistleblowers. Finally, by the 1980s, the buffer of exploitable old-growth forests fell to a critically low point while political tolerance for subsidizing logging on marginal forestlands reached saturation. The intensive management program that cloaked the high harvest levels with a facade of rationality simply became irrational and unacceptable. The result is a rather sudden collapse of timber production, a sudden rise in local and regional unemployment, a lot of contention and bitterness, and a sense that the Forest Service has failed in its fundamental mission to produce commodities sustainably while protecting the nonmarket values of the forests.

All of these results were unnecessary because at every step of the way alternative choices could have been made by responsible people. It would be too easy to blame the failures of this era on a rapacious, short-sighted industry. The fact is, politicians and the agency enthusiastically collaborated with the drive to maximize timber production on the national forests. Besides, many industry leaders felt fully justified by the science of forestry in lobbying for higher timber harvests. A narrow, instrumentalist forestry science might be blamed, but the problem goes even deeper — to the human institutions that selectively adapted and distorted the science in pursuit of economic or political agendas. Alternative scientific paradigms did exist. The Forest Service makes a good target, but it cannot be segregated from the larger political, social, and economic context within which it has operated. It would be easy also to blame Congress or political appointees in the various administrations for their inconsistent policies and their manipulation of the agency through the budget process. Politicians, however, are elected representatives and so it can be argued that Americans got what they wanted — or at least what they deserved. But blaming "the public" is too easy too; it allows those who are the actual decision makers to dodge responsibility for their choices. Economic interests, old-school foresters, bureaucrats, politicians, and the public must all share part of the blame.

But something tied all these disparate elements of society together in such a way that they jointly produced the controversies and failures now confronting us. That something, I argue, was a two-part ideological orientation: first, what Donald Worster calls "economic culture." In his book *Dust Bowl,* Worster argued that three fundamental maxims underlie the ethos of economic culture: (1) *Nature is capital* — "a set of economic assets that can become a source of profit or advantage." (2) *Humans ought to use this capital for constant material self-advancement,* "always seeking to get more out of the natural resources of the world" than before. (3) *The social order should encourage this exploitation of nature for the accumulation of wealth,* "and protect the successful from losing what they have gained." Worster concludes: "America is still, at heart, a business-oriented society; its farming has evolved even further toward the Henry Ford example of using machinery and mass production to make more and more profits. We are still naïvely sure that science and technique will heal the wounds and sores we leave on the earth, when in fact those wounds are more numerous and more malignant than ever."[51]

The second and related factor explaining current problems is a general cultural tendency to reject limitations on resource use and to assume the optimistic regarding our ability to control nature and resolve social problems with environmental engineering. This is the conspiracy of optimism. Assuming the optimistic took many forms and served a wide variety of functions. In the most general sense it involved a collective propensity for Americans to avoid dealing with widespread, complex problems of resource allocation. Rationing could be avoided by expanding the resource base, so any promise to increase the supply of resources was greeted with enthusiasm and relief. The minority who questioned the cornucopians were branded as naysayers or antiprogress or worse. This generalized optimism as applied to resource development and economic growth was usually well-intentioned, but naïve.

For those a little more knowledgeable of national forest issues than the general public, the conspiracy of optimism took on an added dimension. It involved a willful decision to look only at certain pieces of the puzzle, to focus on aspects of resource allocation that offered an opportunity for control while neglecting others that could not be controlled or did not contribute to a preconceived notion of what the finished puzzle should look like. Politicians have been most prone to this tendency, since their function is to establish policy and pursue the possible. Foresters also strongly contributed to this aspect of the conspiracy because they are similarly oriented toward ends and means.

A little deeper into the conspiracy were those who chose not to distinguish between theory and reality. For example, in the early days of resource planning, managers would usually establish a theoretical benchmark of what might be accomplished under ideal circumstances and then adjust their ambitions downward according to practical considerations. Under pressure to expand production to maximum levels, however, some foresters later adopted the benchmark as the goal without worrying excessively about the contingencies necessary to achieving it. Such contingencies included the possibility that nature might throw a curve ball or that Congress might not fund all necessary aspects of the silvicultural program or that industry or the market might behave erratically or that technology might fail or that public opposition might arise — not to mention that the science of silviculture itself might have theoretical shortcomings. The decision to overlook these things when striving for maximum production required a special form of optimism and a collective if tacit agreement not to question the wisdom of maximization. Feeling secure in their foundation in theory, foresters allowed themselves the luxury of blaming the contingencies for any failures in management.

Politicians and industry lobbyists, too, engaged in this willful pursuit of maximization and subsequent dodging of responsibility for problems that arose. Here the conspiracy gets much less benign. For those whose goal was primarily to make profits or stimulate the economy, theoretical calculations of sustained yield simply provided a useful ethical facade over short-term economic objectives. Politicians, for example, would ask forest managers, "What do you need to increase the harvest levels to meet regional market demands?" Optimists in the profession would then develop sets of assumptions and criteria designed to justify the desired level of outputs — within certain constraints. Promises would then be made and harvest levels increased. The whole process became a numbers game, removed from reality. Political demands to maximize production generated veneers of theoretical justifications from professionals in the bureaucracy who were rewarded for their cooperation with budget increases. Well-intentioned forest managers farther down in the agency hierarchy then optimistically tried to achieve the unlikely. When they could not, all the responsible parties claimed not to be responsible. And that is how great promise led to great disappointment.

The current lack of consensus on whether or not national forest management is exploitive, unsustainable, and commodity biased derives from the fact that these judgments are based on definitions which are contestable. To clarify the debate, one needs to analyze the various definitions and assumptions each party employs in making its judgments. How realistic were they? What contingencies did they account for or ignore? Then one should go a step further and look at the pragmatic *function* of those definitions and assumptions, the social, political, and economic *context* of management decisions. What role did the overoptimistic definitions and assumptions play in the management environment? What forces influenced people to side one way or another in contestable management decisions? Finally, one needs to judge the actual historical effects that evolved from the management decisions. Did we achieve a sustained yield of timber? Have we protected non-market resources? Did we succeed in establishing a reserve of public forest-lands managed by responsible professionals dedicated to the greatest good to the greatest number over the long term? If not, why not? These questions drove my investigation.

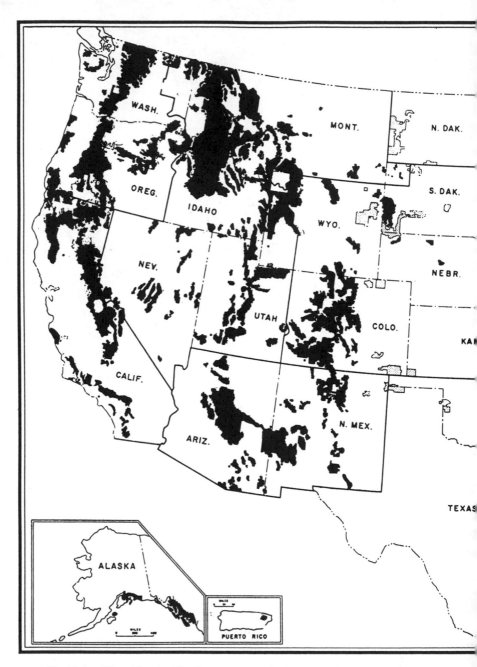

1. The National Forest System. The size and geographic distribution of national forest lands has remained relatively stable since midcentury. This map depicts the national forest system as

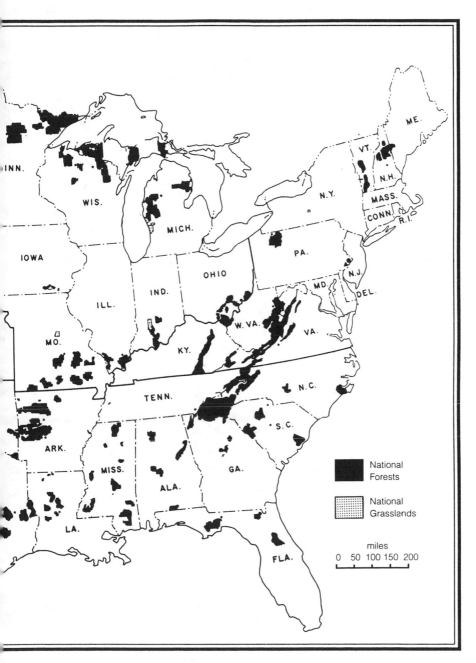

National Forests

National Grasslands

miles
0   50 100 150 200

it stood in 1962 at about the midpoint of this narrative. Some lands in the East and Hawaii have since been added. Source: USDA Forest Service, *Report of the Chief of the Forest Service, 1962*, p. 10.

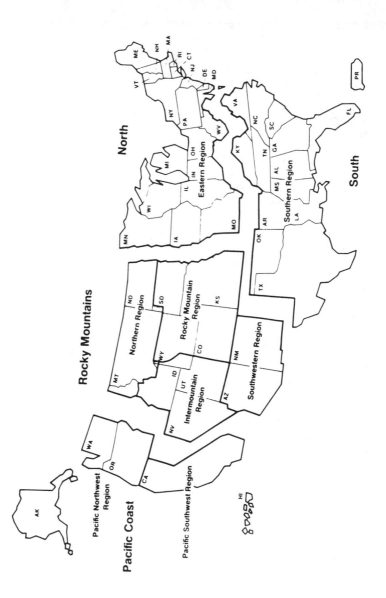

2. Forest Service Regions and Assessment Regions. The national forests are divided into administrative regions with a Washington, D.C., office at the top of the organizational pyramid, regional offices below it, national forest supervisors' offices below them, and district rangers' offices at the foundation of the pyramid. The boundaries of the regions, forests, and districts have often changed and continue to change. This map depicts the Forest Service regional divisions as they stood in 1989. Source: USDA Forest Service, *RPA Assessment of the Forest and Rangeland Situation in the United States, 1989* (inside cover).

A Conspiracy
of Optimism

I

Two Views of the Forest:
Some Philosophical Considerations

In 1959, at the height of the revolution in atomic science and the coincidental flourishing of a literary counterculture movement, British physicist and writer C. P. Snow gave a widely publicized lecture titled "The Two Cultures," in which he argued that "a gulf of mutual incomprehension" separated literary intellectuals from scientists.[1] Snow's often cited essay was provocative not so much for its accuracy as for its symbolic power. By setting up an opposition between two contending ideologies, he simplified a complex social phenomenon just enough to stimulate vigorous debate. Such pedagogical ploys are both instructive and dangerous. Even Snow cautioned, "Attempts to divide anything into two ought to be regarded with much suspicion." While positing this dichotomy between literary intellectuals and scientific intellectuals, Snow recognized that neither "side" was unified. In fact, he admitted, some members of each group "vigorously refuse to be corralled in a cultural box with people they wouldn't be seen dead with."[2] Nevertheless, lumping them proved to be a useful means for identifying an ideological cleavage in society and for proposing a means to bridge it.

In the same spirit of pedagogy, I am cautiously offering another dualism here for discussion purposes: the ecological versus the agronomic views of the forest. There are ample precedents for this distinction. Aldo Leopold in 1949 identified a similar dichotomy, which he called the "A-B cleavage."[3] Environmental historian Donald Worster has referred to the "arcadian" versus the "imperialist" tradition in science.[4] Forest historians have identified a split between "stewards" and "traditionalists."[5] Professional foresters in the late 1980s coined the terms "new forestry" versus "old forestry" and "modernist" versus "postmodernist" to describe divergent approaches to forest management.[6] Leopold's summary of the type A and type B foresters remains classic:

> One group (A) regards the land as soil, and its function as commodity production; another group (B) regards the land as biota, and its function as something broader. How much broader is admittedly in a state of doubt and confusion. In my own field, forestry, group A is quite content to grow trees like cabbages, with cellulose as the basic forest commodity. It feels no inhibition against violence; its ideology is agronomic. Group B, on the other hand, sees forestry as fundamentally different from agronomy because it employs natural species, and manages a natural environment rather than creating an artificial one.[7]

We can conceive of these world-views as comprising nearly separate cultures, although again it is unfair to lump all individuals engaged in forestry into one camp or the other.

Leopold's group A, the "silviculturists" with an agronomic view of forestry, generally maintain an abiding faith in technology, progress, and sustained economic growth. Corollary articles of faith include these: (1) solutions will be found to environmental problems and resource scarcities — the technological fix — without the need to significantly alter the status quo; and (2) trained experts backed by enlightened government policies will be able to sustain high levels of production from the nation's forests to increase Americans' material wealth. In forest management planning, the traditional forestry perspective takes continued economic expansion and population growth as given. Then, based on the assumption that existing levels of per capita material consumption should be maintained or enhanced, it predicts what levels of production will be necessary to meet future demands for forest commodities. Finally, it gears up to meet those future demands to the maximum extent technically feasible through prodigious feats of engineering and intensive management. Progress is equated with economic expansion.

The ecologist does not generally share this rosy assessment of the potential of industrial technology to solve social or environmental problems through expanded production. Beginning in the 1960s, the once nearly unsullied public image of the "scientific forest manager" began to tarnish and the once nearly unquestioned faith in technology faltered, especially after the 1962 publication of Rachel Carson's *Silent Spring,* a revelatory exposé on the ecological repercussions of widespread agricultural pesticide use. Outspoken ecologists like Rachel Carson, Paul Sears, and Barry Commoner characterized the views of the engineers of cornucopia as simplistic, dangerously anthropocentric, and fundamentally inoperable over the long term.[8]

While the ecologist promotes awareness of environmental limits to abundance, the silviculturist strives to overcome limits and create greater abundance. The anthropocentric focus of the latter, the ecologist says, blinds him or her to the external effects of commodity production on the environment, such as damage to water quality and soil stability from road building, the loss of natural biological diversity, and unintentional harm to nontarget species of plants and animals from the widespread use of pesticides and other agricultural chemicals. Since the 1960s, more and more people have come to see technology less as a solution to old problems than as a source of new problems. A growing body of environmental crisis literature — with a long history of precedents — culminated in such classic "gloom and doom" statements as the Club of Rome's 1972 study, *The Limits of Growth,* and the *Global 2000 Report* produced in 1980 by the Carter administration's Council on Environmental Quality.[9] (Past precedents in this genre of jeremiads against unwarranted optimism in human ability to control nature include such classics as George Perkins Marsh's 1864 *Man and Nature,* Paul B. Sears's 1935 *Deserts on the March,* and Fairfield Osborn's 1948 *Our Plundered Planet.*)[10]

Contemporary soil scientist E. L. Stone summarized the ecologist's concerns about overmanaged forests in his keynote address to the Fourth North American Forest Soils Conference in 1973:

> Many foresters and biologists doubt the eventual wisdom or success of what I have termed the domesticated forest. Some doubts spring from an intuitive distrust of simplicity, artificiality, and technology replacing the greater diversity, "naturalness" and regard for ecological constraints that characterize [less regulated forests]. . . . Other doubts reflect the belief that intensified culture necessarily brings intensified pollution.[11]

3

As Stone indicated, ecologists are conservative in their view of the possibilities for biologically engineering ever-greater commodity production from the natural environment on a large scale and over the long term.

In contrast, the faith of the industrial forester in his or her ability to sustain intensive extraction of commodities indefinitely from the forest — be they wood, water, or forage for domestic livestock — requires a studied and persistent optimism. That this faith in intensive management continues to prevail despite biological failures, scientific skepticism, and financial inadequacies indicates the presence of a well-entrenched conspiracy of optimism ensconced at the very ideological core of the natural resources management establishment. For some, the faith in intensive management is genuine; for others it is an economic expediency. The agronomic forestry paradigm reflects both the faith and the economic motive.

The remainder of this chapter traces a path through the ideological groves of the ecologist and the industrial forester, looking at the various ecosystem components — the forest "resources" — from the contrasting perspectives of each paradigm and indicating their management implications. The narrative begins with the most fundamental of forest resources, soil and water, then moves on to a discussion of grasslands, wildlife, and trees, and ends with a general discussion of forestry.

Soil

To someone interested in growing harvestable plant products, such as trees for wood or grasses for forage, soil is thought of as the material foundation for plant growth, a rooting medium for forest vegetation. As such, soil is considered in terms of its utility for growing targeted species. The agricultural perspective, then, is concerned about certain functional characteristics of the soil, such as nutrient content, moisture content, depth, and porosity. By comparing existing soil conditions to the soil requirements of a desired species, the agronomist can determine what types of soil inputs (fertilizer, irrigation, mulching) will be needed to grow the crop most efficiently. Philip Hahn of the Georgia-Pacific lumber corporation expressed this view succinctly:

> In order to expedite the growth rate even more, we are moving in with aerial fertilization. Aerial fertilization is used only in areas where we know we have nutrient deficiencies. . . . We are examining all timber

stands old enough to be fertilized. We are looking at the soil to see what's missing. We can pick out the fertilizers that fit our conditions the best, and then we can order a fertilizer in rail carloads and use helicopters to spread the fertilizer over the various areas.[12]

There are other perspectives on soil beyond this strictly functional view.[13] Soil geographers see it as a physical component of the landscape, with traits that reflect its geologic and climatic setting. These specialists classify and map soils in great and esoteric detail according to inherent physical characteristics that may or may not reflect agricultural potential. Soil is seen as a thing in and of itself in this model. Hydrologists, in contrast, see soil as a "vegetated, water transmitting mantle."[14] Soil in this view becomes a functional portion of the hydrologic cycle, in contrast to its function in relation to vegetation growth. Finally, and most importantly, microbiologists view soil as an ecosystem, a habitat abundant with life arranged in complex relationships. A classic, if somewhat dated, monograph on soil produced by the U.S. Department of Agriculture (USDA) in 1938 pointed out that the upper twelve inches of topsoil comprise the most densely populated zone of life on the planet. Forest soil organisms "vary in size from the microscopic up to the gigantic and in numbers from a few per acre to billions per ounce. They have in reality changed the surface layer of the soil from an aggregate of mineral particles to a mass teeming with organisms."[15] Soil organisms *make* soil. They decompose plant litter, breaking down minerals into forms that can then be absorbed by plants as "nutrients." They absorb moisture, aerate the soil, provide pathways for the transmission of water, and some, like mycorrhizae fungi,[16] even form tight symbiotic relationships with plant root systems that make survival for both possible. According to Paul Ehrlich, "soil thus does far more than prop up plants; it is a delicate system critical to plant growth and thus to the health of entire ecosystems." A wide variety of impacts from industrial forestry activities, including erosion, compaction, misuse of fertilizers and pesticides, burning and exposure, may alter the soil ecosystem, decimating its biota and compromising its plant nurturing capacity.[17] A few inches of topsoil that may have taken nature decades to build can be lost or made biologically dysfunctional in a single day of logging.[18] Managing for sustained yield takes a great deal more caution and care than traditional logging practices have allowed.

5

Water

Water is simpler biologically than soil, but its management is more complex and controversial. There are two major public policy issues related to water management on the national forests: (1) the *quantity* and timing of water flows, which are important to consumptive users like farmers and nonconsumptive users concerned about flood control, river navigation, fisheries, and hydropower generation; and (2) the *quality* of the water, which is important to the thousands of small and large municipalities that extract their drinking water from streams flowing off the national forests, and to interests concerned about recreation and fish and wildlife habitat. The national forests encompass important "headwaters" for much of the nation's surface water supplies, especially in the West, and they provide opportunities for water storage sites, flood control, and even supply augmentation (vegetation and snow-pack manipulation to increase runoff). The Forest Service usually approves proposals by other public agencies and private interests to develop water resources on national forest lands. Water politics in the West are far more powerful than forest politics. Although healthy forests offer a natural means of flood control and water storage, the dominant ideology of technological control for maximum use has long driven water resource decision making. The 1963 *Report of the Chief of the Forest Service* clearly exemplifies this ideology:

> During the year [1963], 230 [water] projects were studied to determine how the projects could best fit into multiple use objectives, to facilitate coordination between the construction agency and the Forest Service during construction, *and to determine how National Forest management practices could be adjusted for maximum project benefit.* . . . Increasing water needs in many areas call for the application of intensive scientific management, whereby various land use practices can improve the quality, quantity, and timing of water yields. . . . Artificial manipulation of snowpack accumulation is being put into practice on an operational basis.[19] [emphasis added]

Watershed and stream flow protection also became subordinated to logging, grazing, and other extractive activities on the national forests, especially after World War Two. The 1963 *Report of the Chief of the Forest Service* introduced its discussion of watershed management with the decep-

6

tively promising statement: "The Forest Service gives prime consideration to watershed protection when it manages timber, grazing, wildlife, and recreation resources and constructs roads, trails, and other facilities." But, in fact, the agency only employed watershed scientists on 39 of the nation's 154 national forests, and those employees were only able to give "analysis and advice" on 300 projects out of literally thousands undertaken that year. As timber harvesting on the national forests rapidly accelerated in the 1950s and 1960s, unprecedented increases in watershed-related problems caused alarm among soil and water specialists.[20] But unfortunately they remained limited to giving advice and consent while the logging intensified and spread into ever more remote, steep, and unstable watersheds. The old controversy over the damaging effects of industrial forestry on water quality and stream flow that spawned the creation of the national forests in the first place evolved into an imbroglio within and outside the Forest Service as industrial timber harvesting increasingly dominated agency management after World War Two.[21]

In contrast to the water developer's view of water as a commodity with only two basic traits, quantity and quality, the ecologist sees water as a crucial component of the forest ecosystem, as fundamental to forest health as soil and sunlight. Water circulates through the forest in a complex hydrologic cycle, performing biological functions like those of blood in the human circulatory system. Underground, when carried through the soil strata, water sustains the life of plants, invertebrates, and microorganisms, dissolves minerals, carries nutrients and waste products to and from organisms, maintains chemical equilibria, and regulates temperatures. Above ground, flowing water quenches the thirst of land animals, provides habitat for fishes, amphibians, and other water-based life forms, transports sediments, and dilutes wastes. In areas where surface water is regularly or intermittently found, "riparian" (water-associated) vegetation flourishes, providing exceptionally rich and biologically productive habitat.

Development activities on the national forests necessarily cause declines in water quality and adversely impact the functioning of the hydrologic system. The crucial policy issue, then, is how much degradation is acceptable. Agronomists tend to accept whatever level of degradation is unavoidable in the efficient pursuit of productivity. Forest ecologists, more cognizant of the important biological roles of soil and water, establish management

7

goals based on maintaining the integrity of ecological processes that support forest health over the long term. Management time scales are a crucial distinguishing factor between the old forestry and ecological forestry. The former generally *considers* the long term (100 years or more) but *manages* for the short term (20 years or less); while the latter *considers* the short term but *manages* for the long term.

Grasslands

A significant fraction of the national forest system consists of grasslands, concentrated in the Great Plains, the Southwest, and the Great Basin. Like forests, grasslands are complex ecosystems. But the range manager intent upon products reduces this complexity to one simple concept: forage. That which is edible to domestic livestock or certain desired species of "game" is good; that which is not edible is considered a "weed" and a proper target for "control." As Harold F. Heady of the College of Natural Resources at the University of California, Berkeley, explained in 1975: "Range management is the control of land systems for the optimal output of goods and services for the range. In a forest-land system, the principle range outputs are forage and herbivorous animals. In general, the ultimate values of the range lie in livestock products, wildlife, and recreation opportunities."[22]

In contrast to Heady, Donald Worster encapsulates the ecologist's view of grasslands in his study of the Dust Bowl of the 1930s with these words: "complexity, adaptation, and loveliness."[23] The ecological perspective appreciates complexity and militates against notions of simplicity in nature. Grasslands are a rich, interconnected web of life, encompassing soil microbes, countless species of herbs, grasses, shrubs and trees, insects, mammals, reptiles, amphibians, and birds, all adapted to the unique grassland environment. The remarkable capacity of living creatures to adjust to changing conditions of their habitat constitutes one of the most fascinating aspects of the natural world and one of the most fertile fields of research for ecologists. Adopting this biological model, ecologists tend to promote human adaptation to natural constraints and warn against excessive simplification of natural systems in forestry and agriculture. The agronomist, on the other hand, takes pride in domesticating nature to make it yield greater human utility. Worster's inclusion of "loveliness" indicates also an esthetic component to the ecological perspective. Natural systems can inspire an admiration and veneration so deep as to be religious. Nature — with a capital N — becomes the very embodiment of beauty, harmony, and symmetry. Respect for nature is born out of love for its forms and functions. Of course, the domesticated "garden" has always served as a paradigm for beauty and symmetry in nature too.

For Worster, and for many ecologists, the moral and behavioral implications behind scientific paradigms are real concerns. Theories are metaphors, Worster said, and metaphors shape values.[24] The theories of range scientists like Harold Heady emphasize utility value and control over natural processes. "Managers have available two kinds of controls over the range system," Heady said, "animal and vegetative. These are the manager's inputs into the range. By choosing the set of inputs, he governs range productivity — i.e., outputs." Animal inputs meant the number and distribution of domestic livestock on the range. Vegetative inputs included "seeding, fertilizing, burning, regulating noxious plants [those unpalatable to livestock], and regulating water."[25] Ironically, however, much of the spread of so-called noxious plants has been due to overgrazing of the ranges and other human interventions in the natural regime (such as fire suppression).[26] If cattle or sheep are not properly managed, they will overeat the most palatable forage, inhibiting reproduction of those plants and allowing less palatable species to proliferate in the newly opened niche. The grazing capacity of the range consequently declines. This process has occurred on most national forest rangelands over the past one hundred years. Attempts to maximize livestock outputs thus often cause reductions in the capacity of the land to sustain those outputs. This is a common result of narrowly utilitarian management regimes. They tend to self-destruct over the long term.

What to do about ranges that are in a deteriorating condition has formed the basis of a public rangelands management debate that has raged unabated for over a century (see Chaps. 3 and 4 below). The ecologist's typical solution to overgrazing is to reduce livestock numbers to a naturally sustainable level — or to eliminate grazing if the rangeland cannot support it without damage — and to restore the range to more natural conditions. In contrast, instead of grazing reductions, the agronomist promotes intensive management and vegetation manipulation to try to artificially restore productivity to the ranges without reducing commercial uses thereof. Phil Ogden, range management professor at the University of Arizona, argued that *desired products* rather than natural conditions should be the range management goal: "There is no basis for establishing excellent condition range as the management goal unless this condition class for a specific range site does, in fact, provide the mix of products yielded and land stability acceptable or desired from the site by interested parties."[27] In other words, excellent range condition might in fact be undesirable from the point of view of a manager seeking to provide specific range outputs, such as more beef.

Ogden was right, of course, in one sense: the degree to which Americans want their public rangelands in an optimal condition to provide soil stabilizing, flood controlling, and wildlife habitat functions as opposed to producing maximum yields of range beef *is* a policy question. Traditional livestock managers make cattle and sheep production the priority and accept degradation as inevitable. Range ecologists emphasize healthy and diverse vegetation and stable soil as the management goal, accommodating livestock grazing only insofar as the health and long-term productivity of the range can be assured.[28]

Wildlife

To the ecologist, wildlife are seen as inhabitants of the landscape living interdependently with each other and their habitat in complex and dynamic communities. The study of wildlife, ecologists say, provides insight into broad issues affecting humans as well as natural communities, issues such as competition and cooperation, environmental adaptation, response to stress, reproduction, dependency, community interaction, and social organization. For example, Paul Ehrlich's popularly known work on human overpopulation grew out of his original research with the ecology of butterfly populations. While ecologists have developed complex conceptions of wildlife-environment interactions, the utilitarian perspective of the agronomist reduces the vast category of forest dwellers into an easily comprehended dichotomy with clearly implied management priorities: forest product versus forest pest. The wildlife viewed as products (or resources) are usually further classified as "game" or "nongame" — those that serve as targets for hunters versus those that only serve as objects for camera- and binocular-toting recreationists. Exemplifying the forest product view, a chapter titled "Forest Wildlife" from a 1975 guidebook on forest resource management sponsored by the Council of Forestry School Executives explained:

Wildlife management is concerned with both the biological production of desired species and the transfer and consumption process by which they are made available and utilized. . . . The production of forest wildlife can be viewed as a two-stage process. The first is genetic production [reproduction of desired species]. The second is use of the wildlife as an input to producing recreation services. At both levels of production, the factory is the tract of land.[29]

Regarding the forest "pest" view, William D. Hagenstein of the Industrial Forestry Association discussed wildlife in a 1977 pamphlet on tree farming under a section titled "Rodents and Mammals." The entire text of his remarks follows:

Of course, we have the usual hazard of animal damage from deer, elk and bear, all of which damage seedlings by browsing, rubbing and bark removal as well as damage by various rodents — mountain beaver, wood rats, mice, shrews, rabbits and other small mammals which browse leaves, twigs, stems, bark and roots and, of course, seed-eating rodents and birds compete with us for the seeds we need for reforestation. These problems seem insurmountable at times; others we're able to do something about.[30]

Until recently, the Forest Service approached wildlife from this product or pest orientation, too. For example, the wildlife section of a 1955 annual report for the Lolo National Forest in Montana talked exclusively about deer management and the local economic benefits derived from hunting and fishing. Under the timber management section was a discussion of "forest pests" with the following passage on porcupines: "The 'porky' feeds on the inner bark of coniferous trees, principally pines. Although he seldom kills a tree outright, the deformities which result greatly reduce the value of the tree for lumber. . . . Hunters, fishermen, and all users of the Forest are encouraged to kill porcupines whenever they see them."[31]

Aldo Leopold wrote about a difference in perspectives among wildlife managers in an obscure essay in 1919 titled: "Wild Lifers Versus Game Farmers," in which he stated, "A first and fundamental distinction between the two is that the Game Farmer seeks to produce merely something to shoot, while the Wild Lifer seeks to perpetuate, at least, a sample of all wildlife, game and non-game. The one caters to the gunner, the other to the whole outdoors-loving public."[32] In 1919, Leopold still considered large carnivores such as wolves "vermin" — a legacy of the game farmer perspective which he came to disavow later in favor of an appreciation of the predator's role in wildlife ecology. He dates his transformation from a poignant experience he had in New Mexico as a game manager engaged in "predator control":

> We were eating lunch on a high rimrock, at the foot of which a turbulent river elbowed its way. We saw what we thought was a doe fording the torrent, her breast awash in whitewater. When she climbed the bank toward us and shook out her tail, we realized our error: it was a wolf. A half-dozen others, evidently grown up pups, sprang from the willows and all joined in a welcoming mêlée of wagging tails and playful maulings. What was literally a pile of wolves writhed and tumbled in the center of an open flat at the foot of our rimrock.
>
> In those days we had never heard of passing up a chance to kill a wolf. In a second we were pumping lead into the pack, but with more excitement than accuracy: how to aim a steep downhill shot is always confusing. When our rifles were empty, the old wolf was down, and a pup was dragging a leg into impassable slide-rocks.
>
> We reached the old wolf in time to watch a fierce green fire dying in her eyes. I realized then, and have known ever since, that there was something new to me in those eyes — something known only to her and to the mountain. I was young then, and full of trigger itch; I thought that because fewer wolves meant more deer, that no wolves would mean hunters' paradise. But after seeing the green fire die, I sensed that neither the wolf nor the mountain agreed with such a view.[33]

The game-farming perspective that defends predator control to maximize hunting opportunities has often created conditions opposite to its intentions. For instance, in areas where predators have been eliminated (such as wolves) the prey population (such as deer) often explodes. Overpopulation then leads to severe overgrazing/browsing, which is followed by range and browse damage and die-offs from starvation. A famous example of this occurred to a deer population on the Kaibab National Forest on the North Rim of the Grand Canyon in the 1920s. This particular tragedy caused Leopold and many other game managers to reconsider their view of wildlife management and adopt a more ecocentric perspective.[34] Again, intensively managing the forest for a particular commodity often backfires, as overuse degrades the capacity of the land to sustain those uses.

Trees

The old adage about not being able to see the forest for the trees indicates a propensity for people to focus not on the whole but on its parts. Accordingly, we will pause here for a discussion of how the ecologist and the silviculturist see individual trees before launching into a discussion of their respective visions of the forest as a whole.

First, to the ecologist, a tree, like an iceberg, is only partly visible. At least half of the tree's "biomass" (living matter) exists underground — out of sight, but not out of mind. The visible structures of the tree are its food-producing portions. "Limbs" of trees, an apt term, hold leaves up to the sky to absorb sunlight. The action of sunlight on the chlorophyll in leaves produces sugars, food for the tree. This sustenance is circulated through the branches and down into the root system, feeding the growth of the tree. Meanwhile, the roots take up minerals and water from the soil to complement the sugars and facilitate the circulation of nutrients. Some ecologists see this as somewhat analogous to the human digestive and circulatory system. They see trees as another kingdom of living beings, eating, drinking, synthesizing essential nutrients, growing often to great size and age, and ultimately falling prey to disease and old age. Perspectives like this can lead one to step outside of habitual cultural assumptions of human exceptionalism and identify — if only briefly — with the natural world.

Beyond this relationship between aboveground and underground parts of the tree, ecologists are also cognizant of additional relationships that each part of the tree carries on with other forest dwellers. A tree is literally a habitat in and of itself. Trees provide a source of food (cones, acorns, nuts, buds, nectar, cambium, sugars, cellulose) for a wide variety of surface and ground dwellers. They also provide shelter and nesting places for insects, mammals, and birds; shade for regulating soil "microclimates" (localized variations in temperature and moisture to which many species are adapted);

safe movement corridors for small mammals like squirrels; and organic matter and nutrients for recycling back into the soil.

One of the most striking features of trees is their longevity. Most trees live much longer than humans do. In fact, some species of trees outlive entire civilizations. The typical old-growth Sitka spruce, Port-Orford cedar, or Douglas fir in the Pacific Northwest was already well-established in its current place on the forest floor when Christopher Columbus sailed into the Caribbean in 1492. The typical old-growth Alaska yellow cedar, western red cedar, and coast redwood were drawing water from the soil and leaving mulch when Europe was just barely emerging from the political chaos of barbarian fiefdoms in the early Middle Ages a millennium ago. These are *typical* ages of the very old trees in the region. The oldest trees on record for these species are even more impressive. Dendrochronologists have counted 2,200 growth rings on the oldest known felled redwood tree, and 3,500 rings on an Alaska yellow cedar.[35]

Relationships between a tree and its surrounding community of life continue after death in important ways. Ecologists consider the amount of time it takes for a tree to decompose into humus and soil on the forest floor an essential component of its biological life cycle. One-third of a tree's functional existence comes after it has ceased to live and grow.[36] A 600-year-old ponderosa pine takes about 300 additional years to decompose and recycle itself into the forest. During these latter years, the tree continues to serve as habitat, food, rooting medium, and as a soil builder for the next generation of trees. A recent issue of *Audubon* magazine featured a photographic essay of forest life amid forest decay titled, "The Tree Is Dead! Long Live the Tree!" The introductory text exemplifies the ecologist's celebration of the entire organic cycle of birth, death, and rebirth:

> Bane of foresters, a dead tree may nevertheless be the richest resource in the woods. Having succumbed to old age, storm, disease, and the hunger of insects, it may remain erect for years, harboring woodpeckers, owls, squirrels, raccoons. But one day it will fall. Mushrooms and seedling trees will sprout, mosses will spread, mice and salamanders will wriggle underneath, sow bugs, slugs, crickets, centipedes, and snakes will move in, ants and beetles will tunnel into the rotting wood. Fungi and slime molds will speed the decay, adding nutrients to the forest soil. The tree is dead, yet it hums with life.[37]

Moss-covered, decaying trees serve as food, rooting medium, and wildlife habitat; they recycle nutrients and organic matter into soil, absorb and store moisture, and slow the flow of potentially erosive surface water during heavy rainfall. Traditional silviculturists sought to eliminate such "waste" of wood fiber by cutting and removing all trees before they could die and decay. *Photo: Breitenbush drainage, Willamette National Forest, Oregon. © 1992 Trygve Steen.*

Eleven-feet diameter old-growth Douglas fir. In silviculture, such a giant is considered over-mature or decadent. Ecologists and others, like Mary Vogel of Ancient Forest Adventures (pictured here), see much more than wood fiber in ancient trees. *Photo: Goddard Grove, Willamette National Forest, Oregon. ©1992 Trygve Steen.*

To the silviculturist, trees are timber. The word "timber" emphasizes the functional nature of a tree as a source of wood fiber. Questions foremost on the mind of an industrial forester when viewing a tree include these: Is the tree a commercially valuable species? How many "board feet" of lumber or cubic feet of pulp are available in the tree? Is it of optimum harvestable size and shape? Would it be economically rational to allow the tree to mature more before utilizing it? Language is a very important indicator of values and ideology. Industrial foresters use a common set of terms that both reflect and shape the perceptions and assumptions of those sharing that vocabulary. Tree species that are not commercially valuable are called "weed trees" or "brushy species," and are rooted out or poisoned like dandelions in a domestic lawn. Oddly shaped trees are "culls," unusable for lumber and again weeded out. Ancient trees with low annual growth rates are "overmature" or "decadent." Natural decomposition is viewed as an "attack" by "pests." In areas where fire or pests have killed trees, "salvage" operations are necessary to harvest wood fiber that would otherwise be "wasted." Indicatively, at the Fourth American Forest Congress in 1953, the president of the American Forest Products Industry, James L. Madden, complained that the national forests were not producing their full timber harvest potential, explaining: "Substantial portions of these public forests are over-mature, and in urgent need of selective cutting and other types of improved operations to forestall losses from the attacks of insects, disease, and the decadence of overmaturity."[38] This perspective forms the foundation of the silviculturist's view of the forest as a timber crop.

Forests and Forestry

Marion Clawson, economist and forestry analyst at Resources for the Future, a "supply-side" environmental policy think-tank in Washington, D.C., published a book on forest policy in 1975, aimed at a popular audience, titled, *Forests For Whom and For What?* His language exemplifies the agronomic-economistic perspective. Because Clawson's stated purpose was to present "facts and ideas" regarding policy alternatives to the layperson, the ideological underpinning of his discourse is worth analyzing.[39] In chapter 4, "Forest Characteristics and Forest Uses," he identified exactly four characteristics of forests relevant to forest policy: (1) land, (2) timber stand, (3) annual growth, and (4) annual harvest. What is missing from this description is significant. Almost the entire focus is wood. Regarding "land," the only nontimber characteristic, Clawson began: "*Land* is obviously needed as a site upon which to grow trees." Land characteristics, he continued, "affect the growth rate one may expect from various species of trees, the difficulties and costs of logging, the difficulties and rewards from uses other than timber growing, the risk of erosion, and other aspects of forest land use" (pp. 26–27). Like the functional view of soil as a rooting medium for plants, land for Clawson was merely the physical foundation for growing timber.

Clawson's description of forest characteristic number 2 is a classic statement of the silviculturist's perspective on trees outlined above:

> *Timber stand* refers to the trees now standing upon the forest land. Trees vary as to species, age, size, degree of rot or other defect, rates of growth, insect or disease infestation, and in other respects. . . . Standing timber may be classified as sawtimber or as growing stock. Sawtimbers consist of those trees in the total growing stock which are large enough in diameter, long enough to provide sawlogs within the total tree length, free enough from defect, and otherwise suitable for sawing into lumber or peeling into sheets from which plywood is manufactured. (p. 27)

In his book, and for much of his career, Clawson advocated the liquidation of commercially marketable old-growth forests on public as well as private lands in order to put the land into production as tree farms. He wanted this accomplished in as rapid a manner as possible even if it meant exceeding sustained yield in the short term. A characteristic of mature forests is that growth and decomposition are relatively balanced. There is as much death as new life. The industrial forester views this as a wasteful, almost tragic lack of productivity. Clawson explained, "if we are to grow trees, we must harvest the stands making no growth so that new trees can become established and grow relatively rapidly. *The vast primeval forests which covered most of the United States when white men first saw them may have been wonderful to behold, but their net growth was close to zero*" (p. 30, emphasis added). Nature appears inefficient from this perspective. Human intervention to improve resource productivity and eliminate waste is thus desirable.

The Forest Service as an organization has historically shared Clawson's view. It is no accident that the agency has always been within the Department of Agriculture. In fact it credits itself with the successful promotion of the concept of tree-farming. William Hagenstein, a prominent proponent of industrial tree-farming since World War Two, admitted that the logging industry moved toward tree-farming in the 1940s partly in response to Forest Service pressures.[40] Throughout its history, whenever the agency criticized loggers for "destructive" timber harvesting practices, it was denigrating not industrial forestry per se, but rather the failure of industry to practice what the agency considered to be a sustainable form of tree farming. The Forest Service and the timber industry have shared a common ideology concerning the nature and function of forests. Foresters for both train at the same schools, belong to the same professional organization (Society of American Foresters), and even share leadership. Many agency leaders accepted employment in private industry after their public tenure (William B. Greeley and Charles Connaughton, for example), while many political appointees in the Department of Agriculture with authority over the Forest Service have come from industry (Ervin L. Peterson under Eisenhower and John B. Crowell under Reagan, for example).[41]

This commodity production ethos that the Forest Service shares with industrial timber producers has dominated the agency regardless of which party occupies the White House. "National forest timber is for sale," stated Lyle Watts in his 1948 *Report of the Chief of the Forest Service:*

Production is not yet up to full sustained-yield capacity on many of the national forests. Substantial areas of mature and overmature timber in the West are still inaccessible and cannot be harvested until access roads are built. . . . With proper cutting practices, harvesting the mature and overmature timber will make room for new growth and growth of thrifty younger trees; instead of remaining in a near stagnant condition, the stand will once more be growing timber.[42]

Five years later, under a Republican rather than a Democratic administration, the perspective was much the same. Incoming Secretary of Agriculture for the Eisenhower administration Ezra Taft Benson spoke to the Fourth American Forest Congress about the purpose of the national forests under his jurisdiction: "Let us not forget that forestry is inseparable from agriculture. Forests are composed of plants, and trees are a renewable crop. . . . The basic objective of the Department of Agriculture for forestry is the highest possible productivity of the land."[43]

Attaining the highest possible productivity entails intensive environmental engineering. Complex ecological relationships within forests are simplified. Roads are pushed into the hinterlands to access undeveloped areas. Old forests are cut over and replaced by fast growing young forests. Diversity is replaced by monocultures of genetically "improved" commercial species. Competitive vegetation is eliminated. Second-growth forests are weeded, pruned, thinned, and eventually harvested, after which the area is once again reforested with commercial monocultures — if all goes well.

Ecologists criticize traditional foresters for concentrating on products rather than processes; for thinking of production in a linear fashion rather than thinking about nature as a closed loop in which one action affects many others in often unforeseen ways; for acting on limited knowledge; for assuming continuing abundance; and for holding an optimistic faith in the efficacy of environmental engineering.[44] The old-style foresters criticize ecologists for being naysayers; for obfuscating simple problems with overly complex issues; for assuming limits to growth and production; and for being unconcerned with economic prosperity.

Economic development is, in fact, at the heart of the industrial forester's perspective — as Clawson once again exemplifies in the concluding chapter of his book in a subsection titled, "How much commercial forest land to withdraw from timber harvest." "Commercial" in this sense means all land — public or private — with "merchantable timber" on it. His phrasing here was deliberate. He could have asked, "How much forest land should be dedicated to commercial timber production?" Instead, he constructed the question in the negative, asking how much land to *withdraw* from harvesting. This implied that all lands, including national forest lands, with marketable timber *ought* to be harvested unless there was some overriding public need or economic rationale to withdraw them from harvest. He explained, "the loss of income from withdrawing low productivity sites is relatively small while the loss of monetary income from not harvesting high productivity sites is large." A collateral implication here is that harvesting timber always generates income. To the contrary, a significant percentage of national forest timber sales do not generate any net income. Most sales are "below-cost" and are thus subsidized by taxpayers. These sales are, in reality, a form of corporate welfare.[45] Regardless, the Forest Service, and indeed the entire forestry profession in general, has always promulgated the view that trees *should* be harvested whenever possible. As recently as 1981, for example, the Northern Regional Office of the Forest Service directed the forest supervisors of the region to determine the national forest lands "suitable" for commercial timber production by assigning all acres as suitable and then subtracting acres specifically determined to be unsuitable. Thus, the burden of proof fell to those arguing why an area should *not* be logged. The domination of the agency by silviculturists and allied professions made establishing lands as unsuitable difficult. Declaring lands unsuitable was made even more difficult by an earlier Regional Office memo directing forest supervisors to assume that "intensive management" practices would render suitable for commercial development all forest types except alpine fir.[46]

If forests are viewed as economic assets that should be developed under a profit incentive to increase material wealth, then Clawson's policy recommendations are mostly rational. Indeed, those who share this perspective believe that reasonable persons ought to be able to sit down and calmly allocate national forest resources to various uses fairly and equitably under maximum net benefit and economic efficiency criteria. National forest policy and resource allocation conflicts arise, however, not over such narrow considerations of what is economically rational, but rather over more fundamental considerations of whether economic criteria should drive decision making and whether the national forests should even be viewed as economic assets in the first place.

Gordon Robinson, ex-chief forester for the Southern Pacific Land Company and later a Sierra Club lobbyist, addressed this very issue in his book *The Forest and the Trees:*

> Good forestry is not a lucrative business. It never was and never will be, because it takes longer than a lifetime to grow high quality timber, longer than anyone can wait for a return on investment. . . . Owners of timberland, confronted with the choice between a high income for themselves and an even higher income for their heirs, will nearly always choose the former. Few of us can afford to be philanthro-

21

pists. . . . The forester, on the other hand, if he loves the forest and has not confused his role with that of the businessman, will resist the temptation to maximize income and will be more concerned with a wide range of environmental factors.[47]

Robinson advocates what he calls "excellent forestry": cutting only select mature trees, reducing clearcuts, protecting soil, preserving biological diversity, and maintaining habitat for native wildlife.[48]

But in Clawson's world-view, the demand for resources appropriately drives forestry decision making, even on public forest lands; if more timber is desired, more should be cut until the maximum technically feasible level of sustained timber extraction is reached. Determination of the "maximum" level can be raised or lowered according to the level of intensity with which the forest is managed and according to how far into the future one expects to sustain production. Higher intensity applications of technology, labor, and capital theoretically allow higher levels of production. This fundamentally rationalist and totally human-centered view assumes that the forest is a reasonably simple and predictable physical system that can be effectively manipulated. Clawson recognized that not everyone shared his vision of national forest management. Besides technical and economic difficulties, he acknowledged that the most serious obstacle to his program was "cultural acceptability." "To many persons, foresters and nonforesters, inside and outside the Forest Service, a marked acceleration of cut of old growth timber will be a traumatic experience."[49] He was right. Intensive tree-farming of the national forests was and remains a controversial proposition.

Within the Forest Service itself, a growing sense of dissatisfaction with traditional forestry practices led to a vigorous debate in the late 1980s between traditional forestry advocates and exponents of a "new forestry." The new forestry pays closer attention to ecological processes and promotes the maintenance of natural biological diversity. Reflecting this intellectual ferment, the newly formed Association of Forest Service Employees for Environmental Ethics (AFSEEE, 1989) sponsored a series of forums on New Forestry in its journal *Inner Voice*. Cheri Brooks, editor of *Inner Voice,* explained: "[Intensive] management is being challenged on many fronts today as we witness dying tree farms at home and abroad; the failure of some clearcuts to regenerate; the increased risk of plantations to insects, pathogens, and fire; poorer quality trees; degradation of water resources; and the loss of biodiversity on an enormous scale. . . . Many scientists are verifying what others have known intuitively for years: tree farm forestry is not ecologically sound."[50] Tim Foss, a thirteen-year veteran of the Forest Service and a timber sale planner on the Wenatchee National Forest in Washington, wrote several articles in the *Inner Voice* on the subject of new forestry. In his essay, "New Forestry — A State of Mind," he summarizes the reasons for advocating a change of thinking regarding forestry:

> In forestry we have a long-standing paradigm of wise use, which is based on the notion that "a managed forest provides more benefits than an unmanaged forest and through proper harvest scheduling, we can maximize these benefits." . . . However, it seems that the owners of the national forests, the American people, are no longer accepting our professional forestry paradigm (it's questionable if they ever did). They are telling us, as evidenced throughout the media, that they see their forests not simply as a source of "outputs" for human consumption, but as a living biological entity that deserves our respect. In short, they want Forests, not tree farms.[51]

Foss then reviewed the state of knowledge regarding forest ecosystems, commenting that traditional forestry research had concentrated on wood production and utilization, leaving basic ecological understanding in a relatively undeveloped state. That began to change in the 1970s, especially with the pioneering work of Dr. Jerry Franklin and others at the Forest Service's Pacific Northwest Forest and Range Experiment Station. Comprehending the interrelated functioning of the various components of forest ecosystems and the importance of maintaining the integrity of those components in order to preserve the health, stability, and long-term productivity of the whole system has led many foresters to advocate caution and a new paradigm of forest ecosystem management: "Tree cutting becomes appropriate only when we leave an intact forest ecosystem when we're done," explained Foss.[52]

Chris Maser, an old-growth forest research ecologist, has questioned the biological sustainability of industrial forestry using an economist's metaphor:

The original old growth forest has three prominent characteristics: large live trees, large snags, and large fallen trees. The large snags and large fallen trees become part of the forest floor and eventually are incorporated into the forest soil, where a myriad of organisms and processes make the nutrients stored in the decomposing wood available to the living trees. . . . The advent of intensive forestry disallowed this finely tuned practice, the reinvestment of forest capital (large dead wood) in future forests. . . . Without balancing withdrawals, investments, and reinvestments, however, both interest and principle are spent and productivity declines.[53]

Jerry Franklin's version of the new forestry (one of several versions, which include Chris Maser's and Gordon Robinson's perspectives, among others) contrasts substantially with the simple and traditional practice of cutting everything that can be marketed. He suggests preserving large, interconnected blocks of wilderness as native genetic diversity reserves and as habitat for species that cannot tolerate human disturbance. "Snags," dead trees that old-school foresters considered to be insect and disease bait, should be retained rather than removed or burned so that they can perform their important tasks of contributing to nutrient recycling, organic soil litter, wildlife habitat, and erosion control. Clearcuts should be reduced to smaller sizes; and in logged areas at least a small percentage of trees should be left standing to provide "vertical diversity" in the second-growth forest. Streamsides should be protected from disturbance to reduce soil erosion and protect the quality of these crucial fish and wildlife habitat corridors. Finally, continued fragmentation of old-growth forests by dispersed cuttings should be discontinued. Needless to say, the new foresters believe the small fragment of old-growth forests remaining (about 10 percent nationwide, depending on your definition of "old growth") should be retained mostly intact rather than liquidated, as the old school tried to do.[54]

Many observers of the debate over resource management now think a new era in forestry has dawned.[55] Indicative of this recognition of the importance of shifting social values is the new "land ethic" canon debated and adopted by the Society of American Foresters in 1991.[56] Additional evidence of mainstream acceptance of changing values is the conference sponsored by the Pinchot Institute for Conservation in 1991 celebrating the centennial of the national forests, from which issued a proceedings pamphlet titled, *Land Stewardship in the Next Era of Conservation*. In the preface, Al Sample of the American Forestry Association observed:

> Shortcomings in natural resource management in the global environment as well as at home have caused many Americans to re-examine the concepts of natural resource conservation and stewardship that seemed to have served us well in the past. . . . We are now beginning to recognize forests as far more than just warehouses of goods maintained for human use and consumption. . . . The concepts of sustained yield and multiple use, which have served us well over the past century, are gradually being rewritten in terms of sustainable ecosystem management. The focus is less on guaranteeing a continuous flow of products and more on maintaining or improving resource conditions so as not to leave forest ecosystems diminished from what they were when they came under our care.[57]

While appearing to be a scientific or technical debate, this is fundamentally a *policy* debate — for which science alone cannot provide an answer. Every prescription for forest management is imbued with values and perceptions and assumptions. National forest policy is partly an ideological issue, partly biological, partly economic, partly technical, and wholly political.

Conclusion

These two somewhat artificially constructed paradigms of the new forestry and the old forestry — the ecologist and the agronomist — are convenient summaries of the great divergence in perspectives characterizing the debate over forest policy and management. There are innumerable positions between these two paradigms and outside these paradigms. The two presented here simply represent the kind of philosophical disjunction that underlies much of the acrimony behind debates over how the national forests should be managed. They symbolize the role of ideology in public policy debates and the philosophical foundations of conflict. Both paradigms were relevant in the 1940s and remain so in the 1990s (and, indeed, have been with us for centuries in various forms).

Although the terms of the debate have changed little, the public's approval of tree-farming on the national forests and its faith in industrial forestry technology has begun to break down in recent decades. The Forest Service, a diverse organization, contains both those who identify with the ecologist's perspective and those who identify with the agronomist, as well as just about every imaginable position in between. But a historic tradition within the Service of enforcing conformity, controlling information, and attempting to project a united front on forest policy and management issues has resulted in effective hegemony for the commodity perspective — at least until very recently.[58] In the 1980s and 1990s, dissenters within and outside the Forest Service have grown increasingly vocal and influential, challenging the traditional hegemony of the industrial forestry perspective in national forest management and proposing a new forest management paradigm that better integrates the ecological perspective with the utilitarian one.[59] At the same time, advocates of the utilitarian perspective have fought equally strenuously to retain their hold on the federal institutions responsible for natural resource decision making. One effective method for influencing decision making is to try to shape the way managers, politicians, and the public *think* about the forest. Ideology and perceptions are a powerful and ubiquitous aspect of the history of natural resources management. In Chris Maser's words: "As we think, so we manage."

2

Historical Antecedents: The Development of Forest Policy before World War Two

When they created the national forests a century ago, Americans were putting wisdom to work. The rapid development of the West in the nineteenth century had been an impressive affair, but it was not universally regarded as an unmitigated success. Particularly troubling to some was the careless, almost frenzied, exploitation of natural resources by commercial enterprises that followed on the heels of the industrial revolution. For centuries, Euro-Americans had felt that the continent's natural resources were inexhaustible and this instilled a laissez-faire attitude on the part of western speculators and resources developers. In such an intellectual climate, wastefulness became a hallmark of American economic activity. The faith that additional undeveloped land — and profits — lay beyond every horizon led to a migratory entrepreneurial spirit that in turn produced transitory economic booms followed by busts. This boom/bust pattern of development was repeated in endless variations throughout the nineteenth and twentieth centuries, especially when the primary economic activity involved the harvesting of some biological or geological resource that nature had provided freely and abundantly. In the case of commercial exploitation of forestlands, a great deal of wealth could be created in a relatively short time by cutting down and marketing logs from America's vast, centuries-old forests. But the bustling communities that developed around logging operations only lasted as long as the sustaining resource held out. When the forests were gone, the companies moved on, leaving behind economically depressed communities with devastated landscapes.[1] During the bust phase of the lumbering economy in the Great Lakes states in the 1890s, Wisconsin established a special Board of Immigration to try to bring settlers back to the northern part of the state where, according to the Board, there were "dozens of cities and villages where the inhabitants have begun to wonder what will become of them when the timber is gone and the mills close down. Everybody has seen settlements very prosperous ten years ago which are now abandoned by almost all their former inhabitants."[2]

Deforestation and capital migration did not just harm the local inhabitants, it also caused economic and environmental problems for people living far removed from the logged areas. On land laid bare in the headwaters of streams and rivers, snow melted faster and rainfall ran off much quicker, increasing the frequency and severity of downstream flooding in wet seasons. Soil erosion clogged river channels with silt, too, and this wrought havoc on commerce and transportation in the early and mid-1800s, as waterways were still the principal means for getting people and goods to market. Channel dredging, a very expensive activity, was constantly required to keep the great commercial river systems like the Mississippi and Ohio navigable. Erosion also seriously reduced the regenerative capacity of the land by degrading the soil conditions necessary for the reestablishment of vegetative cover. The loss of vegetative cover and accelerated runoff decreased the amount of water that infiltrated the top layers of soil, causing springs and streams to go dry more often and for longer periods of time. Fires sweeping through leftover logging debris posed another problem, especially in the Great Lakes states, where the most destructive wave of nineteenth-century commercial logging occurred.[3]

Widely disparate groups began to agitate for some form of governmental intervention to slow forest destruction. The rapid liquidation of forests in the Great Lakes states and the failure of much of the clearcut lands to regenerate caused scientists, economic planners, and policymakers to grow increasingly concerned about future timber supplies. Some of them began to challenge the ideology of unlimited abundance so entrenched in entrepreneurial culture and to raise the specter of a future "timber famine" to bolster proposals for governmental intervention.[4] "Sportsmen" contributed to this early forest conservation movement too, hoping to protect the rapidly declining game populations.[5] Concerns of an esthetic nature as well contributed to forest protection advocacy. Proposed federal land reservations offered an opportunity to preserve some of America's natural beauty. (Historians have long recognized esthetic considerations as integral to national park advocacy, but until recently they have downplayed its role in forest reserve advocacy. America's first national park was Yellowstone, created by Congress in 1872. Perhaps not coincidentally, the first forest reserve was the Yellowstone National Park Timberland Reserve, incorporating 1.2 million acres on the north and east borders of the park.)[6]

Thus, a combination of concerns and problems — declining timber supply, economic booms and busts, resource waste, erosion, river siltation, flooding and drought, wildlife depletion, and esthetic considerations — all led to a movement in the 1880s for a federal forest protection policy that would guard the watersheds of major rivers and "reserve" a portion of federal timberlands from the effects of short-sighted commercial exploitation. A variety of advocates, including scientists, intellectuals, politicians, navigation interests, big game hunters, garden clubs, women's clubs, and chambers of commerce created a critical mass of public will that finally led to the 1891 Act of Congress authorizing the president to set aside portions of the federal government's vast western land holdings as "forest reservations."[7]

President Benjamin Harrison wasted no time using his new authority. Between 1891 and the end of his term in 1893, he established 14 million acres of forest reserves — about 1.5 percent of the billion acres that still remained in federal ownership. (Three-quarters of a billion acres had passed out of federal ownership by 1891.) His successor Grover Cleveland added another 4.5 million acres in two large Oregon reserves in 1893, and then decided to hold off making any additional reservations until Congress established some formal management policy and means of protection. The initial authorizing legislation of 1891 had not done this. It simply segregated certain forest lands from entry and disposal under the public land laws but provided no guidance for what activities if any would be allowed in the reserves. In response to Cleveland's request, a debate over policy and management ensued. Some advocates argued for complete preservation, others advocated scientific management of the forests as tree farms (after the German model, see below), while still others called for the abandonment of the whole reservation idea and return to the traditional system of disposal to state or private ownership.[8] Lacking a clear consensus or a perception of crisis, Congress chose inaction, except to commission a study of the problem in 1896 by the National Academy of Sciences. The academy established a National Forest Commission — including among its members the young, eloquent, and ambitious Gifford Pinchot — which toured the western public lands for three months and then produced a persuasive document advocating substantial additional reservations and a comprehensive policy of regulated use and protection based on European, especially German/Prussian, models of forest management. Cleveland was so impressed he signed proclamations for another 21 million acres of forest reserves just before he left office in 1897.[9]

Cleveland's proclamations precipitated a crisis that led to congressional response. Western politicians, who had grown accustomed to an absence of federal regulation, felt that the reservations threatened local control over the public lands under their jurisdictions. Foul denunciations showered the capitol. All sides marshalled their forces before Congress, and within the year a compromise was enacted into law. The 1897 Organic Act, as it is now called, established the purposes of the reserves: to protect the forests from fires and depredations, to secure favorable water flow conditions, and to provide a continuous supply of timber.[10] Congress log-rolled the bill (an apt metaphor in this case) by incorporating language designed to please all the disparate advocates and opponents of the forest reserves. (Log-rolling was a lumberman's game in which two or more men would stand on a large floating log and spin it in the water using their feet. A group of lumberjacks all working in unison could get a log rolling at a good clip. The trick was to stay on board.) The protectionists, those concerned with river navigability, wildlife, recreation, and esthetics, as well as those concerned with rational timber management, all got language that they wanted. Even those advocating repeal of the forest reserves and local control over development got a number of concessions: Cleveland's 21 million acres of reservations were suspended for another nine months to allow settlers and others to make claims to the lands or resources; those claims could then be traded if desired for a patent — a land title — to an equal amount of vacant public lands elsewhere free of charge. A mere claim could thus be traded for outright ownership. This provision, called the "Forest Lieu" section, quickly became one of the most abused public land laws in history.[11] Another provision in the act allowed the Secretary of Agriculture to sell the timber on the reserves to

30

commercial operators at appraised value, although settlers could continue to cut timber free for personal use. Another provision opened up the reserves to mining. Grazing was already an established use in many of the reserves. Another clause authorized the president to modify, reduce, or dissolve entirely a previous president's reservations. Finally, lands suitable for agriculture were to be opened up to homestead entry.

Perhaps most important for the development of the Forest Service in later years, the 1897 Act gave the Department of Agriculture authority to regulate "occupancy and use" of the reserves. This clause later served as the legal foundation for the agency to implement grazing reductions and fees, to provide campgrounds and summer home sites, and to establish timber harvest regulations. Thus, the seeds of sustained yield policy ("a continuous supply of timber") and of multiple use (timber, favorable water flows, and mining) and of forest preservation (protection from "depredations") are all included in this first national forest "Organic Act." To scientist-advocates like Pinchot who subsequently came to dominate administrative policy for the forest reserves, sustained yield was the key to the whole management system: a philosophy of conservative use that would allow sustained production of timber yet leave the forest unimpaired. Of course, the timber industry would later complain that preservation posed too many constraints on economic production, while preservation interests would complain that production activities impaired the forest. The grand synthesis was easier to conceptualize than implement.

The Progressive Era Legacy

In 1898, Gifford Pinchot replaced his colleague and mentor, German-born forester Bernhard Fernow, as Chief of the Division of Forestry in the Department of Agriculture. The next twelve years of his tenure in that position ushered in a new era in natural resources policy and politics. The basic institutional structure and guiding principles of federal forest management laid down by Pinchot have carried on to the present. Pinchot was America's first native-born professional forester, although he studied Prussian-style forestry in Europe. He and his close friend President Theodore Roosevelt, who unexpectedly became president in 1901 after the assassination of William McKinley, established an enduring policy of natural resource conservation that reflected the values and conditions of contemporary Progressivism: scientific management for maximum efficiency and minimum waste in production, and protection of the present and future public interest.[12]

Pinchot claimed to have invented the term *conservation* in a discussion with some colleagues, purposefully choosing the root verb "to conserve," rather than the verb "to preserve." Conservation meant a utilitarian maintenance of nature's ability to produce goods and services rather than the preservation of nature per se. As Pinchot defined it in 1910, "Conservation means the greatest good to the greatest number for the longest time."[13] Roosevelt's first State of the Union address introduced conservation as a major new policy of his administration and underscored the utilitarian purpose of the forest reserves and the economic focus of conservation: "Forest protection is not an end of itself; it is a means to increase and sustain the resources of our country and the industries which depend upon them. The preservation of our forests is an imperative business necessity.... Whatever destroys the forest threatens our well-being." Preservation, then, did not mean nonuse. In fact, Roosevelt added, "the fundamental idea of forestry is the perpetuation of forests by use" — a curious concept.[14]

Pinchot, too, constantly advocated "preservation through use" and was infamous for his opposition to the establishment of the National Park Service and for his proposal to open up New York's Adirondack State Park to timber harvesting.[15] He railed mercilessly against "the interests" who put personal profit above the public welfare, but he opposed just as vigorously the contemporary efforts by wilderness lovers such as John Muir to reserve certain portions of the national forests for "nonuse," for the maintenance of wild, unmanaged conditions, even in especially scenic areas. While Muir approached nature as a monk would a monastery, Pinchot regarded the natural world as an engineer would a problem. He viewed natural forests as fundamentally inefficient and longed to "improve" them — that is, to enhance their productivity. He believed that through the judicious application of technology, nature could be made to yield increasing benefits to humans. Natural resources left unused or unimproved constituted negligence as wasteful as overuse.[16]

Another central tenet of progressive conservation ideology was the theme of the public interest versus private interest. On this subject, Roosevelt's above-mentioned State of the Union Address stated, "The forest reserves should be set apart forever for the use and benefit of our people as a whole and not sacrificed to the short-sighted greed of a few." This charge was aimed at the anti–big-business element of the growing Progressive political movement. Although Roosevelt was not anathema to big business or big government, he gained support from many of the old populists by railing against selfish business elites and advocating corporate social responsibility. Pinchot felt the same way, saying in a famous policy statement in 1905, "In the administration of the forest reserves it must be clearly borne in mind that all land is to be devoted to its most productive use for the permanent good of the whole people, and not for the temporary benefit of individuals or companies."[17] Pinchot, Roosevelt, and the Progressives in general constantly reiterated this opposition between the long-term public interest and short-term private gain, aligning the federal forest reserves with the former. This simple dichotomy superficially masked two more complex issues, though: it implied, first, that trained foresters in the employ of the federal government would be able to distinguish effectively between public interest and private interest and side successfully with the former; and second, that erratic market forces and political pressures would not interfere with foresters implementing their public interest determinations. Despite this oversimplified rhetoric, Pinchot certainly recognized that individual self-interest did not always comport with community or national interest, and he insisted that government should make an effort to consider the bigger picture – at least in regard to the management of public forestlands. He tirelessly promoted expansion of federal forest ownership as the only viable means for achieving rational resource management and protecting the public interest.

In 1905, Pinchot solidified his control over the forest reserves and secured his role as the prime architect of federal forest policy. With the president's support, and after years of effort, he successfully convinced Congress to transfer the forest reserves from the Department of Interior to his jurisdiction in the Department of Agriculture. Two years later (1907), at Pinchot's request, Congress officially renamed the reserves "national forests" and gave Pinchot the title of Chief Forester of the United States Forest Service. The Chief Forester wanted to emphasize through the name change that the national forests were not "reserved" from use. This utilitarian theme was unequivocally established in 1905 with the famous, oft-cited letter of Agriculture Secretary James Wilson to Pinchot marking the transfer of the forest reserves to his jurisdiction. Pinchot actually wrote the letter for Wilson to sign. In it, he established the fundamental administrative policy for forest management that still is taken as gospel by agency foresters today: "All the resources of forest reserves are for *use,* and this use must be brought about in a thoroughly prompt and business-like manner, under such restrictions only as will ensure the permanence of these resources."[18]

More than simply allowing for use, Pinchot actually promoted an active form of management that sought to transform the forests into a kind of factory of products and services. "The first duty of the human race," he wrote in 1910, "is to control the earth it lives upon."[19] A Pinchot colleague, W. J. McGee, whom Pinchot once referred to as "the scientific brains of the conservation movement," similarly stated that the duty of government scientist/managers was to "progressively artificialize the earth with its life and growth for the benefit of men and nations."[20] This type of philosophy was quite common at the time, but it especially reflected the thinking dominant in Prussian forest science, which American foresters emulated. Pinchot's older colleague and mentor, Bernhard Fernow, came to America from Germany as a professional forester in 1876, rose to the position of Chief of the Department of Agriculture's Division of Forestry, and founded the Cornell School of Forestry.[21] Rebelling against traditional laissez-faire ideology, American Progressives of the time often advocated Prussian forms of social and economic organization. One of the great publicists of Progressivism in the United States, Herbert Croly, held up Prussian democratic nationalism for American emulation. Croly cited Germany as an exemplary model of how a partially nationalized economy, administered by an enlightened executive, could yield the highest levels of productivity and provide the widest distribution of the benefits of that production.[22]

The Evolution of Multiple Use Policy to World War Two

Supporters of the forest reserve idea represented a variety of interests. Accordingly, forest reserve policy had to aggregate these diverse concerns and values into policy statements. Although not specifically codified into law until 1960, "multiple use" can be said to have been integral to national forest management from the beginning. Besides the two main purposes established in the 1897 act — "securing favorable conditions of water flows

[and] a continuous supply of timber" — the government recognized live-stock grazing, wildlife habitat, and recreation as legitimate values or uses of the public forests. Regarding the last two, Roosevelt expressed sentiments shared by many when he said: "Some at least of the forest reserves should afford perpetual protection to the native flora and fauna . . . and free camping grounds for the ever-increasing numbers of men and women who have learned to find rest, health, and recreation in the splendid forests and flower-clad meadows of our mountains."[23] He may have had John Muir in mind, or the Boone and Crocket hunting club that he helped found, when he uttered these words. The president clearly believed the forest reserves served multiple purposes, and that enlightened, responsible, governmental management could provide continuous economic production while at the same time preserve native flora, fauna, "flower-clad meadows," and recreational opportunities. Even Pinchot, who was interested mainly in socially responsible timber production, stated in his 1907 *Use Book* (a procedural manual for forest rangers), "Quite incidentally, also, the National Forests serve a good purpose as great playgrounds for the people. They are used more or less every year by campers, hunters, fishermen, and thousands of pleasure seekers from the near-by towns."[24]

Accommodating these somewhat incompatible interest groups could have presented problems for Pinchot, especially since he clearly favored economic development. But, fortunately for him, he ran the agency during a time when demand for national forest resources was so minimal that conflicts between protection and production rarely arose. In 1910, when national timber harvests reached an all-time historic peak of 40 billion board feet, the national forests contributed only 480 million board feet — a little over 1 percent of national production.[25] Pinchot had to actively drum up markets for national forest timber. In situations where logging or grazing would take place in areas with important watershed, recreational, or wildlife values, Pinchot, establishing an important precedent, promised a style of management that would accommodate everyone's needs simultaneously. With an unflagging optimism buoyed by his faith in scientific management, he insisted that the forests could provide a continuous, carefully regulated, efficient, and profitable output of water, timber, and livestock forage indefinitely, without environmental deterioration, economic dislocation, or impairment of the productivity of the land. This established the ideological pattern for the agency's future. With a profound sense of mission and self-confidence, federal foresters envisioned themselves as unbiased balancers of national interests dedicated to the greatest good for the greatest number. In fact, however, foresters shared an ideological orientation that eventually placed them at odds with large segments of their constituencies.

By the time the phrase "multiple use" actually appeared in agency publications in the 1930s, it had taken on several flexible definitions depending on the audience and the situation. In the 1910s and 1920s, the concepts of coordinated use, dominant use, and maximum public benefits became well-established as the precursors to multiple use. As mentioned above in regard to Pinchot's philosophy, the most optimistic scenario was one in which multiple uses could be harmoniously coordinated to provide the greatest total benefits: "A notable and highly advantageous characteristic of forest land is that [the] major uses are not mutually exclusive. Forest lands may at one time serve efficiently all of these uses." When uses could not be fully coordinated, however, the one most suited to the capabilities of the land might dominate: "dominant and subordinate uses are dictated by the character of the land." The reason for identifying a dominant use in these cases was to ensure "the greatest total output of products, uses, and services." Sometimes, however, commercial outputs might not provide the greatest public utility or value: "The benefits afforded watershed protection, recreation, game and range uses of forest lands, though not so readily appraised, may well represent values to the public far greater in the aggregate than those realized from commercial timber." All of these statements come from the 1933 Copeland Report, *A National Plan for American Forestry,* written by the Forest Service.[26] They indicate an effort by the agency to cover all potential bases with one management concept, the gist of which was to maintain management flexibility.

During the 1930s, management flexibility in practice meant freedom to log wherever logging could be accommodated. The definition of multiple use, too, seemed to be inextricably tied to logging. The Forest Service disqualified as "multiple use" any management scheme that left marketable timber uncut. While a few social welfare economists, recreation specialists, and wildlife ecologists in the Forest Service advocated a broader view of multiple use, the decision-making hierarchy of the agency remained so completely dominated by silviculturists that forest management without timber harvests seemed wasteful. The Forest Service's relationship to the National Park Service exemplified this. The Park Service was always on the lookout for national forest land of high scenic and recreational value to absorb into its own domain. The Forest Service, always in a defensive mode, struggled mightily to fend off such initiatives. Multiple use policy became a weapon in this battle. First, by reiterating the validity of recreational uses of the national forests, the Forest Service could argue that National Park status was not needed to protect these values. Second, because the Park Service forbade extractive uses, including logging, the Forest Service could contrast its own style of management with its competitor's by referring to the former as multiple use and the latter as "single use." For example, the Copeland Report characterized both National Parks and municipal watersheds, where timber harvesting was excluded, as "reservations of public lands under the single-purpose formula," in contrast to the "multiple-purpose management" of the national forests.[27] Although the single-use criticism was a straw dog, it served the Forest Service well. The main problem with the argument is that it implied that forbidding commodity development reduced uses to only one. Of course, national parks provided many of the Forest Service's multiple uses, including watershed protection, wildlife habitat, and all forms of recreation except hunting.[28] The Forest Service's derogatory characterization of noncommercial uses as essentially illegitimate except as supplements to commercial uses began to drive a wedge between the Forest Service and many conservationists, who were less driven by a commodity perspective.

The agency's growing concentration on timber production led to a continuing series of epic confrontations with interest groups working to protect nontimber values. One of the most famous was the decades-long controversy over management of the federal lands on the Olympic Peninsula of Washington state. In 1897, Cleveland created a 2.2-million-acre forest reserve there, which shrank to 1.4 million acres by 1906, largely because of acquisitions by private timber and land speculators. In 1909, by presidential proclamation, Roosevelt designated 620,000 acres of the still-shrinking Olympic National Forest as a National Monument to protect a valuable population of elk (now called Roosevelt elk) that had been decimated by habitat loss and by professional hunters. Although that land was still under the jurisdiction of the Forest Service, logging and hunting were prohibited on the monument by the proclamation. Between 1909 and World War Two, the Forest Service repeatedly lobbied for reductions to the boundaries of the monument in order to facilitate logging. They succeeded in convincing President Wilson, for example, to remove 292,000 acres of rich timberlands from the monument in 1915, ostensibly to allow manganese development for munitions, though in fact no manganese was ever discovered. The agency quickly prepared timber sales, however, and "mined" that resource in the following decades despite a chorus of protests. This led to a contentious battle by local conservationists to have the monument transferred to the National Park Service for safe keeping. Despite vigorous opposition by the Forest Service, the transfer took place in 1938.[29]

Efforts by the Forest Service to log protected areas of the Olympic Peninsula did not end there, however. As if it had not learned any lesson from the Olympic Park battle, the agency tried to log the watershed containing the municipal water supply of the city of Port Angeles on the Olympic Peninsula's north coast, despite many local protests. In response, President Franklin Roosevelt had the area added to the National Park. This seemingly obsessive desire to log wherever feasible, even when watershed or other important values would be harmed, was reflected in a 1940 Municipal Watershed Act (16 USC 552d) passed by Congress with support by the Forest Service. Although never actually enforced, the law discouraged cities like Port Angeles from objecting to logging in their designated municipal watersheds by making them liable for the "losses" to the federal Treasury of any net revenues that might have been gained from foregone timber sales. This law is still on the books. Finally, during World War Two, the agency in tandem with the Pacific Coast lumber industry lobbied (unsuccessfully) to remove large areas of forestland from the Olympic National Park to allow logging.[30] Similar battles occurred over Kings Canyon/Sequoia National Park, Grand Canyon National Park, North Cascades National Park, and others. In a similar vein, Forest Service reductions to its own designated primitive or wild areas to allow resource development also erupted into contentious battles with conservationists.

By midcentury, multiple use had been defined yet it remained an enigma. Robert Wolf, a forester who worked for the Congressional Research Service from the 1950s to the 1980s as a natural resource specialist, recently had this to say about it: "Multiple use is like Silly Putty, a product created accidentally in a G.E. laboratory 50 years ago. Silly Putty can be shaped, but if left for a few minutes it reverts to its indeterminate mass. Multiple use has the same characteristic: it can be stated specifically . . . but it defies meaningful description when one seeks to portray examples on the ground."[31] Rather than a clear management policy, it seemed to be a defense against Park Service incursions and a rationale for maintaining agency management discretion. When put into practice, as noted above, multiple use meant commodity extraction first and foremost, while management discretion meant freedom to manage all commercial forest lands for timber production. Forest and watershed and wildlife preservation had legitimacy only insofar as they occurred incidental to commercial production on the "managed" forest. Ever since Pinchot's tenure, *use* had been the operating philosophy of national forest management. As forest economist David Jackson recently quipped, "The whole concept of multiple use doesn't have the word 'no' in it."[32]

The Evolution of Sustained Yield Policy to World War Two

While the goal of sustainability can apply to the development of any renewable resource, on the national forests the concept was always couched in terms of wood production. Sustained timber yield to Pinchot meant achieving an overall balance of harvests with growth — that is, professional managers would determine how much annual *net* growth a particular forest area supported (overall growth minus overall death and decay) and then limit timber harvests to that annual "growth increment" — thus allowing a sustainable yield of timber. A stable flow of commodities was the focus in this perspective. Biological considerations functioned as constraints on the economic yield. However, by manipulating biological factors, such as the incidence of fire and pests or the species composition of the forest, higher yields might be achieved. This early conception of sustained yield derived from Pinchot's experience with European forestry. There, forests were no longer wild, but rather were fully "regulated."[33]

Pinchot's European-based conception of sustained yield had to be revised in light of the special conditions of America's forests. As the agency developed its first preliminary timber inventories, managers fully confronted the challenging fact that the national forests were wild — completely *un*regulated — and in many places composed predominantly of very old trees. To a forester interested in establishing a sustained output of lumber, these "old-growth" forests had one key undesirable characteristic: they exhibited at best only small annual net growth increments because decay generally balanced out new growth. The ancient forests of America, in the new forestry terminology, were "old and decadent." Foresters eventually decided these conditions needed to be eliminated. In 1922, the Forest Service's E. J. Hanzlick developed a new formula for determining sustained yield based on a combination of annual growth increment *plus orderly liquidation of a portion of the old growth*. This represented the beginning of a shift in emphasis from regulating timber yield to regulating the "growing stock" of the national forests; in other words, the Forest Service began thinking less about managing natural forests and more about converting natural forests into timber plantations.

In the 1920s and 1930s, eminent forester David T. Mason sharpened this trend by defining sustained yield as the achievement of full, long-term productive capacity. This represented a theoretical more than empirical approach to forestry. Actual measurements of growth increment became less important than theoretical calculations of the growing *capacity* of a fully regulated forest. Striving to achieve *maximum* potential yield became the new goal, and natural forests were accordingly seen as an impediment. Such an approach provided the intellectual foundation for the shift from conservative management of timber yields to an aggressive and optimistic manipulation of "growing stock" aimed at achieving maximum yields. Mason also nested his vision of sustained yield in an economic context, promoting the stabilization of timber-dependent industries and communities through sustained economic production, focusing forestry increasingly on economic and social considerations rather than biological ones. Interestingly, Mason had been hired by the Pacific Coast lumber industry in these years to figure out a way to reduce timber production in the region so that lumber prices might rise. Sustained yield was his solution.[34]

Congress adopted Mason's interpretation of sustained yield in 1944 with the Sustained Yield Forest Management Act[35] — supported vigorously by Mason as well as many industry leaders. This law authorized, indeed encouraged, the Forest Service to enter into long-term, noncompetitive contracts with local lumber mills in timber-dependent communities to assure a continuous supply of wood products. Industrial timberland owners usually cut their forests faster than they regenerated, so there was a general fear among government planners of a wood products shortage in one area after another. To entice lumber companies into sustained yield, the government offered an assured supply of logs at minimum appraisal price, and in exchange the private cooperators agreed to a regulated flow of timber. Importantly, the Sustained Yield Forest Management Act legitimized Mason's view that the national forests should function as an adjunct to private commercial forest lands. Industry leaders generally backed the law for this reason and because they hoped the regulated output would relieve overproduction and depressed lumber prices. The Sustained Yield Forest Management Act thus encouraged government-industry partnerships aimed at improving the timber market and stabilizing timber-dependent communities. Such a policy developed logically out of the desire to avoid boom-and-bust economies, but instead of establishing economic stability it simply contributed to an increasing vulnerability of the national forests to the fluctuating demands of the private market.

This experimental policy of government-sanctioned monopoly yielded only five actual "sustained yield units" and one "cooperative unit," as they were called—all of which were mild to dismal failures. Although Forest Service Chief Lyle Watts supported the program fervently, managers in the field pursued it hesitantly. Competing companies objected to the favoritism, and local residents and lumber mill employees often complained about the effects of granting so much power to one operator in the community. Smarting for the first time from accusations that they were "friends of monopoly," the Forest Service stopped pushing sustained yield units after Watts retired in 1953.[36] Even though the law had limited application, the community stability version of sustained yield policy embodied in it became popular with the timber industry and with congressmen from states with national forests as a way to promote more logging on the public lands when private supplies ran low or when biological factors threatened to impose limits.

Sustained yield as a concept proved to be as slippery as multiple use and just as biased toward commercial resource development as the latter. Instead of focusing on maintaining land productivity, it emphasized perpetual yields of products. Sustained yield began as a philosophy of conservative resource husbanding reflecting an ethic of responsibility to future generations, but developed into a philosophy of wealth maximization. When that happened, failure to achieve the original social goals of sustainable communities and economies was perhaps inevitable.

Conclusion

Pinchot's legacy is still hotly debated today. What precedents did he set? How much of today's Forest Service is attributable to his original influence?[37] Certainly, Pinchot was an unmitigated utilitarian concerned almost entirely with economic production values. But he was also something of a social radical who distrusted big business and promoted federal control over the economy to enhance social welfare. Certainly he felt nature should be controlled so as to provide maximum social utility, but he also repeatedly emphasized that timber management should be "conservative" in order to preserve the essential integrity of the forest. In the 1905 Wilson/Pinchot letter establishing policy for national forest management Pinchot stated, "The permanence of the resources of the reserves is . . . indispensable to continued prosperity, and the policy of this Department for their protection and use will invariably be guided by this fact, always bearing in mind that the *conservative use* of these resources in no way conflicts with their permanent value" (emphasis his). Similarly, one of Pinchot's early forestry manuals called for "conservative lumbering to maintain and increase the productivity and the capital value of forest land."[38] One thing seems clear: although Pinchot's emphasis on control and utility remained consistent, the agency's dedication to intensive technological manipulation of nature to enhance production went substantially beyond his precedent.

In 1939 Aldo Leopold, who was growing increasingly alienated from the mainstream of the forestry profession, contributed an essay to the *Journal of Forestry* titled, "A Biotic View of Land." In it, he cautioned his colleagues about the profession's trend toward increasingly intensive manipulations of the forest in pursuit of maximum yields as well as its increasing focus on the utility value of species. Pointing to the new science of ecology as a model, he suggested that foresters should view forests as communities of living, interdependent organisms, and should be more cautious about their wholesale efforts to grow useful species while eliminating the supposedly useless or destructive species. All species have a function in the ecosystem, he said; humans should not assume that they can simply throw away parts of the system with impunity.

Leopold was concerned about biological sustainability; that is, the continuing integrity or resilience of biotic systems. In this same 1939 essay, he argued that the less "violent" the manipulation of the system, the greater the probability that it will remain functional and continue to offer utility value. The tendency toward biological violence and the lack of humility in the forestry profession troubled Leopold. He saw these tendencies as an outgrowth of the Prussian forestry tradition that Fernow and Pinchot had imported, but he noted with irony that the Germans had already begun to abandon their faith in monocultural tree-farm forestry just as American foresters were becoming doubly committed to it:

> Thus the Germans, who taught the world to plant trees like cabbages, have scrapped their own teachings and gone back to mixed woods of native species, selectively cut and naturally reproduced *(Dauerwald)*. The "cabbage brand" of silviculture, at first seemingly profitable, was found by experience to carry unforeseen penalties: insect epidemics, soil sickness, declining yields, foodless deer, impoverished flora, distorted bird population. In their new Dauerwald the hard-headed Germans are now propagating owls, woodpeckers, titmice, goshawks, and other useless wildlife.[39]

Reviewing both the commitment to maximum production forestry and the growing dissention against it, Leopold wondered which path American forestry would take. He offered the hopeful prediction that his colleagues would likely take the *Dauerwald* path some day and observed that "the present dissensions among conservationists may be regarded as the first gropings toward a nonviolent land use."[40] It is sobering to realize that the advocates of nonviolent forestry are only now beginning to influence national forest management. The persistence of the old tree-farm model of forestry and the increase in violent manipulations of the national forests after World War Two cannot be explained as simply institutional inertia. These management regimes were functionally desirable, even encouraged, in the political economy of post–World War Two America.

3

The End of the Forest Service's
Custodial Era, 1945–1948

The seeds of modern industrial forestry and the management controversies of the present day germinated in the early post–World War Two era. There is a remarkable continuity of political relationships and resource problems during the years 1945–92. An in-depth look at this early period illuminates the genesis of challenges now facing the Forest Service. This early postwar era brought sustained economic prosperity and an unprecedented escalation in demand for national forest timber and outdoor recreation. The Forest Service welcomed the increase in demand from both sectors. These additional responsibilities would inevitably lead to increased agency funding and organizational security. Expanded and appreciative constituencies would provide the Forest Service an edge in the competitive struggle for a share of the federal budget pie. But demands for the resources of the national forests quickly outstripped the Forest Service's ability to accommodate them in an orderly and sustainable manner. Rather than discourage demand, however, the agency enthusiastically sought to increase supply through intensive management. This, of course, was a rational response for an organization seeking to expand its activities, budget, and political clout. A later Chief of the Forest Service, John McGuire, observed that all organizations pursue three main objectives: survival, growth, and autonomy.[1] In pursuit of these objectives, the Forest Service promised to deliver upon demand goods and services to interest groups *provided* it received the fiscal, political, and social support it required.

National Forests in 1945: The Legacy of World War Two
During the Second World War the federal government forged the American economy into a war machine, infusing billions of dollars into industrial

44

production to mobilize for the defense of America's European allies. A staggering number of orders for war-related products kept U.S. manufacturers and farmers producing at extraordinarily high levels. Added demands from European allies for food and war materials caused industrial production in America to soar to unprecedented heights in the 1940s. That increased production generated a parallel growth in demand for the raw materials of production: wood, minerals, energy, etc. The national forests held vast stores of these natural resources and so the Forest Service suddenly found itself playing a significant role in the war mobilization effort — even providing consultation to the War Department on the behavior of fire for the latter's strategic fire bombing program.[2] Wood, essential to the war effort in countless ways, became classified as a "critical war material" in 1942. In that year, estimated demand for wood products exceeded estimated supplies by 6 billion board feet (bbf) — an amount nearly three times the year's timber yield from the national forests. To stave off shortages, the War Production Board and the Forest Service worked together to increase the production of timber on both public and privately owned forest lands. For private owners of commercial timberland, the government offered to purchase wood products at prices that guaranteed attractive profit margins for the producer. But declining private inventories of lumber proved insufficient to meet projected needs, so the government simultaneously accelerated sales of timber from the national forests, partly through an incentive program that offered many local mills noncompetitive bid contracts with assured profit margins.[3] Timber sales on the national forests rose from 1.3 bbf to 3.1 bbf between 1939 and 1945, an increase of 238 percent. More significantly, the *proportion* of national forest contributions to the total national timber production economy in that same period doubled from 5 percent to 10 percent. Looking back on the war years, the 1945 *Report of the Chief of the Forest Service* observed that, "in recent years the timber resources of the national forests have taken an increasingly important place in supplying the Nation's forest products. In the years ahead national forest timber will be even more indispensable."[4] World War Two thus marked a new beginning, a period of expanding use of the national forests that accelerated after the war, catapulting the Forest Service out of its previous role as a custodian of the national forests into its new role as a major provider of lumber and pulpwood.

This rapid transition to a production mode, however, posed new difficulties for the Forest Service in fulfilling its self-ascribed mission to harvest trees on a sustained yield basis while simultaneously protecting the national forests and managing them for multiple uses. Each year during the war, acting Chief Earle Clapp and later Chief Lyle Watts warned in their annual *Reports of the Chief* that logging on both the nation's public and private timberlands was occurring in a destructive manner and at an unsustainable pace. (The National Park Service, too, labored under strong pressure to allow development of its mineral and timber resources for the war effort, but the imperious Secretary of Interior Harold Ickes successfully resisted most of the proposals.) The two chiefs charged that private industry was liquidating its old-growth forests with little concern for soil erosion control and reforestation. But ironically, the Forest Service, ostensibly serving as an example of responsible and sustainable resource development, could not ensure sensitive logging practices and prompt restocking of its own cutover lands because Congress and the administration had channeled most Forest Service funds and personnel into wartime production activities, leaving resource protection and rehabilitation needs unmet. Earle Clapp's 1942 *Report of the Chief* discussed how the Forest Service's regular work had taken a back seat to war priorities: "Maintenance of normal standards in the protection and administraton of the 177½ million acres of national forests became increasingly difficult as experienced personnel, both permanent and temporary, were lost to the military and industrial establishments. . . . Because of the war, steps have been taken to curtail drastically the forest-planting program."[5] Lyle Watts, in his first report as Chief of the Forest Service in 1943, put the situation into a larger perspective: "More fundamental and far-reaching than the problem of industrial output is the impact of destructive cutting on the growing stock left to produce wood for the future. . . . There can be no doubt that forest capital and hence forest productivity are being impaired by the war." Looking back on the war's legacy in 1945, Watts observed that forest depletion was "serious," and estimated that wartime timber cutting and losses from fire, storms, insects, and disease exceeded annual timber growth by 50 percent.[6] Reforestation and soil rehabilitation were critical needs in the postwar years.

The Forest Service's postwar plan for forest rehabilitation on a national scale included public regulation of private timber harvesting practices, especially on commercial forest lands held by industrial owners. Taking the view that forests were a "national" resource and that private use of forest lands had repercussions extending beyond property lines and affecting the "public welfare," the Forest Service argued that the public interest demanded regulation of private logging. This proposal had precedents. Every annual *Report of the Chief* from 1941 through 1945 (and most reports dating back to the early 1930s) contained a section advocating public regulation. Bitterly opposed by the timber industry, Congress, with a narrow Democratic majority, debated but never enacted Forest Service recommendations — in part because the antiregulation Republicans had nearly captured the House of Representatives in 1942. Nevertheless, the agency revived the public regulation idea at every opportunity. Watts described the typical, rather modest Forest Service proposal in his 1945 annual report:

> The Forest Service believes that the Federal Government should establish standards of forest practice which would stop premature cutting and other destructive practices and keep the land reasonably productive. It proposes that the Federal Government extend financial aid to States that enact regulatory legislation and enforce specific cutting rules conforming to the Federal standards; and that the Federal Government should itself regulate forest practices in States that fail to do so in a reasonable number of years.[7]

Note that this proposal primarily involved state regulation keyed to federal guidelines, with the federal government engaging in direct regulation only in the event that a state failed to adopt a regulatory program. Note also that federal financial aid is offered as an incentive to states to conform voluntarily. (This technique of offering matching grants had worked admirably well in stimulating states to adopt federal highway standards when building roads.)

As industry had discovered during the war, the federal government's vast resources made it a formidable regulatory agent. Further, the government's liberal use of financial rewards and penalties to woo lesser government jurisdictions and corporations into conformity with federal policies challenged the hegemony of many big corporations that had traditionally dominated state politics and regional economies. Industry leaders were opposed to public regulation on principle and fought tooth and nail against any action that might reduce their freedom in the marketplace or their liberty to do as they saw fit with their property. The Forest Service in turn asserted that the nation's forest lands were too valuable and vulnerable to allow the private market and profit motive to guide decision making. This particular battle over public regulation of private forestry practices (covered in more detail later in this chapter and the next) raged on for seven years after the end of World War Two, with industry finally emerging as victor in 1953, following the election of Eisenhower and the ascendance of Richard McArdle as Chief of the Forest Service.

Although the Forest Service and the forest products industries steadily moved toward a more cooperative relationship in the 1950s, their alliance remained somewhat tenuous. The Forest Service wanted to engage in "sustained yield forestry" as a showcase for industry to emulate, but it had no authority to harvest and process timber on its own. It could only offer stands of national forest trees for sale to industry in specified blocks and under specified conditions of harvest. At the same time, many timber corporations in the West had so depleted their private reserves of profitable old growth (with little regard for sustained yield) that they increasingly turned to the national forests to supply logs to keep their mills running. This mutual dependence between the industry and the agency did not evolve into a smooth, uncomplicated relationship, however. Industry strove to constrict the authority and power of the Forest Service and gain access to national forest timber on its own terms, while the Forest Service jealously guarded its control over the national forests and sought to re-form industry in its own image.

Larger economic, technical, and political changes during World War Two also contributed to this growing, uneasy cooperation between the Forest Service and the timber industry. Under the guidance of the War Production Board, agency and industry learned to work quite well together in pursuit of war production goals. Nationwide, lumber companies were becoming better organized, less transient, more mechanized, and more willing to experiment with intensive "tree-farming." The timber frontier was gone. Commercially viable timberlands in the United States had either been cut over and abandoned already or were being consolidated into large industrial holdings or were under permanent federal ownership. To stay in business, some companies by necessity began to think about cutting their virgin stands at a rate that could be sustained for at least a generation, and to prepare their cutover lands to produce a second "crop" of timber.[8] Traditional cut-and-abandon practices of the earlier migratory lumber industry continued, but proved to be a political liability to many established corporations as the Forest Service pointed to examples of irresponsible forest exploitation to justify the need for regulation. In response, leading lumbermen conspicuously admitted "past" failures, insisted their industry was now changing, and initiated a major promotional effort to establish industrial "tree farms" dedicated to sustained yield production of wood products.[9]

In an effort to head off congressional consideration of federal regulation in 1945, Stuart Moir of the Portland, Oregon–based Western Pine Association wrote to key senators explaining that an "out of control" Forest Service was giving industry a bad rap and should have its wings clipped:

> The U. S. Forest Service presents a very one-sided picture and manipulates the facts and figures to tell only the story they want the public to hear. . . . While the taxpayers' money is being lavishly spent by [the Forest Service] for propaganda purposes, the fundamental purpose for which the appropriations are made, namely the administration and protection of the national forests, is being sadly overlooked.[10]

Moir sent a copy of this letter to his colleague G. Harris Collingwood of the National Lumber Manufacturers Association in Washington, D.C., and appended a handwritten note to it saying: "It is high time we began [sic] to hit hard at the F.S. appropriations[,] demand a close scrutiny of expenditures by proper congressional authority and effect a curtailment of funds for propaganda purposes." In the following years, Moir, Collingwood, and other industry lobbyists aggressively advocated cuts in all aspects of the agency's budget except for timber sales administration, road construction, and fire and pest control, in order to gut the Forest Service's "propaganda" capabilities and focus the agency on selling trees.

Even while such antagonisms remained, the Forest Service and industry grew more alike each other in these years. Many industry leaders began promoting an industrial brand of sustained yield forestry with a fervor and rhetoric that mimicked the Forest Service's own campaigns; while at the same time, the Forest Service began to mimic industry's dedication to maximizing wood fiber growth and harvests. As historian David Clary pointed out, after World War Two timber management "took control of [Forest Service] destiny."[11]

Postwar Housing and Recreation Boom

Radical changes in economic and demographic conditions after World War Two posed new opportunities and new challenges for the USFS. Pent-up demand for housing exploded after 1945, exacerbated by a postwar "baby boom." The ubiquitous American dream of owning a single family home in the suburbs propelled the real estate and construction industries into national prominence and guaranteed that the demand for lumber would remain high for decades to come. During this period, pressure to "open up" the national forests to more logging grew unrelenting. The 1946 *Report of the Chief* began dramatically with the following statement: "Our forests today are not supplying enough timber products. While thousands search desperately for places to live, construction of urgently needed dwellings is hampered by lack of building materials. Lumber is perhaps the number one bottleneck."[12] The report predicted a worsening timber famine if intensive management practices and increased investments were not immediately forthcoming. That year, the total cut of timber from the national forests was 2.7 billion board feet.[13] Nine years later in 1955 the cut was 6.3 bbf, and by 1960 it had reached 9.4 bbf.[14]

The bulk of the increase in national forest timber sales occurred in the Pacific Northwest in what is called the Douglas-fir region, named after the predominant commercial tree species. One Forest Service timber appraiser in Oregon who started with the agency in 1938 recalled that "allowable cut" levels in the region rose dramatically after the war, as did the value of timber. He told of one case in which the Forest Service sold a particular stand of timber on the Willamette Forest in the mid-1940s, and then turned around ten years later and resold the leftover "cull" trees still standing on the site at twice the price of the original good trees.[15]

The Northern Rockies were another major source of timber feeding the postwar housing boom. In the first year after the war, eighty-three new timber access roads were planned for the national forests in Montana and north Idaho. Chambers of Commerce, logging companies, and investors saw an economic boom in the making and scrambled to get a piece of the action. Several hundred individuals and companies tried to move to that region to set up logging operations. They encountered hundreds of existing small and large lumber operators already established, as well as an over-worked and understaffed Forest Service trying desperately to train enough new "timber cruisers" to keep up with escalating demands for national forest timber sales. Although the Forest Service went to extraordinary lengths to accelerate logging on its lands, it could not fully accommodate this flood of profit-seekers.

Business investors, whose fiscal horizons extended only a fraction of the distance required to regrow a logged forest, felt frustration with the Forest Service, which seemed to be sitting on vast stretches of unused forest land. They often enlisted the aid of senators and representatives to prod the agency to offer more timber sales. One disgruntled entrepreneur, Dwight Seymour of Seymour Brothers Lumber Company, called upon Montana Senator James E. Murray for help in 1946.[16] The Seymour brothers wanted a square mile or so of national forest land promised to them as collateral for a loan to move their mill into the Swan valley in west-central Montana: "As we explained before we cannot do a thing without having a source of timber supply guaranteed us prior to our plant construction, that would assure us of several years of continuous operation in order to warrant our investment. There are plenty of other people being serviced by the Forest Department in regards to this matter and we cannot understand why we are not given like consideration."[17] Senator Murray pressed Percy Hanson, the Regional Forester, to "get in touch with the Seymour Brothers and do everything you can toward meeting their requirements."[18] The Forest Service responded in two predictable ways: (1) it yielded to political pressure by adjusting a planned timber sale in Lolo Creek (about sixty miles from the Swan Valley) to make it more acceptable to the Seymour brothers, and then sent bid forms and a conciliatory letter to the loggers; (2) the agency then sent a lengthy letter to Murray explaining how sustained yield and multiple use policies required management considerations that private loggers often failed to understand or appreciate. Regional Forester Hanson pointed out that only about half of the trees in any timber sale area would be cut "in order that there would be a reasonable stock of growing timber left both for future timber growth and to preserve the recreational values which are paramount in this area."[19] Selective cutting, rather than clearcutting, was the dominant practice on national forest lands at the time, in contrast to private industry timberlands, which were mostly clearcut. The Seymour brothers wanted a block of "mature" forest that they could systematically clearcut over a few years and then move on. This was not the Forest Service way — at least at that time.

Such agency limits to how much and how fast timber could be cut from the national forests grated on itinerant businesspeople seeking to invest in the postwar timber boom. Moreover, very few foresters held office in Congress or in the administration, while quite a number of businesspeople and their lawyers did. The preponderance of sympathy in Washington, D.C., halls of power leaned toward the economic entrepreneur. Although Dwight Seymour declined the Forest Service's offer of an 8 million board feet timber sale in Lolo Creek, for reasons unexplained in his correspondence to the Senator, his case is identical to dozens of others, and their net impact on national forest management was devastating. Migratory investors cashing in on a lucrative business climate stimulated by favorable government policies — and promoted by the agency's top level bureaucrats — bulldozed over traditional Forest Service dedication to conservative timber production and multiple use management.

The same prosperity that supported the housing boom also led to an astonishing proliferation in outdoor recreation. Greater expendable income, more leisure time (50 percent more than in 1920),[20] and increasing mobility (the automobile becoming more available and affordable) sent millions of Americans into parks, forests, and waterfronts to enjoy the great outdoors.[21] Furthermore, population growth in the postwar era was not evenly distributed, but was concentrated in the sun belt and especially the West, where the vast majority of the nation's public lands lie. In the 1950s, 87 percent of national forest land was in the eleven western states. One in five acres in this region was in a national forest. Between 1945 and 1953 more people visited the national forests than any other component of the federal land system, including the national parks. Hunting, fishing, camping, boating, and sightseeing generated a demand for roads and facilities, which in turn attracted more visitors and further increased demand. In 1945 the Forest Service estimated that approximately 10 million Americans visited the national forests; in 1950 it was up to 27 million visits, in 1955 almost 46 million visits, and by 1960 the estimate had climbed to 92.5 million — a 900 percent increase overall during a period in which the total population increase was about 35 percent. The Forest Service crowed, "No end is in sight to this astounding surge into the wide open spaces."[22]

Satisfying these various constituencies proved a difficult management task even at this early date. Conflicts among users, environmental constraints, professional biases, imbalances in program funding, and other political exigencies all strained Forest Service relations with users of the national forests and threatened the agency's fundamental mission: to protect the multiple values of the forest and ensure that resource development was sustainable.

Timber Management

As soon as the war officially ended, Chief Lyle Watts announced he would undertake a much needed reappraisal of the timber situation in the United States. In support of this, Truman's budget message to Congress in January 1946 called for a comprehensive natural resources inventory and earmarked $1 million in the Forest Service budget for Watts's forest survey. Truman acknowledged that accurate inventories were a necessary first step toward developing a sound government conservation program. Begun in 1945, this study was completed the following year and presented at a national conference sponsored by the American Forestry Association (AFA). Highlights of the study also appeared in Watts's 1946 *Report of the Chief.*[23] The AFA, founded in 1875 to promote forest conservation, initiated its own national timber reappraisal about the same time under the direction of the industry apologist John B. Woods. The AFA and the Forest Service at the time were not on the best of terms. During the war, acting Chief Earle Clapp had accused the AFA of being a tool of the lumber, pulp, and paper industries.[24] Probably what most irritated him was that the AFA had refused to back his pet proposal for federal regulation of private timber harvesting practices.

As expected, the Forest Service timber reappraisal concluded that quality timber on American forests was being depleted at an alarming rate. The cause: poor cutting practices on private lands, both large industry holdings and smaller woodlots owned by individuals. The agency recommended, once again, public regulation. The 1946 *Report of the Chief*, titled "Timber Shortage or Timber Abundance," explained that while total estimated annual tree growth in the United States almost equaled total drain (from harvests, fires, insects, and disease), the drain was primarily of mature stands of commercially valuable trees ("sawtimber") while new growth often con-

53

sisted of noncommercial species and young, unmanaged (abandoned) stands that would not substitute for the old growth forests in quantity or quality for hundreds of years — if ever. "In trees of saw-timber size — and the bulk of our forest industry depends on saw timber — drain is at the rate of 53.9 billion board feet, while annual growth is only 35.3 billion board feet. Saw-timber drain thus exceeds growth by more than 50 percent."[25]

In the 1946 appraisal, the agency actually rated cutting practices on private lands for the first time. It estimated that on one-third of large indus-trial holdings cutting practices were "good," meaning the owners provided adequately for soil erosion control and reforestation. Practices on two-thirds were classed as "fair," "poor," or "destructive." The agency noted, addi-tionally, that 85 percent of all "commercial" forest lands in private hands were in medium or small holdings and generally not managed with the goal of providing a continuous crop of trees. The largest percentage of poor and destructive cutting practices occurred on these lands. Unfortunately, me-dium and small holdings offered the least promise for reform. The bulk of the future supply of timber would inevitably have to come from industry and public lands. The solution to the future timber supply crisis, according to the Forest Service, involved education, incentives to practice "scientific for-estry," more intensive management by industry and federal agencies, re-habilitation of abused lands, additional public acquisition of forestland, *and public regulation.*[26]

The AFA's report by John Woods likewise acknowledged that timber depletion had occurred and that small ownerships were the single biggest problem, but there the similarity ended. Woods aimed some of his sharpest criticisms at the Forest Service and reserved his most generous praise for the forest products industry. Launching an industry argument that would resur-face repeatedly in the coming decades, Woods's report claimed that the cause of overcutting on private commercial timberlands could be traced directly to the failure of the Forest Service to make its lands fully available to industry. The report stated that 40 percent of the remaining commercially desirable trees in the United States were in public ownership, but that public lands only supplied 9 percent of the total national yield of timber. Ironically, the report recognized that the Forest Service had traditionally held off sell-ing national forest timber at the specific request of industry (to avoid market saturation and competition) prior to World War Two, but it nevertheless asserted that now the agency was irresponsibly withholding timber and inadequately contributing to national needs, thereby forcing industry to exceed "sustained yield harvests" on its own lands.[27]

The larger aim of the AFA report was threefold: (1) put the Forest Service on the defensive; (2) spur an increase in national forest timber sales; and (3) veil industry's desire to substitute public timber for its own depleted forest lands with the charge that the public agencies were not contributing their "fair share" to national wood production. The Forest Service countered by pointing out that 75 percent of the nation's "commercial" forestland was privately owned, including most of the nation's most productive and accessible. That the remaining 25 percent of mostly marginal forestland in public ownership held 40 percent of the nation's total standing timber in 1946 spoke volumes about private stewardship of forests. The agency did not give an inch on its position. Earle Clapp, by this time retired from the Forest Service, characterized the Woods report as "anti-Federal, anti-Forest Service, anti-labor, by implication at least asocial, and pro-forest [sic] industry." Chief Watts publicly panned the report at the AFA's own convention in 1946, calling it misleading and "studded with allegations and innuendoes" that distorted the facts and promoted a false optimism.[28]

Although industry and the agency disagreed on how much overcutting had occurred and who was at fault, they both shared the view that timber harvesting needed to be increased and that more intensive management was needed to maximize the timber yields from both private and public forests. Chris Granger, Assistant Chief in charge of national forest management from 1935 to 1962 (the agency's key timber administrator at the time), recalled that the Forest Service in this period pushed hard to get an active timber sales program going nationwide: "continuing efforts were made by the Forest Service to put all national forest timber working circles under active management. This required initiative on the part of Forest Service land managers to promote the sale of national forest timber, rather than waiting for the business to come to us."[29] A "working circle" was the agency's term for a large block of land dedicated to timber harvesting that encircled a town with harvesting or milling capabilities. In April 1946 a Forest Service Washington Office memo directed all regions of the agency to develop or revise management plans for all working circles in which timber marketing might be possible in the next ten years.[30] The regions were further directed to *maximize* timber sales — without violating "sustained yield" — and to find ways to increase the annual allowable cut through intensive management.

In 1946, sustained yield generally meant that the total volume of wood extracted from the working circle should not exceed the total volume of new growth. These estimates, however, involved wide margins of error and a great deal of discretionary judgment. In practice, foresters attempted to restrict annual harvests to a level that they felt could be sustained indefinitely, based on the sawtimber or pulpwood growth *potential* of the working circle. Intensively managing timber stands theoretically increased their productive potential and thus permitted higher annual allowable cuts. Among the national forest lands that the agency considered "commercial" in 1946, 86 percent still had never been fully inventoried. Timber could not legally be offered for sale without an inventory. Inventories essentially addressed three things: (1) the percentage of commercially desirable tree species in a forest area; (2) the estimated volume of wood in those trees — measured in board feet for lumber and cubic feet for pulp; and (3) accessibility. Up to that time, timber volume had only been vaguely estimated on most of the national forests designated as "commercial" forestland. Part of the function of the 1946 timber reappraisal, then, was to provide the necessary inventory base for an accelerated timber sales program.

In theory, if a working circle had an estimated volume of one billion board feet of commercially marketable logs, and if cutover areas required 100 years to grow new trees to sawtimber size again, then the forester could allow 10 million board feet a year to be cut under sustained yield. But in a real forest, many factors other than cutting affect timber volume: fire, wildlife, insects, and microbes consume a share of the forest, too. Some parts of the working circle may have soil, slopes, or climate conditions that make reforestation of cutover areas difficult or impossible. Reforestation of commercially desired species may not occur. Damage or waste during logging may reduce the actual volume available to market. Plus, the national forests by law had to serve multiple purposes, including wildlife habitat, recreation, grazing, and watershed protection. A responsible public lands forester had to take these and many other difficult to quantify factors into consideration when estimating what the allowable cut should be. However, if the forester was told to assume that the working circle would be managed intensively in the future — that fire suppression by the agency would eliminate 90 percent of the natural fire loss; that greater use of pesticides would reduce insect and disease losses by another 90 percent; that cutover areas would be immediately replanted with genetically engineered, faster growing, commercially desirable tree species; that because of new utilization technology trees could be harvested at 60 years of age rather than 100; that careful logging would increase utilization; and that the negative effects of timber cutting on other multiple uses would be mitigated — then, under these new assumptions, the allowable cut could be much higher. Judgments of whether or not a forest is managed on sustained yield principles thus depend on what assumptions are adopted. As pressure to increase harvests from the national forests grew, and as incentives to meet the rising timber demand filtered down the organizational ladder, agency foresters became adept at altering their assumptions to justify ever higher allowable cuts.

This is essentially what happened as working circle management plans were revised in the years following World War Two. In nearly all cases, the revised plans raised allowable cuts and aimed for maximum timber harvests under intensive management as the Washington Office had requested. The 1948 *Report of the Chief* stated, "In handling the national-forest timber resources the Forest Service is working toward intensive management for maximum continuous production."[31] Ira J. Mason, head of the Forest Service's Division of Timber Management in this period, took the lead in pushing each of the regional offices to promote accelerated timber harvests. Mason also enlisted the agency's Division of Information and Education to help bolster public support for the idea of maximum production through intensive management. He wrote: "The Division of Timber Management needs a campaign to sell intensive forestry on the national forests to the people who will be directly affected by our Timber Management programs. These groups are primarily labor, operators, dependent communities, and local consumers. We need to develop an understanding in these groups of the various things which must be done in order to obtain maximum timber yields from the national forests."[32]

Other forest resources besides trees required attention from the agency. The rush of emphasis on wood products, however, rendered nontimber professionals and user groups increasingly marginal (unless their interests were compatible with timber harvesting, as has often been the case with ranchers). Bernard Frank, an economist and Assistant Chief of Forest Influences in the Washington Office, spoke eloquently for those marginal interests. He reminded his colleagues at a Society of American Foresters meeting in 1947 that many national forests contained little commercial timber, having been established mainly to protect watersheds. This being the case, he found it ironic that professional forestry thinking had nevertheless focused almost entirely on timber values: "Timber conservation has furnished the dominant motive for forest development policies and for public and private expenditures to protect, improve, and maintain the cover." Frank added that "many doubts have arisen as to whether timber considerations alone can safely assure the proper functioning of the forest as a whole." The confidence foresters placed in silvicultural technology needed to be tempered by caution and a concern for the broader public interest in forests, he counseled.[33] Frank perceived the Forest Service moving away from such caution and concern.

As timber production increased on the national forests, discussions of the Forest Service's administrative policy of "multiple use" grew more prominent. Richard G. Lillard's popular and scholarly history of forests and forest policy, published in 1947, explained multiple use as the "latest" government program for managing public lands in the public interest: "This requires a forester to be broad and wise in his management of land. He must see the forest as more than a timber crop. He must solve the interrelated problems of use by wild life, livestock, loggers, irrigationists, wilderness lovers, picnickers, summer-home owners, wood choppers — all on the same parcel of land."[34] This emphasis on multiple use by lay conservationists reflected their fear that timber production values might dominate national forest management and threaten to turn the public's forests into a reserve supply of wood products for industry.

Other indications of a surge of interest in multiple use policy were a session on the topic featured at the 1946 American Forest Congress sponsored by the AFA, and efforts by the Society of American Foresters (SAF) between 1945 and 1947 to develop a formal policy advocating multiple use, which the SAF then submitted as a referendum to their membership in the July 1947 issue of the *Journal of Forestry.* Also at the SAF's 1947 meeting, two presentations presaged a trend toward multidisciplinary forestry that would come of age in the 1970s — one by Walter Mulford, Chief of the

Forest Service's Division of Personnel Management, and the other by H. Dean Cochran of the University of California, Berkeley, School of Forestry. The presentation by Cochran, titled "Future Trends in Federal Employment of Foresters," pointed out that 90 percent of the professionals employed by the Forest Service were trained as "foresters" specializing in silviculture (and a significant portion of the remaining 10 percent were engineers specializing in building timber access roads). Characterizing the recent demand for timber and livestock forage as beyond the current capacity of the national forests to supply, and noting simultaneous increases in demand for water, wildlife, and recreation, Cochran observed that "a common denominator of these use trends is more scientific, technical, intensive management. . . . The increased intensiveness of management in handling especially our timber and our range work has resulted in materially broadening the base of our personnel pyramid, since the end of the war." This quantitatively broadened base of expertise was desirable but qualitatively narrow, he said. In coming years the Forest Service would need more diversely trained professionals to deal with the effects of development on interrelated resources and to manage forest land "for its many and varied uses."[35]

In the other forward-looking presentation, titled "The Decade 1948–58 in the Forestry Schools of the United States," Walter Mulford commented on the "maturing" of the forestry profession and the direction forestry schools should take in the coming decade. Posing the rhetorical question, "Should our master-plan for forestry education include provision for a wide range of specialized curricula?" Mulford answered an emphatic yes. Forestry schools in the United States focused too narrowly on timber management, he said, and failed to adequately prepare students for the forestry of the future. "Phases of wildland management other than tree-forestry should either be recognized as full brothers to tree-forestry in a widely inclusive profession, or they should have the status of independent professions, with schools of their own."[36]

Lewis M. Turner, Dean of the School of Forest, Range, and Wildlife Management at Utah State Agricultural College, had offered a similar assessment two years earlier in the *Journal of Forestry*. Arguing for a broader curriculum in forestry schools, Turner blamed part of the narrowness of the discipline on the Civil Service. Aspirants to government jobs had to take one of two exams available to the profession in 1946: a forester's exam or a range manager's exam. The minimum curriculum requirements attached to each field were narrow in scope. In the case of the forestry option, only one course in either range management or wildlife management was required. Most forestry schools at the time understandably shaped their curriculum to help students excel on the Civil Service exams, and accordingly focused on timber management. Ninety percent of the professionals employed by the Forest Service were trained as timber managers in these highly specialized forestry schools.[37]

Turner complained that outside the academic world most students entering public service needed training in the management of multiple uses on real forests — and they were not getting it. A few schools, especially in the West, had begun to require more coursework in nontimber resources, but even the most progressive still failed to offer an appropriate blend of technical training to prepare graduates for the kind of work they would be involved in on the national forests. At Turner's Utah State, which was progressive at the time, 70 percent of the technical forestry courses students took involved some aspect of timber management, 15 percent involved range management, and another 15 percent wildlife management. Turner thought the *ideal* curriculum blend for western forest managers (except for those working in the Pacific Northwest) would be 38 percent range management, 28 percent timber management, 18 percent wildlife management, and 8 percent each for watershed and recreation management. To achieve such a balance, however, would require changes in the Civil Service exam — perhaps offering a third exam option in wild land management, he suggested — and a commitment from the professional society of foresters to make broader curricula a factor in ruling on forestry school accreditations. Neither of these changes was forthcoming.

Wildlife

A Forest Service press release of April 12, 1944, announced that Lloyd Swift had just been named Chief of the Division of Wildlife Management. "Mr. Swift takes up his duties at a time when the big-game population on national forests is larger than at any time since 1900."[38] Federal, state, and private efforts at fish and wildlife conservation in the twentieth century — and aggressive federal "predator control" programs — had allowed some waterfowl, elk, and deer populations to rebound dramatically, in some cases from near extinction. The year Swift took over, the Chief of the Forest Service reported that "one of the surprising developments of the war period has been the continued, and in some localities the increased, interest in the use of national forests for hunting, fishing, and wildlife study."[39] After the war, wildlife-related recreation virtually exploded, and the national forests provided both crucial habitat and vital recreational opportunities. In 1948, the Forest Service estimated that the national forests supported 16.5 million "man-days" of wildlife-related recreation, a fourfold increase in four years. The national forests then held most of the nation's best trout waters (90,000 miles of trout streams and 1.5 million acres of lakes) and habitat for one-third of the nation's total big game population. In the West, 70 percent of all big game spent some or all of their life on the national forests.[40] These facts make it easy to understand why wildlife conservationists had been at the forefront of forest conservation movements. They even played a central role in lobbying for the creation of the national forests a half century earlier.[41]

Swift, a range manager who specialized in livestock-wildlife interactions, enthusiastically accepted the opportunity to head the Wildlife Division, a position that had been created only a decade earlier. But he was troubled by the way the organization treated wildlife management, and he remained troubled throughout his tenure and into his retirement in 1963. One of his concerns was that the agency consigned wildlife management to a marginal position within the bureaucracy, making it more difficult for wildlife managers to influence policies and decisions. In a 1968 interview, Swift recalled:

> Up until the time that the Division of Wildlife Management was created, in 1936, wildlife was part of range management. And even today the wildlife men in the western regions are in the Division of Range Management. . . . I've always felt very strongly that wildlife must not be a part of range management. Because they are competitive. . . . A wildlife man should be free from this entanglement with range, so that he can fully represent the wildlife resource in the policy making of the Forest Service.[42]

Swift felt that wildlife managers, more than other resource specialists, had a feel for multiple use. "Very often we have timber people who see nothing but timber; range people who see nothing but range. But that's not characteristic of wildlife people. They're pretty sensitive to coordinated land use." But once again, wildlife managers were "not high enough up to participate in policy in a strong way."[43]

If wildlife managers wielded little clout in the agency, they found themselves completely powerless before the Appropriations Committees of Congress. In 1947, Congress totally eliminated the budget for wildlife management for fiscal year 1948. Out of an outlay of nearly $24 million for national forest protection and management, the House Agricultural Appropriations Committee could not find its way to approve even the pittance of $174,000 for wildlife that the administration requested. Timber sales administration, in contrast, was allocated $3.3 million (with a supplemental appropriation of $475,000 added later in the year).[44]

This action by Congress in 1947 was an ironic prelude to a very significant year in the history of wildlife conservation. In 1948, the International Union for the Conservation of Nature (IUCN) organized itself under the auspices of the United Nations Educational, Scientific, and Cultural Organization (UNESCO). The IUCN, comprised mainly of scientists, targeted the disappearance of species and the preservation of natural habitat as its major organizational focus. The Conservation Foundation also got its start in 1948. Aldo Leopold, one of the founders of wildlife management science and a Forest Service employee for many years, tragically died fighting a neighbor's field fire in 1948, just before his classic series of essays on conservation, *A Sand County Almanac,* came out in print. Two popular and influential books published in 1948 — William Vogt's *Road to Survival* and Fairfield Osborn's *Our Plundered Planet* — warned that deforestation, soil erosion, and the exploitation of natural resources threatened the survival of civilization. Both books elaborated themes touched on the previous year in Richard Lillard's *The Great Forest.*[45]

All this concern for conservation, and wildlife in particular, apparently had little effect on the holders of the government purse strings, though. The Forest Service explained to Congress in 1948 that it needed to monitor and inventory wildlife populations and habitat conditions on its 180 million acres nationwide, coordinate with state game and fish agencies in developing and maintaining wildlife habitat, help state agencies manage and police hunting and fishing activities, and integrate wildlife concerns with other management activities. Yet, for the second year in a row, Congress approved no funding for wildlife in the fiscal year (FY) 1949 Forest Service budget.

Swift's own salary had to be paid out of discretionary funds! A House Appropriations Committee report insisted that even though the wildlife budget had been eliminated, Congress did not intend to interfere with wildlife-related work. In the committee's words,

> Last year the committee and the Congress eliminated the budget allocation of $174,164 for the protection of the wildlife resources of the forests. It was indicated in the report, however, that it was not intended to forbid or unduly limit the work in connection with wildlife on the national forests. It was indicated to the Forest Service that they should readjust the allocations of the other work projects shown in their budget statement and effect transfers therefrom in amounts essential for the prudent work in connection with wildlife on the national forests. That policy is to be continued for the ensuing year.[46]

In response, the 1948 *Report of the Chief* lamented:

> During the war, when efforts had to be concentrated on other activities, the Forest Service discontinued practically all wildlife operational projects. A big backlog of needed work and of critical maintenance of prewar developments piled up. No funds have been appropriated directly for wildlife work during the past 2 years, and the backlog is still growing.[47]

Many in Congress felt that the wildlife programs run by individual state governments (with some federal subsidies) were the proper vehicle for game management. But these programs were chronically underfunded in most cases too. Besides, state game and fish departments usually concentrated their efforts on regulating hunting and fishing (law enforcement, essentially), while the Forest Service needed *habitat* management specialists on staff to ensure that wildlife concerns were integrated into development plans. Even minimal wildlife management personnel needs remained largely unmet, however, for the next three decades. The current endangered species program enacted in 1973 can be viewed as a legacy of the failure to properly protect wildlife habitat during the postwar years.

Recreation

The Forest Service felt recreational opportunity was an essential service it supplied to the public — part of its mission. During this postwar era of increased use and active management, however, the agency took to providing this service as though it was engaging in commodity production. Forest Service recreation management focused on construction and development. As with wildlife management's focus on sport fishing and big game hunting, recreation management focused on developed camping and picnicking facilities, beaches, boat ramps, and ski resorts. Undeveloped or nonconsumptive types of recreation — scenery, wilderness, hiking, bird-watching — played second fiddle.

The Forest Service argued aggressively for additional funding to handle the increased demand for recreation. A passage from the 1945 *Report of the Chief* is indicative:

> Now that gasoline, tires, and new automobiles are becoming available [end of wartime rationing], more people than ever before will seek vacations in the forests. The need for picnic areas, campgrounds and organizational camps will be far greater than can be served by existing facilities. Plans are being laid for a large program of construction and development. Meeting this need in itself will provide employment in all forest regions.[48]

Clean and attractive facilities offered a most effective public relations opportunity for the agency. With recreation occurring on every national forest and a national forest in nearly every state, outdoor enthusiasts provided the Forest Service a powerful constituency — if satisfied.

Like an industry, recreation generates direct and indirect economic benefits to local communities. Its clear, quantifiable, and marketable values make investments in outdoor recreation eminently salable to chambers of commerce, politicians, and others who may not engage in recreation themselves. The same *Report of the Chief* quoted above shrewdly pointed out the relationship between recreation and economics:

> Before the war, vacation and pleasure travel was edging toward second place in the Nation's industries — between 4 and 5 billion dollars was expended for that purpose annually. . . . Industries employing hundreds of thousands of people benefit by such expenditures stemming in part from use of forest land. Many business enterprises — vacation resorts, dude ranches, guiding, and taxidermy — depend al-

most entirely on the forest and its wildlife. Indirect benefits accrue to the transportation, food, clothing, fur, firearm, ammunition, sporting goods, automobile, petroleum, publishing, and many other industries.[49]

All these references to economic benefits were designed to encourage support from Congress for greater recreation investments on the national forests. The Civilian Conservation Corps in the 1930s had built an incredible array of campgrounds, roads, trails, and other facilities on national forest lands, but World War Two ended that experiment in youth employment, as it likewise curtailed maintenance of those facilities by the Forest Service. Partly due to gasoline rationing and partly due to other more obvious factors, recreational use of the forests declined 65 percent in the three years following Pearl Harbor, but such use climbed back to the prewar high of 18 million visits again by 1946. Two years later, visits to the national forests topped 24 million. Existing visitor facilities were greatly strained because recreational use concentrated in the areas with developed camping and picnicking sites.[50] That year Lyle Watts complained: "This heavy public use is overtaxing many existing national-forest recreation facilities and making the job of clean-up and maintenance very difficult. Since the war there have been virtually no funds available for development of additional public recreation facilities to relieve the overcrowded conditions on existing areas."[51]

The Society of American Foresters' annual meeting in 1947 included a session on recreation, and among the panelists were two Forest Service men who made prescient predictions about the future of forest recreation, while jabbing the profession for its overemphasis on wood products and dollar values. The American people demand forest-related recreation, they said, and foresters are going to have to learn to live with it. Rocky Mountain Regional Forester John Spencer put it this way: "There is no point in trying to explain this recreational urge of our people. Its existence and its imperious demands are demonstrated facts which we cannot ignore."[52] But most professional foresters had nonetheless resisted accepting recreation as a co-equal partner with timber production. Ray Bassett, Chief of the Forest Recreation Section in Milwaukee, chided the conference participants, "As a group foresters have done little to promote intelligent, productive use of the forest for recreation, or even to manifest much interest in it. It has been largely forced upon them by public demand."[53]

Part of the problem with the profession (the Forest Service not excluded), Bassett explained, was that foresters tended to assign mainly material values and objectives to forests and their management. "We have been thinking for a long time in terms of goods rather than of people, of natural resources rather than of human resources and needs. Society now seems to be trying to establish the proper relationship between these two points of view. The impetus is coming from the people."[54] Despite the fact that recreation was clearly a money-making industry, other equally important nonmaterial values associated with recreation had to be understood and accommodated when planning for the multiple use management of the nation's forests. Spencer warned that "the degree of emphasis to be given recreation . . . cannot be safely based on a dollars and cents comparison of recreation with other resources."[55]

This view of recreation as a public good with associated economic, psychological, and spiritual values set it apart from — in a sense, above — other material uses of the forest, according to its advocates. In the tradition of Frederick Law Olmsted's "parks for people" philosophy, Spencer added, "Play is not a luxury, it is a complement to work, especially in this age when more and more of man's active life is confined within the artificiality of steel and concrete structures and molded by the pressure of a complex civilization." Bassett went further, elevating recreation to the status of a social movement "about to take its place alongside education as a democratic prerequisite."[56]

Orienting management decisions toward public desires as opposed to orienting them toward profit and production has always been a policy prerogative of Congress and the agencies with jurisdiction over public lands. The new recreation constituency began demanding the government act on this prerogative. Bassett and Spencer were on the cutting edge of an attempt to renegotiate priorities and values in national forest management, to push the professional society of foresters in a new direction, to elevate nonmarket recreational values to a higher status in the decision-making calculus, based on public demand for such values. With comments aimed at the Forest Service hierarchy, Bassett asserted, "The continuity and adequacy of a forest policy rest wholly on the attitude of mind of the American people and the thinking of those people is not influenced so much by fear of a shortage of inch boards or two-by-fours as it is by the hope or desire to spend a happy vacation in a scene of unimpaired forest beauty." Bassett and Spencer's promotion of "public demand" as a criterion for decision making proved to be a double-edged sword, however. When Bassett claimed, "The public forester must satisfy the public desire," his words directly paralleled those of lobbyists for the timber industry who claimed "the nation demands lumber at reasonable prices."[57]

Conflicting demands for forest resources had to be settled by establishing priorities. In Spencer's Rocky Mountain region, as in southern California and the eastern national forests, recreation was fast becoming the dominant use.[58] Which of the multiple uses should receive priority when conflicts occurred was a growing concern. This issue, which the Forest Service for obvious reasons insisted should be settled on a case-by-case basis, would increasingly plague forest managers in coming decades. Interest groups, dissatisfied with agency decisions, hammered the Forest Service repeatedly in the 1950s and then fought it out in Congress and the courts in the 1960s and 1970s. The agency tried to contain these battles and keep the decisions from being carried over their heads, to no avail.

The problem of reconciling competing uses had not overly troubled the Forest Service before the war. Much less activity took place on the forests during this "custodial" phase of Forest Service history, and what did occur was spread out over such a vast domain that there seemed to be plenty of resources and opportunities for everyone. After the war, with the unprecedented surge in both timber production and outdoor recreation, conflicts among user groups increased and debates about priorities and dominant use appeared much more frequently. Bassett and Spencer anticipated this and expressed to the SAF convention-goers their own hopes for the future. Bassett suggested that "in the long range planning of public wildlands in particular, recreation should be given the benefit of the doubt where there is a question as to which are the present and prospective dominant, codominate and subordinate uses."[59] Fearing that too much emphasis on meeting present demands for lumber and pulpwood might foreclose prime recreational opportunities for the future, Spencer argued that public agencies should adopt a conservative view and keep as many options open as possible:

Public forest management, unlike that of individuals or corporations, is not limited to the benefit of an immediate generation, but is projected far into the future where people yet unborn may enjoy a full measure of the things we guard today. . . . If we err at all it must be on the conservative side of overestimating the recreational needs of the people.[60]

Grazing

One of the most widespread uses of national forest land, especially in the West between the Rocky Mountains and the Sierra Nevada and Cascade ranges, was (and is) domestic livestock grazing. While the Forest Service accepted grazing as a legitimate use of forest lands, it never accorded to grazing the high priority that livestock owners felt they should have. And to the great consternation of the agency, stockmen in the West had the capacity to object vociferously to Forest Service policies. Political allies of the graziers, furthermore, could effectively bribe, mandate, or intimidate the agency into treating graziers more favorably.

The majority of the national forests in the arid West — the desert Southwest, the Great Basin, and southern California — were designated primarily to protect watershed values. Much of the area suffered from heavy overgrazing in the late nineteenth century by an unregulated livestock industry taking economic advantage of the free forage on federal lands. When the Forest Service entered the scene as a new landlord, graziers resented the interference and resisted the agency's efforts to charge fees and bring livestock use down to levels necessary to protect watersheds.[61] Although some individual ranchers learned to work with the Forest Service and appreciate its efforts, a lifelong antagonism developed between the organized livestock industry and the agency. Because of their early, effective penetration of local and state governments, western livestock interests wielded extensive political clout, way out of proportion to their numbers and their economic importance, and they could make life miserable for the Forest Service when they wanted to. The late 1940s was one of those times when the western livestock industry organized a sustained attack on the Forest Service, other federal land management agencies, and on regulation and public land ownership in general.

The science of grassland ecology had come of age in America in the 1930s, stimulated by ecologist Frederick Clements's work on the Great

Plains. Backed by new knowledge, grassland ecologists energized conservation thinking and infused public agencies with a renewed commitment to better manage commercial use of the rangelands. Despite its commitment, the Forest Service remained frustrated with its range management program throughout the midcentury. A long history of failure to get livestock grazing down to "carrying capacity" stimulated a firm resolve to make changes, but something always blocked progress. The World War One "beef shortage" had attenuated Progressive era attempts to reduce stocking levels on the forests and led to extensive overgrazing in the name of the "war emergency." Then, just as the agency began making progress in reducing numbers in the 1920s, the Depression hit, forcing it to make concessions to rural communities on hard times. World War Two did not repeat the overgrazing disaster of the first war, but a lack of funds hamstrung continued reform efforts during the war years. Historian William D. Rowley found that "a sense of frustration with the control that national events exerted over serious range management appeared in departmental memoranda."[62] One of those memoranda came from retiring Regional Forester Clarence N. Woods of the Intermountain Region in Ogden, Utah. In December 1942, he wrote to Chief Lyle Watts complaining that after thirty-five years of grazing management a large portion of the rangelands in his region were still in unsatisfactory condition. His impatience with the situation came through in his language:

> There is no more difficult job on a national forest than that of RM [range management] on districts with much depleted range, which inevitably presents big grazing problems. It requires, in a high degree, patience, diplomacy, familiarity with RM, courage, aggressiveness and persistence to handle big grazing problems successfully. . . . I know we have been told that good PR made it imperative that we go slow. Surely, it's poor PR to countenance depletion of the natural resources.[63]

Others in the agency bolstered Woods's conclusions, but the Washington Office nevertheless could not countenance the "stridency" with which Woods promoted reductions in livestock use. Washington is a political arena and graziers had friends in high places. The Washington Office chastised Woods for his impatience and intemperance, causing him to respond angrily in May 1943, "I am much disturbed, for the good of the Service, and for the cause of conservation, at the attitude of the WO [Washington Office]. It is my judgment, after much consideration, that the WO is in certain very important things showing a decided timidity, fear, attitude of appeasement."[64]

The officials in Washington were in a tough position. The more the Forest Service tried to regulate grazing, the more the graziers harassed the agency through such powerful members of Congress as Patrick McCarran of Nevada, Frank Barrett and Edward Robertson of Wyoming, and Wesley D'Ewart of Montana (all ranchers themselves). During the war, Senator McCarran staged a series of hearings on the Grazing Service (shortly to become the Bureau of Land Management) and its range policies. The hearings mainly served as a soapbox for ranchers and their congressional allies to excoriate the agency. The result was an emasculated Grazing Service powerless to regulate use of the public lands under its charge.[65] The lesson was not lost on Forest Service leaders. In an attempt at appeasement without surrender, the Washington Office in 1944 transferred Edward P. Cliff from the Fremont National Forest in Oregon to headquarters. He had training in forestry as well as range and wildlife management; plus he possessed an invaluable ability to get along well with ranchers while still accomplishing reductions. The Washington Office brought him in to serve as Assistant Chief of Range Management. He stayed there two years before being moved to Ogden to serve as Assistant Regional Forester in charge of range and wildlife. (Cliff eventually rose to become Chief of the Forest Service between 1962 and 1972, holding tenure during the rise of the modern environmental movement. His conciliatory style, old-school outlook, and his defense of clearcutting made him an object of vilification among conservation groups that would have been his allies in the 1940s.)

In a 1981 oral history, Cliff recalled that although times were rough during the 1940s, the agency made significant progress in grazing management reform.[66] New studies firmly backed reductions recommended by the agency, making it easier for range managers to argue their point; and more money began flowing after the war for actual range management, allowing the agency to design and subsidize new, more effective grazing systems (utilizing added fencing, pasture rotations, reseeding, etc.).[67] As a sign of the times, the first professional organization of range conservationists, the Society for Range Management, formed between 1946 and 1948.[68] With increased confidence and tentative backing from the Washington Office, line officers in the field began to institute some long-needed and painful grazing reductions. In many cases, the adjustments went smoothly. In others, trouble brewed. Late in 1945, Colorado's Routt National Forest Supervisor Charles Fox had sent a blunt letter to grazing permittees, announcing with apparent finality that "for one reason or another our ranges in general are overstocked and on many not only have inferior [plant] species become established, but active erosion is occurring." After explaining that he would have to close grazing entirely on some areas to begin the process of rehabilitation, he warned, "a few years of nonuse will not do the trick; neither will a reduction of a few hundred head here and there. The situation calls for rather drastic action, and as land managers responsible to the people of the United States, there is no alternate course open to us. We must ask that substantial reductions be made."[69]

The local Grazing Advisory Board (made up of ranchers) protested the decision as well as Fox's "dictatorial" manner. The permittees affected by the decision protested to their congressmen, while the Colorado legislature the next month passed a resolution calling for an investigation of the Forest Service's grazing reduction policy. Fox's frustration with the resistant permittees and the agency's "go slow" policy was shared by many other land managers. Similar episodes erupted all over the West. While upper levels of the agency were trying to get line officers to avoid exacerbating tensions, line officers were trying to get more support from their superiors for firm, immediate action.[70] The Arizona legislature in the meantime had passed a resolution similar to the Colorado one, and New Mexico would soon follow suit. The organized livestock associations in 1945, 1946, and 1947 repeatedly passed resolutions proposing that national forest rangelands and other public lands be turned over to the states for eventual sale to ranchers and others.[71]

Senator McCarran, Senator Robertson, and Congressman Barrett (who would later become a senator) introduced various bills in the 79th Congress (1945-46) that would have redefined grazing privileges as a vested right, given stockmen much greater influence in range management decision-making, and made provisions to allow for the transfer of certain public rangelands to state ownership, with additional opportunities for private purchase.[72] None of these bills passed, but the effort sobered the Forest Service and conservationists. A great outpouring of both support and opposition arose over what critics called the "Great Land Grab." Public awareness especially developed around a series of hearings organized in several western states in 1947 by rancher-congressman Frank Barrett of Wyoming, who chaired the House Interior Committee's Public Lands Subcommittee. The hearings, dubbed by the *Denver Post* as "Stockman Barrett's Wild West Show," offered a forum for unruly mobs of ranchers and ranchers' opponents to harangue the Forest Service and each other. Barrett conducted himself partly like a backwoods preacher of the private enterprise faith and partly like a lawyer (which he was) in vituperative attacks on the Forest Service, delivering long-winded diatribes against swivel-chair bureaucrats, long-haired intellectuals, and communists. The western papers had a field day, and so did a popular, influential editor of *Harper's* magazine, Bernard DeVoto.

Throughout 1947 and 1948, DeVoto and many of his friends and colleagues carried on a virtual war of words with the ranchers.[73] It was a classic confrontation. DeVoto wrote his most influential essay, "The West against Itself," for the January 1947 issue of *Harper's*. A perspicacious reflection on western history and the western character, it took direct and penetrating aim at McCarran, Barrett, and Robertson. From then until 1954, DeVoto periodically used his editorial column in *Harper's,* "The Easy Chair," to blast efforts to despoil the nation's natural resources.

In "The West against Itself," DeVoto argued that public lands ranchers lived a romantic dream of independence. Claiming to be hardy, self-sufficient pioneers, they railed against eastern capitalists, but were actually willing dependents, peons of bankers and railroads and slaughterhouses, beggars on the public rangeland. With grazing systems subsidized by tax dollars, they fought blindly to maintain excessive numbers of cows or sheep on their public land allotments, resulting in range deterioration that ultimately worked against their own interests. This was the irony of the West against itself: "The West does not want to be liberated from the system of exploitation that it has always violently resented. It only wants to buy into it."[74]

DeVoto perceived a second irony in the ranchers' request for federal handouts (such as range improvements, water development, and predator control) while simultaneously demanding hands off. "It shakes down to a platform: get out and give us more money. Much of the dream of economic

liberation is dependent upon continuous, continually increasing federal subsidies — subsidies which it also insists must be made without safeguard or
regulation."[75]

More irony, still: The only force preserving the West's renewable natural
resources from total liquidation by foreign (that is, eastern) exploiters was
the federal government and its public land agencies. Yet western ranchers,
miners, lumbermen, politicians, and economic boosters usually sided with
the plunderers, vilifying the very people who strove to put the West's economic development on a sustainable basis. In DeVoto's inimitable words,

> So, at the very moment when the West is blueprinting an economy
> which must be based on the sustained, permanent use of its natural
> resources, it is also conducting an assault on those resources with the
> simple objective of liquidating them. The dissociation of intelligence
> could go no farther but there it is — and there is the West yesterday,
> today, and forever. It is the Western mind stripped to the basic split.
> The West as its own worst enemy. The West committing suicide.[76]

The rest of DeVoto's essay described the McCarran, Barrett, and Robertson
bills mentioned earlier and the public land privatization objectives of the
organized livestock industry. He concluded with a political call to arms to
the public, warning that the land grabbers could only succeed with public
support and would fail if an informed citizenry denounced their efforts. That
was in January 1947, a few months before Barrett's "Wild West Show"
began.

After a preliminary hearing in Washington, D.C., Barrett's Public Lands
Subcommittee traveled to Billings, Montana; Rawlins, Wyoming; Grand
Junction, Colorado; and Ely, Nevada. Events started out well for Barrett and
his cohorts, but by the end of the circuit the tables had turned. Sensing the
ghost of DeVoto's January 1947 personal attack on his policies, Barrett rose
to his feet in the Rawlins hearing and denounced the "scurrilous" remarks
made about him and his colleagues by certain eastern editors. (DeVoto
actually hailed from Utah.) The journalists, however, had the last word.
Extensive media coverage and the poison pens of DeVoto, his protege Wallace Stegner, Art Carhart, William Voigt, and others whipped up pro-conser-
vation sentiment and forced the congressional sponsors of the hearings to
publicly recant many of their more radical proposals. DeVoto's critical re-

construction of the most unflattering details of the hearings in his "Sacred Cows and Public Lands" (*Harper's,* July 1948) helped to generally discredit the whole affair.

In the end, the Barrett committee made six rather moderate recommendations to Secretary of Agriculture Clinton Anderson, only one entailing any change in existing grazing policies. That one asked for a three-year moratorium on grazing reductions until a thorough study of range conditions and justifications for the proposed reductions could be made. Anderson politely accepted the five noncontroversial recommendations in a letter to Barrett while rejecting the sixth with a detailed vindication of the Forest Service.[77] DeVoto observed, "The secretary's letter was just, courageous — and final."[78] Anderson resigned that year from his post in the Truman administration and won a seat in the Senate from his home state of New Mexico, besting Republican General Patrick J. Hurley in the election. This was bad news for the ranchers, as the defeated Hurley had been an outspoken champion of their cause. In a gutsy speech before the New Mexico Cattle Growers Association that election year, Anderson predicted that the future was not in the graziers' hands: "If there is going to be a battle, who has the most votes?" he asked, "the livestock ranchers or a combination of conservationists, game protective associations, public power enthusiasts, and the water interests? Who is going to come out second best?"[79]

Nevertheless, the graziers continued their campaign relatively unabated for another four years, their spirits dampening only after realizing that their goals of reining in the Forest Service would not receive even the support of the pro-business Eisenhower administration in 1953.

Forest Service Budget Politics

What the Forest Service claimed it would like to do and what the Forest Service had the capacity to do were usually at odds. Management capabilities are limited by knowledge, technology, environmental factors, social factors, and, perhaps most of all, budgets. Integrated multiple use–sustained yield management plans require supporting budgets, but while resource management planning is ostensibly a professional exercise, budgeting is almost wholly political. The elimination of the wildlife budget in fiscal years 1948 and 1949 provides a case in point. Another example is the livestock industry's threat in 1948 to have Congress slash the Forest Service's range management budget if the agency continued to advocate reductions.[80] While periodic negotiations of public policy are important milestone markers, the real proof of commitment — or lack thereof — to established forest policies is to be found in the annual funding process. Budget negotiations and allocations are an oft-neglected but absolutely crucial aspect of national forest management history.[81] Political ideology, economic objectives, and resource allocation priorities all constellate around the funding process. Congress will often direct an agency of the federal government to achieve some objective and then unabashedly fail to provide the necessary funds for the agency to accomplish its mission. There is also often a conflict between the congressional committees that *authorize* spending levels for government programs and the appropriations committees that actually *approve* the annual budget. The former usually (not always) authorize spending levels adequate to get a specific job done — such as reforestation — in a specific period of time; while the latter determine spending priorities based on overall budgetary considerations for that year. Because Congress is a complex corporate body with a constantly changing membership, this inconsistency is understandable, even inevitable; nevertheless its effects are destructive. Worse, the failure to integrate policy with appropriations is often deliberate. Again, this is Congress's prerogative.

With the 1946 midterm elections, Republicans gained a majority of seats in Congress and with that majority came chairmanship and control over the various committees. A new so-called fiscal conservatism (against social spending and government economic activism, except in the realm of defense spending) reigned when budget negotiations began in January 1947. Timber industry representatives were the most active public participants in Forest Service budget hearings in the 1940s, and in some cases the only public participants. Sometimes this occurred by congressional design, since committee chairmen accepted testimony by invitation only. Examining the testimony of industry lobbyists and appropriations committee members is instructive.

President Truman's FY 1947 budget — his first postwar budget, submitted to Congress in January 1946 — called for a 25 percent increase in funds for "forest protection and management" and a 250 percent increase in funds for roads and trails, the latter slated almost entirely for building new timber access roads. These proposed increases were especially significant in that

Truman, who was aggressively looking for ways to reduce the federal deficit that had ballooned during the war, had proposed a cut of 9 percent from the Department of Agriculture's overall budget (the Forest Service's parent organization).[82] While the timber industry approved of funding increases for timber sales, access roads, and fire and pest control, other parts of the budget made them nervous. Concerned about the general growth in the Forest Service's budget, Stuart Moir of the Western Pine Association wrote to his friend Harris Collingwood at the National Lumber Manufacturers Association (NLMA) just after the president's budget came out, complaining that "the USFS has grown gradually larger and larger and with it they attempt to regulate everyone else's business and autocratically say 'do it our way or else.' "[83] (The NLMA represented fourteen regional associations of lumber manufacturers nationwide, the largest, most influential lumber lobbying organization in the country, then and now. It changed its name to the National Forest Products Association in the 1970s.) Moir suggested they scrutinize how the 4 million additional dollars for national forest protection and management was to be used and attempt to block funding for land acquisition, regulation proposals, and the agency information and education program. Following through on this suggestion the next year, NLMA's executive vice-president, Richard Colgan, Jr., appeared before the House and Senate Agricultural Appropriations Subcommittees to deliver a statement of industry policy regarding the Forest Service budget. His testimony exemplifies the prevailing political and economic ideology among industry leaders in this postwar period and deserves extended treatment.

Prefatory to his comments on the Forest Service budget, Colgan stated, "The lumber industry is in full sympathy with the announced policy of the present Congress that the Federal Budget must be balanced, that the national debt must be reduced, and that taxes must be lowered. To accomplish this purpose, a bold and fearless approach that will result in the elimination of unnecessary activities, wasteful practices, and extravagances must be taken. *I feel that the very existence of our form of Government depends upon such action*" (emphasis added).[84] This exaggerated linking of the Forest Service budget with the survival of American political institutions reflected a general ideological opposition to federal regulation. The institutions Colgan and others felt were at risk were traditional private property rights, relatively unregulated markets, and the freedom to accumulate wealth. They saw the

Forest Service as one manifestation of a centralizing and dictatorial impulse in government *hostile to private industry* that had to be nipped in the bud if possible.

Beyond this ideological position, Colgan offered some specific suggestions to eliminate those "unnecessary activities" and "extravagances" of the Forest Service. First, the timber sales program was inefficient, spending 28 percent of its receipts on the administration of the sales. Congress should cut that budget by one quarter yet retain the same level of sales. (This tactic backfired, as will be explained shortly, and consequently Colgan supported full funding for the timber sales program in his testimony to the same committee the following year.) The Information and Education branch of the agency, "which spearheads the great Forest Service propaganda effort," should be gutted. Employing Cold War metaphors in a colorful peroration, Colgan stated, "Funds allocated for salaries of personnel in the national, regional[,] local forest supervisors and rangers offices are being used to blanket the countryside with the Forest Service ideologies of Federal Control and Regulation. These field employees through appearances at meetings and forums; through press releases and articles; by land, by sea, and by air attempt to develop public sentiment in favor of more power for the Forest Service" (p. 5).

Industry lobbyists were also concerned about federal land acquisition. They wanted the Forest Service to *sell* some of its commercial timber lands, not acquire more. Colgan recommended that a budget item of $1 million for land acquisition be eliminated. The Forest Service had another method of acquiring additional lands, however, which did not involve direct appropriations, and the NLMA wanted that stopped, too. This other method went by the indicative title of "stumps for stumpage." Congress had authorized the agency in 1922 to acquire cutover private lands in order to rehabilitate them, and to pay for those lands by allowing the owner to cut and haul off designated national forest timber of equal value in exchange for the land. Industry and agency foresters referred (and still refer) to standing marketable trees as "stumpage," with "stumps" being what is left after harvesting the trees. Thus, "stumps for stumpage" meant trading denuded land for national forest timber. The agency justified this practice by arguing that *someone* had to be responsible for reforesting cutover lands if the owners failed to do it. The Forest Service could regulate how the owner cut national forest timber and at the same time acquire and rehabilitate land that would have sat eroding and unproductive. Where private enterprise failed to protect the public interest, the Forest Service should step in. This practice used national forest trees as capital to purchase relatively worthless private lands, under the expectation that the forest capital on both the federal land and the cutover private land could be renewed in 100 years or so as a second "crop" of trees matured.

Colgan admitted that his industry had mixed feelings about stumps for stumpage: "To be sure, this procedure is welcomed by some members of the lumber industry who have benefited by acquiring raw material for their sawmills at a very attractive figure" (p. 5); but he saw the practice mainly as another somewhat devious method for agency self-aggrandizement. (A total of 2,325,206 acres had been acquired by the Forest Service from 1930 to 1946 — a little over 1 percent of the national forest land base.) For the record, Colgan also submitted a resolution from the Senate and House of Representatives of the state of Oregon opposing, like the NLMA, further federal land acquisitions via stumps for stumpage — a display of industry's political clout at the state level.

The last item Colgan targeted for budget cuts, ironically, was roads. Access roads on the national forests, other than designated through highways, were paid for by two methods: (1) direct funding from Congress, and (2) reimbursements to timber purchasers who built access roads themselves under Forest Service guidelines. As in the case of stumps for stumpage, the reimbursement for timber purchaser built roads came not as cash, but as logs — that is, if the purchaser built the road instead of the Forest Service, the cost of building the road was deducted from the price the purchaser paid for the national forest timber. If the estimated costs of building the road were high enough, the timber sale contract could be purchased from the Forest Service for little more than a nominal fee. The NLMA supported timber purchaser built roads and generally opposed Forest Service built roads. They believed that the primary function of roads should be to access timber. Roads built for other purposes were seen as superfluous. Colgan actually complained that the Forest Service had recently spent appropriated road funds to "build up the road system on the . . . national forests without regard to the end expediency in getting out so-called urgently-needed timber" (pp.

9–10). He argued that the Forest Service should use appropriated road construction funds only to access virgin timber and only in areas where the roads "cannot be built by buyers of government timber" with purchaser road credits. In other words, appropriated funds should be used whenever the costs of building the roads exceeded the value of the timber to be extracted. To minimize the construction of roads for nontimber related purposes and to maximize the construction of timber purchaser roads, the NLMA suggested lopping $7.5 million off the $12.5 million road budget — so long as that reduction did not affect the amount of timber to be cut on the national forests.[85]

In contrast to these recommended budget cuts, the NLMA proposed increases in a budget category referred to as "forest protection." Over the years "protection" of the forests came to mean the protection of *timber* from destruction by fire, insects, and disease, so that the economic value in the "stumpage" could be marketed. Both industry and the Forest Service wholly adopted this narrower interpretation of the 1897 Organic Act's mandate to protect the forests. As Colgan proclaimed: "we urge that you do not decrease appropriations covering forest protection . . . for these natural enemies of the forests destroy merchantable timber" (p. 11).

The Forest Service was not merely a passive participant in this effort by industry to slash part of its budget. When Congress actually did cut its timber sales funds (though not as much as the NLMA suggested), agency foresters in the field informed national forest timber purchasers that the promised level of sales could not be sustained because Congress had cut its budget. If they, the timber purchasers, wanted sales returned to desired levels, they would have to press for more funding. This considerably irritated industry lobbyists. Moir and another colleague in Portland, Oregon, wrote to George Fuller of the NLMA's Washington, D.C., office in February 1948 advocating a change in strategy for the upcoming budget hearings. Moir's colleague wrote, "it seems to Stuart and I that as a matter of tactics they [the Forest Service] should be given what they request for timber sales this year and the Committee should obtain a statement from a responsible U.S.F.S. official that this will meet their needs."[86] When Richard Colgan testified before the House Subcommittee on Agricultural Appropriations at the end of February 1948, he recommended that the full appropriations requested by the Forest Service for timber sales be granted, adding, "the Forest Service should certify this amount is sufficient to administer sales up to the allowable cut on the national forests and that mature, harvestable timber will not be withheld from the market because of insufficient funds to service sales."[87]

This initiated a pattern of full industry support for Forest Service timber sale budget requests that has continued unabated to the present day. It also initiated a pattern of expectation by Congress that its timber appropriations would result in firm timber harvest quotas. Eventually Congress would come to use the annual appropriations process overtly to set its own politically configured timber harvest targets, regardless of Forest Service management plans, and in spite of conflicting policies of sustained yield, multiple use, and environmental protection.[88]

Conclusion

During World War Two and the years immediately following, the Forest Service found itself in a strikingly new environment in which the national forests were suddenly in high demand. Interest groups, including loggers, ranchers, wildlife managers, recreationists, and others, began laying competing claims to forest resources and leaning on the agency to accommodate them. The agency felt ambivalent about these new interest groups, sometimes viewing them as valuable allies and other times as troublesome antagonists. It quickly discovered, however, that the best way to encourage supportive alliances and avoid antagonisms was to acknowledge the validity of everyone's claims and try to satisfy demands to the greatest degree possible. Satisfying demands usually required capital investments in such things as roads, livestock developments, and recreation facilities; and the main sources of capital for these investments were timber sales, grazing fees, and direct appropriations from Congress. With 90 percent of the professionals in the agency trained as foresters at that time, selling timber met no organizational obstacles and provided substantial revenues that in turn stimulated more silvicultural investments. Furthermore, the agency discovered that politicians would readily consent to federal investments that brought immediate economic stimulation, as logging and road contruction did, and so it learned to tie its appropriations requests to economic production goals. This proved to be an ominous development, as the Forest Service slowly became a pawn in the larger chess game of economic policy. In one sense, then, the transition to a production mode empowered the agency, yet in another sense it ironically led to a loss of autonomy. In the next decade, the Forest Service would become thoroughly occupied by efforts to expand its reach without compromising its independence.

4

Forestry, Freedom, and Fiscal Conservatism, 1949–1952

National forest politics cannot be divorced from broader political culture. Nature, unfortunately, does not serve as an anchor to which political whims are tethered. Because forestry is a long-term affair requiring consistency, and politics is a short-term affair requiring constant compromises, the two make terrible business partners. Partisan political culture continually impinges on Forest Service activities inhibiting multiple-use, sustained-yield management. The Korean War and an anti–New Deal conservative backlash had a profound impact on the national forests between 1949 and 1952, especially in budget negotiations. Political relations in these years were not exceptional, however. Throughout the postwar era, Congress consistently supported Forest Service efforts to sell more timber without simultaneously supporting the rehabilitation activities necessary to make the increased harvests sustainable.

The Setting during Truman's Second Four Years

The year 1949 marked the beginning of Truman's first duly elected term as president, although he had already served essentially a full term since Roosevelt's death in 1945. That year also heralded the return of a Democratic majority in Congress, narrowly elected on Truman's short coattails. The Republicans of the 80th Congress (1947–48) enjoyed only the briefest tenure at the helm of Congress before Democrats regained the positions of leadership. Despite the enviable situation this put the Democrats in, the party's nominal leader, Truman, still had trouble getting his domestic proposals through. On many issues Republicans and southern Democrats had established an informal but effective "conservative coalition" in both the Senate and House of Representatives, formed as early as 1938 (following Franklin Roosevelt's disastrous attempt to pack the Supreme Court with liberals). This so-called fiscal conservatism extended primarily to social programs, however. National defense and most forms of domestic economic development continued to receive the benefits of liberal federal largesse. Although the Democrats retained both houses of Congress until the election of Eisenhower in 1952, the conservative coalition actually strengthened after the 1950 midterm elections. As the Cold War heated up in the late 1940s, especially during the Korean "Police Action" of 1950–52, domestic programs in the national budget felt the squeeze. All these factors affected Forest Service management priorities, its labor force, its budget, and even its lobbying tactics, as well as the lobbying tactics of the timber industry.

Despite the Korean War, which led to relatively static Forest Service budgets and a shortage of personnel, the years 1949–52 witnessed new record levels of timber harvesting and recreation activities on the national forests. In fact, the demand for these two products and services so far outstripped the agency's capacity to supply them that social tensions and ecological disasters resulted. The agency broke past timber harvest records every year, and due to a substantial rise in lumber values it annually exceeded timber revenue records by an even more substantial margin. The 1949 *Report of the Chief,* for example, noted that although the fiscal year 1949 timber harvest barely topped the FY 1948 harvest (because of delays in logging in the West due to heavy snows), the receipts from the sale of timber nevertheless had increased substantially from $20.6 million to $27 million (p. 43). In the following years, receipts rose even faster. By 1950, the Washington Office had begun enthusiastically counting the number of forests for which revenues exceeded expenditures, and by 1952 Assistant Chief Chris Granger, the timber pivot man of the agency, boasted that the national forests were finally self-sustaining (although that was not really an accurate assessment).[1] Though the Forest Service welcomed Granger's announcement as an effective tool for defending budget requests, it would eventually regret having initiated the argument that the national forests could be run like a business. As Edward Crafts, who became Assistant Chief for Programs and Legislation in 1950, later observed:

83

The Forest Service found, in the limited thinking that it was encountering from the appropriations committees on [Capitol] Hill in those days, the late forties and early fifties, that Congress was thinking of whether things paid for themselves purely in terms of dollars. Therefore, the Forest Service could plead, "Well, if you appropriate this many million dollars to us for the management and planting of trees, we'll return this many million dollars to the treasury." . . . Congress bought this lock, stock, and barrel, and the Forest Service then found itself locked in because this did become the pattern for justification of its appropriations. Consequently, the Forest Service was continually pushed to cut more and more timber in order to raise more and more revenue in order to get more and more appropriations. This was and is [speaking in 1971] a vicious cycle and as wrong as it can be.[2]

As recreation pressures on the forests similarly mounted, recreation-oriented conservation groups began to develop effective lobbying campaigns and acquire their own congressional sponsors, as the timber and grazing industries had. But, interestingly, the congressional sponsors of recreation were often the same people advocating for the lumber and livestock interests. Mike Mansfield (D-MT), for example, championed recreation development and wilderness preservation, as well as increased logging and subsidies for range revegetation to benefit graziers. The new political catchphrases of the day, borrowed from foresters, were "multiple use" and "intensive management." By promoting multiple use, politicians could befriend all the pressing constituencies, and with intensive management there was to be more of everything for everyone.

This optimistic vision ran into obstacles first and foremost in the budget office of the president and the appropriations committees of Congress. While the production half of the agency's land management mandate got a significant funding boost, the rehabilitation and protection half of their mandate stagnated. For example, rather than eliminating the World War Two–era backlog of denuded lands needing reforestation, the acreage in need of such rehabilitation nearly doubled between 1946 and 1953 from 2.2 million acres to 4 million acres.[3] Richard McArdle, who became chief of the Forest Service in 1952, explained, "Most of the imbalance in national forest resource development can be attributed to policies and attitudes of budget

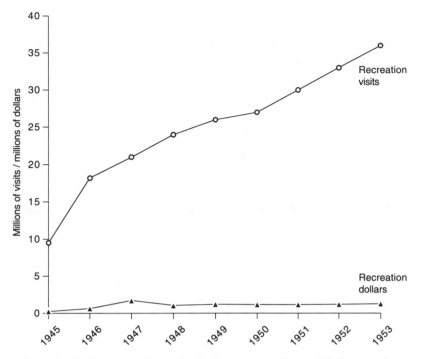

3. Recreation Use Compared to Recreation Funds, 1945–1953. Source: U.S. Congress, Senate Appropriations Committee, Subcommittee on Agricultural Appropriations, Hearing on H.R. 5227, 83rd Congress, 1st sess., April 22, 1953, pp. 361–63.

people. . . . These budget people had no real understanding of the need for orderly development of public land resources and seemed uninterested in learning anything about it. . . . It was like talking to a stone wall," he continued. "These people were prone to allocate money to activities that brought in money, timber sales being the outstanding example. They would save money by cutting our requests for activities such as recreation and wildlife."[4] (See fig. 3 to compare recreational use with recreation funding between 1945 and 1953.) In response to this problem, the Forest Service turned to the development of long-range resource management plans as a way to underscore the bigger picture in resource management and to help in lobbying for more integrated, balanced funding. National resource development programs emanating from the Forest Service inevitably emphasized the need for more intensive management in order to meet public demands — in other words, more inputs in order to achieve greater outputs.

Truman, Congress, and the Forest Service Budget in 1949

A serious rash of postwar price inflation troubled the nation in the late 1940s, and Republicans blamed it on government deficit spending under previous Democratic administrations. At the same time, a residue of Depression era fear of unemployment subtly but powerfully influenced economic decision making under both Truman and his successor, Eisenhower. Truman's State of the Union address included a statement on his administration's natural resources development policy, with an added message directed at what he expected to be a cost-cutting Congress: "In our present dynamic economy, the task of conservation is not to lock up our resources but to develop and improve them. Failure, today, to make the investments which are necessary to support our progress in the future would be false economy."[5] Truman hoped to maintain employment and prosperity while simultaneously balancing the budget. Predictably, his administration planned to accomplish this by increasing taxes rather than by cutting expenditures.[6] In his "Economic Report to the Congress" of January 7, 1949, he repeated his concern for making necessary investments in natural resource development: "While we must deal promptly with the problem of inflation we must not unduly hold back undertakings that are needed to preserve and develop our employment opportunities and our productivity in later years.[7]

The Forest Service, however, had to compete with a host of other natural resource development agencies for funds and to contend with an administration that emphasized water development in particular — not one of the Forest Service's strong suits. (Truman aggressively supported the grandest of water development schemes, including a Columbia Valley Authority and a Missouri Valley Authority, patterned after the Tennessee Valley Authority, only bigger.[8] These schemes never materialized.) Of the government's total natural resources–related expenditures proposed in Truman's budget, the Atomic Energy Commission (then considered a natural resource agency) and the nation's two federal water development agencies, the Army Corps of Engineers and the Bureau of Reclamation, received 80 percent of the budget allowance. A dozen other agencies had to split the remainder.[9] Despite all the rhetoric about building up a sustainable natural resource development program, the Forest Service budget allowance recommended by the Truman administration for the next fiscal year (FY 1950) actually cut funding for national forest protection and management slightly from the previous year's level. (Forest Service activities that were lumped under "protection and management" included all salaries and expenses related to the multiple uses: timber sales administration, timber stand improvement, recreation, reforestation, range, wildlife, soil and watershed management, construction and maintenance of facilities, and a few smaller items. Until the mid-1950s, the president's budget office and Congress lumped these items together, allowing the Forest Service a fair amount of discretion in dispersing the funds. The agency's extensive research program, its cooperative forestry programs, fire fighting, road construction, land acquisitions, and other items fell into distinct budget categories within the Forest Service's total budget.)

After its deliberations on the president's budget, Congress settled on a final figure of $26.3 million, a little less than the administration's request, and nearly half a million less than the previous year's appropriation.[10] Having failed to compete successfully for a larger piece of the federal pie, Forest Service leaders in Washington sought ways to make their funding requests more attractive and defensible.[11] One of these efforts was a new economic analysis strategy that tried to incorporate more nonmarket values and benefits as an alternative to the strict "costs-returns" methods of accounting common at the time. In a then unusual procedure, the agency monetized such amenity values as recreation and wildlife, and placed a dollar value on the water flowing off the national forests. Adding those "returns" to the actual cash receipts for timber sales, grazing leases, and other rents, the study concluded that returns amounting to $412 million resulted from an operating budget of $58 million. Chief Watts advertised these conclusions in his 1949 *Report of the Chief* in a section indicatively titled, "Returns Greatly Exceed Costs."[12] Unfortunately for the agency, Congress remained unimpressed. Those wielding the budget axe were interested in activities that generated direct returns to the treasury rather than indirect economic benefits.

Timber

During Truman's second term, both Congress and the Forest Service continued to actively promote the sale of logs from the national forests to accommodate timber industry demands. A palpable enthusiasm infused hearings and reports whenever the topic of timber production came up. Both the agency and Congress always remembered, however, to append discussions of timber production with a qualifying reference to sustained yield; but the reference often remained just that. Congress still lacked commitment to invest the necessary capital and labor for a sustainable high-yield timber production program within the context of multiple use management. As Assistant Chief Edward Crafts told the Society of American Foresters in December 1951, "The preeminence of the policy for acceleration of timber sales has diverted men and money from needed work for the balanced development of national forest resources. As a result, needed timber stand improvement, reforestation, insect and disease control, as well as recreation, range, and wildlife management work is being delayed."[13]

Timber purchasers more than shared the enthusiasm for national forest timber sales. Their aggressive promotion of increased harvests from the national forests took on the character of a crusade, immeasurably aided by the Korean conflict, which was officially declared a "National Emergency" by Truman on December 16, 1950. A policy statement on federal forest contributions to national defense by the National Lumber Manufacturing Association (NLMA) in August 1950, just after war broke out, included the following:

> During World War II the national forests contributed not more than 3½ billion board feet in any one year. As C. R. Granger, Assistant Chief of the U.S. Forest Service, in charge of national forests, pointed out to the House Appropriations Committee on January 26, 1950, the timber harvests on national forests could be increased to 6 billion board feet a year if they were placed under proper management, and under intensive management the annual yield from the national forests could be raised to 10 billion feet a year. The present emergency demands that these forests be placed under such management without delay, and that all efforts of the Forest Service be concentrated on this objective.[14]

Not satisfied with the maximum "allowable cut" permitted by the Forest Service under sustained yield guidelines, the NLMA used the Korean War to justify a departure from sustained yield: "If some over-cutting should occur in a few working circles, cutting can be reduced to a level after the emergency, and especially during a depression, to compensate for the overcutting. Proponents of the policy of reserving national forest timber to meet

88

emergencies should now recognize that the most pressing emergency we may ever face may now be upon us."[15]

In July 1950, Truman had issued a directive requiring agencies of the federal government to modify their programs "wherever practicable to lessen the demand upon services, commodities, raw materials, manpower, and facilities which are in competition with those needed for national defense." He hoped to avoid the confusion and expense of creating a plethora of new government organizations to deal with the war — as had occurred in World War Two. Plus, he hoped to keep international and domestic tensions down by trying to avoid the appearance of full-scale mobilization. Taking advantage of Truman's message, the NLMA suggested that "all activities of the Federal forestry agencies which are not necessary to an early solution of the war emergency should be reduced or eliminated. This would mean postponing educational work, wildlife management activities, recreational developments, new research, and any existing program which is not contributing to the solution of the emergency."[16] The sale of timber from the national forests assumedly qualified as an activity contributing to the solution of the emergency.

As if responding directly to this industry policy statement — and to Truman's directive — the Forest Service had Edward Crafts deliver its own statement at the Society of American Foresters convention in 1951. Crafts, with realistic foresight, argued that "what we are calling an emergency now will come to seem like the normal situation." (As he predicted, the Cold War continued for decades.) "Public forest policy therefore must be geared to long-term considerations," he added. "It must recognize the long-term nature of the timber-growing enterprise, and the length of time that may be necessary to adjust the forests for the proper implementation of a long-range policy." Other resource programs, especially reforestation, timber stand improvement, and range rehabilitation, according to Crafts, "may be of as much or more importance than immediate timber sales."[17]

Timber industry lobbyists, especially the lumber manufacturers, focused their energies on the Forest Service because the national forests contained much of the nation's remaining valuable old growth "sawtimber."[18] As mentioned earlier, this industry position represented a major shift: NLMA lobbyists who had opposed the sale of national forest timber up until the early 1940s (trying to keep competition down and prices up), now spoke critically about the national forests not contributing their "fair share" to the lumber supply burden, disingenuously blaming the Forest Service for the overcutting that had earlier occurred on private lands: "Those who may point with pride to vast Federal forest areas of virgin and old-growth timber that have been safeguarded from cutting, and then point with scorn to cut-over private lands, often fail to realize that in substantial degree such cut over private lands are a direct result of the failure of Federal forests to meet their equitable share of the total lumber demand."[19] Unwary listeners bought this argument.

Also urging increased access to the national forests, the Forest Industries Council — a public relations organization then sponsored by the NLMA, the American Paper and Pulp Association, and the American Pulpwood Association — adopted the following forest policy statement in June 1951: "The F.I.C. believes sound public policy during times of emergency requires the immediate development of plans for the maximum utilization of publicly-owned stumpage. These plans should include consideration of overmature stands now degenerating in areas now locked up for lack of ready access in Alaska."[20] Alaska's timber was chiefly used for pulp and paper, and thus of special interest to the FIC's pulpwood associations.

The Forest Service and Congress had, of course, already been considering how to exploit Alaska's great Tongass National Forest. In 1948 the agency had awarded a fifty-year, 1.5 billion cubic feet timber sale contract to the Ketchikan Pulp and Paper Company (an affiliate of the Puget Sound Pulp and Timber Company). The pulp mill to be built as part of the contract was expected to eventually employ 800 persons and produce 300–500 tons of pulp daily for fifty years. The Forest Service boasted that year, "This pulp-timber sale is the fruition of thirty years of effort on the part of the Forest Service to bring a pulp and paper industry to Alaska. Providing a stable major industry with year-round operation and employment, the Ketchikan development marks the first step in opening up the territory's huge pulp-timber resources, the largest untapped resources of the kind on the continent." The Ketchikan contract was the first of five such timber sales then in the planning stages.[21] As an economic incentive to the company, the Forest Service agreed not to reappraise the value of the timber being cut until 1964, and then only in five-year intervals thereafter. With sharp rises in timber values occurring, this promised to be an enormous economic boon to the company. Of course, the agency emphasized that the timber would be cut on a sustained yield basis with environmental values protected.[22] (Later, wholesale clearcutting of entire watersheds on the Tongass led to a showdown between industry and environmentalists and to passage of the 1980 Alaska National Interest Lands and Conservation Act, in which the timber industry won congressional endorsement of continued subsidized clearcutting on some portions of the Tongass while environmentalists won wilderness designations on other portions. Efforts to further reform timber management on the Tongass culminated in 1991 with the passage of the inaptly named Tongass Timber Reform Act — a compromise that did not slow the cutting.)[23]

The volume of timber cut off the national forests as a whole rose from 3.7 billion board feet (bbf) in FY 1949 to 4.6 bbf in 1951, and to 5.1 bbf in 1953.[24] During this time, national forest contributions to total U.S. timber production remained at about 10 percent, the level reached in 1945.[25] The Forest Service was not being pushed into accelerated timber production against its will, as Crafts explained to the SAF: "This acceleration in timber sales is deliberate. It would be even greater if additional manpower for preparation of timber sales and facilities for carrying out the sales were available."[26] The shortage of manpower alluded to was largely a result of Truman's demand that federal agencies minimize their personnel needs while simultaneously maximizing their production of war-related materials. With very few additional funds and an essentially static personnel base, the Forest Service had to shift personnel and cut corners to accommodate this 30 percent increase in timber harvests or else risk being criticized for not contributing adequately to the war against communism. This resulted not only in neglect of other multiple uses, as Crafts had mentioned, but in serious environmental problems related to poorly planned, inadequately managed timber sales. By 1952 a huge backlog of abandoned "slash" left over from logging operations in California national forests posed a critical fire hazard.[27] With the emphasis on construction of new timber access roads, existing roads deteriorated, causing substantial erosion and sedimentation problems, especially in California where severe storms in 1950 knocked out numerous roads and bridges.[28]

Although the Forest Service complained that a shortage of professional foresters hampered their timber sale program, a lack of timber access roads apparently constituted the main obstacle to raising the allowable cut. "The national forests are still woefully deficient in suitable road mileage needed for maximum utilization and proper management of the timber," Watts said in his 1951 annual report. "Construction of approximately 4,000 miles of main timber-haul road mileage would make accessible enough timber to increase the sustained annual cut to a total of some 6 billion board feet each year." At the time this statement was made, the national forests already bore 22,664 miles of highways and 111,256 miles of what the agency called "forest development roads" — enough to crisscross the nation east to west nearly forty-five times.[29] It is significant that Watts did *not* characterize the lack of funds for reforestation, erosion control, and multiple use management as an "obstacle" to higher timber targets. These programs were apparently desirable but expendable. Only a shortage of access roads, timber sale funds, and, to a lesser extent, personnel limited timber harvests.

Prompted by a press conference held by the regional forester in California, an article in the *San Francisco Chronicle* in August 1950 reported on the agency's proposed accelerated road construction program and what it meant for California's national forests: "The annual timber yield from national forests in California can be [doubled] to more than a billion board feet if Congress gives the U.S. Forest Service money to build logging roads, Perry Thompson, regional forester, said yesterday. The increase will come from virgin stands in the Sierra, Six River and Trinity National Forests." The reporter then parroted a perspective that the agency and industry diligently and defensively sought to promulgate in this era of growing controversy over national forest logging: the view that building roads into virgin forests and harvesting the ancient trees constituted forest conservation and resource protection. "Good roads are an integral part of the Forest Service's preservation of natural resources plan," the reporter stated.[30]

To maximize the timber access road system, the Forest Service encouraged both timber purchaser roads, wherever feasible, and agency-built roads where conditions made purchaser-built roads impractical or undesirable. Industry appreciated this dual system, especially as the timber companies sought access into ever more remote and rugged forest areas in which road construction costs exceeded the value of the timber. What the agency called "main timber-haul roads" (4,000 miles of which it ideally hoped to build in 1952) were usually major arteries through vast roadless areas from which a network of timber purchaser roads could then be extended, like veins on a leaf, at an affordable cost to the logging companies. In 1949 the agency had suggested that Congress invest $100 million over the next five years "for main tap roads to open up remaining large stands of national forest timber."[31] These major arteries also served to increase the ability of smaller logging operators to bid on national forest timber sales, since small companies usually did not have the financial resources to construct the larger roads themselves. The representatives of the big companies found that competitive bidding could still be kept to a minimum, however, if enough timber were offered for sale. Thus, accelerated road construction reduced competition, minimized price escalation, and kept industry mills running at full capacity.

The coordinated campaign for more road funds paid big dividends by the end of Truman's second term. In FY 1950, Congress made available to the Forest Service $13.3 million for forest roads; in FY 1951, $16.9 million; in FY 1952, $18.9 million; and for FY 1953 the figure jumped to $24.3 million.[32] In comparison, the entire budget for national forest protection and management—of all resources—in FY 1953 amounted to $39.8 million (not including roads). These road funds and additional timber purchaser credits built nearly 6,000 new miles of roads between FY 1951 and FY 1953, even though a significant portion of the road budget went to maintenance and reconstruction (54 percent of the existing road mileage was in "unsatisfactory" condition in 1950). The line item in the budget covering road construction is officially termed "forest development roads and trails," but this is a misnomer. In contrast to the 6,000 new miles of roads, the trails system actually declined in those same years by 8,389 miles.[33] Trails, offering no contributions to economic production, benefited little from this orgy of spending on the "transportation" system.

As the volume of logs hauled off the national forests escalated, growing numbers of individuals and groups concerned about nontimber resources questioned whether the harvesting was taking place in a manner sensitive to other values and whether it was truly sustainable. Some even questioned whether commercial exploitation of the national forests was appropriate at all. Forest Service spokespersons went to great lengths to allay public concerns, though many agency employees privately labored under the same concerns themselves. California Regional Forester Perry Thompson, in his

1950 interview with the *San Francisco Chronicle,* reiterated that careful selective cutting rather than the more destructive clearcutting would be practiced on the lands newly opened up to timber harvest.[34] Similarly, in a *Journal of Forestry* article in 1949, ex-chief Earl Clapp had argued that protecting the forests for the future required "the greatest emphasis on selective cutting, which removes only the larger and more mature trees and leaves the smaller trees for future growth. . . . Clearcutting," he continued, "and clearcutting in its modified form of leaving only a bare minimum of seed trees, must be reduced to an absolute minimum."[35] Within about a decade, however, clearcutting replaced selective cutting as the harvest method of choice for most timber sales on the national forests (see Chapter 6).

Reforestation, a Casualty of the Korean War

Widespread soil erosion and inadequate forest regeneration on both public and private forestlands provided impetus for federal government cooperative reforestation programs which the Forest Service administered. The agency offered free advice along with tens of millions of free or cheap tree seedlings to states and private owners of forestlands to encourage reforestation. In 1950, thirteen national forest nurseries disseminated 45 million seedlings. But in that same year, due to a lack of funds, only 45,428 acres of the Forest Service's own *four million acre* backlog of deforested land got replanted. The year before, only 44,000 acres had been planted. Chief Watts dryly observed, "The present rate of tree planting obviously falls far short of what would be required to accomplish the job within a reasonable time."[36] Ironically, Congress liberally supported reforestation subsidies for industry lands while neglecting its own showcase, the national forests.

The Forest Service had been clamoring insistently for more reforestation funds since the end of World War Two, yet its reforestation budget remained static even as its backlog of cutover lands expanded. In response, Senator Clinton Anderson, former Secretary of Agriculture, came forward in 1949 with a legislative proposal to help the Forest Service with this neglected but essential aspect of its sustained yield forestry program. With scarcely a political ripple, the Anderson-Mansfield Reforestation and Revegetation Act,[37] sailed through Congress and was signed by the president on October 11, 1949. The law declared that it was the policy of Congress to accelerate and provide a continuing financial basis for replanting programs on the national forests, and it authorized — did not appropriate, only authorized — gradually increasing funds for reforestation and range revegetation in amounts that would theoretically be sufficient to eliminate the backlog of denuded national forest lands within fifteen years. The act authorized reforestation appropriations of $3 million starting with FY 1951, rising to $10 million for FY 1955 and thereafter until 1965. To aid in rangeland revegetation, the law authorized $1.5 million in FY 1951, with gradually increasing amounts up to $3 million for FY 1965.

Politicians hardly gained political advantage opposing such laudable intentions, and hardly suffered political liabilities for *authorizing* without appropriating such funds. Fiscal conservatives could support the principle of resource rehabilitation, while opposing annual appropriations to accomplish the work on the grounds that fiscal economy was of greater immediacy, or that other priorities beckoned. Unfortunately, these same fiscal conservatives continually supported accelerated sales of timber and sustained high levels of livestock grazing, while ignoring the effect such lopsided priorities had on long-term productivity and the sustainability of resource development.

In response to the Anderson-Mansfield Act and strong lobbying by the Forest Service, the president's Budget Bureau agreed to nearly double its FY 1951 budget request for reforestation and range revegetation — less than the full authorized amount but significant progress nonetheless. The president's budget asked for $2.1 million for reforestation and $1.2 million for range revegetation. But, ironically, the House Appropriations Committee extended only a small gesture of support, earmarking $1.6 million and $914,229, respectively, in its appropriations bill, while keeping the overall budget for national forest protection and management static. Since reforestation and revegetation were part of the national forest protection and management budget, other programs had to be cut to make up the difference. The Forest Service complained. The Senate Appropriations Committee, which took up the budget bill next, responded by raising the national forest protection and management allowance high enough above the House level to allow the reforestation and revegetation increases without cuts to other programs.[38]

At this point in the funding process, Cold War considerations and a revolt of fiscal conservatives threw everything out of whack. The curmudgeonly Senator Styles Bridges (R-NH) and thirty-six supporters attached an amendment on the Senate floor to the whole federal budget bill stipulating that the total appropriations agreed to by the Senate and House conferees would be reduced across the board by 10 percent, *except* for budget items affecting the military, Atomic Energy Commission, Veterans Administration, and the Post Office Department. The House had not passed any such amendment, so when the conference committee met, the two bills had to be compromised. The conferees agreed to an overall cut of $550 million (not the full 10 percent), but instead of an across-the-board cut, the committee mandated that the president, through his Budget Bureau, make the decisions on where to eliminate $550 million of spending, "without impairing national defense." Truman subsequently complained in a message to Congress that this "unwise and dangerous" departure from standard budgetary practices indicated "a failure by the Congress to exercise its proper responsibility for enacting appropriations."[39] Understandably, Truman did not like being put on the hot seat.

For the Forest Service protection and management budget item, this conference committee bill lopped off most of the boost in funding provided in the Senate bill, settling on a figure only a few hundred thousand dollars above the previous year's request and less than what was needed to keep up with the rate of inflation. As a final insult, the Budget Bureau excised that tiny added increment when making its congressionally mandated cuts. The reforestation budget as finally allocated out of this convoluted set of actions actually declined from $1.2 million to $1 million.[40] So much for good intentions.

The next year (1951), a coalition of Republicans and southern Democrats in the House led their own drive — similar to the Senate the previous year — to reduce federal expenditures, partly by forbidding the Interior and Agriculture Departments to fill more than 25 percent of employee vacancies in FY 1952. The increased emphasis on timber harvests, coupled with a static protection and management budget for fiscal years 1952 and 1953, and declining professional staff due to the Korean War, kept reforestation programs again on the back burner. The backlog of denuded forest land and overgrazed ranges piled higher and higher. By 1960, just five years before the 1949 backlog was to have been eliminated by the Anderson-Mansfield Act, areas of the national forests classified as "nonstocked or poorly stocked" had climbed to 4.4 million acres, and Senator Anderson was back at the drawing board sponsoring another reforestation and revegetation act (see Chapter 9).

Federal Aid to Graziers

The two architects of the Anderson-Mansfield Reforestation and Revegetation Act of 1949 were both from western states with large amounts of national forest land supporting intensive grazing. The revegetation part of their act was designed not just to stem erosion on overgrazed lands, but to increase grazing capacity by reseeding deteriorated lands with monocultures of grass species preferred by cattle, such as crested wheatgrass (a nonnative species from Eurasia which has very little wildlife habitat value). Reseeding, a form of intensive management, offered range managers an alternative to simply reducing livestock numbers. As Watts's 1950 *Report of the Chief* explained, "The Forest Service is not relying alone upon reductions in numbers of livestock as a means of protecting and improving the range. Just as rapidly as appropriations are made available by the Congress the funds are used to rehabilitate the ranges through reseeding operations and the construction and maintenance of range improvements." In 1950, the agency reseeded 67,000 acres of national forest rangeland and contemplated similar treatment of 4 million acres over the next fifteen years, contingent upon receipt of Anderson-Mansfield Act funds.[41]

Thus, like cooperative reforestation and "stumps for stumpage" programs, revegetation funds subsidized the rehabilitation of lands degraded by commercial exploitation. This, in essence, allowed the graziers to transfer some of the external "costs" of their operations onto the federal taxpayer, and to continue damaging the grasslands by overgrazing, with the expectation that intensive management and infusions of federal money would artificially restore range productivity. Again, the conspiracy of optimism played a significant role here. National forest reseeding programs on overgrazed ranges have, in fact, proven notoriously ineffective over the long term, unless accompanied by significant changes in the management regime or reductions in grazing levels. The real problem is that *proposals* to engage in reseeding and other forms of intensive management forestall the implementation of grazing reductions — regardless of whether the proposals are actually funded or successful. The technological fix becomes an excuse to delay direct action on the cause of the resource damage. Then, if the range does not improve, politicians can conveniently be blamed for failing to budget the agency adequately for intensive management. This is the basic flaw in the ideology.

The FY 1951 budget negotiations resulted in some additional revegetation money, though much less than the agency had hoped for, as well as a new fund for cooperative range improvements. The House Appropriations Committee approved a $200,000 boost in the Forest Service's range reseeding program for FY 1951 in response to the Anderson-Mansfield Act, but then the committee mooted its action by making the additional funds contingent on the Forest Service raising grazing fees to offset the increase. Of course, this could not be done, because grazing fees were determined by a congressionally mandated fee formula tied to the price of beef and to rancher ability to pay. An earlier Congress had designed the formula specifically to keep public lands ranchers in the West (a tiny minority of livestock producers nationwide) from going belly up in the "free market." Forest Service grazing fees, according to the required formula, were substantially below fees paid for grazing on comparable private lands in the vicinity of the public lands. These artificially low grazing fees engendered intense controversy (and still do today).[42] Bernard DeVoto, excoriating public lands ranchers again in 1951, decried, "For every dollar a stockman pays to graze his stock on national forest land, one who leases privately owned grazing land pays at least three dollars, some times as much as six dollars. The public, including you, pays the difference; it subsidizes the user of forest ranges by writing off two-thirds of his grazing fee. It then spends part of what it does get improving the range for him."[43]

The last sentence in the quotation above referred to the new cooperative range improvements program authorized by Congress in the Granger-Thye Act of April 24, 1950. This law authorized the expenditure of a percentage of grazing fee receipts for range improvements. Cooperative range improvements most often took the form of pasture fencing, livestock watering development (ponds and springs), and access roads. Due to record high prices for beef that year, grazing fee receipts totaled almost $3.4 million (one-tenth the amount of receipts from timber sales).[44] Since the agency's range management *and* reseeding programs cost $1.7 million dollars in 1950, the range management program was theoretically in the black — so long as all the external costs of soil erosion, water pollution, loss of productivity from overgrazing, and impacts to wildlife were not factored in. (The grazing management program has run substantially in the red for the past several decades now, exacerbating the grazing fee controversy.)[45]

The Granger-Thye Act passed between the time the House completed its work on the FY 1951 budget and the time the Senate began its deliberations, so the House did not consider it in its budget. But the Senate, in its 1951 budget negotiations, set up a budget line item for these "Cooperative Range Improvements." The conference committee, ironing out differences in the House and Senate versions of the FY 1951 appropriations act, accepted the Senate's creation of the Granger-Thye cooperative range improvements budget item, but set the spending authorization at only $700,000. (That $700,000 later survived the Budget Bureau's $550 million congressionally mandated reduction.) In addition to this special fund, the agency spent $715,000 out of its FY 1951 general appropriation for reseeding, virtually the same amount it had spent the previous year. Although making incremental advances, the agency's plan to reseed four million acres of rangeland in fifteen years remained way behind schedule. As Watts reported in 1951, "At the present annual rate of appropriation it will take 65 years to complete the range-revegetation program for the national forests."[46]

More Range Wars

During all these Cold War budget negotiations, another range war was heating up out West. This time concentrated in the Rocky Mountain Region, ranchers again raised accusations that the Forest Service was acting unreasonably and dictatorially. Ed Cliff, who had been sent to the Intermountain Region headquarters in Ogden, Utah, in 1946 to help pacify ranchers during the late 1940s range wars, was transferred to Denver in 1950 to take over for retiring Regional Forester John Spencer. The transfer was controversial both within and outside the Forest Service. The Assistant Regional Forester in charge of Range and Wildlife Management in Ogden at the time, Earl Sandvig, had a reputation as a "hard-liner," while Cliff had a reputation for being conciliatory toward graziers. Sandvig had been in the Denver office since 1944 and had developed a tight network inside and outside the agency of supporters dedicated to eliminating overgrazing. Ranchers called him the "scourge of the West." As the Denver Office in the late 1940s fearlessly implemented necessary livestock reductions, communities in the Rocky Mountain states again polarized into those who defended and those who vilified the Forest Service. An anecdote Cliff tells of his arrival in the Denver office reveals the tense political situation he was sent in to ameliorate:

> I hadn't been in the office of the Regional Forester in Denver more than a week, when I was called upon by Senator Eugene Milliken. Milliken, the minority leader of the Senate, and a very powerful Senator, had generally been friendly to the Forest Service over the years. During the Christmas recess, 1949–50, Milliken had come to Colorado to do some politicking. . . . He came into my office about the end of the first week in January, when I was just getting settled down in the chair, and brushed past my secretary and marched into my office and planted himself in a chair in front of me, and he was livid with rage. I've never seen an angrier man. He said, "I have been over in western Colorado to try to talk to my people. I haven't been able to discuss anything that I wanted to discuss. All I've been doing is listening to complaints about harsh Forest Service treatment. . . . This kind of foolishness has got to stop."[47]

Perhaps most troubling to the Forest Service, ranchers had spread the inflammatory rumor that the agency ultimately planned to eliminate all livestock grazing from the national forests, using incremental grazing reductions as a strategy. When the powerful Democratic Senator Joseph O'Mahoney of Wyoming (a veteran New Deal liberal from a conservative state) heard such rumors advanced as gospel truth among his stockmen constituents, he demanded an explanation from Chief Watts. Watts wired him back:

> [It is] difficult for me [to] understand why such misunderstanding persists in view [of] my repeated public statements to contrary. Forest Service regards use of National Forests for grazing of domestic livestock as one of the most valuable uses. Our policy is to provide range for as many stock as is consistent with protection of watershed and forage resources and relation to other important national forest resources and values. Will appreciate your assistance in gaining general public understanding of Forest Service policy in this matter.[48]

But O'Mahoney was not pacified. Cliff recalled that the senator got "so fed up with hearing the tirades that were coming to him from his constituencies that he finally demanded a moratorium on grazing reductions." Chief Watts told him no, and the senator exploded. Cliff called on the senator personally to try to smooth things over and got a tongue-lashing himself.

In Cliff's oral history, he characterized himself as taking a more "democratic" approach to grazing problems, as opposed to what he called the "direct action" approach of Sandvig and others, although he claimed to have supported the decisions of the hard-liners even while criticizing their implementation methods: "I have no reason at all to quarrel with the objectives that Earl Sandvig had and what he was trying to accomplish, in the way of making adjustments on the ranges. They were correct, sound. I supported them, virtually all of them. But I didn't agree with the approaches that he was following — the direct action, the gung ho, do it now, get it accomplished approach." Cliff preferred to slow down, negotiate, and try alternatives to reductions, such as revegetation.[49] Cliff peddled technological optimism. Pressure from politicians like O'Mahoney reduced support within the agency for hard-liners like Sandvig. The Washington Office clearly backed Cliff and Cliff clearly did not back Sandvig and his allies. Rather than playing ball, some of the hard-liners continued to defend their generally quite defensible decisions and actions, eliciting aid from supporters in the *Denver Post* and in the conservation community who accused higher-ups in the agency of buckling under to pressure. The situation was intolerable from a purely administrative point of view and Cliff, being in the position of authority, moved to eliminate the sources of contention.

Several transfers were effected, including Sandvig in November 1951. To keep the move from appearing too much like a reprimand, Sandvig got his choice of destinations: Portland, Oregon. Sandvig's protagonists, including ex-Forest Service employee Art Carhart, who made a personal appeal to Chief Watts on Sandvig's behalf, raised hell over the transfer, claiming that this accommodation of disgruntled ranchers would set range management back on its heels and encourage other livestock operators to similarly target offending range managers for removal. These protests altered nothing. In the end, the Forest Service efficiently left a clean slate by transferring Cliff out of the region too, a few months after Sandvig. Cliff, however, hand-picked his and Sandvig's successors in order to ensure that his alteration of the status quo would remain as the new status quo.[50] And it did.

Watershed Management and Soil Erosion Control

Related both to overgrazing and logging is the problem of soil erosion. Healthy watersheds retain their soil, and thus their biological productivity, and provide the highest quality water and optimum flow rates. Protecting watersheds is a primary function of the national forests — sometimes considered *the* primary function in the arid West. Every *Report of the Chief of the Forest Service* in the 1940s and 1950s had a theme, and the 1947 report, titled "Forests and the Nation's Water Resource," focused on watershed protection:

> Virtually all of our national forests are sources of water of the highest importance for industrial, agricultural, domestic, and recreational use. National Forests west of the Great Plains include many of the high-altitude areas that are the source of 90 percent of the water of the Western States. The watershed services of national-forest lands at the sources of western rivers transcend all other values attached to these lands. There is no substitute for these services.[51]

The report went on to describe how poor grazing and logging practices had resulted in siltation of streams, degraded water supplies, flash floods, and a loss of soil fertility. It noted that large rivers important for commercial transport like the Mississippi required extensive and regular dredging because of sedimentation, and that huge, expensive reservoirs in the West like Lake Mead behind Hoover Dam would have their useful life cut drastically short because of silt buildup. The report also pointed out that cities in North Carolina with watersheds half denuded spent an average of $27.00 per million gallons treating their municipal drinking water, while Asheville, N.C., with an intact watershed spent about $8.50 per million gallons treating its water.

The Forest Service has completed numerous scantly publicized studies of erosion resulting from logging on its own lands. In September 1950, an in-house agency newsletter briefly noted the results of a study of soil erosion from normal logging practices on the Coweeta experimental forest in North Carolina. Logging had ceased in 1948 at the forest and since that time 1.3 acre feet of soil had been lost per acre of logging road surface. "Wood products valued at $1,465.70 were hauled over the 2.2 miles of logging road. Had the soil that was eroded from this road been sold for the prevailing 'fill' material price of $1 per cubic yard, the revenue would have been five times the value of the wood products which were hauled over the road."[52] The lost opportunity costs of that eroded topsoil to future forest growth and the added costs related to stream sedimentation further increase the disparity in this economic equation.

Despite the obvious social and ecological centrality of watersheds, the most neglected of all national forest management programs then (and now) is soil and water protection. The 1949 *Report of the Chief* cautiously yet optimistically asserted that problems of erosion, flood control, and sedimentation were "receiving careful consideration in the administration of the national forests." But that is about all they received. Production of commodities inevitably took priority over protection of watersheds, as national forest development accelerated in this postwar period of prosperity. As ranchers forced delays in grazing reductions and loggers penetrated virgin forests, the need for a strong watershed protection program grew acute. While Congress put $4 million into timber sales administration in 1949 and $10 million into logging roads, watershed management received only $47,411 — the smallest appropriation in the entire budget, less than two-tenths of 1 percent of the national forest protection and management budget. For FY 1950 and 1951 the funding level remained unchanged. For a value that transcended "all other values," soil and water protection seemed to be remarkably unimportant to federal budget architects.

Conclusion

Watershed management symbolized the larger plight of the national forests in this postwar period of rapidly accelerated production. Intensive management of the resources for a high sustained output of commodities required a federal investment balanced between resource extraction and resource rehabilitation. Agency leaders had a reasonably accurate idea of what a balanced investment entailed, and they regularly informed the administration and Congress of their opinions on the matter. Nevertheless, resource extraction activities advanced at a much more rapid pace than resource protection and rehabilitation, even after the (Korean) "war emergency" excuses had fallen away.

Congress's original intent was for the national forest system to be secured from unsustainable economic exploitation and dedicated to serving public purposes — such as watershed protection — not adequately protected by the institutions of private property and market transactions. Optimistically, the agency believed it could intensively develop resources without environmental degradation, encourage multiple use of the national forests without creating conflicts, become a major player in the market economy without becoming captive to it, and secure funding for resource rehabilitation as readily as resource extraction. This optimism strengthened in the following years even though historical events offered little justification for it.

5

Transition to the "Businessman's Administration," 1953

In January 1953 the first Republican administration in twenty years took the reins of government. Both houses of Congress went Republican in the 1952 elections too, giving the party an obvious even if narrow mandate.[1] America had happily, overwhelmingly elected a war hero, and the Republican party, rebounding from near death in the 1930s, believed that its day had again arrived. Rebelling against the trend toward a powerful, interventionist federal government, the Republican party promised voters it would get government off the back of private enterprise, eliminate the frightful federal debt, and propel America into a new era of prosperity. The federal government would be a "partner," rather than an Orwellian Big Brother, encouraging individual initiative and greater local and state control over economic life. Gone were the days of creeping socialism, nationalized industries, strangling federal regulations, and free-loading social welfare programs. Or so many businessmen and Republican party leaders hoped.

While campaigning, Eisenhower stated that he did not want "federal domination of the people through federal domination of their natural resources."[2] After his election, he loaded his administration with business leaders who opposed federal controls but nevertheless favored federal support for economic development. When they preached "partnership," they meant a form of government-business cooperation in which the government facilitated economic development but did not direct the flow of benefits, constrain the accumulation of wealth, or demand specific social or environmental outcomes. This ideology dovetailed nicely with the objectives of the timber, grazing, mining, and other extractive industries.

Eisenhower's Team

"There was a clean sweep when the Eisenhower administration came in," recalled Edward Crafts, who served as Deputy Chief for Programs and Legislation from 1950 to 1962.[3] The president's choice of New Hampshire governor Sherman Adams as his top executive assistant proved especially advantageous for the logging industry. Adams had spent two decades in the lumbering business prior to entering politics, including a stint as executive director of the Northeastern Lumber Manufacturers Association. Only a year earlier, in an article in *American Forests,* he had likened federal regulation of private forestry to "national socialism," and argued that if controls ever proved necessary, they should be kept "as close to the grassroots of government as possible" — where they would be amenable to local influential businesspeople, of course.[4] Eisenhower picked Ezra Taft Benson, a member of the "Council of Twelve Apostles" of the Mormon Church in Salt Lake City to be Secretary of Agriculture. (Benson would later become president of the Mormon Church and a member of the John Birch Society.) He had a master's degree in agricultural economics from Iowa State University and had served as Executive Secretary of the National Council of Farmer Cooperatives, where he achieved a reputation for defending collective self-help among farmers while opposing federal aid programs. Although not a Republican party activist, Benson nevertheless had impeccable conservative credentials: he had actually favored arch-conservative Senator Robert Taft over Eisenhower for the Republican nomination in 1952. Oregon's governor Douglas McKay filled the slot of Secretary of the Interior. McKay, like Adams, had used the *American Forests* forum as a stump on which to rail against federal regulation of forestry in 1951:

> We want no federalization of our Oregon forests. . . . We are all neighbors here in Oregon, whether we work for the state or for industry, and we want to run our own affairs as every true son of the West has done for a century or more. Let those who would impose carpetbagging, socialized, push-button forestry on us first look to their weapons, for they will get a fight in Oregon.[5]

Among other responsibilities, McKay, as Interior Secretary, had authority over Bureau of Land Management timberlands in the Northwest. Eisenhower at first appointed Earl Coke as Assistant Secretary of Agriculture with direct oversight over the national forests, but in November 1954 Ervin

L. Peterson took over the job, staying through the remainder of Eisenhower's two terms. Peterson likewise had ties to industry and had grown up in Coos Bay, Oregon, the self-proclaimed "Timber Capital of the World" after World War Two.[6]

This team of businessmen and industry advocates ably implemented the Republican party's natural resource policies during the next eight years. They promised to run the federal bureaus like businesses, reducing expenditures, raising revenues, and promoting economic efficiency. Social welfare was expected to automatically follow from economic prosperity, while programs designed to protect the "public interest" in natural resources would be implemented through a "partnership" policy with a lessened federal role. A meeting between prominent lumber lobbyists and Secretary Benson during the first few weeks of the new administration kicked off this era of cooperation between industry and government, with Benson promising an end to Forest Service proposals for regulation and the lumbermen in turn extending support for the newly appointed Chief of the Forest Service Richard McArdle. McArdle, to his advantage, had been Assistant Chief in charge of cooperative forestry and generally opposed federal regulation.[7]

The forest management priorities of the Eisenhower administration were abundantly clear: standing trees represented unutilized economic capital and the public interest would best be served by harvesting that capital and putting it to economic use.[8] On lands capable of being harvested, every other resource or value became subordinate. While speaking at the American Forestry Association's Fourth American Forest Congress in October 1953, Secretary Benson disparaged notions of conservation that included preservation or nonuse. "*Conservation* means *management,*" he said, "I hope we no longer have any citizens who look upon conservation and preservation as synonymous terms." He commended the concept of multiple use, but emphasized that timber was an agricultural crop and that wood production should dominate on forest lands: "As forest managers, we must not become so imbued with *all* resources that we fail to make the land yield up to its full potential of the resource for which it is best fitted."[9]

"The Myth of Idle Resources"

Notable in the 1950s was a concerted effort by many industry and government leaders to characterize unexploited resources as wasted assets, tragically deteriorating for lack of national will to utilize them. This ideology served the important function of promoting public acceptance of the extensive logging occurring on national forests. Most Americans assumed the public lands were nature reserves, protected from exploitation. Outrage often resulted when this was found not to be the case. So, the promoters of national forest development sought ways to reverse people's natural assumptions and convince them that clearcutting was conservation and natural forests were unproductive and undesirable. While most politicians and many Americans came to accept this view of conservation promoted by foresters, the ideology did engender dissent. One of the dissenters was professor L. G. Hines, head of the Department of Economics at Dartmouth College in New Hampshire, who gave an address titled "The Myth of Idle Resources" at the Eighteenth North American Wildlife Conference in March 1953. Hines pointed out that it had become commonplace to assert that conservation implied development, that "idle" resources were wasteful. And he warned, "to an alarming degree emphasis upon full use or 'full employment' of all resources diverts attention from the important consideration of the type of use that may be appropriate for given resources, and affords a basis for attack upon conservation programs by those who wish to bring all resources under commercial exploitation." Hines criticized two ideologies then dominant in natural resources policy: (1) the belief that the dynamics of supply and demand in a free market would automatically optimize socially beneficial resource allocation, and (2) the belief that technology would inevitably solve resource scarcity and environmental degradation problems. Against the former, he argued that the distribution of goods and services in a free market economy was based not on social need but upon ability to pay, and as long as income remained so inequitably distributed among Americans, "ability to pay" would remain a socially unsatisfactory method of allocating resources. Besides, he added, powerful interests constrained consumer choices and consumers "may unwittingly provide patronage for the irreversible depletion of resources."[10]

Hines then identified two particular problems that the free market could not resolve: (1) some natural resources provide their highest long-term social value when kept commercially idle, and (2) some resources require periodic nonuse in order to remain productive over the long term. He pointed out that unfettered market mechanisms too often failed to protect against overuse of lands that might best be left idle. The market furthermore offered "no effective means by which an individual can express his desire for commercial nonuse of resources." What lands should be kept idle? Marginally productive lands that degrade easily into nonproductivity or that require constant heavy subsidies of nutrients, energy, and capital to keep them productive. "When commercially idle, these land areas may provide social benefits, such as watershed protection, sanctuaries for wildlife, and public hunting grounds, that are clearly of greater importance than the intermittent private gains resulting from commercial exploitation." Even on productive lands, soil, ground and surface water, timber, and other resources often require periodic disuse or idleness to maintain their productivity, otherwise, an "artificially high" output is obtained for the present generation at the expense of resource productivity in the future. Increased productivity through the intensive application of technology induces an inflated optimism, he said, that fuels the arguments of those who would "refute the claim for the necessity of conservation."

Hines dismissed the arguments of "technological enthusiasts" as based largely on "faith and selected illustrations," and he warned against their unfounded confidence in the capacity of natural resources to absorb ever greater levels of use. He concluded:

> The needs of mankind cannot be revealed and met within the perimeters of the market economy alone, but require conscious appraisal of social goals and the means of obtaining them. High in the scheme of social goals to fulfill basic human needs must be a definite provision for idle resources — idle to permit replenishment of productivity and to provide an emergency buffer for a future that seems more uncertain than ever before.[11]

But voices such as Hines's were the exception rather than the rule. Most foresters and politicians adhered to the dogma that idle resources were wasted resources, and they maintained an unswerving faith in the human capacity to enhance natural forest productivity in pursuit of maximum utilization.

"Growing Trees in a Free Country"

In anticipation of the promised era of enhanced cooperation between the federal government and private industry, the Forest Industries Council (FIC) — representing lumber and pulp associations responsible for four-fifths of all timber production in the nation—distributed a comprehensive new forest policy statement in the fall of 1953 to policy makers in Washington, the media, and the public. The FIC hoped its statement, titled "Growing Trees in a Free Country," would set the agenda for the future of both public and private forestry in America. Prefaced with the assertion that "private enterprise and initiative can provide the most effective management, use and renewal of our forests," the FIC's pamphlet set forth nine broad objectives for obtaining a "continuous and adequate flow of products from all forest lands": fire protection and insect and disease protection for all forest lands; expansion of intensive forest management to ensure "full use"; a preference for private ownership over public ownership; management of public forest lands according to the principles practiced on the high-yield private industrial forests; timber tax reform; improved and expanded state forestry departments; "maximum utilization of each tree that is cut and of all forests which should be harvested"; and more research into commercial management and utilization.[12] Some of the FIC's appended explanations of these general goals deserve a closer look for what they reveal about the psychology of lumber lobbyists in those years.

Under goal number 3, the FIC placed forest management decisions wholly on an economic foundation: "Sound forestry advice and practice must be guided by the basic economic principle that 'it must pay.' " Of course, many advocates of public resource management argued precisely the contrary, that good forestry in fact usually did not pay, thereby justifying the need for public forests to be managed by public agencies in the public interest.[13]

Under goal number 4, encouraging private ownership of forest lands, the FIC referred to the 19.5 percent of "commercial" forest land under federal control as "excessive," and encouraged a congressional study to determine "whether our entire economy would be strengthened by restoring [to private ownership] some federal forest lands." The term "restoring" here was a curious turn of phrase. The vast majority of federal timberland had *never* been privately owned.

Under goal number 5, "urge better management of public forests," the FIC defined better management as attaining the maximum annual allowable cut in order that the national forests contribute their "full share to the wood economy of the United States." Interestingly, the FIC did not include accelerated reforestation of the 4 million acre backlog of cutover and burned areas on the national forests as part of its definition of better management. It wanted considerations of economic efficiency to determine whether denuded national forest lands should be artificially restocked. "Since no dependable data are available as to the areas needing planting *and their economic potentialities,* the Council finds itself unable to recommend an increase in current plantings on these lands" (emphasis added). But the Forest Service based its determinations of allowable cut, which industry wanted maximized, partly on the assumption that nonproducing commercial forest lands would be restocked with commercial species — regardless of the cost. It was thus inconsistent for industry lobbyists to proclaim their approval of higher harvest levels while not supporting the reforestation efforts that made those high harvest levels theoretically sustainable. Looking back on this period, retired Chief Richard McArdle complained, "the forest industry people who were continually pressuring us to increase the cut on the national forests, never once went to Congress during my time [1952–62] to ask them to appropriate money for building up the forest resource — only for money to make timber sales."[14] Granted, it was perhaps economically irrational to reforest many of those denuded lands, but then the allowable cut determinations should have been lowered accordingly. Needless to say, no one involved in timber management in the agency hierarchy wanted to abandon any technical assumptions that supported higher harvests or give up the budget and personnel dedicated to reforestation work.

Building roads to access virgin stands of timber also figured prominently in the FIC's definition of "better management." Goal number 8, encouraging maximum utilization of all trees, advocated massive road construction to salvage the otherwise "wasted" wood fiber in the ancient forests of the Pacific Northwest. With rhetoric designed to instill distaste for old-growth, the FIC complained, "a major element of timber loss now exists in the old-growth forests in public ownership. Where roads are lacking or because of inflexible management plans, over-mature timber is permitted to die and fall and insect-ridden, diseased and windthrown trees are permitted to deteriorate instead of being salvaged promptly."

Under the goal of forest tax reform, the FIC advocated changes in federal and state tax laws to provide incentives for private investment in sustained yield forestry. A related goal, though not mentioned in the FIC pamphlet, was to get financial institutions to recognize timber as collateral on loans to industrial tree farmers for forestry work. Through the extraordinary efforts of the Western Forestry and Conservation Association, an industry group centered in the Pacific Northwest, Congress amended the Federal Reserve Act in 1953 to authorize national banking institutions to accept timber as collateral. Representative Harris Ellsworth and Senator Guy Cordon, both Republicans from Oregon, sponsored the legislation. The act authorized loans based on up to 40 percent of the market value of the standing timber, to be repaid in two years or mortgaged out over ten years. The timetable for repayment obviously was inadequate to serve as an investment incentive for reforestation, since trees require a minimum of forty to eighty years of growth to reach merchantable size. In fact, the law as written served as an incentive to liquidate forest capital, so the sponsors added a toothless stipulation that only forest lands "properly managed in all respects" would qualify for the loans. Incredibly, the act made the banker/lender responsible for determining whether standards of forest management were satisfactory![15] The lender's interest in management of course centered on whether the "stumpage" was adequately protected from fire, insect, and disease, not whether cutover forests were restocked for the next generation's use. This change in the lending laws reinforced continued short-term economic speculation in forest lands, leading eventually to the widely criticized liquidation of private forests in the 1970s and 1980s by corporate raiders who took on massive debt in hostile takeovers of timber companies and then clearcut the "forest capital" to repay the loans.[16]

Edward Cliff, Assistant Chief for national forest protection and management in 1953, reflected this same industrial desire to maximize timber harvests and accelerate road construction in his budget testimony to the Senate Appropriations Committee that year. He told the committee he was disappointed that the national forests were producing at only about 80 percent of their maximum sustained yield capacity, and he hoped to increase the cut by another 30 percent within a year or two. "The main reason why we are not cutting up to the full capacity is . . . the lack of accessibility of some of our larger and more remote timber operating areas. The need is for access roads to open that up for orderly harvesting."[17] Much of this accelerated harvesting was anything but orderly. In the rush to meet impossibly high harvest quotas with inadequate staffing, the Forest Service fell drastically short of its multiple use, sustained yield management goals. Ed Cliff's alter ego in the agency, Edward Crafts, later lamented:

> Frankly I was quite dissatisfied with Forest Service timber management policies . . . the use of stumpage in lieu of money to build roads, the chopping up of the hillsides with too many roads, and resulting erosion, excessive cutting . . . use of clear-cuts instead of selective cuts, excessively large blocks of clearcut timber, failure to require adequate regeneration measures, failure to require adequate slash disposal and erosion control measures. This is a whole list of things that I thought the Forest Service timber management people were far too easy on with the timber industry.[18]

For the forest industry, growing trees in a free country really meant liquidating forest capital in a free market.

Roads and "Natural Enemies of Timber Abundance"

Developing the economic assets of the national forests to their "fullest potential" required roads, as Cliff had explained and as McArdle emphasized in his 1953 *Report of the Chief*.[19] Timber access road construction accelerated at an astonishing pace during the 1950s (see fig. 4). In fact, all kinds of federal and federal-state road construction projects flourished during this era. The interstate highway system was born in the mid-1950s, partly justified at the time as a national defense measure. Upon arrival in Washington in January 1953, the fiscally conservative Eisenhower administration asked for a *90-percent increase* over the Truman administration's $11.3 million request for timber access roads, despite a whopping $10 billion overall reduction to the $78.6 billion federal budget.[20] Secretary Benson acknowledged that the $10 million increase in the road budget represented an "urgent need for carrying out a two-year program for the building of access roads into [insect] infested and threatened areas" to allow "salvage of dead and infested timber." He pointedly remarked that this increase would be "a nonrecurring item after the second year of operations."[21] But in fact these increased funds initiated a timber production momentum that allowed no backsliding. Instead of returning two years later to the original $11 million road budget, the administration requested *$24 million* for roads for FY 1956, the maximum then allowable by law. Having run into a ceiling,

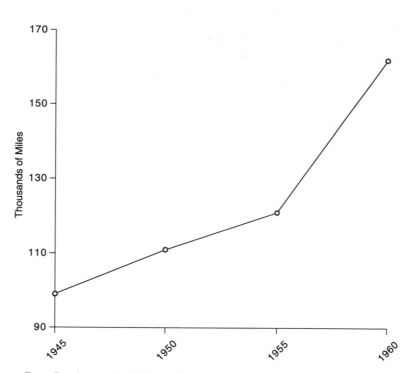

4. Forest Development Road Mileage Totals. Source: U.S. Forest Service, *Reports of the Chief of the Forest Service.*

Representative Harris Ellsworth, a Republican from the timber-producing state of Oregon, introduced a bill in 1953 that would have made available an additional $25 million annually in Treasury loans to build timber access roads on the national forests, to be repaid with timber sale receipts. He explained that he wanted to facilitate road construction into national forest backcountry in order to capture the economic value from otherwise "worthless" lands.[22] Ellsworth's bill failed, but other bills increasing the road budget authorization passed in subsequent years.

This drive to salvage insect-infested timber reflected a peculiar mind set: an industrial forestry vision of intensively managed and fully utilized timber resources. Proponents of this vision abhorred the thought of dead and dying trees decaying in the forest without being utilized. The value to the forest ecosystem of decomposing trees did not enter the picture at all. America could not afford to be so wasteful. Worse yet, every dead or decaying tree attracted "pests" and "diseases" that threatened nearby healthy timber.

Complicating matters, the Forest Service based its calculations of sustained yield and allowable cuts on the assumption that intensive management would progressively increase the level of "protection" from fire, insects, and other natural decomposers. This assumption of greater protection led to a second assumption that more timber would be available for harvest in the future, which in turn led to the crucial decision that more timber could be cut today without exceeding sustained yield. Consequently, large fires or natural, periodic outbreaks of spruce bark beetles, white pine blister rust, and other pests threatened to upset sustained yield calculations and motivated the agency to attack vigorously these "natural enemies of timber abundance." Fire and pest control were thus aimed to protect the market values of the timber as well as to preserve the integrity of the agency's increasingly optimistic calculations of sustained yield.

The Forest Service approached the naturally occurring spruce bark beetle outbreak of the early 1950s as if it were a national emergency justifying extraordinary measures. These measures included huge federal subsidies for rapid bulldozing of timber access roads into high elevation areas of the northern Rockies, the spraying of DDT mixed with oil on some timber stands, the harvesting of other stands, and a "temporary" departure from sustained yield. Ed Cliff testified before the Senate Appropriations Committee that approximately 600 million board feet of timber worth $4,800,000 had already succumbed to the beetle. Fearing that the "epidemic" would spread too fast to allow orderly salvage harvesting, the Forest Service decided to attempt to excise the whole infestation in one fell swoop. Charged with the rhetoric of urgency, Cliff explained, "In order to do the job, we should log 460 million [board] feet this summer, which means we have got to get those roads in pretty fast." Since it was already the end of April, Senator Cordon skeptically asked Cliff how his engineers could possibly build the necessary roads in just a few months. "What do they do — just bulldoze them in?" he asked. In a response that revealed the lack of caution accompanying this rapid acceleration of harvesting, Cliff replied, "We plan on pushing these roads in just as quickly as possible, and if we hit tough going, such as a rock bluff, we will go around it. If we hit certain places which need bridges, we will build temporary bridges." Cliff carefully underscored, however, that this was nevertheless a permanent operation designed to support future logging: "We want to build [roads] on locations, however, which are permanent as far as alinement [sic] and grade are concerned, so that the investment can be salvaged and used later to log out other timber that is in the same area."[23]

Forest Service engineers determined that the 1953 operation in the northern Rockies would require about 750 miles of new roads, only 280 of which could be feasibly built by timber purchasers. Thus, the agency needed funds from Congress to construct 470 miles of main haul roads from which the purchasers could build spur roads. The cost of these 470 miles of logging roads to be punched into the high elevation mountains was estimated to be $9.9 million. This investment plus the timber industry's additional 270 miles of roads (paid for by the government in reductions from the timber sale price) would access only $4.8 million worth of timber; clearly not a cost-effective operation, even without the expenses of preparing the timber sales and reforesting the areas added to the equation. Anticipating potentially embarrassing queries from the Senate Appropriations Committee about the economic irrationality of this road expenditure, Cliff suggested that 6–12 billion board feet of spruce on the seven national forests of Montana and north Idaho might ultimately be threatened by the bark beetle if action was not taken immediately.[24] He thus shifted from the standard defense that roads were revenue generating to a new defense based on the flawed assertion that valuable assets would be "lost" without an emergency subsidy. In the first place, these "assets" were only marginally valuable; in the second, dead trees left on the forest were not lost, but rather conserved for use as wildlife habitat and for nutrient recycling.

The use of DDT in this battle against the bark beetle went unquestioned, as did essentially all uses of pesticides which became quite widespread on the national forests in the 1950s. Manufacturers claimed the new chemicals were safe and managers considered them wonderful technological advances essential to the effort to maximize productivity. Montana's Lolo National Forest casually announced in 1955 that it planned to spray 102,000 acres aerially with DDT the next year to control spruce budworm, mainly because the insect damaged the esthetic appearance of young conifers used by the local Christmas tree industry.[25] A history of southwestern national forests written in 1988 noted that large-scale DDT treatments for bark beetle and budworm occurred in Arizona and New Mexico in 1950, 1953–56, 1958, 1962, 1963, and 1966.[26] Cliff had led a battle against spruce bark beetles in the Colorado Rockies in 1951. His biography includes a fascinating account of the politics and mechanics of attacking that problem. In Colorado, half a million acres of trees were individually treated with DDT mixed with fuel oil. Interestingly, Cliff admitted that cold winter temperatures — not the pesticides — actually broke the epidemic.[27] Two decades later, an official team of Forest Service researchers in Wyoming would discredit this practice of timber harvesting for spruce bark beetle control as both ineffective and destructive, but at the time "salvaging" dead and dying trees was widely accepted as appropriate and desirable.[28]

These "emergency" salvage operations actually set the stage for future timber harvests in areas that otherwise might not have supported profitable development. Rocky Mountain spruce and fir at the time were considered commercially worthless. Higher quality timber (mainly lower elevation ponderosa pine) was so readily available that no market had yet developed for these "inferior" species. The first sale of insect-damaged spruce in the northern Rockies salvage campaign occurred on Montana's Flathead National Forest, and the stumpage sold for $1 per thousand board feet — essentially a giveaway. The late University of Montana forestry professor Arnold Bolle argued that the Forest Service consciously used salvage sales subsidies at that time to create new markets for its low value timber so that the old undesirable forests could be cleared away and replaced with plantations of desirable species.[29]

Congress eventually approved more than four-fifths of Cliff's requested budget increase for salvage roads, going the extra mile by giving the agency half of it right away in a Supplemental Appropriations Act passed in June 1953. Ironically, in July, the "Washington Lookout" column in *American Forests* magazine observed that Eisenhower's budget and Congress's action on it strengthened the perception that this was a "businessman's" administration[30] — if businessmen were running the national forests, these costly salvage sales in marginal timberland would never have occurred.

Sustained Yield in 1953: A Whole Proposal; Half a Budget

While the federal government seemed willing to help protect state and private forests from fire so the timber could be cut and marketed, it did not appear so willing to help ensure that there would be future crops. While cooperative state and private fire control efforts got funded at $9.4 million, cooperative tree planting programs received only $447,000. Similarly, Congress essentially gave the Forest Service a blank check to fight fires on the national forests — amounting to $10.5 million in FY 1954 — and approved over $5 million to combat insects and disease and more than $6 million to administer timber sales. But for replanting 4 million acres of denuded forest land and reseeding another 4 million acres of deteriorated rangeland, Congress approved only $1.3 million, not enough to deal with new problem areas let alone start to eliminate the backlog. The 1949 Anderson-Mansfield Act authorizing increased funds for these two rehabilitation activities clearly had little effect on actual funding levels. In fact, Cliff informed the Appropriations Committee, "The authorization under [the act] has never been met either for reforestation, or range reseeding." Eisenhower's proposed budget actually called for a $384,500 *reduction* in these activities (a 20 percent cut) while recommending a $340,000 boost to the timber sales budget. Ed Cliff again faced questions from the Senate Appropriations Committee on this subject. He explained that these reductions originated at higher levels of the administration (the Budget Bureau) "as a result of a very serious effort to try to cut down on the budgets" — although, as we have seen, these efforts were quite selective.[31] Awash in a veritable flood of road-building funds, the agency suffered compensatory cuts elsewhere. Higher echelons of the government seemed willing to pay to protect existing economic assets on the forests but balked at reinvesting in future assets. Once again, the Forest Service found itself with a budget supporting maximum production and minimum renewal.[32]

The agency itself must assume part of the blame, however, for having helped the Budget Bureau establish priorities. As Cliff explained, "We cannot walk away from forest fires. We cannot neglect public recreation areas to the point where health is in danger. We have contractual obligations to meet in making timber sales, and we should be selling more timber. This [reforestation and range revegetation program] is one place where we could defer some of the development work even though we feel that it is highly important to get along with that job." This comment slightly unnerved Senator Henry Dworshak (R-ID), a conservative who nevertheless expressed concern for the present generation's obligations to the future when he asked Cliff, "Are you not, through your sustained yield program and reforestation, keeping abreast of the requirements for timber in this country so that you are not denuding our forests?" Cliff could only respond, "Our progress in re-forestation of the national forests has been rather slow, Senator."[33]

The American Forestry Association's Partnership
with Industry in 1953

Because the American Forestry Association (AFA) could not be so easily dismissed as a selfish economic interest, industry aggressively sought the association's backing on key issues. Industry advertisements heavily supported the AFA's magazine, *American Forests,* and industry leaders enjoyed significant representation on the AFA's board and among its membership. These connections were exploited to great advantage in 1953. That, of course, put the AFA in a touchy political position, as the organization purported to represent a broad cross-section of forest advocates. The masthead of *American Forests* proclaimed the association was "independent and non-political," and dedicated to "intelligent management and use of forests and related resources of soil, water, wildlife, and outdoor recreation." The AFA's statement of purpose also explicitly recognized both the economic *and social* values of forests. In 1953, however, the editorial page in *American Forests* took a markedly narrower approach to forest policy. Using masterfully tactful language, a series of editorial essays promoted timber production over other resource uses and economic considerations over social ones. Ed Crafts later flatly asserted that the AFA was at the time "controlled" by industry. (He added that the Society of American Foresters was also generally spineless then, confining itself to technical matters to avoid controversy.)[34] Indicatively, the AFA often took positions contrary to other private conservation organizations during the Eisenhower administration.

In 1953, the AFA sponsored a conference at Higgins Lake, Michigan, to update their 1946 assessment of the forestry situation in America. An editorial titled "Challenge at Higgins Lake" in the June issue of *American Forests* explained that the purpose of the conference was to draft "a workable program that will accelerate the growth of more and more trees in an economic climate that provides private initiative with the greatest possible encouragement." It made no mention of the problem of protecting soil and water resources in the context of intensive timber production or of balancing multiple uses on the national forests. To the contrary, the editorial praised the Eisenhower administration's boost to the Forest Service's timber access road budget, remarking that "the new administration is serving notice that it intends to emphasize *first things first* in forestry"[35] (emphasis added).

Curiously, a representative of lumber interests used the same phrase at another AFA sponsored conference that October in a talk ostensibly on multiple use: "We of the Western Pine Association's Conservation Committee believe in the realistic approach, putting first things first." Using industrial tree farms as an example for federal land managers to emulate, the spokesman, E. R. Aston, continued, "The private owners handle our tree farms on a priority basis of multiple use. We decide what is the highest use, be it Christmas trees, poles or posts, sawlogs, pulpwood or grass."[36] Multiple use in his mind meant determining which of several forest crops was best suited for a particular plot of land and then growing that crop. If other values were served in such an agricultural system, so much the better. But first things first.

The AFA editorial also asserted without explanation that the great increase in timber access roads supported by Eisenhower would not only produce more revenue, but would "eventually provide greater support for parks, wildlife and kindred programs — with less money coming out of the taxpayer's pocket in the process."[37] It is certainly debatable whether the timber salvage operation in Montana and Idaho put any money in the taxpayer's pocket. Beyond that, this oblique reference to parks and wildlife benefiting from timber roads signified nothing more than a superficial nod to multiple use. In his talk on multiple use, the lumberman from the Western Pine Association offered a similarly superficial description of industrial multiple use management: Where unfavorable environmental conditions do not support dense stands of timber, he explained, the lumberman can grow both trees and grass, allowing grazing and lumbering to thrive side by side. "Often wildlife prospers too in such areas, and you have fine recreational changes, which are encouraged on tree farms. And certainly the water crop is safe where these other uses flourish."[38] Such statements indicate a failure by many (not all) industrial foresters to consider multiple use and integrated management seriously.

Although the three dozen men who attended the Higgins Lake conference represented a broad cross-section of professionals from federal agencies, state agencies, private industry, and academia, they were virtually all foresters or economists, with the exception of a couple of journalists and a wildlife advocate, Ira Gabrielson. Other than Gabrielson, not a single leader from any non–forestry-aligned conservation group attended. And judging from the results of the conference, a majority of them probably felt quite comfortable with the sentiments expressed in the *American Forests* editorials and the views on multiple use espoused by Aston.

The recommendations of the Higgins Lake conference were printed in the August issue of *American Forests* and in the proceedings of the American Forest Congress.[39] Essentially they concluded that America needed more intensive forestry to produce and harvest more trees to meet growing demands; that the national forests should supply a larger percentage of total wood products than before; and that national forest lands should be inventoried to see whether the public interest might be served by turning over some tracts to private ownership. America could not afford to leave land idle or allow inefficient forestry practices to retard the achievement of maximum sustained yield. Aston noted, "I've been reading the Higgins Lake statement and I can say we Western Piners are pretty much in accord with it."[40] Edward Rettig of Potlatch Forests, Inc., of Idaho seconded Aston's approval and especially backed the boundary study proposal. Secretary Benson ironically commended the Higgins Lake proposal for its "broad outlook."[41] The Forest Service officially reserved its opinion on the Higgins Lake statement, while retired Assistant Chief Granger lambasted it. Conservation groups tended to ignore it. A minority report from the conference complained that the new Higgins Lake statement softened the AFA's earlier support for state regulation and appeared too enthusiastic about privatizing productive forestland. All in all, the AFA's new Program for American Forestry effectively supported Eisenhower administration priorities and the policy of cooperation with timber executives.

National Forest Boundary Reevaluation —
A Strategy to Increase Timber Production

The Forest Industries Council (FIC) had already recommended a congressional study to determine whether some federal lands should be "restored" to tax-paying private ownership to improve production and strengthen the economy. The U.S. Chamber of Commerce, too, a close ally of the National Lumber Manufacturers Association in Washington, D.C., had joined the crusade to reduce federal land holdings in an August 1952 article in its publication *Washington Report,* in which it printed a map showing the percentages of federal lands in each state accompanied by the statement, "Federal land empire deprives states of taxes on 24 percent of U.S." Although the tax issue was spurious, the proposal to turn commercially marketable resources over to private owners posed a real threat to the Forest Service and other federal land agencies.

Robert Sawyer, a western conservationist and editor of the Bend, Oregon, *Bulletin,* criticized the Chamber's position in the March 1953 issue of *American Forests.* In an essay titled, "The Whole Story," he pointed out that millions of acres in that 24 percent of the United States held by the federal government were lands "no one would ever want or be willing to own or pay taxes on. There is no tax loss on these lands." Furthermore, he continued, millions of acres of forest land had been divested by the federal government into the hands of private citizens or corporations and, "after being raped of their timber, went back to the 'federal empire' on the solicitation not of a federal bureau but on that of their private owners." Finally, Sawyer reminded his audience that although taxes are not paid on these federal lands, "numerous financial benefits in lieu of taxes . . . do come to the states where they lie" — such as the program by which 25 percent of revenues earned from national forests are returned to the counties of origin, "in lieu of taxes."[42] This in-lieu-of-taxes program resulted in local political jurisdictions vigorously supporting revenue generating activities on the national forests as a way to fatten their own coffers — a fourth side to the classic iron triangle.

The Eisenhower administration took a politically safe middle-of-the-road position on national forest land disposal. In a speech before the American Forest Congress sponsored by the AFA in 1953, Secretary Benson announced that the administration was opposed to any enlargement of the total area of the national forests, but that they fully intended to maintain "the basic structure" of the national forest system. He said his department was "engaged in a critical review of national forest boundaries" to see where some lands might be divested and some acquired. The decision on land tenure changes would, of course, be based on "what is shown to be in the best permanent public interest *as the result of thorough economic studies of each situation*"[43] (emphasis added). Proponents of privatization were unsure whether to be encouraged or discouraged by these statements.

Backing the FIC's call for a boundary study, and reflecting industry's view of the purpose and need for such a study, the AFA Board of Directors passed a resolution in January 1953, stating, "the national forests would be strengthened by a realistic and impartial review of their boundaries, state-by-state, in the light of progress in forest management."[44] The "state-by-state" phrase reflected an industry view that the boundary study should be controlled at the local level and kept out of the hands of the Forest Service. (Another industry position held that the review should be in the hands of Congress, since both the House and Senate were now controlled by Republicans. More on this below.) The phrase "in the light of progress in forest management" referred to the industry view that new harvesting technologies, greater wood utilization capabilities, and a booming market now rendered once marginal areas of the national forests commercially viable. These commercially viable national forest lands, according to industry, might be "better managed" under private ownership.

Like Benson, the AFA added to its resolution the qualifying statement, "The essential integrity of these federal properties must be preserved as part of our basic national policy." What "essential integrity" meant, of course, was anybody's guess. Regardless, astute observers recognized the hidden implications behind the language of the resolution. One of the nervous onlookers was ex-Assistant Chief Chris Granger, the Forest Service's timber management expert who had just retired in 1952. He wrote complaining to Secretary Benson that this looked suspiciously to him like the land grab attempts of the livestock industry. He and Leo Bodine of the National Lumber Manufacturers Association debated the merits of AFA's position in essays in the April issue of *American Forests*. At the AFA's Forest Congress later that year, Granger arrived still steaming and delivered an impassioned speech defending public forest ownership. His arguments centered on three main themes: (1) the boundary study was really a smokescreen over a large scale disposal scheme to turn over all productive forest lands to private industry, ultimately to the detriment of the public interest; (2) divesting productive timberlands to private ownership would "gut" the national forests and "wreck" orderly sustained yield management; and (3) divestment of revenue producing lands would end Congress's willingness to fund the Forest Service at adequate levels to allow for protection of nonproductive lands and nonmarket uses and values.[45] His arguments were hard to refute.

Advocates of disposal simply retorted that "commercial" timberlands properly belonged in private hands as a matter of economy and principle.

A March 1953 editorial explaining the AFA's resolution on the boundary study noted, "The Association finds itself in disagreement with that school of thought which urges that the status quo on federal lands be frozen." The school of thought referred to included Chris Granger, Bernard DeVoto, Arthur Carhart, and others who opposed federal land disposal flat out, as a matter of principle, in hopes of nipping the movement for privatization in the bud. Freezing the existing land pattern, according to the AFA editorial, would be "at odds with the whole spirit of forestry progress in a dynamic free society."[46] Pregnant words. "Forestry progress" again referred to industry's advancing capacity to utilize previously marginal forestlands — lands that now might be better managed under commercial ownership? — and "free society" of course meant freedom for industry executives to accumulate wealth without undue restrictions by government.

Opposition to expansion of federal land holdings was to a large degree an ideological issue, just as opposition to disposal often was. Industry (and some academic) critics of the Forest Service charged that federal bureaucracies were economically inefficient by nature and inconsistent with "the American way of life" — that is, private enterprise pursuing profit in a free market. Even conservation groups of the era generally shared this allegiance to capitalist modes of production, although they wanted specific portions of the American landscape segregated from market exploitation. Taking a generally conservative position, the Izaak Walton League in 1953 stated: "The League opposes, with minor exceptions, the sale or other disposition of the national forests to the states or to private interests; at the same time, it is of the opinion that except under extraordinary and now unforeseen conditions, the system need not be expanded by creation of additional national forests."[47] Additions to the national forest system had an extremely tough row to hoe in this climate. Albert Hall observed in his "Washington Lookout" column of *American Forests,* "Acquisition of additional lands for national forests appears to be temporarily halted, with only the usual $75,000 appropriation for rounding out boundaries. . . . The authority to utilize receipts, under special acts for land acquisition has been withheld."[48]

As it turned out, only insignificant portions of the national forests were divested during the 1950s. The system in fact experienced a small net gain in acreage during the decade, from 181.2 million acres in 1953 to 185.6 million acres in 1960, even though industry and the administration consistently opposed funds for acquisition. Americans liked their public lands and did not want them turned over to commercial interests for unregulated private development. Congress, under pressure from nontimber interest groups, especially recreationists, approved meager but valuable funds for the purchase of private inholdings within national forests. Even the AFA backed a proposal in 1955 to acquire nearly a hundred thousand acres of land inside national forest boundaries in Arizona, despite its 1953 resolution opposing further expansion of the system, and despite the consternation it generated among industry lobbyists who thought they had firmly secured the association's endorsement of their antiexpansion policy.[49]

Even though the proponents of privatization lost the war, they won their practical objective of increasing timber harvests on the national forests. As Chris Granger indicated, the Forest Service feared it might lose the bulk of its most productive timberlands if disposal schemes were successful, and that concern stimulated even more aggressive promotion of intensive timber production as a defense against the charge that it managed its lands inefficiently. In the long run this served industry better than if the lands had been privatized; this way, loggers could purchase timber in marginally productive areas made available to them by taxpayer subsidized roads.

The Year of Transition for Grazing and Recreation Interests

Edward Crafts recalled a few years after his retirement from the Service in 1962 that the relative emphasis given to resources changed in the 1950s: "Grazing lost ground, timber increased in importance, [and] recreation began to come of age, although it had a hard road ahead of it." Recreation had a hard road, he explained, because most agency personnel were foresters who had advanced through the ranks via "the timber route" and who were "slow to sense a real future in the recreational field."[50] This timber bias contributed to a less than enthusiastic commitment to the grazing program too, at least at the agency's national level.

The key event marking the decline of clout for the grazing industry on national forest issues was the defeat of the D'Ewart Grazing bill in 1953. Sensing, like the timber industry, that Eisenhower's election heralded their day in the sun, graziers were doubly disappointed when they failed to get sufficient support from Congress and the administration for their recycled attempt to establish grazing leases as vested rights; "stability of tenure," as they called it. As soon as Wesley D'Ewart (R-MT) and Frank Barrett (by then in the Senate) introduced what critics called "the Stockman's Bill,"[51] the old network of antigrazing conservationists came out of retirement and launched another attack. Art Carhart warned in one essay, "They Still Covet Our Public Lands"; Robert Sawyer, testifying before Congress in May 1953 on behalf of the AFA, told the lawmakers not to be "hoodwinked" by this attempt to turn control of the national forest ranges over to graziers; and Chris Granger, retired from the Forest Service but still defending it, wrote in *American Forests,* "The public must vigorously oppose all efforts by any group to obtain anything which smacks of vested rights in the public lands."[52] The Forest Service took this threat seriously. McArdle dedicated his 1953 annual report to the subject of grazing. Crafts, the agency's point man on legislative matters, fell into the thick of the controversy and later revealed some of the remarkable political machinations surrounding the D'Ewart bill:

> Livestock interests pushed this bill very aggressively. The Forest Service prepared very strong adverse reports and strong adverse testimony. These were suppressed in Secretary Benson's office by Assistant Secretary Coke, whether on the direction of the Secretary I never knew. The Forest Service was ordered to destroy this material. . . . Hearings were held by both House and Senate but the transcripts were never printed and the Forest Service was not allowed to testify. The Eisenhower administration nearly came down with a favorable position to the stockmen on this matter, but it came to the attention of [presidential assistant] Sherman Adams, who was shrewd enough to read the public posture involved and directed that the Administration take no position on these bills, which it never did.[53]

Although the Forest Service did not attend the hearings, many other opponents of the bills did, along with journalists who publicized the debate. Things went poorly for the graziers. Carl Shoemaker, the National Wildlife Federation's Washington politics specialist, told a gathering of state game and fish commissioners in June, "After a five-day hearing in Washington in the House and a one-day hearing in the Senate, I think I can predict without any equivocation that the Stockman's Bill is as dead as the heath hen and the dodo."[54] Crafts considered this defeat to be "a major turning point" in the relationship between the Forest Service and ranchers.

The same year, 1953, saw a modest but promising turning point in the Forest Service's relationship with the growing recreation constituency. Slowly but steadily recognizing the large role recreation would play in the national forest's future, the Service began to more aggressively court recreational users and to defend increases to the agency's abysmally inadequate recreation budget. Testifying before the Senate Appropriations Committee, Cliff explained that most recreational facilities had been built during the 1930s and maintenance was now ten to fifteen years behind schedule due to a lack of funds (and partly due also to the fact that there was no longer a Civilian Conservation Corps to perform the grunt labor). Worse yet, use of the facilities was already at about twice their originally designed capacity. "The facilities for taking care of human refuse are inadequate, and we are getting into a situation where public health is seriously threatened in many areas. The pollution of the streams and creation of garbage-disposal and refuse-disposal problems are becoming almost insurmountable."[55] In response, both Eisenhower's Budget Bureau and Congress supported incremental increases to the recreation budget, although they were not nearly as much as the agency asked for and were much less than the increases in timber sale administration and road construction funds.

As yet, recreation interests had not effectively garnered sufficient political support to balance the clout of economic development interests. The production and prosperity ethos so imbued popular culture that individual dissenters were successfully isolated and ignored. But as more and more Americans got out into the "Great Outdoors," they learned to love their national forests not for the wood produced but for the pure pleasure of experiencing a natural forest environment. Bernard Frank, a speaker at the AFA-sponsored American Forest Congress in 1953, eloquently expressed this reverence for America's disappearing native forests:

> The impact of the majestic solitude of an undisturbed forest is one of
> the deepest spiritual experiences man can know. It cannot be realized
> in an environment that has been artificialized by human interference,
> no matter how skillfully the scars may be disguised. We are fortunate

that we can yet gain this refreshment and so enlarge our perspectives. It is our responsibility to ensure that those who follow us shall be able to do so also.[56]

Timber production — especially of the industrial variety that made use of ever larger blocks of clearcuts — created its own opposition. As logging marred scenic views and turned favorite camping, picnicking, and hiking areas into smoldering, eroding forest graveyards, individuals became outraged and complained to their local papers, politicians, and conservation societies. The grass-roots public lent support and new direction to an expanding wildlife, wilderness, and recreation advocacy movement starting in the 1950s. Later in the decade, as conflicts escalated, the prevailing consensus for high yield production on the national forests began to break down.

An example of the criticism that would soon become commonplace appeared in an address by Paul Herbert, Vice-President of the National Wildlife Federation, at the American Forest Congress of 1953. Herbert charged that "multiple use" was at best a facade. "I am convinced that often wood production is receiving too much emphasis in the management of publicly owned forests." The problem, he said, was the preponderance of silviculturists at the helm of the agency. Reiterating earlier concerns about the narrowness of forestry school curriculum, Herbert revealed that of the twenty-seven forestry schools then functioning in the United States, only one required its students to take a course in water conservation, only three a course in forest recreation, and only eleven a course in wildlife management. All of them, however, required many courses in silviculture. He blamed not just the forestry schools for failing to take multiple use management seriously, but also the Society of American Foresters which held responsibility for accrediting the schools, *and* public forestry agencies like the Forest Service for "not requiring as a prerequisite to employment a technical knowledge in other than wood production."[57]

At the same conference, in the same multiple use session with Paul Herbert and Bernard Frank, the Forest Service's Ed Cliff half-jokingly remarked, "There are some of us who very often get caught in the crossfires when conflicts occur, and sometimes we think that the multiple use results in multiple abuse of the public servants who are trying to practice it." The audience chuckled, but Cliff's talk, "Multiple Uses on National Forests," did little to assuage the concerns of noncommercial interest groups. Reflecting the high yield production ethos, Cliff defined multiple use management as "the integrated development and use of all the resources and values of the land to the fullest possible extent." But then he seemed to contradict himself: "Timber production is given priority over other uses on the most important areas of commercial forest land, with recreation, livestock grazing, and wildlife being integrated as fully as possible without undue interference with the dominant use."[58] The problem, to recreation and wildlife advocates and to towns dependent on clean water from national forest watersheds, was that intensive management had not lived up to its promise in mitigating the negative effects of forest development. Also, areas subjected to it (commercial forest land) kept enlarging in response to market pressures. The Forest Service seemed always to find timber production to be the appropriate dominant use wherever there was a demand for it.

Noncommercial interest groups accordingly grew distrustful of the Forest Service's claimed commitment to multiple use. Picking up on the concept of "dominant use" — as applied by foresters to timberlands — some recreation advocates called for the zoning of national forests into areas emphasizing different dominant uses. For example, Howard Zahniser of the Wilderness Society, who also spoke at the AFA Forest Congress, argued that multiple-use management "should be applied in consistence with the zoning principle." Specifically in reference to wilderness, he continued, zoning would allow the administrator "to devote a particular area to a special purpose and yet maintain it within his multiple use forest."[59] The agency opposed such zoning proposals as an impingement on its management flexibility, not admitting that designating "commercial timberland" areas on the national forests accomplished the same thing. In practice, agency leaders argued for the need to preserve "flexibility" most often during debates over wilderness designations. That is why eventually environmental groups pushed Congress to legislatively zone areas of the national forests for noncommercial purposes and thus take away the agency's flexibility.

Conclusion

The Forest Service found itself in an increasingly uncomfortable position in the Eisenhower era. Although it threw itself wholeheartedly into timber production, its industrial beneficiaries remained discontented and some-times hostile. At the same time, nontimber interest groups felt increasingly marginalized and even betrayed, growing at first wary, and then hostile. Within the limits of their own professional biases, most employees of the agency genuinely believed they were committed to multiple use and that imbalances in management were not really their fault. As Ed Crafts later explained, "As for the criticism that has been felt by the Forest Service so greatly in recent years, particularly on timber, much of it is merited and much of it isn't. The Forest Service has been doing what Congress made it do. . . . I think a great deal of the fault rests with Congress and the higher authorities in the executive branch. This gets right into the heart of multiple use."[60] To a significant degree he was correct, but the issue was not so simple. Under potent incentives to increase production, the agency chose to endorse a forest science orthodoxy based on the ethos of maximization and technology-intensive crop-agriculture forest management. Other forestry paradigms existed but were not adopted. Perhaps the problems caused by budget imbalances would have been less severe had the agency maintained a conservative stance and not encouraged the ethos of maximization.

6

Getting Out the Cut, 1953–1960

The key development in national forest management in the 1950s was the full maturing of intensive timber extraction and the contingent evolution of technical and ideological rationales for raising allowable cut levels, including the widespread adoption of clearcutting as an alternative to selective cutting. During the 1950s, timber production from the national forests shot up from 3.5 billion board feet to 9.3 billion board feet. At the same time, the percentage of national forest contributions to total U.S. timber harvests climbed from 10 percent to 15 percent. In the Pacific Northwest, national forest contributions to regional timber production in this decade jumped from 21 percent to 35 percent.[1] Though the Forest Service expected the demand for and the supply of wood products to continue to rise at the same rapid rate in the following decades, in fact they both leveled off. For the following thirty years, the volume of timber removed from the national forests as a whole remained at decade averages of 10–12 billion board feet, although that level of production, which was based on optimistic assumptions, could not be sustained into the 1990s. National forest contributions to total U.S. cut and Pacific Northwest cut averaged 16 percent and 30 percent, respectively, for the 1960s–1980s.[2] Due to the rapid acceleration of harvests in the 1950s, the problems of that decade were particularly acute. Under great pressure to "get out the cut," and lacking the experience, personnel, and funding to manage the high harvest levels with care, the Forest Service often caused or allowed irreversible damage to watersheds, streams, and wildlife habitat. The visual effects of the dramatic increase in logging also shocked forest visitors and rural residents. As Ed Cliff, Assistant Chief in the 1950s, recalled, "People became enraged when there were changes in scenic values due to logging, road building, and other development."[3] Conflicts over increased production eventually led to a struggle to renegotiate national forest policy, culminating in the 1960 Multiple Use–Sustained Yield Act (the subject of Chapter 8). The Eisenhower years fully established the modern era of timber production and timber related resource problems on the national forests. Issues covered in this chapter — raising of the allowable cut, old-growth forest liquidation, below-cost sales, and road construction — foreshadow the major national forest controversies of the 1980s and 1990s. Problems begun in the 1950s are only beginning to be resolved today.

Redefining and Raising the Allowable Cut

For national forest managers, sustained yield was an unquestioned, rock-solid policy foundation for the management of commercial resources on the national forests. Its definition, however, proved exceedingly flexible. Corporate timber executives had noticed that the Forest Service regularly accused them of not practicing sustained yield forestry and were understandably anxious to end their days as whipping posts. Defensively touting the success of their tree farm program, they then took the offensive by accusing the Forest Service itself of not practicing sustained yield. Turning the traditional definition of the policy on its head, industry lobbyists insisted that the failure to achieve *maximum* allowable harvests of timber meant a failure to achieve sustained yield.[4] The Forest Service found this new interpretation of sustained yield and allowable cut unusual but nevertheless helpful in their pleas for a larger organizational budget, and after 1953 even the agency consistently referred to the allowable cut not as a maximum to stay below but as a minimum to strive for. Deputy Chief Ed Crafts identified this new interpretation as one of the great mistakes the Forest Service made in this period, blaming it partly on pressure from industry and Congress but partly on the agency itself.[5]

With the Forest Service generally accepting allowable cut determinations as a floor rather than a ceiling, industry — with the cooperation of timber administrators in the agency — then sought ways to raise this crucial calculation. Timber purchasers were well aware of the assumptions the Forest Service used to determine the allowable cut, and rather than simply demand higher harvest levels — which could be interpreted as a lack of support for sustained yield — they instead demanded a revision of the data and assumptions used to determine the allowable cut. The Forest Service based its sustained yield calculations partly on assumptions regarding accessibility and timber demand (how much could be feasibly marketed in a given region). With rapidly rising demand and advancing road construction technology, ever more remote areas of the national forests could be added to the harvestable timber base, permitting an increase in the allowable cut. Lodgepole pine, for example, was considered worthless before World War Two, so the agency did not even count it in timber inventories. In eastern Oregon, by 1950, the same stands of lodgepole pine left uncounted fifteen years earlier were selling for higher prices than premium ponderosa pine had fetched before the war. Commenting on this and similar situations across the nation, the 1951 *Report of the Chief* explained, "These examples show the effects of improved markets on the expansion of management to remote areas of the national forests and to hitherto unused species."[6]

A second strategy for increasing the allowable cut was to reappraise timber inventories. Forest Service determinations of the volume of desirable "merchantable" timber in a forest considerably affected its allowable cut calculations. Not all species of trees were marketable, so not all trees counted in inventories. But, with the rise in lumber prices and demand, new markets opened up for lower quality species of trees. Industry lobbyists demanded that the agency update its timber inventories to include all theoretically marketable timber volume. When the agency did so, the rise in estimated volume then justified an increase in the allowable cut. Unfortunately, while the agency agreed to consider all potentially merchantable wood fiber in its sustained yield calculation, industry did not always agree to buy or use all the wood fiber in its lumbering activities. Instead, loggers often concentrated on removing the higher valued trees, leaving behind much slash and subsequently demanding additional harvests to make up for the shortfall. As Chief McArdle recalled,

There was never a week that I wasn't being beat upon to raise the amount of timber which could be cut. . . . The allowable cut figure these people wanted to establish included timber that could be easily reached and timber that was entirely inaccessible, timber that was usable under present-day conditions and timber that was not usable, small trees and large trees, good species and poor species, trees that would probably never be cut under any timber sales practice, and so on. In brief, they wanted the allowable cut figure to be based on everything. This led to misunderstandings because the timber they wanted to cut was the best timber and only the best.[7]

Beating upon McArdle to raise the cut apparently yielded results. In April 1953, Assistant Chief Edward Cliff told the Senate Appropriations Committee that the full sustained yield potential of the 73 million acres of designated commercial timberland on the national forests was "a little over 6½ billion board feet of timber each year." Just six months later, the *Report of the Chief* claimed the sustained yield capacity was "at least 6.9 billion board feet." Two years after that, the commercial timberland base had been increased from 73 to 85 million acres (new assumptions and additional access roads) and the allowable annual cut was estimated to be nearly 9 billion board feet. The year Eisenhower left office (1961) national forest lands classified as commercial topped 95 million acres and the allowable cut had been raised to 11.2 billion board feet. The actual harvest of timber rose on a parallel trajectory from 5.1 billion board feet in 1953 to 6.3 billion in 1955 to 8.3 billion in 1961.[8]

The Gifford Pinchot and Boise National Forests

In 1949, the Forest Service renamed the Columbia National Forest in south-central Washington state the "Gifford Pinchot" National Forest in honor of the agency's founding father, who had died in 1946. Making it an event, the agency released a press packet and held a joint ceremony with the Society of American Foresters at a campground on the forest where a memorial plaque was unveiled and speeches given by Chief Lyle Watts, Washington Governor Arthur Langlie, Pinchot's wife and son, and other celebrities. The press release gave a glowing description of the forest's resources, starting with the observation that the area was "of outstanding scenic beauty." It then emphasized the "high economic importance" of the forest's range, wildlife, watershed, and recreational resources, adding that "its greatest resource is some 16 billion board feet of commercial timber." The press release concluded this discussion of resources by underscoring Pinchot's philosophy of multiple use as the greatest good for the greatest number: "The Forest Service policy of multiple use management looks to permanent maintenance and wise use of these various resources for local and national benefit." An important reference to timber production was also included. It read, "Managed for sustained yield, the timber growth is estimated to be sufficient to yield perpetually *an annual cut of 200 million board feet*"[9] (emphasis added).

That was in 1949. Under new intensive management assumptions, a massive timber access road construction program during the Eisenhower years, and indomitable pressures to increase production, the allowable cut and actual harvest levels on the Gifford Pinchot Forest rapidly exceeded this 200 million board feet (mmbf) sustained yield estimate. By 1956, timber planners on the forest had increased the allowable cut by more than 50 percent to 313 mmbf annually. The actual harvest that year was 236 mmbf, already well in excess of the 1949 estimated maximum. By 1958, they had further increased the allowable cut to 395 mmbf and had harvested 262.6 million. Then, a tremendous boost in harvesting the next two years pushed the actual cut to 440 mmbf in 1960, exceeding the allowable cut limit by 12 percent! This incredibly accelerated production of timber continued unabated into the 1960s. By 1962, the timber planners felt it was finally necessary to revise the allowable cut *downward* to 381 mmbf, reflecting the overcutting that had occurred, yet logging continued on its upward climb, reaching 559.5 mmbf in 1968 at the end of President Lyndon Johnson's term in office.[10]

Scrambling to resolve this disparity but under pressure to accommodate timber demand, the Gifford Pinchot forest supervisor approved a higher allowable cut determination of 416 mmbf in 1971 to be achieved by unprecedented applications of intensive management. Despite the fact that the funding necessary for the proposed level of management always fell short, harvest levels remained in the 450–500 mmbf range for most of the 1970s and 1980s. This timber sale program involved clearcut logging of ten to twenty square miles of forestland *per year* between the 1960s and 1989.[11] By the late 1980s, old-growth forests with trees over 200 years of age remained on only 9–14 percent of the forest (depending on how "old-growth" is defined). According to ecologist Peter Morrison, all but 30,000 acres of that old growth (2 percent of the forest) were ecologically "fragmented" into small, isolated, vulnerable blocks by 1988. Wilderness designation protected only 8,000 acres of that old growth, and at 1980s harvest levels Morrison predicted the unprotected areas would be logged out by the year 2008.[12]

In his history of national forest management in the Intermountain Region (Region 4), Thomas Alexander found similar events widespread throughout southern Idaho, Nevada, Utah, and western Wyoming. He told a story of how Ira Mason, head of the Forest Service's timber management division in Washington, D.C., had visited the ponderosa pine region of southwest Idaho in 1950 to see whether timber production could be increased there. Harvests on the Boise and Payette National Forests already exceeded sustained yield calculations (by 11 percent on the Boise and 46 percent on the Payette), posing a serious policy conflict as well as an obstacle to higher harvests, so Mason concentrated on determining whether the theoretical allowable cut could be revised upward. He ventured into the field for a rather cursory inspection, after which he concluded that the sustained yield capacity was much greater than local timber managers thought. Mason told the responsible officials to prepare a new timber analysis report. A team made up of national, regional, and local Forest Service timber planners, with the cooperation of representatives of Idaho state government and the Boise-Payette Lumber Company, came out with a proposal in 1953 to *triple* the allowable cut for the area's forests. On the Boise Forest, the allowable cut in 1952 was 38 million board feet; the 1953 plan suggested raising that to 131 million board feet. Contrary to this special national/regional team's recommendation, the local Boise Forest timber staff independently suggested that the allowable cut should not exceed 85 million board feet if multiple use values were to be protected. Bureaucratic and political demands for wood production won out, however, as a Boise Forest timber management plan of 1956 increased the allowable cut to 130 million board feet (the harvest level already exceeded 100 million board feet). The Boise Forest Supervisor then tried to unilaterally raise the allowable cut even higher to 185 million board feet.[13]

This accelerated harvest had many repercussions nationwide. New personnel streamed into the Forest Service as its timber budget grew — organizational expansion always being desirable to a bureaucracy. Unfortunately, they were virtually all assigned to timber management. Alexander found that increased timber sale appropriations funded thirteen assistant ranger positions on the Boise and Payette Forests in 1953 alone. Timber "cruisers" who marked trees to be cut worked year long, ceaselessly, in snowshoes in the winter, to keep up with the sales schedule. They eventually perfected the paint gun to speed up the process. But marking would grow less important as the agency increasingly substituted clearcutting for selective logging in order to get the cut out even faster. To help achieve higher timber targets, the Washington, D.C., Office authorized the Boise Forest to adopt a new harvest procedure in 1955 called "unit area control" — classic obfuscatory language that simply meant clearcutting ("even-age management" has been another common euphemism for clearcutting).[14] Forest Service administrators resorted to jargon here because most of them had spent their careers criticizing clearcutting on private lands. Within a few years, however, the agency had closed this credibility gap by developing scientific rationales for clearcutting, such as the argument that Douglas fir trees only regenerated in full sunlight, a theory with a germ of truth that was eventually stretched to extremes to justify ever larger blocks of clearcutting. Such rationales developed very rapidly. In 1958, George Craddock, Chief of the Management Division of the Forest Service's Intermountain Forest and Range Experiment Station, said at a Society of American Foresters meeting, "Clearcutting is essential to the regeneration of the densely growing forests of western white pine, spruce, fir, and lodgepole pine in Idaho and Montana."[15] Ironically, Craddock's presentation was on watershed problems in the region caused by overgrazing and destructive logging.

Increased harvests required roads, and in many cases the prevailing harvest technology required a particularly dense pattern of roads. In the unstable soils unique to the Intermountain Region, the frantic pace of road construction led to massive erosion and stream sedimentation. Watershed and wildlife specialists began to complain vociferously. The agency responded by initiating some studies of the problem, and by trying to lay out logging roads a little more carefully, but timber production advanced unabated. Craddock's address to the SAF, cited above, reviewed the watershed restoration problems faced by the Forest Service in the Intermountain Region: Besides widespread damage from overgrazing, other restoration problems included controlling excessive "surface runoff and erosion" caused by clearcuts and by "poorly built logging roads, gullied skid trails [where logs were dragged across the ground], and compacted log landing areas. Corrective action on this part of the problem is moving too slowly," he said. When Craddock focused on future prevention of watershed deterioration, his prognosis grew distinctly pessimistic: "Demands for more timber are extending logging operations into remote, steeply sloping headwater lands having a high erosion potential. Tested watershed protection standards for many of these lands are not yet available." Besides losing precious, essentially non-renewable topsoil, sediment that washed off logging areas ended up in streams, where it killed fish and ruined spawning habitat, and in reservoirs, where it cut short the usable life span of expensive water development projects. Craddock dourly reminded his fellow professionals, "The public has already invested 5 billion dollars in storage dams, reservoirs, canals, power plants, and other water projects. . . . All of the developments are subject to damage by floods and sedimentation. There is thus an urgent need for more adequate watershed protection guides for . . . preventing a repetition and extension of the damaging mistakes of the past." [16]

Despite such voices of concern, timber production on the national forests continued to accelerate at a rate constrained only by market demand and the availability of funds for timber sales and roads. The Forest Service and everyone involved in advocating increased timber production, however, genuinely felt they were contributing to a better, more prosperous America. Hitherto unexploited national forest assets were being put to work building homes across the nation, lumber mill towns remained temporarily stable, and the economy remained strong. The process of putting assets to work seemed economically sound and socially appropriate. (The social desirability angle hinged to a large extent on the issue of homebuilding. The rise of suburban tract home development in the 1950s, such as Levittown, Long Island, contributed greatly to escalating demand for lumber and to the belief that lumber production made a special contribution to social welfare and quality of life in America. Social critics, of course, took aim at the conformism and lack of quality associated with these mass-produced suburban developments. John Keats, in 1956, wrote a soft polemic against the proliferation of "ticky-tacky" housing developments in his book, *The Crack in the Picture Window*. He wrote colorfully of "square miles of identical boxes" in "fresh-air slums" all across America. Cheaply built, for esthetics each one offered only a plate glass window in the living room — a picture window — framing in its view "the box across the treeless street.") [17]

A Long-Range Plan for Timber

The Forest Service announced in 1952 that it was undertaking a massive reappraisal of the forestry situation in America to revise its earlier forest appraisal of 1945–46. Estimating that it would take at least two years to complete, this Timber Resources Review (TRR) would "bring up to date the information on timber resources, re-analyze prospective requirements, supplies, and growth of timber, appraise today's timber-conservation programs, and chart a course for American forestry." Because this appraisal would serve as a new foundation for allowable cut determinations, timber industry lobbyists hoped to exert a strong influence on its development — taking advantage of the Eisenhower spirit of cooperation.

The main problem from the timber industry's perspective with past Forest Service timber appraisals was not so much the factual aspects of them, but rather the policy recommendations that accompanied each assessment. Every past timber appraisal by the Forest Service had blamed private owners of forestland for resource problems. Every past appraisal had also recommended public regulation of private forestry practices. Industry lobbyists supported the development of factual information regarding standing inventories, growth, and drain; but they were determined to block policy initiatives and opportunities for what they termed "propaganda." Diligently pursuing this negative agenda, they turned the Forest Service's two-year effort into a five-year struggle. Ed Crafts, who directed the TRR, recalled, "With the exception of a few outstanding leaders in the industry, I would say that the organized timber industry, in general, sniped at the Timber Resources Review all the way through. They questioned our techniques, demanded and succeeded in getting repeated meetings and hearings, they objected to this, delayed that, and there was just constant difficulty and harassment." Crafts also admitted that industry successfully confined the TRR to a "technical analysis," getting program and policy "completely omitted."[18]

The TRR advanced to the draft stage by 1955 and to a final product in 1958, published under the title, *Timber Resources for America's Future*. Significantly toning down the "timber famine" rhetoric traditional to previous reports, it nevertheless revealed a significant problem in supply and demand: although total forest growth essentially balanced total drain, too much of that growth was of poor commercial quality. Supplies of large, old-growth "sawtimber" valuable for lumber were still on a precipitous decline, and second growth (and third growth) forests in certain regions would not mature in time to avert temporary economic downturns, implying that present harvests exceeded "sustained yield" in these regions. The report further emphasized that even though great progress had been made in reforestation, especially on industrial tree farms (aided by federal cooperative planting programs), approximately one-quarter of the nation's commercial forest land remained inadequately stocked while another 50 million acres were virtually denuded of forest.[19]

According to industry lobbyists, this recycled "gloomy timber famine" language was unnecessary and unjustified. In a speech titled "The Great Guessing Game," Alf Nelson of the National Lumber Manufacturers Association told the Western Pine Association in Portland, "our timber resource situation is basically sound and its future bright." He criticized the TRR for its faulty and dangerous implications citing technological advances of recent decades that had led to greater timber utilization efficiency. The NLMA delivered a copy of Nelson's speech to its media contacts in the lumber trade with a cover sheet summarizing his points and quoting some of his more colorful passages. Nelson's language represents a classic expression of industry's carefully constructed timber supply optimism juxtaposed with its own gloom and doom fears of political despotism that leaders of the lumber business disseminated to the grassroots business culture:

> A leading forest economist warned today that "timber famine" forecasts of the U.S. Forest Service "could lead to government dictatorship" of the nation's forest resources. . . . While these forecasts have proved "as thin as the homeopathic soup that was made by boiling the shadow of a pigeon that had starved to death," there is danger that such "gloomy statements" may discourage consumer use of forest products and set the stage for "unwarranted and undesirable" legislation or forestry programs, he asserted.[20]

One aspect of the TRR did please industry: it presented a formidable argument for increasing timber production on the national forests and advocated an exponential step-up in intensive management. Chief McArdle summarized the tone of the document and its implications in a foreword to the final report: "To meet future timber demands will take earnest effort. Meeting those needs will require not only early action but *an intensity of forestry practices that will startle many of us*. There are no grounds for complacency. What we do in the next 10 or 20 years will determine whether we shall grow enough timber to enable our children and their children to enjoy the timber abundance that we ourselves know"[21] (emphasis added).

The Ideology of Intensive Management in the 1950s

How did foresters conceive of the means for achieving the "prompt and very substantial expansion and intensification of forestry" that the TRR demanded?[22] First, according to the TRR, harvest all old-growth forests. Decay in these forests generally canceled out new growth, so they added little or nothing to the national inventory of "growing stock." Young, rapidly growing stands on the other hand yielded large increments in annual growth. Since higher growth rates could justify increases in the allowable cut, these "overmature" and "decadent" ancient forests had to go. Second, build an adequate system of roads both to gain access to all commercially usable timber and to support protection of that timber from fire, insects, disease, and wildlife. Depredations from fire and forest pests actually "destroyed" more volume of wood on the national forests each year than industry harvested, the report claimed. Third, promptly and successfully replant cutover lands and burned areas, replacing the wasteful natural diversity of forests with an efficient stand of commercially desirable species. Fourth, "improve" the growing timber stands: use traps and poisons to protect seedlings from wildlife damage; use hand labor and herbicides to remove competing "weed" trees; and periodically thin the stands to promote vigorous growth of only the best trees. Applying this kind of intensive forestry to nearly a hundred million acres nationwide would require an astounding investment of capital, labor, machinery, and chemicals. But foresters in this age of technological optimism did not shrink from the task. Even when necessary investments in tree seedling regeneration failed to keep pace with investments in harvesting, defenders of this rosy vision of engineered timber abundance never wavered.

The one task in this litany of intensive management practices receiving the most attention and support, other than road construction, was harvesting old growth. (This issue would receive top billing in the debates over national forest policy again in the 1980s.) Appropriately, the Society of American Foresters sponsored a technical conference on "Converting the Old-Growth

Forest" for its annual meeting in 1955. At the conference, no one questioned the value nor the inevitability of this "conversion" of old growth to younger stands; speakers talked only of methods and mitigations. The Regional Forester for Alaska, A. W. Greeley, offered a decidedly uninspired appraisal of the public's interest in old growth. There were exactly three issues of concern to the public regarding the harvesting of old growth, he said: (1) maintaining "a consistent level of employment and economic activity in forest-based industries at the highest feasible and sustainable level" (note the approval of the maximum production ethos); (2) assuring "ample provision" for "nontimber products and services" (a nod to multiple use); and (3) eliminating avoidable damage and correcting unavoidable damage during logging (a nod to forest protection). He never acknowledged in his discussion of nontimber values and damage prevention that old growth might be more useful for these purposes in an intact state. His discussion of nontimber values offered only this salvo: "The public interest requires that some minimum amount of these 'other' products and services be provided from forest land." This minimum provision for "other" uses and values was to be provided "while the old growth conversion process goes on" in pursuit of "maximum timber production."[23]

Assistant Chief (soon to become Chief) Ed Cliff wrote a public information pamphlet in the late 1950s titled, "The Care and Use of National Forests," in an apparent attempt to address growing criticism from some conservation groups of its timber program. After implying that forestry was a technical issue better left to professionals, Cliff explained how harvesting old growth was both inevitable and proper: "The first and probably most important fact which must be faced is that trees and lesser vegetation are organisms; thus temporary. Each has its optimum life for utilization and if not utilized dies."[24] This was a classic utilitarian perspective that offered no recognition of the essential soil-building and nutrient-cycling role dying trees play when left in the forest to decay, nor any recognition of the fact that many Americans valued the national forests more in their natural state than in the form of two-by-fours.

While industry and the Forest Service fought over a number of issues, the leaders of both agreed that old growth must be converted. At the 1955 SAF conference at which Greeley spoke, E. P. Stamm, a prominent forester with Crown Zellerbach Corporation in Portland, Oregon, threw caution to the wind in his advocacy for old growth liquidation. "There is no argument but that complete utilization of timber resources is necessary," he pronounced confidently. Specifically directing his comments at the Forest Service and Bureau of Land Management, Stamm said the "problem" of getting rapid liquidation of old growth was "particularly acute on federally owned lands." He then quoted ex-chief William Greeley (who had become a spokesman for the West Coast lumber industry), saying that although sustained yield had traditionally been a check against overcutting, it was "high time we applied it just as seriously as a principle of management to prevent *under-cutting*"[25] (emphasis his). Under a section of his paper titled, "Management Means Roads," Stamm emphasized a common industry theme: "The large volumes of big old growth, rugged topography, and long distances from woods to market . . . all spell ROADS, MORE ROADS, AND BETTER ROADS in big, red capital letters." The lack of roads meant "fantastic losses to the regional and national economy." He acknowledged that industry's private timberlands were generally accessible and the primary need for road systems was on federal lands. While 95 percent of the road mileage on Northwest national forests had been built by timber purchasers, with road costs deducted from their timber sale contracts ("roads for stumpage" program), Stamm stressed a growing need for federally funded "main access roads" into areas where the costs of the roads exceeded the value of the timber to be removed. He concluded with the aphorism: "lack of management is synonymous with mismanagement."[26]

A few protesting voices among resource management professionals rose to challenge the ideology of these engineers of cornucopia. Speaking for the dissenters, Justin Leonard of the Michigan Department of Conservation wrote in 1956, "Our mastery of material skills still far exceeds our ability to comprehend the outcome of the exercise of these skills."[27] W. Winston Mair, Chief of the Canadian Wildlife Service, endorsed Leonard's sentiments in an address to the Western Association of State Game and Fish Commissioners, also in 1956, adding his own doubts that humans were sufficiently aware of their place in the "web of life" to utilize natural resources intelligently. His talk, titled "Toward an Ecological Conscience," argued that wildlife populations served as indicators of forest and range health, and that wildlife declines assuredly warned of the deteriorating health of the ecological system as a whole. When one looked beyond certain well-stocked game populations which were specifically managed for production — like a crop — one discovered a frightening decline of species. Mair quoted Aldo Leopold, "We stand guard over works of art, but species representing the work of aeons are stolen from under our noses." The source of this decline in wildlife and ecosystem health, Mair suggested, was "the general philosophy that everything must have a dollar value to be worthy of consideration."[28]

Advocates of an ecological conscience, like Leonard and Mair, usually adopted a somewhat defensive posture when speaking during the 1950s. The cult of cornucopia held such sway over public opinion and especially professional opinion among foresters that people like Leonard and Mair could be perfunctorily dismissed as "nay-sayers." Mair's discomfort showed through as he emphasized several times his appreciation of social and economic progress and his faith in human beings.[29] Those who dissented against the status quo were excluded from the halls of power and remained on the margins of policy debates.

Roads and Revenue

As previously noted, the whole intensive management scheme depended on roads. Justifying the construction of a "dense" transportation system in turn depended on the Forest Service's ability to generate revenue from timber made accessible by those roads. In fact, to a certain degree the whole Forest Service budget had become dependent on timber sale revenue. Without it, as the Forest Service feared, Congress would likely have been even more stingy with its appropriations for other national forest resource programs. Thus, exponents of increased timber harvesting never failed to point out the revenue potential of increased timber sales and the need for more roads to get at that timber. Although the revenue argument had severe limitations, its exponents in the Forest Service, industry, and Congress all conspired to ignore them. Each group in this "iron triangle" had a stake in national forest timber production that was served whether the sales were profitable or subsidized. More production meant more personnel, money, and prestige for the Forest Service; industry got public timber to keep their mills rolling and profits accumulating; senators and representatives stimulated the economies of their states with federal dollars, pleasing influential constituents and gaining cannon fodder for the next election battle. Testimony to the Senate

Appropriations Committee by H. Robert Hansen, a California lumberman, exemplifies these mutually dependent relationships:

> At the rate of cutting which we must practice on our own lands in order to maintain our operation at full scale and to keep all of our people employed — our privately owned timber will soon be gone. Standing all around us . . . are some two million acres of federally owned National Forest timber. Most of this timber is virgin old growth and much of it is over mature. . . . The reason for the failure of this timber to be sold and cut is the lack of funds by the Forest Service for construction of main access roads and lack of sufficient personnel to prepare and administer the timber sales. Failure to harvest valuable overripe timber . . . is a grievous crime. If the timber is not soon made available to us many of our people employed in the lumber industry will be without employment.[30]

Hansen justified his support for more timber roads by claiming they were not expenses but rather "extremely wise *capital investments* which will be returned very rapidly to the federal treasury *in hard cash* realized from the sale of standing timber"[31] (emphasis in original). This defense of the timber program as revenue generating, however, was misleading. Timber sales (and grazing programs) in most regions actually lost money. In California in 1958 the Forest Service spent over $25 million managing the national forests — primarily engaging in timber production or protection — but took in only $11.6 million in receipts. It spent $8.6 million constructing and re-habilitating roads and bridges alone. California national forest timber was expensive to access and of only moderate commercial quality. The Forest Service valued the 1 million board feet of timber cut out of California national forests in 1958 at $11.8 million. The same volume of national forest timber in Washington state that year was valued at $17 million. Timber cut from Oregon, Alabama, Georgia, South Carolina, Mississippi, and Texas national forests commanded twice the value per thousand board feet as California timber. Yet California national forests provided the third highest timber yield of all forty states with national forests.[32]

Essentially, the Pacific Northwest's valuable old growth and the South's fast-growing, lucrative pine plantations generated enough revenue to subsidize the timber sales program of California and virtually every other region.

When the Forest Service crowed that its revenues exceeded its expenditures for national forest protection and management, it only mentioned total U.S. receipts and expenses. The regional breakdown would have proved embarrassing. The data on regional costs and expenses were known to industry lobbyists — available in annual statistical booklets produced by the Forest Service at the request of industry representatives[33] — and certainly members of Congress knew the details, too, yet everyone judiciously sidestepped the issue. Political "log-rolling" in Congress required the broadest possible distribution of federal largesse to maintain a critical mass of support for federally sponsored development projects, and since forty states contained national forests, it was reasonably easy to gather support for general increases in the Forest Service roads and timber sales budgets (and later the recreation budget), so long as those increases were distributed fairly widely throughout the national forest system. But that meant uneconomic logging on marginally productive forests. The Forest Service, for its part, certainly did not want its operations to become lopsided by a concentration of its production activities only in the profitable regions, so they supported a broad-based harvest program with some regions subsidizing others. Plus, the agency's quasi-religious dedication to averting timber shortages demanded that every feasible acre yield wood products.[34] If that required federal subsidies, so the argument went, then the public interest justified it.

Figure 5 shows statistics related to revenues and expenses for each Forest Service region, derived from the "Reports on National Forest Timber Resource Operations" for the second half of Eisenhower's term in office (FYs 1957–60).[35] These reports listed timber sale revenues and total revenues for each forest and region, but unfortunately only listed total expenses for each forest and region without identifying timber-related expenses separately. The figures are nonetheless revealing. Timber receipts accounted for virtually the entire revenue base for seven out of ten regions. Only the Rocky Mountain, Southwestern, and Intermountain regions (Regions 2, 3, and 4) had any significant sources of revenue besides timber. In these three regions grazing receipts made up 30–40 percent of revenues. Also, the three Pacific Coast states (Regions 5 and 6) and the Southeast (Region 8) generated over three-quarters of all revenue (virtually all from timber). Finally, expenses exceeded revenues for every region except the South and the Pacific Northwest, by nearly a factor of two in most cases. The three regions with signifi-

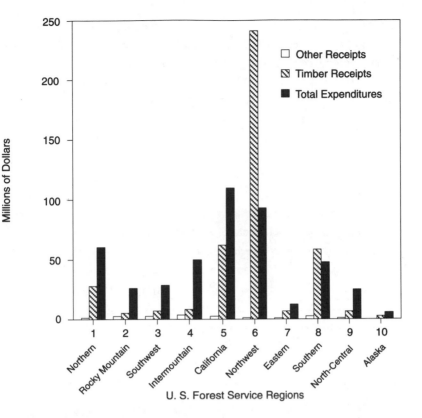

5. National Forest Receipts and Expenditures, 1957–1960 Source: U.S. Forest Service, Washington Office, "Report on National Forest Timber Resource Operations," 1957–60.

cant grazing topped the list of money losers, with expenses occasionally exceeding revenues by factors of three and four.

In addition to these direct logging subsidies, a second questionable economic characteristic of the timber program was the "roads for stumpage" scheme. As mentioned, approximately 95 percent of timber access roads in Oregon in the 1950s had been built by timber purchasers under this program. National forests in regions outside the Northwest and South usually required a much larger percentage of government funded roads. For example, the Forest Service built or rebuilt 118 miles of roads in Idaho's national forests in 1958 while the cut that year equaled half a million board feet. In Oregon the same year, more than three times as much timber was harvested yet the Forest Service built only 71.5 miles of roads.[36] The Forest Service justified this practice of trading "stumpage" for roads as a capital investment, arguing that the higher values and lower costs of the second "crop" of timber would make up for any losses in the original sale. But that justification fell apart under scrutiny. A second crop of timber takes 60–120 years to mature and the expenses of road maintenance during this long interim period invariably exceed the surplus value of the second growth timber after harvest costs are factored in. (The U.S. General Accounting Office recently analyzed and rejected the agency's claim that road costs are recouped by future harvests.)[37] Politicians and foresters who understood that the revenue argument was specious (with the exception of the Southern and Northwest regions), supported the timber and road programs as a kind of social/corporate welfare, a way to stimulate or sustain local timber-dependent economies and transform otherwise idle resources into market commodities. To see this liquidation of forest capital as being in the long-term public interest required faith in the Forest Service's ability to renew that capital by engineering second crops on these often marginal cutover lands and to get them profitably to market in the future. Alas for these optimists, reforestation efforts often failed, roads deteriorated, topsoil washed into streams and rivers, and the high levels of production required ever greater subsidies to sustain them. Many of the indirect costs of timber production would be absorbed by the environment or passed on to future generations.

Was this veritable orgy of road building really in the public interest? Did Americans want the national forests to be managed for maximum production? Was it the function of the national forests to serve as a supplemental supply of timber for an industry that repeatedly failed to manage its private lands for sustained yield? Many, of course, answered a qualified, "yes." Others challenged this management course. Willis Evans of the California Department of Fish and Game warned the Society of American Foresters in 1959 that neglect of watershed values in timber management had contributed to "resource abuses" that threatened both sustained yield and fisheries resources in the Northwest. The advent of tractor logging and the harvest of old-growth stands in remote and steep areas, according to Evans, had resulted in rapidly accelerated soil erosion and destruction of salmon and steelhead habitat. "The great bulk of sediment which is carried downstream from logged watersheds can often be traced to improper location and construction of road systems."[38] The Forest Service was well aware of the

contribution of roads to stream sedimentation, and had already begun experiments to measure the erosion rates of various logging practices. A two-
decade experiment begun in 1952 in three adjacent watersheds in a rugged
region of western Oregon documented that a clearcut area using "high-
lead" cables instead of roads to lift the logs out averaged three times the
erosion rate of the adjacent undisturbed watershed, while the roaded and
logged area averaged 109 times more soil loss than the undisturbed forest.[39]
But studies of this type did nothing to slow the logging.

Besides the problem of soil loss and stream sedimentation, logging affected soil productivity and forest regeneration capabilities in other ways.
Exposure to the drying effects of sun and wind reduced soil moisture, often
making it more difficult for seedlings to get established, especially in arid
regions. Even worse, compaction from logging machinery, especially on
skid roads, radically reduced soil porosity and permeability, leaving remaining topsoil in a less productive and more unstable condition. Roads caused
by far the worst episodes of erosion, compaction, and productivity losses. A
study by a Weyerhaeuser soil scientist and a University of Washington
professor published in 1955 measured the precise changes in macroscopic
soil pore space and soil permeability on logged areas of Weyerhaeuser's tree
farm, and contrasted tree seedling survival and vigor on skid roads with
adjacent cutover areas off the skid roads. They found that permeability was
reduced 35 percent on the cutover areas and 92 percent on the skid roads,
while soil pore space showed a loss of 11 percent on the cut areas and 53
percent on the skid roads. Importantly, skid roads comprised *one-fourth* of
the total logged area on average. These studies further showed that 78
percent of seedlings survived on the unroaded clearcuts, while only half the
seedlings planted in the skid roads survived. Of those that survived, 41
percent of the seedlings on the skid roads were rated "poor quality," while
only 12 percent on the unroaded clearcut were rated poor.[40]

Conclusion

Willis Evans argued in his presentation to the SAF in 1959 that managing
for high yield production under the profit motive did not protect the public
interest in forests — unless profit and wood production were defined as the
sole public interest. On both private and public lands, he warned, "Too often
the immediate economics of a situation rather than sound long-range con-

servation principles dictate the actions taken." As an alternative he suggested that all forest lands should have two fundamental management principles applied to them: (1) use of any resources should not impair the basic health and productivity of the forests; and (2) use of any one resource should not impair the productivity of other related resources. "The basic fact that the soil belongs to mankind, not to any one generation or any one group currently using it, is a concept that will eventually be adopted by a thinking people concerned with tomorrow."[41]

Evans's proposal challenged the ideology of the free market. It would have led to less ambitious timber production on the national forests and forced industry to absorb ("internalize") more of the environmental costs ("externalities") related to timber extraction.[42] Evans admitted that protecting soil, water, and wildlife would "inevitably increase the cost of timber harvest," but "prevention is far more economical than corrective action after damage has been done."[43] Besides, practically speaking, soil once lost cannot be feasibly replaced on a large scale. But, as Evans feared, economic motivations and the ideology of full utilization prevailed. Those who argued that remote areas of the national forests should remain remote — to save money, protect soil, provide clean and stable water flows, preserve wildlife habitat, and offer primitive recreation opportunities — formed a small and uninfluential minority. Contrary to the Forest Service's own policies of multiple use and sustained yield, a breakneck acceleration of timber sales and old-growth forest liquidation vastly outstripped related programs in reforestation, erosion control, and wildlife habitat management during Eisenhower's administration. While unable to alter this trend, conservationists in this period did make headway in getting Congress and the Forest Service to expand the national forest recreation program, but only insofar as it did not interfere with getting out the cut. The next chapter explores the efforts of conservationists to improve the balance of multiple uses.

7

The Fight to Protect Nontimber
Values, 1953–1960

During the custodial era of national forest management, wildlife habitat, soil, water, and wilderness were preserved almost without effort. Lack of management was good management for these values. Suddenly, after World War Two, the custodians of the public's forests took advantage of new market opportunities and began intensive extraction of the timber resource affecting the quality of these other forest resources and values. Nontimber interest groups then had to organize to defend the environmental values they had traditionally enjoyed during the custodial era. The timber industry, however, had a head start in establishing influence in the forest policy arena. Shrewdly, conservation organizations (usually with Forest Service support) mimicked the tactics of the lumber lobby: just as industry had acquired federal subsidies for roads and below-cost sales, recreation advocates sought federal funds for recreation development; just as the national Timber Resources Review had documented the "need" for accelerated logging, a comprehensive wildlife and recreation plan unveiled by the Forest Service in 1957 documented the "need" for more attention to these latter two resources; and, finally, just as industry strove to disseminate the ideology that natural forests were undesirable, conservationists responded with their own intellectual defense of wilderness. Despite some Forest Service efforts to cultivate recreation and wildlife constituencies, these two groups felt increasingly marginalized. The mid-1950s marked a distinct watershed in relations between conservation groups and the Forest Service, as well as between two disparate wings of the conservation movement.

Failed Attempts to Earmark Funds for Recreation in the 1950s

As the timber program shot forward, recreation management and maintenance of facilities advanced little. Yet, recreational *use* increased at a pace
exceeding even timber demand. Despite repeated pleas to Congress from
conservationists and the Forest Service, funds for handling these problems
remained scarce. Consequently, many recreation advocates supported efforts to bypass the administration's Budget Bureau and the congressional
appropriations committees with bills authorizing the return of certain percentages of national forest receipts automatically to the agency for recreation management. This form of supplemental earmarking of funds from
national forest receipts had long been approved for timber-related programs,
such as road construction and timber sale area rehabilitation activities, as
well as for grants to counties in lieu of taxes.[1] But earmarking funds for
recreation, in contrast, faced insurmountable opposition. While some lobbyists and policy makers opposed earmarking on principle, others defended it
as a tried and true method of assuring stability of funds for important programs. Whether recreation deserved such a boon was the real issue to be
decided. A bill introduced by Representative Boyd Tackett (D-AR) in 1949
had initiated the effort to set aside 10 percent of national forest receipts for
recreation. Tackett's bill did not pass, and after he retired Republican Representative Howard Baker of Tennessee carried the torch during the first Congress of the Eisenhower administration. Baker tried twice with H.R. 1972 in
1953 and H.R. 8225 in 1954 to replace the failed Tackett bill. In 1955, after
Democrats recaptured the House and Senate in the midterm elections, Representative Lee Metcalf (D-MT) introduced a third incarnation, H.R. 1823.
All failed.

Howard Baker's bills of 1953 and 1954 would have returned 10 percent
of receipts, with a cap at $5.5 million annually, for recreation and wildlife
habitat management. Speaking in favor of his bill in 1953, Baker mentioned
that the near doubling of recreation use between 1945 and 1953 without
adequate resources to manage that use had led to a number of recreation
sites being closed down in 1952 as health menaces. Congress had a responsibility, he said, to make the national forests available to the nation's recreating public, and to do so in a way that protected both soil and water as well as
public health.[2] As did advocates for increased timber sales, Baker asserted
that government had a responsibility to satisfy public demands for goods

and services from the national forests. This market-like argument helped in appealing to members of Congress inclined toward viewing natural resource management in economic terms.

Supporters of the bill at the hearing in 1953 included the International Association of State Game and Fish Commissioners, the National Wildlife Federation, the Izaak Walton League, the Wildlife Management Institute, the Sierra Club, the General Federation of Women's Clubs, the Appalachian Mountain Club, the Outdoor Writers Association of America, and many others. Reflecting this demand and supply perspective, William Voigt of the Izaak Walton League pointed to the increasing development of private lands and the posting of "No Trespassing" signs, which made it doubly important that the government make a "strenuous effort . . . to find ways and means of putting, and keeping, our national forests in the best possible condition to carry the present and future burden."[3] Even more overtly economic in its focus, the American Automobile Association testified in favor of the bill, arguing that, "In evaluating the recreational value of the national forests, the economic importance of travel should not be overlooked." A study by the association had found that "75 million Americans, nearly half the national population, take a vacation trip during the year. Of that number, 66 million travel by passenger car. These motor vacationists spend nearly $10 billion during the course of their journeys, and no less than 26 states now rank travel among their three biggest dollar earning industries."[4]

These economic arguments carried some weight, and figured prominently in future recreation advocacy. Industrial interests, and others who wanted recreation clearly subordinated to commodity production, countered that outdoor tourism ought to pay its own way on the national forests if it was to compete with activities such as logging, which, they said, generated a significant amount of revenue. Recreationists retorted that camping, picnicking, and sight-seeing did not consume resources (mostly but not entirely true), and that theirs was a not-for-profit use that benefited a broad section of the public, and therefore revenue generation should not be an issue. Besides, argued the Conservation Director of the state of Minnesota, these were public lands — why should the people have to pay to go and enjoy the use of their own property?[5]

The Forest Service did not testify at the 1953 hearing on the Baker bill. It had supported the Tackett bill under the Truman administration, but the

Eisenhower administration prohibited the agency from supporting the Baker bill now. Opponents of the bill at the hearings were few and included the National Lumber Manufacturers Association, the American National Cattleman's Association, the National Wool Growers Association, and, interestingly, the American Forestry Association. All four took the position that earmarked funds were a fiscally unsound practice and should be opposed on principle. Three of the four, in particular the AFA, qualified their opposition with statements that they supported wildlife and recreation programs as legitimate. But, as the NLMA argued, national forest receipts "belong to the general public . . . and before any portion of them is spent for some special purpose, we believe that the expenditure should be fully justified, substantiated, and supported by evidence before the Appropriations Committee in Congress."[6] This, of course, was a safe position for timber industry representatives to take because Congress had shown itself to be quite generous with federal funds for roads and timber sales. On the other hand, as William Voigt pointed out in his testimony, "It is obvious that Congress has been reluctant to grant sizable direct appropriations for [recreation and wildlife]. There always seems to come along someone with a more persuasive manner or a more touching story of need for the tax money in the Federal Treasury."[7] The hint of sarcasm in his tone revealed his frustration with the direct appropriations avenue of funding.

After a nudge from the timber industry, Eisenhower's Budget Bureau took the most active role in blocking the Baker bill, enlisting the aid of the Agriculture Department in clamping down on any overt aid the Forest Service might have lent supporters of the bill. Secretary Benson wrote to the House Agriculture Committee, "The department is in sympathy with the objectives of this bill but believes the needs covered by it should be considered along with other needs and financial resources, as part of the regular budget process." Without administration support the bill was doomed. A few weeks after the 1953 hearing, the House Agriculture Committee reported the bill unfavorably and the Senate declined to schedule a hearing on a similar bill.[8]

Oddly, although George Fuller of the NLMA stated in response to a question from a member of the Agriculture Committee that the bill would have virtually no effect on timber harvesting activities, his association still lobbied quite aggressively against it. The next year, 1954, Fuller sent a copy of Howard Baker's new version of the bill, H.R. 8225, around to association members with a cover letter asking them to contact their congressmen and express opposition.[9] Stuart Moir of the Western Forestry and Conservation Association wrote to Alf Nelson of the NLMA at the same time, warning that the Natural Resources Committee of the Portland Chamber of Commerce had been lured into endorsing the new Baker bill. According to Moir, who had a well-deserved reputation for federal agency bashing, it was Forest Service rhetoric regarding the deterioration of recreational facilities that had inspired this endorsement by the Portland Chamber. He felt the agency's ulterior agenda was self-aggrandizement, and in pursuit of this goal it was "gaining support from tourist-eager Chambers of Commerce and like organizations." He concluded with a warning and a plan of action:

> The activities of Chambers of Commerce need watching, for the Forest Service have [sic] a tremendous appeal to the public through recreation, rather than an appeal along sound business lines. This work of education must start right with company employees and with the communities. Otherwise, the forest industries are going to be taken for a ride on every whim of public inclination, particularly when it is agitated by a money-hungry Forest Service.[10]

Nelson thanked Moir for the warning and sent a copy of Moir's letter to representatives of the U.S. Chamber of Commerce in Washington, D.C., which shortly issued a formal statement to Congress opposing the Baker bill.[11]

The NLMA need not have worried. The second Baker bill died in committee, just as the first one did. However, as the NLMA's Alf Nelson accurately predicted, "If this bill is not passed in the current session of Congress it will undoubtedly come up in the next Congress. *It is a perennial*"[12] (emphasis his). Sure enough, another incarnation of the Baker bill appeared early in 1955, as the 84th Congress opened its first session. In fact, by 1956 thirteen bills were pending before the Agriculture Committee dealing with recreation uses on the national forests. Republican Howard Baker reintroduced his 1954 bill (now titled H.R. 3742), but Democrat Lee Metcalf's nearly identical bill (H.R. 1823) received the bulk of attention in the newly Democratic-controlled Congress. In regard to his bill, Metcalf explained, "Time after time sincere efforts have been made to get appropriations suffi-

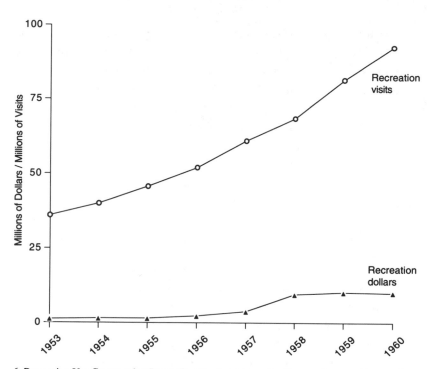

6. Recreation Use Compared to Recreation Funds, 1953–1960. Source: for recreation use figures: U.S. Forest Service, *Reports of the Chief of the Forest Service;* for funding: U.S. Congress, Senate, *Congressional Record* 106, pt. 9 (June 8, 1960): 12079–82.

cient to meet [recreation and wildlife] needs. The needs never have been
met." He hoped enactment of his bill would "end this meager hand-to-
mouth existence of our forest recreation facilities."[13]

Momentum built for Metcalf's bill, helped along by the considerable
publicity power of the Outdoor Writers Association of America, which had
endorsed it. Through popular magazines and newspapers, the public became
increasingly aware of outdoor recreation opportunities on the national forests — especially hunting and fishing. Americans also heard much about the
"urgent" need for facilities maintenance and development.[14] The reality of
deteriorated facilities and sky-rocketing public use, and the consistent shortfall in the Forest Service recreation budget allocations, built up increasing
public and political support for earmarked funds (see fig. 6). Seeing the
handwriting on the wall, and hoping to avoid victory for the advocates of
earmarked funds, Agriculture Secretary Ezra T. Benson and Assistant Secretary Ervin L. Peterson announced in 1956 that they had authorized the Forest

Service to study recreation demand and supply, and to prepare a five-year recreation development plan. The department distributed a press release announcing this just two weeks before the new hearing on the Metcalf bill was scheduled to begin.[15] The timing was deliberate. At the hearing, the Forest Service, speaking on behalf of the Agriculture Department, told the committee that until its study was completed "legislation in this field affecting the national forests would be premature."[16] Consequently, the Metcalf bill languished in committee while the administration promised to move forward with a recreation program. Even though the Forest Service already had the data on recreation development and maintenance needs and had already estimated the costs, the actual recreation program was not released until January 1957, after the adjournment of the 84th Congress and the death by neglect of the Metcalf bill.

The proposal to set aside 10 percent of receipts for recreation did not surface again in the next Congress, but the momentum for more attention to recreation could not be turned back. The Eisenhower administration eventually responded by supporting the Forest Service's five-year recreation program, "Operation Outdoors." In this case, the recreation advocates lost the battle but won the war.

Operation Outdoors: The Forest Service's First National Plan for Recreation

With the Baker and Metcalf bills apparently doomed, recreation advocates and the Forest Service turned to long-range planning as the next best tactic for improving recreation funding. On January 17, 1957, the Forest Service proudly announced its five-year recreation management program, Operation Outdoors — a small-scale parody of the earlier Timber Resources Review. The program proposed to "double camping and picnicking facilities in the national forests within the next five years."[17] Not coincidentally, Operation Outdoors came out just days after the president's budget message, which included rhetorical and budgetary support for the recreation plan. Without that support, Operation Outdoors would not have been published. Forest Service management proposals that specified a need for additional funding could not be released without clearance from the president's Budget Bureau — unless Congress specifically requested such information over the heads of the administration.[18]

Operation Outdoors once more effectively focused attention on recreation supply and demand problems in outlining the need for funds. John Sieker, Chief of the Recreation Division from 1947 to his retirement in 1964, recalled in an interview the year he retired that Operation Outdoors successfully led to a *tripling* of recreation funds in just a few years. The Forest Service had asked for $85 million spread out over five years to upgrade and expand facilities. Starting with FY 1958, the administration and Congress approved about three-quarters of that request, boosting the recreation budget from $4 million to over $9 million in that one year. Funds continued to climb slowly during the remainder of the Eisenhower term. Operation Outdoors also expanded the agency's support base in the public. When asked if public pressure had made any difference at the time, Sieker responded, "The general public helped a great deal. A lot of letters were written and a lot of organizations supported Operation Outdoors. And, of course, it was also helped by the fact that at the same time the Park Service was coming out with Mission 66." [19]

The National Park Service had already initiated a ten-year plan — "Mission 66" — to accommodate rising demand for outdoor recreation. The Park Service's program raised the visibility of efforts to recognize recreation as a major and legitimate activity on public lands. *Competition* with the Park Service in fact had partly motivated Operation Outdoors. One element of the Park Service's Mission 66 plan included proposals to transfer national forest lands of high scenic and recreational value to the Park Service for management. The Forest Service had been fending off attempts by the Park Service to acquire national forest lands for decades. [20] Operation Outdoors served as a politically advantageous display of the Forest Service's commitment to recreation, helping it avert challenges from the Park Service.

This significant jump in Forest Service recreation funding went to more than just facilities construction: it supported the development of a full-fledged recreation management staff for the first time in Forest Service history. To function as a true multiple use agency, the Forest Service needed a balanced and diverse staff, representing the various natural resource professions and uses. As pointed out earlier, prior to the late 1950s agency managers only represented professional expertise in building roads and managing timber. A semblance of a recreation staff had been built up during the 1930s with Civilian Conservation Corps labor, but that dissolved during World War Two, leaving the Forest Service with an unfilled void after the war. Starting from scratch in the mid-1940s, the agency first hired a few landscape architects to provide consultation in campground design, then tried to get at least one or two recreation staff people in each of the ten regional offices. The boost in funding in the late-1950s finally allowed the agency to get recreation managers out onto most forests and, later in the 1960s, into many of the District Offices, too.[21]

The need for better recreation management was not confined to the national forest lands — as the Park Service's Mission 66 program showed. Forests, parks, wildlife refuges, Bureau of Land Management lands, Tennessee Valley Authority projects, Army Corps of Engineers and Bureau of Reclamation projects, and state and private lands all shared in this surge of public use. In 1956, some of the recreation group lobbyists, particularly Joseph Penfold of the Izaak Walton League and David Brower of the Sierra Club, began pushing for a coordinated nationwide review of recreation resources and needs, to support a coordinated national recreation program.[22] Given the recent success of Mission 66 and the momentum added by the Forest Service's Operation Outdoors, this tactic was perhaps predictable. Unexpectedly, however, it came to fruition — and rapidly. In January 1957, Senator Clinton Anderson (D-NM), by then a veteran conservation advocate, introduced S. 846, "For the establishment of a National Outdoor Recreation Resources Review Commission [ORRRC]." Within about a year, the bill became law.[23] Unlike the Baker and Metcalf earmarking bills, the legislation establishing ORRRC did not commit the administration to anything more than studying the problem, so opposition was slight. The ORRRC represented an umbrella agency for recreation assessment and planning on all public lands with recreation potential.[24] The ORRRC produced its first plan in 1962, and so it did not really affect events in the Eisenhower administration except to further raise the visibility of recreation issues.

Planning for Wildlife

Like the Baker and Metcalf recreation bills, Operation Outdoors was supposed to have a wildlife component, but, lacking the political support that recreation enjoyed (animals don't vote), the wildlife portion of Operation Outdoors got put on hold. The Forest Service called Operation Outdoors "a double barreled program" (an ironic metaphor) aimed at solving both family recreation and wildlife management problems. Campground and picnic area development and maintenance constituted part 1. "Part 2 will be released later," the agency promised. Operation Outdoors part 2 sat on the shelf, despite complaints from wildlife groups, until the Kennedy administration rolled into office. In 1961, with support from the new president, the Forest Service finally received the go-ahead to release the wildlife plan. Like recreation funding, the wildlife budget increased after 1957, but proportionately it remained minimal, increasing from $694,000 in 1957 to $839,000 in 1958 to just over $1 million for the rest of the Eisenhower term — as compared to an escalation in the timber sale budget from $11 million to $20 million in the same years.

One of the stumbling blocks to a more aggressive wildlife management program on the national forests was the legal convention that states, not the federal government, owned wildlife within their state's jurisdiction, regardless of who owned the land. The national forests may have provided key habitat, and hunting and fishing grounds, but state departments of fish and game administered regulations regarding the "taking" of wildlife. Often the Forest Service worked well with state fish and game managers, but just as often the two wrangled over management priorities or resource extraction activities that affected habitat. A pressing need during this time of increasing forest development was to integrate wildlife habitat considerations into timber and range planning. In an effort to force wildlife considerations to the bottom of the priority scale, those who stood to lose from increased attention to wildlife (loggers and ranchers) often challenged the authority of the Forest Service to engage in wildlife management. A series of administrative and legal decisions since the 1930s had incrementally affirmed limited authority for the Forest Service to manage wildlife and its habitat on the national forests, but the extent of that authority was circumscribed and remained open to debate.[25] For their part, national forest managers considered wildlife management one of their mandates and cooperated with state wildlife managers whenever they could, but wildlife remained a very low priority.

Foresters in the 1950s (and to some degree in the following three decades) primarily conceived of wildlife management as a subsidiary function of timber and grazing activities. Perhaps the best indication of this general bias is found in the 1955 Society of American Foresters symposium on converting old-growth forests. This topic, which now raises heated debates over endangered species and the maintenance of viable populations of game and nongame wildlife, then attracted only technical considerations of game enhancement and the control of forest wildlife pests. At the symposium, the SAF's Division of Forest–Wildlife Management sponsored a panel on "The Effect of Logging Old Growth Timber on Wildlife." Five of six panelists discussed either the benefits of logging on certain big game populations or else the problems that rodents and other mammals posed to reforestation.[26] The one anomalous presentation out of these six offered a characteristically resigned analysis of the deleterious effects of logging on salmon in the Pacific Northwest. Interestingly, this latter presentation, by P. W. Schneider, Director of the Oregon State Game Commission, excused timber production while detailing its destructive impact on fisheries. In an obvious display of political finesse, he opened his talk by expressing concern over the future of fisheries in Oregon while simultaneously acknowledging that timber production ruled in his state:

> The question of the influence of the inevitable and progressively increased logging activities to the carrying capacity of Oregon streams for fishery production has concerned the fishery workers in the Oregon State Game Commission for several years. The influence of such necessary and essential lumbering activities in our number one industry to Oregon's economy has an impact in varying ways to both anadromous and resident species of salmonoid fishes and may affect such values in various ways.[27]

Schneider explained that logging altered natural stream environments in six ways, *all* harmful to fish habitat: (1) logging increased exposure of water courses to the sun, raising water temperatures and harming cold water fish like salmon and trout; (2) it caused erosion, leading to greater turbidity and silting of spawning beds; (3) it sometimes reduced insect populations (a food source); (4) it made stream flows unstable and erratic; (5) it altered water chemistry; and (6) it exposed spawning and rearing grounds to humans and other predators. Treading carefully across politically dangerous soil, Schneider employed others' research to make his points about the deleterious effects of logging and road building on streams. He concluded with a summary of five guidelines for keeping damages to a minimum, including road construction guidelines and a request for better coordination with the Game Commission when private companies and public agencies engaged in what he called "necessary and essential lumbering activities."

Wildlife management in the 1950s was still an evolving young discipline playing second fiddle to forestry at universities and in public agencies (with a few notable exceptions, such as the pioneering research on the grizzly bear taking place at the University of Montana's School of Forestry). Politicians considered funding for wildlife management programs on federal lands an expendable luxury. Funds for wildlife research primarily went to economic production related studies — for example, research on game animals (viewed as a crop), research on the damaging effects of wildlife on market resources, and research on the impacts of logging on fish habitat. The view that wildlife had a right to exist without regard for their commercial value or that natural biological diversity ought to be preserved had not yet taken hold in the wildlife management profession and had as yet made no headway in the political arena. These policies evolved in the wake of the new "environmental movement" of the 1960s and 1970s, resulting most significantly in the passage of the Endangered Species Act in 1973. In the meantime, wildlife managers and wildlife advocates struggled unsuccessfully to transcend their marginal and subordinate status.

Zoning for Wilderness

In 1958, national forests totaled 187.9 million acres. Eighty-eight and a half million of those acres had been designated commercial timberland — 47 percent of the total. That percentage had been steadily increasing since World War Two. The remaining 100 million acres comprised inaccessible lands; grasslands and scrub woodlands of the arid Southwest, usually intensively grazed; and rock and ice in the high Sierra, Cascades, and Rocky mountains. A relatively small amount — 14 million acres in 1958, just over 7 percent of the national forests — had been designated as "wilderness," "wild," or "primitive" by the Forest Service (these were the agency's own formal categories), and nearly all of that was noncommercial forest or rock and ice. These protected areas were in large blocks widely scattered throughout the West. The agency had established them mostly on its own initiative, due to the efforts of Aldo Leopold, Robert Marshall, and Arthur Carhart, who advocated wilderness preservation while working for the Forest Service in the 1920s and 1930s. (Marshall went on to found The Wilderness Society in 1935.)

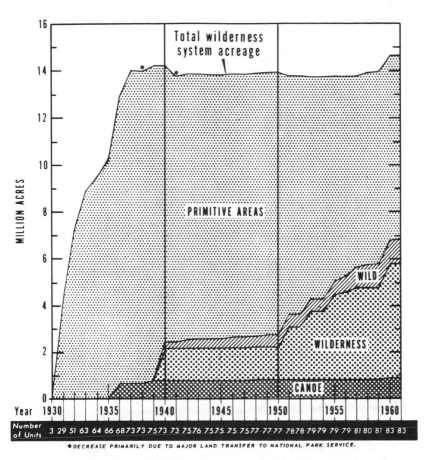

7. Growth of the National Forest Wilderness System, 1930–1961. Source: U.S. Forest Service, *Report of the Chief of the Forest Service, 1961*, p. 14.

While the acreage dedicated to intensive timber production constantly increased, total acres designated primitive, wild, or wilderness remained at the 14 million acre level from 1935 to 1958 (I will call all of these areas "wilderness" here for the sake of simplicity). Many of the protected areas actually suffered a loss of acreage as access roads, lumbering activities, and in some cases recreational resorts chewed away at their edges. The fact that the number of wilderness areas increased from sixty-six in 1935 to eighty in 1958 while the acreage remained static reflects this fragmentation (see fig. 7).[28] A specific example is New Mexico's Gila Wilderness, established as a result of herculean efforts by Aldo Leopold in the 1920s, but split in half in the mid-1930s by a forest development road (the "North Star Road"). Conservationists fought off numerous attempts by the Forest Service in the 1960s and 1970s to further reduce the acreage in these two remaining wild areas, finally succeeding in permanently establishing the boundaries in the 1980 New Mexico Wilderness Act.[29]

While the Forest Service as a whole supported — even defended — wilderness preservation,[30] it remained too amenable to boundary adjustments to accommodate development for the peace of mind of wilderness advocates. Besides, the agency felt 14 million acres was adequate for the foreseeable future.[31] As timber harvesting expanded into "de facto" wild areas and ever larger blocks of clearcutting became standard practice, recreational users reacted against the esthetics and environmental effects of this intensive production by celebrating and promoting the protection of natural forests. Henry Harrison, assistant director of recreation for the Forest Service in Washington, D.C., told the Society of American Foresters in 1958, "We all know that some of our timber harvesting operations are distasteful to the forest recreation visitor. Freshly clearcut areas look like devastation." In the typical agency manner, however, Harrison finished with the observation that such negative public reactions exhibited ignorance of silvicultural science and an inability to "look ahead ten years" and imagine — like a forester — a fully stocked and thriving young stand. Other foresters inside and outside the agency unabashedly argued for the extension of logging into parks, recreation areas, and wildernesses. Outspoken Yale professor of forestry Herman H. Chapman, who had trained fifteen academic generations of forestry students, advocated timber management in national parks, wilderness, and other natural areas in an essay published in *American Forests* in February 1958. Chapman excoriated as "utterly ignorant" a statement made by National Park advocates in *The Living Wilderness* (Autumn 1957) that old forests and decaying trees had long been a healthy and proper part of the natural environment and that there was no need for humans to improve upon it now. Chapman, adopting an anachronistic Judeo-Christian theme, stated that the wilderness enthusiasts were ignorant of the necessary and proper role of man as nurturer in this Garden of Eden.[32]

Such statements prompted wilderness advocates and other skeptics of the industrial cornucopia vision to endorse the concept of legislative zoning of portions of the national forests for noncommodity uses. Howard Zahniser of The Wilderness Society first approached the Forest Service and friendly congressmen like Hubert Humphrey and John Saylor with a proposal for wilderness legislation in 1955. He had decided that Forest Service designation was too insecure and the agency too enthusiastic about intensive management to entrust it with wilderness preservation.[33] At first the agency opposed congressional designation of wilderness, partly because it did not want to lose any management flexibility and partly because the Eisenhower administration opposed wilderness legislation. Wilderness supporters feared that the defense of "management flexibility" really represented a desire to retain the freedom to reclassify areas of wilderness as commercial timberland and open them up to logging when market conditions warranted. To a degree their fears were warranted. The concept of nonmanagement jarred the 1950s sensibilities of professional foresters, and market pressures repeatedly showed an uncanny ability to overcome agency promises to protect nonmarket resources.

The debate over wilderness legislation carried on for eight years from the introduction of the first Humphrey bill in 1956 to the passage of a Clinton Anderson sponsored bill in 1964. Advocates of "full utilization" successfully stalled progress on the bills for many years. The increasing strength of a "new wave" of environmental activists in the sixties and the coming to power of a Democratic administration in 1961 that favored wilderness legislation eventually led to success for the supporters — but only after a series of weakening amendments and loopholes had been added (see Chapter 10 below). In the meantime, controversies over Forest Service development proposals in designated or de facto wild areas drove an ever widening wedge between conservationists and the Forest Service.

Historian Susan Schrepfer described an incident in 1954–56 involving a California national forest that marked a turning point in Sierra Club relations with the agency. Several insect infestation "salvage" sales had been planned for a high use recreation area that contained trees of only marginal value. The first sale left behind such visual devastation that it galvanized opposition, with David Brower leading the charge. Brower scrutinized the official rationale for the salvage sales and found that the Forest Service's own entomologist's report as well as an independent entomological analysis had determined that the forest was healthy and that the insect populations were at normal levels. Still, the agency insisted on going forward with logging, and they wooed Sierra Club support with "show-me" trips for the club's board of directors and special meetings in which they promised to log more carefully than they had with the first salvage sale. The Board members agreed to withhold opposition to the sales partly because they believed the agency's promises, partly because they wanted to maintain good relations with the forest managers, and partly because they felt timber management in recreation areas was an inevitability. Brower, on the other hand, felt as if the Forest Service had been disingenuous about its motivations for the timber sales — he believed that salvage operations were a cover for extending logging into marginal lands and recreation areas — and he felt the agency had been manipulative in its solicitation of the club's support. Eventually most of the board came around to Brower's position rather than vice versa. Although the second salvage sale went forward in 1956, making that particular battle moot, the old "gentleman's" network and client relationship that had evolved between the agency and the Sierra Club slowly dissolved into distrust and recriminations.[34]

Such episodes occurred all over the country and caused as much internal controversy within the conservation movement as external conflict with the agency. Clearly, conservationists were not of one mind. Political scientist Grant McConnell wrote an essay in 1954 titled, "The Conservation Movement — Past and Present," in which he noted that centrifugal forces were scattering the old Progressive conservation coalition in disparate directions. Looking about for some hint of unity in the new directions the movement was taking, he settled on the observation that the one apparent commonality seemed to be opposition to commercial exploitation of natural resources. Wilderness preservation advocacy symbolized this new focus. He also noted that the new wave of movement leaders turned more to Aldo Leopold and John Muir as role models than to Gifford Pinchot and the Progressives.[35] These conservationists coming of age in the 1950s found a different kind of Forest Service to deal with than their predecessors and different challenges to contend with regarding public land management.

Production versus Preservation Antagonisms — Industrial Public Relations

A growing antagonism between the timber industry and organized recreation and wildlife interest groups required the lumber lobbyists to dedicate additional efforts to public relations in the 1950s. In particular, they courted the pro-recreation Outdoor Writers Association of America to advertise industrial commitment to "multiple use." In the struggle between interest groups to claim the majority and shape public perceptions, industrial lobbyists adopted the rhetoric of the Forest Service to great advantage. Weyerhaeuser's recreation manager, Kramer Adams, told the SAF conventiongoers in 1955, "Most private land owners are now practicing true 'multiple use.' "[36] The American Forest Products Industries, Inc., a Washington, D.C.–based public relations arm of the lumber, pulp, and paper associations, put out a series of pamphlets beginning in February 1955, titled "Story Tips for Outdoor Writers." Each pamphlet featured a half dozen summaries of human interest stories portraying industry in its best light.

The first story tip out of bulletin no. 1, titled "Hiawatha Never Had It So Good," told of how the Hiawatha Hunting Club in Michigan had decided to sell patches of old-growth timber on its 36,000-acre hunting ground for a local pulp company to cut, under the expectation that (1) the club could generate some much needed revenue, and (2) the cleared areas would create new food sources and allow the deer herd to increase. The writer of this story tip effused, "To hungry deer the drone of a powersaw or the crash of a falling cedar in Mackinaw county means 'food.' " Appealing to pecuniary instincts, the writer noted that "$20,000 worth of timber products" had been removed the previous year: "To club members this means more hunting to enjoy and more wampum in the club treasury. Hiawatha never had it so good."[37] (The writer neglected to mention how much of that $20,000 in product value the club actually received after the costs of removing the timber had been deducted.)

Another story tip in the same bulletin queried, "Porcupine . . . Friend or Foe?" It cited Forest Service statistics on timber damage caused by porcupines (one of their food sources is the cambium of trees) and then elaborated on the menace these spiny mammals posed to logging operations: "Porcupines also put logging trucks, tractors, and even trains out of commission. When machinery is parked at night, the porcupines cut air hoses on trains, gnaw tires on vehicles, and chew insulation from ignition wiring." This story served to bolster industry-backed "rodent control" programs.

A third story tip, titled "Youth Learns about Logging," opened with the following anecdote: " 'Gee, they even gave us a chance to run a power saw!' This comment from a husky Northern California high school boy typifies student interest in the Redwood Region Conservation Council's annual 'Junior Logging Conference.' " At the conference, 120 "lucky" boys (no girls) got to "live and eat like loggers for three days," participating in demonstrations of logging techniques.[38]

Like the claim that timber harvesting benefited wildlife, industry similarly claimed that timber harvests benefited recreation, too. Bulletin no. 2 (May 1955) included a story tip titled "A New Kind of Management for Recreational Forests" with the following argument: "Protecting a recreational forest from fire and from cutting does not necessarily keep it in the best condition for recreational use. Foresters today believe that even recreational forests have to be managed scientificly [sic], according to the silvicultural requirements of the trees, to maintain desirable conditions. This is a new concept."[39] Characterizing timber harvesting as a tool to be used for *enhancing* recreation and wildlife values was an attempt to retain the maximum amount of forestland available for cutting, in direct response to recreation and wildlife advocacy groups promoting the designation of areas of the national forests off-limits to extractive uses.

The American Forest Products Industries widely distributed these *Story Tips for Outdoor Writers,* and some found their way into major publications. The business section of the *New York Times* carried an article on its front page in October 1956 headlined, "When Forest Industries Open Their Lands to the People, Thousands Thankfully Take to the Woods." The author of the article mentioned the American Forest Products Industries and, like Kramer Adams of Weyerhaeuser, credited the forest industries with having enthusiastically adopted the policy of multiple use: "The trend toward wider acceptance of public use of private timber land is in line with the philosophy of 'multiple use' of industrial forests. This philosophy regards timbergrowing as the primary purpose of the forests but recognizes that it is compatible with other values, such as recreation, scenic beauty, wildlife preservation and soil and water conservation."[40] While opening up industrial lands for recreational use represented a genuine effort at better public relations, the adoption of multiple use policy was mostly window dressing. As noted above, industry's view of multiple use meant logging in wildlife refuges and recreation areas — in fact, it meant logging wherever timber values made it feasible. Industrial foresters always considered wood production a forest's primary function, with other multiple uses incidental. Timber harvesting *was* multiple use management.

Private memos from timber lobbyists in these years best reveal industry's undisguised views on multiple use. California timber executive Robert Hansen, in a 1959 letter to the Forest Service's Regional Forester in California, Charles Connaughton, said he was convinced that emphasizing "multiple use" offered "our best approach" to countering the lobbying efforts of the Sierra Club and getting more funds for national forest timber sales and roads. Perennial industry spokesman William Hagenstein (with the Industrial Forestry Association on the West Coast at the time) wrote to Alf Nelson and Ernest Kolbe, warning that a recently announced U.S. Fish and Wildlife Service survey of hunters and fishermen spelled "nothing but trouble" for the forest industries. He worried that the result of the survey would be "demand for less and less timber management in the national forests and more and more wildlife management, game refuges on State lands, recreational provisions, and all the other development needed for providing for the nimrods and Waltonians." With unerring foresight, Hagenstein added, "In three years take this letter out of the file and see if my forecast isn't at least partially correct." If anything, he underestimated the explosive public demand on federal land agencies to protect wildlife, wilderness, and recreational resources on public lands.[41]

Conclusion

The multiple users of the national forests began to really feel the pressure of conflicting demands during the Eisenhower era. Timber and recreation interests especially grew to perceive each other as entrenched opponents, each jockeying for position in the struggle over how the national forests would be managed. Forest Service leaders, on the other hand, genuinely believed there were enough resources for everyone, especially if Congress approved funds for intensive management. But timber and recreation lobbyists did not always share the agency's optimism, nor were they content to sit back and let the Forest Service call all the shots regarding forest management decisions. While industry lobbied heavily and successfully for maximum timber sale and road budgets, recreation interests pushed, mostly unsuccessfully, for earmarked recreation funds and wilderness zoning. Both endorsed long-range planning as a strategy for getting more of what they wanted and for helping the Forest Service to get more public and political support for its numerous programs.

Superficially, all interest groups agreed with the Forest Service that multiple use was an appropriate national forest management policy — so long as multiple use meant they would get more of the use they were interested in. All groups also supported the policy of sustained yield — even though nobody was quite sure what it meant or how it should be applied. In this context of escalating conflict and confused policy consensus, it became apparent that some clarification of the fundamental purposes of the national forests was needed. The next chapter discusses the struggle between interest groups and the government to redefine national forest policy, culminating in the passage of the Multiple Use–Sustained Yield Act of 1960.

8

Multiple Use and Sustained Yield:
Debated and Defined, 1955–1960

Conflicts between user groups made public relations difficult for the Forest Service. The lumbering, grazing, recreation, wildlife, and water interests whom the Forest Service sought mightily to serve repaid the agency's efforts with vituperation. Increasingly, each constituent user group hammered the agency for failing to provide for their needs, and attempted to redefine the agency's policy rhetoric to their own advantage. For example, the timber industry adopted a definition of "sustained yield" that meant maximum feasible production of timber, and a definition of "multiple use" that implied a hierarchy of uses with timber dominant and others subordinate. The Wilderness Society and the Izaak Walton League proffered a nonhierarchical definition of multiple use that implied equal consideration of all uses — water, wood, forage, wildlife, and recreation — including wilderness recreation. Sustained yield, to this latter group, usually meant biological sustainability more than sustained economic production. The Forest Service's definitions of multiple use and sustained yield, which had previously been consistent with the industry view, grew more ambiguous in the late 1950s; that way agency leaders could retain the maximum amount of flexibility in applying them. As interest groups engaged in rhetorical and political battles to define these policies to their liking, the Forest Service struggled to keep control over both policy interpretation and management decision making.

One useful means for retaining control, ironically, involved accommodating user groups as much as possible. Lobbyists from the interest groups could take their complaints directly to political superiors in the administration or to Congress and convince them to demand certain actions from the agency or to punish it for failing to make certain accommodations. Consequently, the Forest Service bent like a willow to and fro with the winds of public demands. Accommodating interest groups, however, never lessened the quantity or stridency of external demands or criticisms, causing the Forest Service in frustration to alternate its cooperation with a stubborn and sometimes bitter intransigence. An organizational schizophrenia resulted, confusing observers of the agency — including scholars. Had interest groups "captured" the Forest Service? Or had the agency successfully avoided capture and maintained centralized policy control?[1] The answer is both yes and no to both questions, depending on the context. In its only partially successful effort to maintain control, the Forest Service gave in to user demands when necessary and bucked those demands when feasible or desirable. This, of course, does not mean that the agency had no biases of its own or that it straddled the middle ground of policy debates, as is often assumed. Management decisions were made within the context of a politically constrained organization that was occupationally dominated by foresters. In addition, the Forest Service had to contend with changing administrative policies and priorities, partisan politics, and an annual budgeting process keyed to economic development rather than to resource management needs. Within this complex environment a struggle over redefining national forest policy ensued.

Debates over multiple use and sustained yield reflected an underlying struggle over management priorities on the national forests. The existence of the debate itself signified a growing lack of consensus as well as a recognition by interest groups and the Forest Service that whoever influenced policy definitions gained influence over future management priorities. Each group's definition thus dovetailed with its view of how the various forest uses should be reconciled and prioritized. Even among agency leaders, no two definitions were alike. Due partly to agency information and education campaigns in the 1950s, the general public quickly and enthusiastically, if confusedly, adopted the multiple use–sustained yield nomenclature too. Inconsistencies of understanding became increasingly obvious as interest groups sparred with the Forest Service over interpretations of the agency's responsibilities under these policy mandates. For the sake of clarity alone, a formal definition seemed necessary. Defining these policies became a high stakes game.

The Forest Service held the ideal position in this debate. Characterizing itself as the original and true defender of the two policies, it effectively claimed the political center, referring to its critics as "special interest" lobbyists. The agency repeatedly characterized the timber lobby as promoting "overuse," while it branded the wilderness lobby as a "single-use" interest. Both appellations were rhetorical ploys designed to build the perception of a continuum on which the Forest Service occupied a reasonable middle ground. So long as the agency controlled definitions, the user groups were at a disadvantage. Legislation became the obvious recourse for interest groups seeking to advance their own definitions of multiple use and sustained yield.

Even in the legislative arena, though, the agency held advantages. First, it had long maintained close, respectful relationships with key policymakers in Congress. Second, the Forest Service could credibly claim to have originated the principles of multiple use and sustained yield at its organizational inception in 1905. Thus, Congress as a whole extended a special deference to the agency in this debate. The first bills promoting multiple use appeared in 1954, initiated by dissatisfied recreation and wildlife advocates. At first the agency hesitated to support congressional action, perhaps covetous of its administrative discretion and afraid a legal definition might get out of its control. But by 1958, Chief McArdle had decided legislative sanction might be to the agency's advantage in the contentious climate of demands. Getting a green light from the Eisenhower administration, the Forest Service jumped into the fray, aggressively courting congressional allies and capturing the political vanguard. While the precedents had been multiple use bills, the Forest Service bill of 1958 added references to sustained yield, making it the first "multiple use–sustained yield" bill.[2]

The First Multiple Use Bills

The proposal for a multiple use bill in the 1950s first came from wildlife advocates and, ironically, it arose from the ashes of the livestock industry's failed 1953 attempt to secure grazing rights — "stability of tenure," as ranchers called it — on the national forests. This interesting story requires a bit of background information: Congress had not specifically enumerated grazing as one of the fundamental purposes for which the national forests were established in 1897 — only water and timber held that honor — so in the

173

1940s graziers sought legislative recognition of their interests. Actually, they wanted grazing privileges converted into grazing rights, but they failed to accomplish that ambition. In 1950, the Granger-Thye Act[3] formally recognized grazing as an approved and legitimate function of national forest management, without establishing grazing rights. When the Eisenhower administration arrived in 1953, the western cattle industry again tried to secure rights to the range with the ill-fated Barrett-D'Ewart "stockmen's" bill. Republican Senator George Aiken and Republican Congressman Clifford Hope attempted to come up with a substitute bill that would address the livestock industry's concerns but get around the formidable opposition of conservation groups and the Forest Service.[4] Hugh Woodward of the National Wildlife Federation and Elliot Barker, director of the New Mexico Department of Game and Fish, were among those negotiating language for the new bill.[5] The final draft of the Aiken-Hope Grazing Bill (S. 2548 and H.R. 6787) eliminated "vested rights" language for graziers and added a clause recognizing wildlife and recreation as legitimate functions of the national forests. On March 8, 1954, Aiken's bill passed the Senate, including the following statement: "It is hereby declared to be the policy of Congress that the Secretary, in carrying out the provisions of this Act, shall give full consideration to the safeguarding of all resources and uses made of these lands, including grazing, mining, recreation, timber production, watershed conservation, and wildlife."[6]

Another section of the bill provided for a multiple use advisory board (patterned after the grazing advisory boards the livestock industry had earlier succeeded in getting established), made up of representatives of the various user groups. The advisory board would provide input on national forest policy and management to the Secretary of Agriculture. Conservationists strongly supported the advisory board concept, as it offered a formalized role for them to comment on and monitor agency decisions. At the time, public input procedures were informal and very limited.[7] With these clauses added to the grazing bill, the National Wildlife Federation, the Western Association of State Game and Fish Commissioners, and the American Forestry Association, among others, dropped their opposition. Although termed a "grazing bill," ranchers at this point could see no value in it for them, so they did not promote it. In fact, the bill would later be referred to as the first "multiple use" bill, even though the specific phrase did not appear in either the title or the text.

Although the Senate passed the Aiken bill, the House of Representatives failed to approve Hope's companion bill before the end of the session, so the measure died in that Congress. But the chances of success for a similar bill in the next Congress actually improved with the midterm congressional elections that year. D'Ewart lost his reelection bid and Democrats captured a majority in the House in an election year charged with political rhetoric about natural resource issues. Immediately after the elections, Woodward, Barker, Perry Egan of the International Association of Game and Fish Commissioners, and other wildlife conservationists drafted a new bill that retained the multiple use language of the Aiken bill but left out the grazing issues that had spurred the original legislation. They sent drafts around to other conservation groups for comments and sought congressional sponsors. In an accompanying analysis of their multiple use bill, Woodward and Barker explained their reasons for pushing new legislation:

> The conservation organizations have long given lip service to the multiple use doctrine as applied to national forest lands. Such multiple use has never been recognized by Congress and has no statutory authorization. Until the Congress . . . establishes the multiple use of national forests as a national policy for the administration of all national forest lands and directs the Secretary to administer said lands in accordance with such principle, the national forest personnel is handicapped and limited.[8]

By the middle of 1955, three nearly identical multiple use bills patterned after the Woodward-Barker draft had been introduced by congressional Democrats, one by Clem Miller (D-Calif.), one by John Blatnik (D-Minn.), and one by Lester Johnson (D-Wisc.).[9] Miller added to his bill the caveat, "the conservation of water and watersheds shall be of primary importance." This phrase was perhaps to be expected of a congressman from California — a state chronically short of water supplies. His bill also, importantly, listed wilderness as one of the multiple uses (again, not surprising since the Sierra Club's headquarters were in California), and included a provision for a multiple use advisory council. Without the backing of grazing interests or the support of the Forest Service, Miller's bill and the other two companion bills got put on the back burner. Reporting in June 1955 to the Western Association of State Game and Fish Commissioners, Carl Shoemaker of the National Wildlife Federation accurately predicted that the bills — which his organization supported — were "unlikely to receive consideration in the first session of the 84th Congress."[10] Historians of the Multiple Use–Sustained Yield Act (MUSY) have tended to neglect these early bills and attribute the initiative for MUSY to the Forest Service. Part of this is due to the Forest Service itself, which took credit for the ultimate passage of MUSY in 1960. Not having supported the first multiple use bills, agency lobbyists conveniently left them out of their legislative history discussions. Private conservation groups deserve more credit than they have been given for initiating multiple use legislation.[11]

Although lacking a majority, the Miller/Blatnik/Johnson bills did stimulate debate. One group paying attention was the National Lumber Manufacturers Association. Reporting on a February 17, 1955, conference he had with Chief McArdle, NLMA lobbyist Alf Nelson explained to his boss Leo Bodine that "the multiple use bill . . . is the proposal advanced by the wildlife-conservationists group. . . . I asked McArdle how he felt about the proposed measure and he said, 'Just between you and me, I don't like it.' He said that the Advisory Council provision of the measure was just 'window dressing' and the real purpose was to try to get into law as a major use wildlife and recreation activities."[12] It would be unfair to accept Nelson's word on what McArdle actually said, but the fact remains the Forest Service withheld support for these bills for years. When the agency decided to go all out for a bill in 1958, it stubbornly backed only the version it had written — introduced by Harley O. Staggers (D-WV) in the House and supported in the Senate by Hubert Humphrey (D-MN). Interestingly, Staggers asked the Forest Service to write a bill for him to introduce because his Republican opponent in the election of 1958 had been publicly accusing him of neglecting forest conservation and recreation issues in West Virginia.[13]

Although the multiple use bills made no headway in 1955, support for them continued to grow. Senator Humphrey, a leading figure at the time in conservation politics and a friend of both conservation groups and the Forest Service (not a difficult balancing act before the 1960s), introduced his own multiple use bill the next year, also patterned after the Woodward-Barker draft, including the proposal for a multiple use advisory council.[14] His bill, however, did not mention wilderness as a multiple use, as the 1955 bills had. Instead, Humphrey introduced that year the first bill specifically designed to establish a national wilderness preservation system — something The Wilderness Society's Howard Zahniser had been promoting for a couple of years with major support from the Sierra Club's David Brower.[15]

With bills in both the House and Senate and an influential legislator (Humphrey) as a cosponsor now, Forest Service leaders had to make a decision. With legislation perhaps imminent, they would risk having interest groups define their central policies for them if they did not get involved. An obstacle and a concern each stood temporarily in the way, however: First, the administration and specifically the Budget Bureau had to be convinced to support a Forest Service legislative proposal, otherwise the agency was obliged to remain mute or simply reactive. Second, some agency strategists felt that going for legislation posed too many risks. If multiple use failed to win endorsement, the adverse legislative history might make future multiple use management more difficult; and what if the bill favored certain uses over others or circumscribed Forest Service management discretion? Why not just try to kill the multiple use bills and leave well enough alone? These issues were debated among the top brass of the Forest Service for quite some time before McArdle finally made the decision to push for an administration bill. At that point (1958), as Harold Steen observed, the agency typically closed ranks. Staggers got his bill written and the Forest Service got Budget Bureau cooperation after great effort and support from Assistant Secretary Ervin Peterson and Secretary Ezra Benson.[16] Significantly, the Staggers bill added a clause referring to sustained yield. Crafts recalled in 1970 that sustained yield policy actually concerned the Forest Service more than multiple use at the time, but, "unfortunately," multiple use dominated the debates.[17] For the immediate interests of user groups, multiple use may have been the more important issue, but Crafts correctly identified sustained yield as the more important long-term policy. Multiple use really represents *people* management, while sustained yield cuts to the core of *resource* management.

Now, with the Forest Service on board the legislative bandwagon, all the interested parties participated in one debate, expecting eventual legislation. The stakes had been raised, and the struggle to define multiple use and sustained yield heated up.

The Society of American Foresters Forum on Multiple Use

Attuned to this policy debate, the Society of American Foresters (SAF) dedicated its 1958 annual meeting to the subject, "Multiple-Use Forestry in the Changing West." Special presentations by agency employees, industry, and conservationists outlined their various views on multiple use and highlighted their differences. Donald Clark of the Forest Service's Rocky Mountain Regional Office in Denver opened the multiple use panel at the start of the conference. His comments accurately reflected the fears, hopes, and general attitude of the Forest Service in this contentious environment. Clark observed that the West had changed rapidly and dramatically in the past ten to fifteen years. A sharply higher rate of population growth (much higher than the national average), new defense industries, a new efficient transportation infrastructure (including the interstate highway system), the development of vast hydroelectric energy sources in the Northwest, economic prosperity and a rising standard of living, all contributed to rapid development and increasing demands on the natural resources of the West.[18] As a result, Clark said, "single-use resource interests" were jockeying for advantageous positions, and their conflicts "brought into sharp focus the need for multiple-use management." But Clark's definition of multiple use remained hazy. It involved, he said, "harmonizing forest uses to secure optimum values to meet the needs of people."[19] Thus, for Clark, multiple use was essentially a philosophy of the public forest manager as a public interest negotiator: adopting a broad view, the forester would objectively choose a balanced course of action between the demands of the special interests, optimizing as many public benefits as possible. This concept of national forest manager as professional middleman served the agency well and helped it deflect charges that it, too, was a special interest with its own biases. Multiple use offered a defense against critics, from the timber industry to the wildlife associations to the Park Service.

The presentation by Steele Barnett of Boise-Cascade Corporation (Boise, Idaho) predictably focused on economic issues. He pointedly noted that "the application or misapplication of the concept of multiple use to public lands can and does affect the economy of this area, and particularly the lumber industry."[20] The key to the proper application of multiple use, he acknowledged, lay in how the concept was defined, and there did not yet appear to be "a workable definition." Barnett outlined three common ways of defining multiple use: (1) equal emphasis on all uses at all times; (2) rotation of uses over time (harvest timber in an area today, manage the area for wildlife tomorrow, and build a campground there a decade later); and (3) zone different areas to different uses. All three of these definitions, however, wasted valuable assets, he claimed. The best form of multiple use, according to Barnett, would instead be a process whereby all land values were considered and then the forest area dedicated unswervingly to the "highest value" use.[21]

Who defined value? How was "highest value" to be determined? Barnett's reference to forests as "assets" foreshadowed his view that "value" entailed commodity or market values only. By the third paragraph of his paper, he was ready to assert that "logging — or the harvest of the forest crop — is perhaps the greatest use to which the land may be put." Indicatively, he titled his presentation: "Logging — The Key to Forest Management." For public forest management as well as private forestry, Barnett advocated the ultimate commodity perspective: "the aim of forest management should be to get the greatest possible growth in the shortest possible time from the forest and at the same time leave the smallest amount of timber standing as a permanent capital investment." Elaborating on this undisguised defense of virtual deforestation, Barnett argued that such a style of management was economically sensible: "regular heavy cuts over a large area at periodic intervals are better than no cuttings or continued light cuttings over the same area. From a business standpoint this makes good sense. It means lower inventories and consequently less risk, less investment in protective measures, lower costs, and greater returns and greater growth per acre."[22]

Back to multiple use: an "extremist group of nature lovers," according to Barnett, made this utilitarian policy problematic. Motivated by "whim and personal prejudice," these extremists advocated setting aside millions of acres as wilderness where roads and development would not be allowed. Barnett rose to the challenge: "As trained land managers, we foresters should object most strenuously to measures such as this which deprive us of one of our greatest tools — accessability — and which will so limit our possibilities of management." He offered as a counter to the wilderness esthetic his own opinion that "a well managed stand being wisely harvested is more attractive than an unused stand standing idly by and representing waste of valuable assets." In a prediction remarkably wide of the mark, he then cautioned foresters not to put much stock in the fickle and certainly "transitory" business of nature tourism. Logging was the essence of forest management *and multiple use,* he said. "Since forest management is focused upon utilization, logging becomes the focal point of management. It is the key that unlocks this wonderful resource to be used for and by the people, and the key that unlocks vast areas of scenic beauty to the bulk of the population."[23]

Another timber industry spokesman on the opening panel of the conference brought in family values in his perspective on multiple use. Fred Sandoz of the Booth-Kelly Lumber Company in Oregon said that multiple use should be "immensely expanded" in the interests of the American family. "Multiple use would then be defined as 'the greatest good to the greatest number of families for the longest time.' " An appropriate Pinchotism. But what was the greatest good to families? "Timber production and the use of forest products benefits more families by direct and indirect employment, profits to stockholders, and taxes than any other use."[24]

One of Barnett's "extremists," Howard Zahniser, gave a presentation at the SAF convention defending wilderness preservation legislation. Countering wilderness detractors, Zahniser argued that "wilderness is not a special use of lands but rather a character that land has. It can have this character and still serve any of various purposes." Like the timber lobbyists who argued that logging *was* multiple use, Zahniser pointed out that wilderness areas supported multiple use: "watershed protection, recreation, scientific research . . . fishing and big game hunting . . . pack trips, hiking and camping." (Six years later, in the Wilderness Act, Congress would also determine that grazing and all its associated developments were compatible with wilderness too.) *Unlike* the timber lobbyists, who were dissatisfied with 95 million acres of the national forests designated as commercial timberland, Zahniser said he *would* be satisfied with only 14 million acres of wilderness, about 8 percent of the national forest land base, while consigning the remainder to "important uses that unavoidably destroy wilderness."[25]

In a nutshell, multiple use for the timber industry meant maximum economic stimulation through more wood production. For recreation and wildlife interests, it meant greater protection for the nonmarket multiple uses and values that had been generally neglected in the drive for wood and forage production. For the Forest Service, when all the rhetoric was stripped away, it meant "get off our backs and let us do our job as we see fit." To convince others to accept this point of view, the agency essentially promised maximum production of all multiple uses through intensive management. While asking interest groups to be patient, it asked Congress to extend to it adequate authority, funding, and discretion to meet identified public "needs." In other words, the Forest Service sought with its definition of multiple use to maintain the status quo that allowed it wide discretion, while commodity interests sought to firmly establish their priorities and noncommodity interests sought to alter the priorities.

Despite efforts to characterize themselves as occupying the neutral middle ground in this debate, Forest Service spokespersons readily revealed their allegiance to the industrial forestry ideology of full commercial utilization. After explaining the agency's general perspective on multiple use, Regional Forester Donald Clark, mentioned above, continued: "True, there are large opportunities for investment on the present national forest acreage, investment to increase and to capitalize more on the productivity of these forests. . . . By such means every acre must be brought more nearly into full production." Adopting a favorite argument of the timber industry, Clark asserted, "Public recreation development can be enhanced and made more safe through timber stand improvement and harvest of trees before they become overmature."[26]

The following year, 1959, California Regional Forester Charles Connaughton addressed the multiple use issue with a widely distributed Forest Service public information pamphlet explaining the concept as the agency applied it. Again, he characterized the Forest Service as a negotiator of public demands, but holding as its ultimate goal "full utilization."[27] Whenever harmony among multiple uses could not be attained, Connaughton explained, "minor uses must be adjusted to exclude conflict with the major or dominant use or uses." Ideally, all uses might be complementary: "If all values and services can be used to a maximum without conflicts the ultimate is obtained."[28] But this rarely happened, and so the forest manager had to juggle user demands and establish some priorities. Connaughton's statement reflected the timber industry's own hierarchical notions of multiple use priorities, and this made wilderness interests doubly committed to "zoning" areas off-limits to development.

Into this confusion, came a diverse collection of opinionated representatives, senators, and additional interest group lobbyists trying to influence legislation as the passage of the Multiple Use–Sustained Yield Act grew imminent in 1960.

Final Debate Over the Multiple Use–Sustained Yield Act of 1960

Virtually every conceivably related interest group testified at the hearings or sent statements for the record. It was an odd situation, though, in which no one could afford to really oppose a bill providing for multiple use and sustained yield of national forest resources; so, would-be opponents expressed their concerns in polite statements regarding specific wording of this clause or that, cloaked behind the rhetoric of support for the principles embodied in the bill. The timber industry desperately tried to get language reiterating the priority of timber and water as established in the 1897 Act. Recreation and wildlife advocates tried to keep references to priority out of the bill, since they knew their interests were not considered priorities. Ranchers felt generally ambivalent about the bill, since they stood neither to lose nor gain from it. Wilderness supporters sought specific language recognizing wilderness as legitimate; their position supplemented a simultaneous effort to get Congress to pass a separate law establishing a national wilderness preservation system. Politicians mostly advocated whatever their key constituents wanted, although a common and safe position was to simply endorse maximum accommodation of all uses, as the Forest Service did. Spokespersons for each of these positions filled the hearing record. In the end, the "safe" position prevailed.

During the final House Agriculture Committee hearings in March 1960, Assistant Secretary Peterson dodged commitment to any of the user groups, claiming, "One of the basic concepts of multiple use is that all of the named resources in general are of equal priority." McArdle, likewise, added later in the hearing that the agency had never extended priority to any specific resource — a view not likely to command consensus among resource users! Furthermore, McArdle added, the bill only recognized existing policy and would not alter management emphases. "This legislation would neither downgrade nor upgrade any single resource." Getting statutory recognition for multiple use and sustained yield would simply "protect national forest resources from possible future overutilization as the result of economic pressures, or those of single-interest groups." Thus, McArdle offered no commitment to anything but agency discretion.[29]

According to Secretary Peterson, the definition of sustained yield, however, did imply a commitment to "produce the maximum sustained yield of the products [a forest area] is best suited to grow."[30] This definition did not resolve legitimate questions about the meaning of sustained yield. Did sustained yield imply no decrease in the yield of products and services over time? Against what time frame? Did it likewise imply no increase? How was sustained yield to be determined? Under what economic and technological assumptions? To answer some of these concerns the bill was amended to include a definition of sustained yield written reluctantly by the Forest Service, which had resisted defining the terms in order to maintain maximum discretion: " 'Sustained yield of the several products and services' means the achievement and maintenance in perpetuity of a high-level annual or regular periodic output of the various renewable resources of the national forests without impairment of the productivity of the land."[31] This meant *increased* production to the highest feasible level, sustained there in perpetuity. As Ed Cliff explained in his memoirs:

> You could have sustained yield at a low level or at a high level. There was no legal definition of just what sustained yield was. It could vary, depending on your philosophy, your starting point, and how much of an investment you wanted to make in sustained yield. The Multiple Use–Sustained Yield Act defined sustained yield as sustained production of resources at a high level.[32]

Timber industry lobbyists politely ignored Forest Service references to "pressures for overuse" in this debate, while they hammered on the danger of "single use" pressures and pushed hard for one specific change to the bill: an amendment that would "clarify" the priority of timber production among the multiple uses. Of course, asking for this straight out might appear selfish and suggest a lack of commitment to multiple use, so they more tactfully offered language that simply reiterated the 1897 Act's reference to water and timber as the primary purposes for which national forests were to be established. H. R. Glascock of the Western Forestry and Conservation Association (a timber group with headquarters in Oregon) succinctly stated, "Surely the Congress will want to have it made clear that the new act is within and supplemental to, but not in interference with the basic act of 1897."[33] The industry hoped this old reference to the purposes for *establishing* forest reservations might be extended to mean that after establishment the forests would also be *managed* primarily for water and timber. Ralph Hodges of the NLMA forthrightly announced, "we believe the basic 1897 law under which the national forests are managed should not be superseded or amended to diminish the priority given therein to water and timber production on the national forests. Multiple use of forest land through maximum utilization of every acre has long been the objective of foresters and land managers whether public or private." Hodges then argued that to allow effective management, all lands should have a "clear statement of the basic purpose" to which it is dedicated, implying that an equal priority definition of multiple use was unworkable. He approvingly quoted a company policy statement describing a "commonly held" industry perspective on multiple use: "Although the primary use of the forest land is for the production of timber, it is company policy to make the land available for secondary uses which are not detrimental to the maximum growth of new tree crops."[34] Hodges wanted the national forests managed under the same principles.

The graziers expressed support for the bill but asked that the reference to "range" in the enumeration of multiple uses (outdoor recreation, range, timber, watershed, and wildlife and fish) be changed to "grazing" or to "range for livestock." Range was a resource, grazing was a use. The cattle and sheep growers wanted use to be emphasized. After all, concerns for the health of the range had led to grazing reductions in the past. Plus, rebounded populations of deer, antelope, and elk in recent decades had begun to compete with livestock use of range and browse. Ranchers wanted grazing of livestock to be given top priority among range uses.[35]

William Welsh, of the National Reclamation Association, representing water development interests, supported the bill with the caveat that "watershed protection and the production of water [should be] given top priority over all other uses of the resources of the watersheds of the entire West." The association also opposed any further designation of parks or wildernesses.[36] David Brower and the Sierra Club had recently prevailed in a landmark battle against the proposed Echo Park Dam in Dinosaur National Monument, a pet project of the water development interests, by arousing public outrage over this "invasion" of a National Park wilderness.[37]

The half dozen major conservation groups at the time all sent representatives to the hearings (except the Sierra Club), expressing support for the bill. While not advocating priority consideration for wildlife or recreation, these lobbyists reminded Congress of the need for additional attention to wildlife and recreation to "catch up" with neglected resources and deteriorating visitor facilities. Representatives for most of these groups, including the National Wildlife Federation and the Izaak Walton League, also called for an amendment recognizing wilderness preservation as a legitimate multiple use.[38] Joseph Penfold of the Izaak Walton League added an especially poignant commentary on the danger of resource overuse. Finding an appropriate quote from Gifford Pinchot, Penfold stressed that conservation meant *conservative* use — as distinct from the dominant interpretation of "maximum use." (Conservationists quoted Pinchot the way Christian scholars quote the Bible. They still do. And like the Bible, Pinchot's writings are voluminous enough and diverse enough to provide a quote for just about any lobbyist's agenda.) Penfold proposed only one management priority: "permanence" of the resources. In a display of lobbying skill, he knocked the graziers and lumbermen without actually mentioning them, and then followed with an exaggerated compliment to the Forest Service for standing up to overuse pressures:

> The pressures from those who would exploit the resources for individual gain or who would expand their particular forest use in disregard of other forest resources and needed uses has been unrelenting. . . . The pressures have been there, sure enough, but the Forest Service has done a remarkable job of building men of stature, who can withstand pressures, even though not equally exerted at all times from all sides.[39]

Penfold's reference to the inequality of pressures was purposeful. He had just quoted a Forest Service chief who had recently joked that he was "held upright by pressures from all sides." Penfold's response implied that he did not fully accept the agency's view that outside pressures were balanced with the Forest Service holding to the middle ground. He further stressed the importance of considering social and environmental values — not just economic values — when making public land management decisions, and he anticipated a future generation of national forest timber harvest critics by suggesting that ecological considerations of productive capacity should play a much more prominent role in developing resource management plans.[40]

Interest groups did not present their perspectives in a political vacuum. Like high school debate teams, they put their most eloquent voices before Congress in hopes of affecting policy decisions to be made by the legislators. Hearings constituted controlled rituals simulating public participation in government. The most telling and important opinions, however, were those expressed by the politicians — the formal policymakers of the federal government. Although opinions of members of Congress regarding MUSY were diverse, three perspectives clearly dominated: (1) recreation use was legitimate, had been neglected, and should be boosted; (2) economic uses were of primary importance (recreation being a kind of economic use) and should be boosted to achieve full utilization; and (3) all multiple uses should be maximized to the highest degree feasible — under "sustained yield" principles. Each of these three perspectives were considered entirely compatible with each other, and MUSY was expected to embody them all. The law offered something for everyone and promised to reconcile conflicts to everyone's near satisfaction without resorting to rationing or specific land allocations. This optimistic perspective represented the "safe" political position mentioned earlier.

Even those members of Congress interested in all the multiple uses endorsed economic utilization as the first order of business. Legislators commenting on the bill almost universally exhibited allegiance to the ethos of maximized production. As J. Edgar Chenoweth (R-CO) noted, "All groups who are interested in obtaining the maximum use of our national forests appear to be in full support of this proposal." Representative Henry Aldous Dixon of Utah displayed the antiwilderness feeling common among supporters of MUSY: After recounting the revenue gained from timber sales, grazing fees, and other water and land use permits on the national forests in Utah, Dixon praised logging, grazing, and water development as the "true" multiple uses. Acknowledging approvingly that millions of vacationists visited Utah's national forests each year (seven times as many visitors as the total population of Utah!), Dixon gruffly condemned the High Uintas "primitive area" in Utah as a waste of resources, since only a small fraction of the public made use of it. "We favor legislation that prevents any small user group from completely dominating or withdrawing from use any segment of the multiple resources of these forests," he explained. MUSY offered this protection, thought Dixon, and thus, he concluded, "Our support for this legislation is strong indeed." Representative Robert Sikes (D-FL) echoed Dixon's remarks, made an unflattering reference to "pressures for recreation, wilderness, and park use," and culminated his testimony with the battle cry, "our forests must be protected from . . . the impact of pressure groups for a single use."[41] Chenoweth, Dixon, and Sikes represented the point of view that reserving an area for nonconsumptive uses and values constituted the withdrawal of that area from multiple use. They saw activities such as intensive grazing and clearcutting as true multiple use, even though these activities significantly reduced a forest's value for watershed protection, harmed many kinds of wildlife, detracted from esthetic and recreational values, and eliminated the wilderness condition.

Many congressmen, like Harley Staggers of West Virginia, conspired to avoid conflict and hard choices by optimistically asserting that Americans could "have it all" with intensive management and multiple use. "As population pressures mount in this country, each segment of forest land users foresees problems in meeting future needs. There is a strong temptation to solve individual problems in each field by asking for land dedication to meet the particular use with which that segment is concerned. Obviously, this is no solution." But was it obvious? In truth, the Forest Service's version of multiple use satisfied almost no one. Dedications of certain forest lands to specific priority uses seemed to be the direction everyone was headed to resolve conflicts: commercial timberland, wilderness, municipal watershed, salmon spawning stream — each designation carried implications of priority use that set expectations, reduced confusion, and lessened conflict among users. Nondedicated areas were battlegrounds. A vague policy of multiple use that left full discretion to the Forest Service to establish or shift management priorities exacerbated the competition among users. Optimistically asserting that uses were complementary served only to sweep the real issues under a rug of rhetoric. But the Forest Service did not want Congress deciding which areas of the national forests would be dedicated to which priorities; and Congress, conversely, did not want to make these tough decisions anyway. So both shared in a conspiracy of optimism, claiming that establishing priorities and resource use limits could be avoided simply by expanding the resource pie.

Passage of the Multiple Use–Sustained
Yield Act and Its Significance

After the House Agriculture Committee hearings in March had been completed, passage of MUSY followed rather quickly. A few compromises were made to remove obstacles and the bill sailed through in just three months, becoming law on June 12, 1960. The House Agriculture Committee added to Section 1 of the bill the language requested by the timber industry: "The purposes of this Act are declared to be supplemental to, but not in derogation of, the purposes for which the national forests were established as set forth in the Act of June 4, 1897 (16 U.S.C. 475)." The Senate Agriculture and Forestry Committee accepted this language. On the other hand, the House committee refused to include the wilderness language requested by Zahniser and others. As an alternative, it stated in its committee report that outdoor recreation *included* wilderness "as has been the policy . . . in the past." The Senate diverged and added a clause to Section 2 of the bill stating, "The establishment and maintenance of areas of wilderness are consistent with the purposes and provisions of this Act." The conference committee then accepted this Senate statement about wilderness. The Senate Committee also added, and the conference committee accepted, a new Section 4 in which multiple use and sustained yield were specifically defined — the definitions written by the Forest Service.[42] The sustained yield definition included the phrase about "high level . . . periodic output" discussed earlier. The definition of multiple use included the following significant phrases: "some land will be used for less than all of the resources . . . with consideration being given to the relative values of the various resources, and not necessarily the combination of uses that will give the greatest dollar return or the greatest unit output."[43] This last sentence served as a mild rebuke to industry lobbyists who insisted that only production-oriented activities were legitimate.

In the final analysis, the Forest Service got its existing policies endorsed and its management discretion preserved in a five paragraph law, the significance of which no one could agree on. At the time of its passage, the agency touted MUSY as "a major legislative landmark in the history of the Forest Service."[44] User group strategists were ambivalent. No one was really sure what had been won and what had been lost. The Sierra Club had been the only major conservation organization refusing to endorse the bill. Michael McCloskey, then a recent graduate from the University of Oregon Law School, explained the club's concerns in an article he wrote for the *Oregon Law Review*, published in December 1961.[45] In a departure from the prevailing consensus, McCloskey argued that the law was in fact unimportant, "patently ambiguous," and merely added confusion to an already obscure subject. In this view, he was largely correct. He also felt, as a lawyer, that the clause stating that MUSY was "supplemental to and not in derogation of" the Act of 1897 firmly established timber and water as the dominant uses. McCloskey's legal crystal ball was a little cloudy in this case. While timber did remain dominant, it was for other than legal reasons. He further argued that the Forest Service had failed to protect its designated wilderness areas from encroaching development, that due to its timber production bias it could not be entrusted with such a charge, and that MUSY's maintenance of wide management discretion perpetuated rather than resolved the problem. From this point on, the Sierra Club sought, somewhat successfully, to have agency discretion incrementally constrained where environmental protection was a goal. Many other environmental groups eventually followed suit.

Timber lobbyists were generally dissatisfied with MUSY too. In April 1960, after the House Agriculture Committee had approved the law but before the Senate committee had acted, the NLMA's Committee on Forest Management and its Forest Advisory Committee met for a special session in San Francisco. All the familiar and prominent industry lobbyists attended: Bernard Orell, Ernest Kolbe, Richard Colgan, Alf Nelson, Ralph Hodges, Mortimer Doyle, William Hagenstein, and many others. McArdle and California Regional Forester Charles Connaughton also attended. Nelson's formal minutes of the meeting indicate that the principal issues discussed were the desire to maintain the priority of timber and water, and the potential public relations repercussions of opposing the bill. Asked to elaborate the Forest Service position, McArdle reiterated the standard lines about wanting statutory endorsement of Forest Service policies to strengthen the agency's ability to resist pressures for overuse and single use. He also admitted that recreation pressures provided the strongest single motivation for the legislation. Interestingly, he warned the assembled industrialists that recreation pressures would predominate in any showdown at the polls, but he reassuringly added that most agency employees were still oriented toward timber management and that the highest sustained yield production of timber remained a primary agency goal.[46]

After McArdle's presentation, the NLMA committees went into "executive session" and discussed strategies and public relations. According to Nelson's minutes, many of those present expressed concern that MUSY, even as amended to preserve the priorities in the 1897 Act, did not really establish timber priority. McArdle, in fact, had flatly stated that the 1897 Act's priorities only applied to the establishment of new national forests and not to their subsequent management. The point was debatable. But industry lobbyists did not want to debate, they wanted a clear pronouncement that timber production was the priority function of the national forests. What should the NLMA do? Accept the bill as written? Try to seek amendments in the Senate? Nelson's minutes recorded the decision as follows: "It was felt that further efforts to seek clarification of timber and water as basic purposes of national forests would be construed by Congress and the Forest Service as an objection to the legislation. Therefore, it was decided that the industry had no alternative except to support the bill as amended."[47] Bernard Orell of Weyerhaeuser apparently struggled to convince a critical mass of industry moderates to override the hardliners and endorse the legislation. Edward Crafts, who orchestrated Forest Service lobbying activities, said Orell went "way out on a limb" to get industry to back the measure and deserves substantial credit for its passage.[48]

Members of Congress, not surprisingly, heaped praise on the act. Catherine D. May (R-WA) predicted the legislation "will be another milestone in the wise, orderly, and thoughtful management of these public properties." Representative Robert Barry (R-NY) called MUSY "one of the most important pieces of legislation that has come before this House since I have been a member."[49] Ironically, however, the main significance of the law proved to be its insignificance. Due partly to the actions of Congress itself, management of the national forests went forward in a manner that was anything but wise, orderly, thoughtful, and sustainable.

Conclusion

MUSY can be considered the last major victory for the Forest Service in its struggle to retain full discretionary control over national forest management (discretion within budget constraints, of course). After 1960, legislation became increasingly prescriptive. The act further symbolized the continued hegemony of the expanding pie ideology among politicians and agency leaders. For many of the Depression and World War Two generation, the commitment to full utilization was visceral. Representative Harley Staggers, the sponsor of the Forest Service MUSY bill in 1958, spoke for a large number of his contemporaries when he said: "When the supply of natural resources and ability to produce fall to the point where government's chief function is the rationing of too few resources among too many people, democracy cannot survive."[50] Against the backdrop of such fears, political support for maximum production translated into support for the "American way of life." Little wonder that sustained yield technical issues such as soil nutrient depletion, stream sedimentation, biological diversity, third generation forest vigor, and economic stability in the next century made so little impact on so many policymakers. Such fears also help explain hostility toward wilderness. Political leaders of the 1950s in America still feared fascism, communism, and the specter of recurrent economic depression. Production and prosperity meant social stability and the preservation of liberty. Wilderness, theoretically, threatened full production — even if in fact no opportunities for commercial exploitation were present.

Walter Prescott Webb, a leading historian of the American frontier and influential opinion-molder, published in 1951 a reinterpretation of the history of Western civilization, titled *The Great Frontier,* that reflected these assumptions and fears. Treading a path blazed by historian Frederick Jackson Turner in 1893, Webb argued that the institutions of political democracy and economic liberty had evolved as a result of contact with the frontier and its abundant availability of work, its superabundance of (ostensibly) unappropriated material resources, and its "windfall" bounties freely available in the form of goods produced by nature without human labor (such as old-growth forests). These three characteristics — opportunity, material resources, and windfall bounties — made it possible, he argued, for individuals to remain free and self-reliant, and for American civilization to prosper without excessive labor class strife and without recourse to economic socialism. But, he warned, America was slowly becoming a frontierless Metropolis. The machine age, advancing technology, and expanding production had reached the end of the open-spaced frontier. "Man had through his own ingenuity and industry not only caught up with his work, but he had in a sense also run out of stuff to work on, the stuff of unlimited area." The future looked bleak for America's cherished traditions of liberty and democracy.[51]

To opinion leaders and politicians in the 1950s, such pessimistic assumptions had the weight of two world wars, a bloody revolution in Eastern Europe, and a global economic depression backing them up. This pessimism, ironically, nourished a complementary optimistic attachment to the expanding pie ideology, infusing the technological cornucopians with mission fever. Expanding jobs and production meant saving democracy. Throwing up regulatory roadblocks in pursuit of social goals was an insidious form of creeping socialism. Just around the corner, however, loomed a great revolution in thinking — a casting off of these older fears, the development of a more sophisticated understanding of the social and environmental responsibilities that should attend economic development, and the adoption of a new ethos in which the "American way" meant not maximum production but rather maximum enjoyment of life and its amenities. The rise of the environmental movement in the following decades embodied this new thinking.[52]

The slow but steady reorientation in public values took a long time to filter up the hierarchy of the Forest Service and into the halls of political power, however. The agency remained dedicated to its intensive management orientation while federal budget managers continued to approve lopsided funding that favored economic development without adequate environmental protection. MUSY coincidentally became law in the same year the Forest Service began to implement its first fully integrated nationwide multiple use management plan. The plan, released in 1959 and called "Operation Multiple Use," embodied an unequivocal commitment to maximum production and full utilization, and it established the precedent for all subsequent comprehensive management plans the agency has produced since. In the next chapter we discuss this program and its fate in the budgeting process. Developed in the midst of the debate over the purpose of the national forests, Operation Multiple Use is an apt focal point for discerning the reality behind the rhetoric of Forest Service and political commitment to multiple use and sustained yield.

9

"Operation Multiple Use" and the Continued Disjunction of Planning and Funding

In the 1950s, the Forest Service learned that pursuit of its management goals, especially in the budget process, could be enhanced by developing long-range plans. The Timber Resources Review had been successful in getting increased funds for timber sales and roads. Operation Outdoors led to a tripling of recreation funds between fiscal years 1957 and 1959. But what about wildlife? water? grazing? What about underemphasized aspects of the timber program, such as reforestation and stand improvement? What about neglected resource protection activities, such as watershed rehabilitation and soil erosion control? The Forest Service decided in the late 1950s that it was time to develop a comprehensive, integrated, long-range management program for *all* resources and activities. This had never been done before. The need was manifest, the potential benefits obvious, and the time ripe.

Between 1956 and 1959 the Forest Service collected data from its line officers in the field on resource production potential, management needs, and budget estimates for fully integrated multiple use management. In submitting to Congress the resultant Operation Multiple Use (also called the "1959 Program for the National Forests"), Assistant Secretary of Agriculture Ervin Peterson characterized it as the "first . . . fully coordinated, comprehensive program for the entire national forest system." Chief Richard McArdle explained that the program was keyed to the appropriations structure as well as to the work loads of the rangers at the lowest levels of the agency. "It is the first time that we have ever had anything which was coordinated and integrated clear across the board."[1] The program included

193

short-range (ten years) as well as long-range (to the year 2000) management proposals for each of the national forest resources. A paradigm of the production ethos, the 1959 program boldly stated that "all of the renewable resources are to be utilized at a high sustained level of productivity." Pointing out that the national forests were "revenue producing properties" and that "their vast resources are in great demand," the agency turned wholeheartedly to intensive management as the means to increase outputs to meet those new demands: "Management must become progressively more intense and more adequately supported by research findings if the national forests are to keep pace with economic needs and national growth."[2] But intensive management, as everyone recognized then, required significant investments to make it work — if indeed it could work at all. Unfortunately, while Congress, the administration, and agency heads in Washington praised the 1959 program, they simultaneously undermined it in the budgeting process.

Unbalanced resource development during the 1950s had originally led the Forest Service to produce Operation Multiple Use. In it, the agency underscored the interrelatedness of the various programs to drive home the need for more balanced funding. As Assistant Secretary Peterson stated in his testimony before the House Agriculture Committee, "We should not develop one resource and lag behind in another. . . . True multiple use requires that intensified development and utilization proceed at an orderly and coordinated pace among all resources — a balanced program of development." Some activities were "now out of balance," he admitted, and therefore the 1959 program accordingly called for "much greater intensification of some activities . . . to reestablish this necessary balance."[3] It was no mystery which resources had historically received exceptional attention. In hearings on the 1959 program, Representative Harlan Hagen (D-CA) complained that recreational development had lagged while timber harvesting surged ahead. In particular, he chastised the agency for building so many single purpose timber access roads: "This creates problems because one of the justifications for opening up new forest areas is that more people will use them." Secretary Peterson responded somewhat haltingly but honestly that "our present program has had some imbalance . . . in recent years. As you know we have been under some pressure to sell timber. . . . We have built roads to the extent that we could to open up new timber areas, but have not simultaneously done the other management things . . . in the newly opened areas where our objective was primarily to make available timber." Hagen then asked what the Service planned to do about the problem of increased soil erosion in areas of timber harvesting. Chief McArdle, admitting the problem but offering no solution, answered, "We want to sell all the timber we can. There are returns to the Treasury for selling timber, but at the same time we have felt we have in many places gone a little fast and have not done the other things that need doing."[4]

To help restore balance, the agency proposed to step up annual timber harvests only one and three-quarters times above the average harvest level of the previous ten years, while undertaking a reforestation program at nineteen times the previous decade's level, and an erosion control program at *ninety-six* times the ten-year level[5] (see table 1). What is important to note about these figures is not the individual levels of intensified activity for each resource, but the comparative levels of accelerated activity among the resources. To meet full expected demand for national forest timber in the succeeding ten to fifteen years, the agency called for a 75 percent increase of its current timber sales program, but to ensure that such an intensified timber harvest program could be sustained over the long term and not cause unacceptable damage to other forest resources, the agency called for an acceleration of other mitigating programs by 2,000 to 10,000 percent!

Some of these proposed high levels of accelerated management were actually rather conservative. For example, McArdle told the Agriculture Committee that the nineteenfold intensification of reforestation would only accomplish three-quarters of the "needed planting job." Such increases were viewed by land managers as not only reasonable, but necessary to the sustained yield program. Even more telling was the program's proposal for soil surveys, badly needed to determine conditions and trends so that appropriate management plans could be devised. To this end, the short-term program conservatively aimed to complete soil surveys on just one-fifth of the total area needing them. Yet, like the reforestation program, to accomplish this relatively modest goal the agency needed to increase the level of activity for soil surveys nineteen times over recent levels.[6] Such accelerations in management intensity seemed incredible at first glance. For a sense of scale, Forest Service Chief Richard McArdle told members of Congress that the short-term reforestation program required "planting an area larger than

Table 1. Needed Step-Up in Short-Term Program
(Selected Comparisons)

Activity	Unit	Past 10-year Period	Short-Term Program	Needed Step-Up
Annual timber cut	Billion board feet	6½**	11**	1¾
Reforestation and stand improvement	Thousand acres	762	14,750	19
Soil surveys	Thousand acres	1,750	33,000	19
Erosion control	Miles	250	24,000	96
Range analyses and management plans	Number	3,126	5,664	2
Reseeding and noxious plant control	Thousand acres	–750	4,400	6
New family campground and picnic units	Number	5,398	102,000	19
Road construction	Miles	24,788	90,000	3⅔
New dwellings and service buildings	Number	796	5,440	6¾

Source: Data from House Agriculture Committee hearings on the "Long Range Program for the National Forests," 86th Cong., 1st sess., May 14, 15, 1959, p. 32.
**FY 1958 data.

Connecticut"; and that forest stand improvement measures were needed on 17,000 square miles, an area twice the size of Massachusetts.[7] More alarmingly, these intensive management programs implied commensurate increases in program budgets. Anticipating criticism that his program represented an unrealistic wish list, McArdle defended the agency's cost estimates as "conservative," saying, "we have tried throughout this plan to keep our costs at the lowest possible level. We have not tried to view this as a letter to Santa Claus."[8]

By making this graphic comparison between various levels of needed program acceleration, the agency displayed clearly for Congress the grim reality that the national forests were being developed at such a pace and in such a manner that the long-term health and productivity of the resources could not be guaranteed. While still championing "full utilization" of the forest resources, the agency unequivocally reminded economic development boosters that sustained yield — the crux of scientific forest management — required an unyielding commitment to replanting cutover areas and protecting forest soils.

Timber and Roads in Operation Multiple Use

Over the long term (to the year 2000), the Forest Service Program anticipated increasing timber harvests on the national forests to 21.1 billion board feet (bbf): two and a half times above the 8.6 bbf cut of 1959. Over the short term (ten to fifteen years), the agency proposed to achieve a "full sustained yield cut" of 11 bbf. It is important to fully understand the high level of management intensity implied in this latter number, which may seem modest in comparison to the former. A close look at two elements of the short-term timber program — fire and pest suppression, and road construction — serves as an illustration. In 1952 the estimated "loss" of timber due to fire, insects, and disease equaled *92 percent* of the total estimated timber growth that year.[9] To achieve the 11 bbf harvest without exceeding sustained yield required much more effective protection against such losses. (The Forest Service hoped ultimately to reduce or eliminate fire, death, and decay from the forest ecosystem, replacing them with a harvesting program, in order to reach the maximum yield.) For the short term, the agency required a 50 percent increase over their current level of protection from insects and disease, and at least a doubling of their fire prevention activities. Fire suppression and prevention activities already comprised the second largest budget item, exceeded only by road construction. With this mere doubling of fire prevention efforts they optimistically hoped to expand fivefold the acreage of national forests receiving full fire protection (from 23 million acres to 125 million acres); they hoped to reduce the buildup of flammable "hazardous debris" (logging slash, brush, and dead trees) by engaging in controlled burning of nearly 4 million acres, by felling and removing dead trees and brush on another 357,000 acres, and clearing and maintaining 12,000 miles of "fire breaks"; finally, they hoped to completely modernize their fire prevention equipment and technology, including the construction or reconstruction of sixty-two aircraft landing fields.[10]

The road construction program provided support infrastructure for the entire intensive management plan. The Forest Service repeatedly cited the lack of an adequate road system as the primary obstacle to further increasing resource production on the forests.[11] Here, the scope of development becomes most graphic and the bias toward commodity production most evident. In 1959 there were 24,400 miles of designated highways under various jurisdictions traversing national forest land — enough paved highway to go from New York to Los Angeles and back four times. Another 149,700 miles of mostly unpaved "development roads" crisscrossed the forests, providing access for the many forest users. If these roads were stretched end to end along the equator, they would circle the Earth six times. If spread out uniformly over the entire national forest system, they would equal more than a mile of road for every two square miles of forest. However, 14 million acres of the national forests were designated wilderness and at least another 40 million were still completely roadless, so in reality this 174,000-mile road network represented a very dense transportation system concentrated in the one-half of the national forest system designated as commercial timberland. The contributions of this immense disturbance to stream sedimentation and its effect on forest ecosystems and wildlife habitat are incalculable.

Operation Multiple Use required still more roads. By the year 2000, the Forest Service hoped to construct an additional 392,600 miles of forest development roads, primarily to give loggers access to previously inaccessible areas and to support intensive fire and pest control programs. Total forest development road mileage by the year 2000 would equal 542,000 miles. (By 1990, the Forest Service had revised its estimate of the total forest development road needs down to 403,000 miles, to be completed by the year 2040. Eighty-five percent of that had been built.)[12] In contrast to the road construction program, Operation Multiple Use proposed a net *reduction* in mileage for the national forest trail system, from a total of 112,200 miles in 1959 down to about 80,000 miles by the year 2000.[13]

If any one element of the total proposed timber management and protection program outlined above fell short, the whole sustained yield house of cards would collapse. If a drought hit a timber producing region, as happened periodically, causing a series of disastrous fire seasons, then the balance would be upset. If a resistant disease infestation hit, as occurred periodically, then the balance would be upset. If the agency failed to effectively reforest newly harvested areas in steep or arid slopes, as often happened, the balance would be upset. If Congress did not provide adequate funds for soil erosion control or normal reforestation efforts, as it consistently failed to do, the balance would be upset. Yet, rather than advancing conservative timber targets buffered against fiscal, technical, and environmental failures, and unforeseen contingencies, the agency based its production proposals upon optimistic assumptions of full program implementation and complete effectiveness of intensive management practices. With dedicated political support, the Forest Service achieved its short-term, high-yield harvest goal of 11 bbf seven years ahead of schedule, while resource protection goals and nonmarket values, as usual, remained underfunded and behind schedule.

Soil and Water in Operation Multiple Use

Certainly the most important resources of the forest are soil and water, yet they are the most consistently neglected and abused. Soil generally is not a market commodity and so it receives little attention, but it supports the entire biotic system of the forest and is significantly affected by commodity development. Water is a little different. It is treated as a market commodity, but in most cases (not all) it does not become one until it leaves the forest boundary. Water flows naturally off the forest into the thirsty reservoirs of its appropriators. No roads, chainsaws, or flatbed trucks are required to ship it off the national forests. But that does not mean that water is unused on the national forests. Like soil, it is an essential foundation of forest ecosystems, a fact clearly recognized by ecologists but often forgotten by policymakers and those interested mainly in resource development.

Long-term and short-terms plans of action for soil and water reflected those of the timber plan: intensive, accelerated, and optimistic. The 1959 program called for a two-sided approach. On the one hand, it called for intensive efforts to improve water *quality* and stabilize eroding soil by replanting clearcuts, overgrazed areas, and roadsides, thereby slowing the flow of water off watersheds. On the other hand, the program simultaneously called for efforts to increase the *quantity* of water runoff to enhance the supply of water to consumers and dealers downstream. This contradiction in goals was recognized but not resolved in the program. The agency suggested it would seek to achieve both goals simultaneously, but implied, appropriately, that soil and watershed *stability* would receive priority: "Protection of the watershed . . . will continue to be a primary objective. Quantity of water yielded will receive major consideration."[14]

The degree to which the Forest Service remained true to this expressed priority in actual practice is another question. In fact, the emphasis on full utilization usually put water production ahead of both water quality and soil retention. An example of this is found in a report presented at the 1958 Society of American Foresters convention by three Forest Service watershed researchers in California. On the San Dimas Experimental Forest east of Pasadena, they had "deadened" and sold to a fuelwood dealer all the trees in the riparian-woodland zone along a stream — the rarest and most valuable habitat for wildlife in the arid regions of the West. Following up with applications of herbicides to kill leafy vegetation, the researchers hoped shallow-rooted grasses would eventually replace the more water-consuming trees, thus increasing streamwater runoff. In a second experimental watershed nearby, they tried another treatment in which 40 percent of the entire watershed was aerial sprayed with a mixture of "Agent Orange" and Tebuthiron (2,4-D and 2,4,5-T) to kill all the woody vegetation. "Follow-up spraying" would take place for two subsequent years, again in hopes that grasses would replace the trees and allow increased water runoff for consumption by the growing southern California megalopolis. The report never mentioned any concern over water quality but did point out that soil erosion on the deforested slopes posed a serious problem. "We must do much more work of a basic nature in the field of watershed hydrology and in soil stabilization," they acknowledged, but "at the moment we are concentrating on one question: Can southern California chaparral watersheds be managed for more water on a practical basis?"[15]

Regarding structural soil and water improvements, the agency stated that in addition to the 4.4 million acre backlog of denuded lands needing replanting or reseeding, they also needed to stabilize 10,000 miles of gully and channel erosion, control soil loss on 14,000 miles of "substandard" roads and trails, stabilize sheet erosion on 1.3 million acres, and clean up 170 polluted streams. While the program's long-term goals for water resources were couched in terms that implied a clear intent to engage in positive action to maintain healthy and stable soil and water conditions, the specific short-term objectives, for the most part, offered proposals for studies, inventories, more plans, and reactive mitigations rather than specific commitments to forceful protective measures.[16] This emphasis on research and planning functioned and still functions too often today as a bureaucratic or political evasion.

Range Management in Operation Multiple Use

The Forest Service objective for range management in the 1959 program was to eliminate overgrazing.[17] Most illuminating about this goal, however, were the methods proposed for achieving it. In line with its emphasis on high levels of production and intensive management, the 1959 program determined to avoid simple reductions of livestock use in overgrazed areas and instead proposed to balance use with capacity "by building up forage production through reseeding, other range improvement measures, and better management." The range program's summary expressed this reliance on intensive management best: "These policies can be furthered by intensifying management of all range allotments; obtaining and maintaining desirable forage to high capacity; constructing, rehabilitating, and maintaining range improvements needed to attain intensive management on all ranges; and making adjustments in numbers of livestock or seasons of use when necessary."[18]

Short-term investments of capital and labor required to meet these range goals with a minimum of livestock use reductions included vegetation manipulation on over 4 million acres of rangeland (to discourage plants unpalatable to livestock and to reseed overgrazed areas); construction of 18,000 miles of new fences and 9,500 new stock watering ponds or springs; reconstruction or rehabilitation of existing livestock developments; and the completion or revision of allotment management plans for every grazing allotment on the forests. Of course, this range rehabilitation program was intimately tied to the soil and watershed program. Overgrazing had traditionally been the major contributing factor in erosion, pollution, and other watershed problems, although by the late 1950s accelerated timber production competed for that dubious distinction.

Recreation and Wildlife in Operation Multiple Use

Recreation and wildlife habitat goals were considered in tandem and similarly slated for intensive management in the 1959 program. The wildlife program cited the continued explosion in recreational use of the forests, including hunting and fishing, and adopted a long-range goal based on meeting the demand for wildlife sport commodities: "the wildlife habitat will yield a fish and game population adequate to meet the . . . tremendous increase in sportsmen use." To meet the demand for wildlife resources and mitigate the effects of other resource development activities on wildlife habitat, the Forest Service planned to "improve food and cover" on 1.5 million acres of key habitat areas, clear or burn on another half a million acres, and improve degraded riparian ecosystems along 7,000 miles of streams and 56,000 acres of lakes.

The same demand and supply oriented bias imbued the recreation goals: "National-forest recreation resources will be so developed and managed that the kind, quality, and quantity of their development and maintenance will be sufficient to keep abreast of this tremendously increased demand."[19] Keeping abreast of increased demand was a tall order. The agency's national recreation plan published in July 1957 — "Operation Outdoors" — had predicted 66 million national forest visits by 1962. By the end of 1958, that estimate had already been exceeded. Plus, funding to implement Operation Outdoors had fallen way behind schedule. Frustrated, the Forest Service reiterated in its 1959 program the recreation site development and maintenance objectives outlined in the already outdated 1957 recreation plan, and added a proposal to inventory recreation resources and develop recreation management plans for each administrative unit in the national forest system. The Outdoor Recreation Resources Review Commission created in 1958 had requested these recreation resource inventories from all federal agencies, prefatory to developing a national multiagency recreation management program. As a result, the Forest Service refrained from developing the recreation management part of the 1959 program in any greater detail.

The Reforestation Deficit

In the first four decades of the Forest Service's existence, acquisition of cutover and abandoned private timber lands and primitive or nonexistent fire control capabilities burdened the Forest Service with a substantial backlog of areas needing reforestation. (Actually, from an ecological point of view it may be preferable to allow natural reforestation in fire charred and logged areas rather than artificially restocking commercial species. But the agency based its increasingly optimistic allowable cut levels partly on the assumption that all productive lands would have commercial stands of timber on them available for future harvests, so nonstocked or understocked lands threatened sustained yield.) Land acquisition programs, authorized under several laws including the 1911 Weeks Act and the 1924 Clarke-McNary Act, added substantial acres to the national forest land base in the 1930s. In 1937 and 1938, for example, the Forest Service acquired over 3.5 million acres *per year* through purchase, exchange, or donation. The great majority of these lands came to the agency as denuded or otherwise abused lands in need of intensive care. Replanting programs undertaken by the Civilian Conservation Corps in the 1930s took a large bite out of this backlog, but the planting programs were partially offset by an increase in fire losses associated with widespread drought conditions and by additional cutover lands newly acquired from states or private owners.[20]

During World War Two, the reforestation program went into a hiatus as Congress reallocated the agency's budget to emphasize war related production rather than conservation. In light of this, the 1945 *Report of the Chief of the Forest Service* suggestively stated that the agency expected "a large postwar program of reforestation," to make up for lost time, reiterating that "planting should be recognized as an integral part of national-forest administration."[21] But instead of eliminating the backlog of nonstocked and poorly stocked lands, the agency faced a growing deficit. This prompted Senator Clinton Anderson and Representative Mike Mansfield to sponsor the Anderson-Mansfield Reforestation and Revegetation Act of 1949. But due to continuing budget constraints, the backlog continued to grow. In 1960,

Anderson and Mansfield (the latter now a senator) were once again back on the stump, calling for an acceleration of the reforestation program in Senate Joint Resolution 95. The Senate Interior Committee held hearings on the resolution in 1960 — significantly, the same year that MUSY was enacted, and the same year that funding for Operation Multiple Use became a major issue.[22] It was also an election year, with the Republican incumbent retiring and the two parties competing mightily to please voters. The hearings, run by congressional Democrats, became a venue for Eisenhower administration bashing, although the Democratic Congress had little to brag about in its own record.

The Forest Service's Timber Resources Review of 1958 had determined that, nationwide, 48 million acres of federal, state, and private lands with a commercial forestry potential needed some form of reforestation. Forty million of those acres were private lands, 4.4 million were national forest lands, and 2.4 million were state and local government lands.[23] At the request of Senate Interior Committee Chairman James E. Murray (D-MT), the Forest Service calculated how long it would take each above-mentioned jurisdiction to replant its denuded lands at the 1958 rate of reforestation (assuming no new lands were added to the deforested inventory). The results were remarkable. At the 1958 rate, state and local governments would replant their 2.4 million acre backlog in 32 years; private owners, in 44 years; the Forest Service, *169 years*. Of course, newly deforested lands constantly increased the inventory, so the reforestation program actually required even more effort than that to eliminate the backlog. As Chief McArdle explained in the hearings, "Additional plantings would have to be planned to accommodate failure in planting which can normally be expected [as well as] additions to the [4.4 million acre] plantable area [caused] by fire, pests and clearcutting."[24]

In his testimony in support of S. J. Resolution 95, Senator Wayne Morse, a Democrat (ex-Republican) from the timber producing state of Oregon, quoted ex-Chief of the Forest Service Lyle Watts, also an Oregonian, saying: "Our generation has an obligation to the next, to use its resources wisely and not hand our children a depleted, worn out country." But instead, Morse asserted, the Eisenhower administration "has failed in its responsibility for our public lands." For illustration, he cited Forest Service statistics for the state of Oregon showing that at the current rates of reforestation, counties would eliminate their backlog in 7 years, the state would eliminate its backlog in 14 years, and private industry would accomplish their reforestation needs in 20 years. He sarcastically suggested that if the Assistant Secretary of Agriculture, Ervin L. Peterson, also an Oregonian, could not convince the administration to match the counties' record, then maybe he should shoot for the state record. "Or if an even more modest accomplishment were in order, he could fall back on what private enterprise is doing in Oregon and try to complete the national forest job in 20 years. But no — it will take 300 years to do the job for the national forests at the rate we are going. I rest my case for Senate Joint Resolution 95 on the record."[25]

Morse also mentioned the importance of healthy forests to water quality, a theme picked up by Representative Lee Metcalf (D-MT), a cosponsor of S. J. 95 in the House. Pointing out that Montana's forests protected many of the headwater streams of the Missouri and Columbia rivers, Metcalf warned that "as we permit the deterioration of that timber, we underwrite the destruction of our soil and our water resources from Astoria, Oregon, to New Orleans." He also presented reforestation statistics, broken down by forest, for his own state. The eleven national forests in Montana showed variable rates of reforestation, so that at the 1958 rate of planting, the backlogs would take from 27 to 2,430 years to be eliminated. "In recent years, the Federal Government has been resting on its oars, as budget requests have declined," Metcalf charged. "The record shows that this decline is directly related to the party in charge of the administration." Metcalf then cited statistics showing that under Franklin Roosevelt and Harry Truman, tree planting in the national forests averaged 74,920 acres a year; while under the Eisenhower administration the average was 22,100 acres a year.[26]

Senator Mansfield (Democratic Whip and cosponsor of S. J. 95), had some words of praise for McArdle and Peterson even as he blasted the administration for negligence. He lauded the Chief and Assistant Secretary for their "courage, understanding, and patriotic judgment . . . in laying on the line the facts and their implications for our Nation's forest resources." But in regard to the administration, Mansfield charged: "This failure to meet our resource responsibilities is the work of small minds. . . . I refuse to accept the premise that our nation is so poor that it cannot replant its public forests."[27]

Eisenhower's Bureau of the Budget apparently did not find these argu-

Table 2. Reforestation on National Forest Lands

Fiscal Year	Area Needing Planting (acres)	Area Planted and Seeded (acres)*	FUNDS		
			Authorized by Anderson-Mansfield Act	Presidential Budget Request	Appropriated by Congress[†]
1950	4,636,258	29,040	—	$1,422,160	$1,357,643
1951	4,610,632	25,576	$3,000,000	$2,205,118	$1,163,535
1952	4,590,920	19,702	$5,000,000	$1,160,206	$1,264,686
1953	4,567,000	23,980	$7,000,000	$1,182,991	$1,162,333
1954	4,354,546	12,454	$8,000,000	$925,020	$834,520
1955	4,540,776	13,770	$10,000,000	$450,235	$867,650
1956	4,522,602	18,174	$10,000,000	$900,000	$1,230,000
1957	4,501,500	21,102	$10,000,000	$1,130,000	$1,500,908
1958	4,475,000	26,500	$10,000,000	$2,183,000	$2,228,600
1959	4,436,293	38,707	$10,000,000	$2,186,000	$3,015,000
1960[‡]	—	—	$10,000,000	$3,255,000	$3,455,000

Source: Data provided by U.S. Forest Service, adapted from table printed in Senate Interior Committee hearing record on Senate Joint Res. 95, 86th Cong., 2nd sess. (April 22, 1960), p. 26.

*Reforestation work accomplished in timber sale areas with Knutson-Vanderburg Act funds not included.

[†]Under national forest protection and management activity in Forest Service appropriation.

[‡]1960 figures taken from *Congressional Record*, 86th Cong. 2nd. sess. (June 8, 1960), pp. 12079.

ments compelling, though. In a prehearing exchange of letters between the Budget Bureau's Director Maurice Stans and Interior Committee Chairman Murray, Stans reiterated the administration's opposition to passage of S. J. 95. While claiming to recognize the need for an adequate reforestation program, he maintained that acceleration of the program was "dependent on overall budgetary considerations and the relative urgency of the needs of other programs requiring the expenditure of federal funds."[28] In 1960, the Forest Service was authorized by Congress to spend as much as $10 million for reforestation and stand improvement on the national forests. Under budget ceiling constraints set by Eisenhower's Budget Bureau, the agency forwarded a budget request of $4 million to the Department of Agriculture for FY 1960, the Agriculture Department sliced that to $3.3 million and sent it to the Budget Bureau, which further cut it to $3.2 million. Congress finally voted to appropriate $3.4 million (see table 2). For the agency's cooperative reforestation programs (aid to state and private forest owners), Congress had authorized expenditures of up to $2.5 million in FY 1960. The Forest Service requested $1.3 million, the Department shaved that down to $792,000, while Stans's Budget Bureau hacked another half a million off that. Congress approved the Budget Bureau request of $290,000.[29]

Assuring the Future Failure of Sustained Yield

During hearings on the 1959 Program for the National Forests, University of Maryland Professor of Economics Spencer Smith spoke for the newly formed conservation lobby "Citizens Committee on Natural Resources" about the vital importance of the funding process in policy implementation: "The true test will come not necessarily on the program and its dimensions, as we have it now, but when we start to appropriate money to implement various aspects of this program." Underscoring this sentiment, Joseph Penfold of the Izaak Walton League concluded his comments at the hearing with the prescient remark, "without solid and realistic implementation with funds, the program is little more than a pious generality."[30] But could multiple use and sustained yield rise above the level of pious generality within the existing political economy?

As mentioned earlier, Operation Multiple Use sought to restore "balance" and catch up with neglected resource rehabilitation needs. Senator Karl Mundt (R-SD) asked hypothetically which projects the Service would give priority to if Congress made "some extra unbudgeted funds" available in FY 1960 for implementing the program. Peterson responded: "In my opinion, one of the essential things which needs to be done is to bring the several aspects of national forest management into balance each with the other." Peterson continued, "We have run ahead in timber sales, while not going as fast proportionately in planning for wildlife habitat, for protection of watersheds, for tree planting, rehabilitation of cutover and burned over and denuded lands, and so forth." When asked the same question by Senator Murray, Chief Richard McArdle responded: "I think I would give more attention to the tree planting and timber stand improvement operations that have been lacking for so long. I would try to get caught up on meeting our recreational needs. And I think that I would try to give more attention than we have been able to give for watershed management, particularly in the control of soil erosion."[31]

For FY 1960, however, Eisenhower's Budget Bureau and the congressional appropriations committees ignored this sound advice. First, a look at the president's budget: The administration proposed an overall $6.7 million *decrease* from the previous year's funding level, ostensibly in pursuit of a balanced budget.[32] Moreover, this $6.7 million cut actually represented a $59 million reduction from the agency's own budget request for FY 1960.[33] This attitude toward the overall funding of Operation Multiple Use prompted Senator Frank Church to observe wryly: "The administration's response to leadership is too often a brochure followed by an inadequate budget."[34] More importantly, the slashed budget did not reflect an across the board cut. All programs were not affected equally. "Balanced budget" ideology obscured a more complicated policy of favoring some programs over others. The president's budget included a $1 million cut to the recreation program, while timber sales got a $4 million *increase*.[35]

Ironically, the proposed increase in timber sales came at a time when the price of timber was declining dramatically. Even more ironically, the actual volume of national forest timber harvested was falling, too. With stumpage values dropping, however, logging companies were buying more timber even as they were cutting less. The year 1958 had record timber sales, with 8 bbf sold (excluding Alaska), but a poor year for timber harvests, with 6.4 bbf cut (an 8 percent decline from 1957).[36] The price the government received for timber it sold declined from an average of $16.57 per thousand board feet (mbf) in 1957 to $14.67 per mbf in 1958. By February 1959, when the FY 1960 budget negotiations were taking place, the price had declined further to $11.85 per mbf. As a result, timber sale receipts for 1959 were expected to fall by $10–12 million — equal to 10 percent of the total timber revenue. Despite these low prices and the depressed lumber market, the Forest Service and the administration still advocated increasing sales on public forests to a record 10 bbf in FY 1960.[37] In contrast, the administration asked for a 15 percent reduction in the recreation budget at a time when Representative Harold Ostertag of New York could say, "I have been told by my constituents that it is often as hard to get a picnic table in a national forest as to get tickets to a Broadway hit."[38]

Short-term revenue generation and economic stimulation provided the rationale for the Eisenhower budget. Despite depressed prices, Assistant Secretary Peterson optimistically predicted that the higher timber sale level might return as much as an additional $10 million to the federal treasury that year. (He did not mention how much potential revenue would be lost by selling timber at such low prices in a saturated market.) Peterson added that the economic activity to be generated by these additional sales would be beneficial for rural communities with a logging-based economy.[39] Most members of Congress apparently shared this attitude, especially the economic stimulation rationale, since many of them probably realized that a large percentage of timber sales actually lost money.

The effort to use the national forests for economic stimulation and job enhancement went beyond the corporation-promoting, "trickle-down" advocacy of the Republican party. Democratic liberals like Senator Hubert Humphrey also attempted to manipulate the national forest budget for job stimulation. Humphrey hoped forest development would ease "the pains of chronic unemployment" in rural areas in his home state of Minnesota by creating "greater national forest resource yields and services." In his testimony on the FY 1960 budget, he unabashedly suggested that increased funding under the 1959 program "could be used for land development and forest road and trail construction in the Superior and Chippewa [national forests in Minnesota] thus . . . providing employment for the thousands of area residents idled by job layoffs and job shutdowns."[40]

Senator Robert C. Byrd (D-WV) echoed these sentiments while questioning Forest Service witnesses about the number of additional jobs that would result from implementing the program. Edward Crafts estimated that the Forest Service would hire about 3,000 new employees per year for the first five years if full funding was approved. One-third of those 15,000 jobs would go to "professionals." Crafts also noted that the Forest Service usually contracted out for much of the "non-recurrent" construction and other project needs, so that spin-off economic benefits to local communities could be expected. The senator then revealed his desire to target additional national forest funding mainly to those areas of the country with unemployment problems rather than to those areas of the forests needing the work most urgently. "What I am trying to get at," Byrd said, "is this: Were we only to appropriate additional moneys to implement the overall program . . . only in those areas of substantial unemployment, what would be the additional funds needed? And what would be the number of additional jobs that would be provided?" Peterson quite understandably responded, "I would hope that whatever action the Congress may now take . . . would be related to the program rather than directly to the unemployment situation."[41] Such admonitions, however, fell on deaf ears.

The record of *actual congressional appropriations* for the Forest Service, while somewhat of an improvement over the administration budget discussed above, nevertheless remained way out of balance with what the Forest Service claimed was necessary to ensure sustained yield and a balance of multiple uses. In reference to a whopping $24 million request for construction of timber harvesting roads, Congressman Don Magnuson (D-WA) opined "I do not think the authorizations are big enough. As I said this morning with reference to the timber sales program . . . this is all a money making investment. Within reason, whatever we put into the road program is going to come back with a profit."[42] Congress subsequently voted to approve $28 million for roads, *a 17 percent increase over the agency's request,* equivalent to a fifth of the total budget allocation approved by Congress. In contrast, in the final appropriation the Forest Service got substantially less than it requested for reforestation, soil and water management, wildlife, and recreation.

Negotiated in 1959, the FY 1960 budget was a disappointment to the Forest Service, coming as it did in the year they unveiled their comprehensive program for developing the national forests. However, agency leaders regrouped in 1960 and pushed even harder for full funding for FY 1961. To

Table 3. Funds Needed to Implement Operation Multiple Use Compared to Eisenhower's FY 1961 Budget Request

Appropriation Item	Maximum Annual Funding Level (to be reached by end of 5th year)	Total in President's 1961 Budget Request	Percentage of Maximum Annual Level Provided
Timber sales administration	$26,786,000	$20,175,000	75.3
Reforestation and stand improvement	$40,997,000	$3,465,000	8.5
Recreation — public use	$30,712,000	$14,830,000	48.3
Wildlife habitat management	$7,033,000	$1,270,000	18.1
Range management	$6,820,000	$3,000,000	44.0
Range revegetation	$3,453,000	$1,600,000	46.3
Range improvements	$4,779,000	$1,965,000	41.1
Soil and water management	$10,611,000	$1,615,000	15.2
Forest fire protection	$28,778,000	$14,345,000	49.8
Insect and disease control	$9,000,000	$5,018,000	55.8

Source: *Congressional Record — Senate*, June 8, 1960, vol. 106, pt. 9, pp. 12082; provided by the Forest Service.

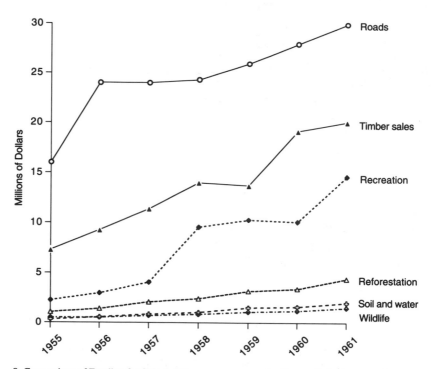

8. Comparison of Funding for Selected Programs, 1955–1961. Source: U.S. Congress, Senate, *Congressional Record* 106, pt. 9 (June 8, 1960): 12079–82.

aid their lobbying efforts, they published a 42-page booklet of estimated costs for Operation Multiple Use,[43] and announced that FY 1961 would be the first official year of implementation of the 1959 program. But again these efforts had little impact. Once more, the Eisenhower budget for FY 1961 substantially favored timber sales and roads while gutting most other programs. In fact, the Budget Bureau allotted the agency *more* than it had requested for timber sales. (Table 3 allows a comparison of the Forest Service's Operation Multiple Use budget with the President's FY 1961 budget.)

Generally following the president's lead, Congress also approved more than the agency requested for timber sales in FY 1961 and substantially less than it requested for reforestation, soil and water, wildlife, and recreation.[44] In the final analysis, the long-range plan had helped the Forest Service acquire a small overall increase in funding, mostly by promising increased commodity production (jobs) and increased recreational services; but the much more important effort by the Forest Service to promote greater bal-

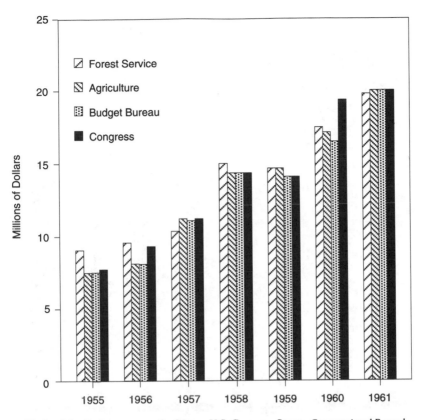

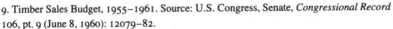

9. Timber Sales Budget, 1955–1961. Source: U.S. Congress, Senate, *Congressional Record* 106, pt. 9 (June 8, 1960): 12079–82.

ance in multiple use management and sustainability in resource production abjectly failed in its goals. (See figure 8 for graphic contrasts among the actual funding levels for selected management activities for FYs 1955–61. See figures 9 and 10 to compare Forest Service budget requests, Agriculture Department allowances, Budget Bureau allowances, and congressional appropriations for those same years for timber and recreation.)

Conclusion

The funding process is a window into the world of state sponsored resource development. The central reality of that world, as shown here, is that the federal government willingly funds, even subsidizes, activities that generate

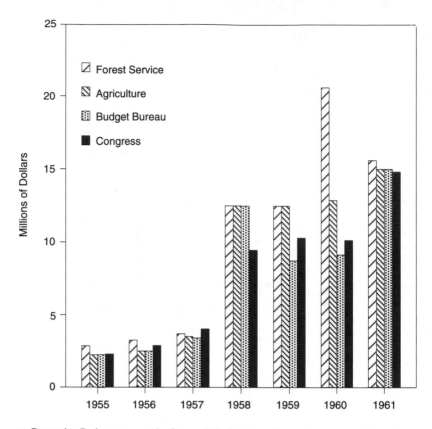

10. Recreation Budget, 1955–1961. Source: U.S. Congress, Senate, *Congressional Record* 106, pt. 9 (June 8, 1960): 12079–82.

revenue or economic benefits, or that enjoy widespread popular support, while neglecting those activities that do not meet one of these criteria. No matter how carefully and explicitly the Forest Service argued for balanced, integrated funding, the separate parts of the national forest program were singled out and favored or neglected according to political designs or ideological agendas, which generally meant lavish funding for the most ecologically destructive programs — road building and timber harvesting. This limited decision-making calculus ignored the external "costs" of unbalanced resource management and foiled legitimately negotiated public policies of sustained yield and multiple use. Just as deplorable, the timber sale program only *appeared* to be a money-maker at that time because creative agency accounting lumped all timber sales together to disguise the money-losers and often confused receipts with profits. Those beating the revenue-generation drum also left out the costs of reforestation, soil erosion containment, and damage to wildlife, recreation, and water quality. The forest environment and future generations would absorb these costs without compensation. The Eisenhower administration, and Congress, and even the Forest Service, supported a policy of clearcutting old-growth forests to generate federal revenue and economic goods for dependent industries that had often liquidated their own timber reserves. This rapid sale of public timber came at the expense of healthy ecosystems, sound forest management, sustained yield, and balanced multiple use. Liquidating America's natural resource capital for narrow and fleeting benefits betrayed one of the fundamental principles of public forest management: the obligation of the present generation to use resources wisely and not leave for posterity a "depleted, worn out country."

IO

Patterns of the Fifties Repeated
in the Sixties

Without skipping a beat, the trends in national forest management set between 1945 and 1960 extended into the 1960s, 1970s, and 1980s. To be sure, some controversies increased in tempo while others moved into the background, but the fundamental political and economic context remained the same. No resolution of any major conflicts or lasting change in management emphases marked these later decades. The public debate over the meaning of multiple use, over management priorities, and over the concept of zoning continued. Except for greater attention to recreation, which was a trend of the 1950s anyway, nonmarket resources and values continued to be neglected in the funding process and, to a lesser degree, in management planning. Although a growing cross-section of the public — including ecologists, philosophers, and environmentalists — challenged traditional forest management practices and assumptions, a commodities management approach to the national forests coupled with a commitment to "full utilization" continued to enjoy ideological hegemony in the forestry profession and the agency until the late 1980s.

The rise of the modern "environmental movement" intensified demands for recreation development, which were accommodated in large part when not in conflict with resource extraction objectives. Environmentalists also made wilderness preservation nearly as American as apple pie (in small doses, of course), and successfully promoted a number of legislative constraints on Forest Service management discretion. These constraints, however, had only a minor impact on forest management. Congress, the Forest Service, and commodity interest groups held tenaciously to the belief that ever higher levels of all multiple uses were achievable, sustainable, and reconcilable with environmental protection. The conspiracy of optimism remained an essential link between the Eisenhower administration and the two Democratic administrations that followed it.

Rise of the Environmental Movement

During the 1960s and 1970s the American conservation movement entered a new phase. Novel groups sprang up, some old groups changed their approach or faded into the background, and traditional alliances broke apart. The change was so obvious that the movement received a fresh new name, "environmentalism," and its advocates became "environmentalists" instead of conservationists. Older groups like the Sierra Club, the Wilderness Society, the National Wildlife Federation, and the Audubon Society altered their tactics to take advantage of new public sentiments, expanded their memberships dramatically, and took the vanguard of the environmental protection movement. (Despite a common appellation, the movement was not monolithic.) Other old-line conservation groups that did not adjust as rapidly, such as the American Forestry Association, became junior partners or dissenters from the new orthodoxy. New groups like the Natural Resources Defense Council, the Environmental Defense Fund, and Friends of the Earth sprang into prominence.[1]

Continuing the trend that had begun among some conservation groups in the 1950s, the leaders of the environmental movement of the 1960s and 1970s abandoned the traditional alliance between their groups and the Forest Service. Both the new environmentalists and Forest Service leaders lost respect for each other, and antagonism escalated. Historian Samuel Hays, in his book *Beauty, Health, and Permanence,* characterized the traditional "conservation" movement as a coalition of scientists, technicians, and government leaders interested in efficient, socially responsible development of resources. In contrast, he said, the environmental movement stressed environmental protection and "quality of life" rather than efficient production.[2] This generalization is reasonably accurate, although to the former coalition of technicians and politicians might be added progressive leaders of industry. Industry apologists, especially after World War Two, recognized that the social and environmental ideals embodied in conservation philosophy enjoyed so much public support that it behooved them to jump on the conservation bandwagon. The public generally perceived conservationists as "good guys," so industrialists often referred to themselves as "true conservationists," seeking thereby to improve both their public image and to favorably influence the definition of conservation. Industry's partial success in shaping conservation ideology in the 1940s and 1950s helps explain the advent of the new term "environmentalism" in the 1960s and 1970s. People needed some shortcut method for distinguishing between conservation as advocated by industry and the Forest Service, versus the conservation advocated by the National Wildlife Federation or Sierra Club. The classic "efficient production" definition of conservation which the Forest Service continued to adhere to in the 1960s had more in common with industry's concern for economic stability than with the environmental movement's growing concern for ecologically stable (naturally diverse), healthy (unpolluted), and attractive environments. So, while the Forest Service and environmentalists broke apart, the uneasy codependent relationship between the agency and the timber industry remained strong, if rocky.

One of the characteristics of the new environmental movement, Stephen Fox has argued, was its professionalization and bureaucratization, made possible by the remarkable growth in membership during the 1960s and 1970s. This growth, paradoxically, followed a shift of focus from the natural world to humans. Fox, like Samuel Hays before him, traced the popularity of environmentalism to its growing concern for *human* quality of life. This new concept of quality of life had less to do with the accumulation of commodities than with a desire to experience a healthy, enjoyable, and satisfying life, which included outdoor activities, reduced stress, and a cleaner environment. Increased memberships in the new or reformed conservation groups led to increased budgets, which led to large, well-trained staffs producing books and glossy magazines and maintaining an effective lobbying presence in Washington, D.C. While the professionalization of the environmental groups gave them more political clout, it also led inevitably to compromises, which in turn contributed to a rebirth and proliferation of more radical grassroots environmental groups in the 1980s — the kind of groups that Fox refers to as the "amateur tradition," following paths blazed by John Muir and David Brower — the groups that Dave Foreman, co-founder of Earth First! refers to as "visionary groups" that "proceed from a biocentric philosophy . . . [and] dare to demand what was once [politically] off-limits." [3]

Contributing to the growth and strength of the environmental movement in the 1960s was a collection of advocate-scientists voicing concern over environmental pollution, the world's burgeoning human population, and unsustainable rates of natural resource consumption. When Professor Paul Ehrlich warned of the "population bomb," America suddenly took notice. The phrase instantly entered the English lexicon. Family planning advocates came out of the closet. New groups, including Zero Population Growth, which spun off from the Sierra Club, advocated birth control and steady state demographics and economics. When Rachel Carson and Barry Commoner warned of the toxic side-effects of much of America's technologically engineered cornucopia, Americans vowed to consume less, recycle more, and better regulate chemical use and industrial waste. E. F. Schumacher summed up the movement with a radical new aphorism— "Small Is Beautiful" — intellectually compelling because it was so anomalous to the prevailing ideology of "Bigger Is Better."

All these developments strongly affected Forest Service public relations. The new environmental scientists were deflating the balloon of optimism that held aloft the agency's vision of proper forest management. Ironically, the same deference for scientists that contributed to public acceptance of intensive management for maximum production in the 1950s now contributed to widespread questioning of the faith in technological fixes and a growing skepticism toward the merchants of optimism. Setting the tone for her book *Silent Spring,* Rachel Carson quoted E. B. White: "I am pessimistic about the human race because it is too ingenious for its own good. Our approach to nature is to beat it into submission. We would stand a better chance of survival if we accommodated ourselves to this planet and viewed it appreciatively instead of skeptically and dictatorially."[4]

This repudiation of the ideology of endless growth and maximized production threatened the foundation of forest management as practiced by the Forest Service. Indeed, since World War Two the agency had constructed its entire organizational edifice on the assumption that increasing demands for resources had to be met with increasing application of machines, labor, chemicals, and capital. Abandoning the commitment to intensive management would have undermined the carefully constructed facade of sustainability and might have resulted in reductions to the agency's size and functions. Forest Service defensiveness in the 1960s and early 1970s can thus be seen as an attempt to conserve ideology as much as resources, and to sustain the organization as much as long-term yields of products and services. Perhaps the agency should not have been expected to respond otherwise.

The Forest Service was only one actor in this conspiracy play, however. As mentioned earlier, business interests joined as coconspirators for obvious reasons: technological optimism maintained the supply of national forest logs and grazing permits at higher levels than would otherwise have been allowed. Members of Congress who did not join the conspiracy stood to lose development subsidies for their district or state, and thus stood to lose votes at home. More importantly, they would lose bargaining power in the legislative log-rolling process. Building consensus by the ubiquitous "you scratch my back and I'll scratch yours" method meant that only team players achieved influence in Congress. (It also meant that legislative policies and appropriations bills were based more on considerations of political feasibility than on coherence.) Finally, local governments in the vicinity of national forests supported the conspiracy because forest development meant jobs for local residents and tax revenue. If development appeared not to be sustainable, the conspirators assumed a technological fix would be invented in the future, or they pragmatically chose to maintain the status quo at the expense of the next generation.

Continued Imbalance in Resource Management

The Forest Service, though led by a new chief in the 1960s, continued its policies of the 1950s unabated. If anything, it promoted timber sales with even more fervor than before. In fact, timber production in the coastal and inland northwest (Regions 1 and 6) actually peaked in the late 1960s. In 1962, a year after the new Kennedy administration had settled in, Richard McArdle retired as Chief of the Forest Service. As with the timely departure of Lyle Watts in 1952, McArdle's retirement was intended to reduce the possibility of the chief's position becoming part of the political spoils system. The Forest Service had succeeded in promoting agency heads up through the ranks of its professionals and hoped to keep it that way. The president has authority to designate the chief, but traditionally presidents simply ratified the agency decision. As a consequence, internal debates over who would replace the chief were always charged with political ramifications.

When McArdle announced his plan to retire, he gave Secretary of Agriculture Orville Freeman a list of three desirable successors to choose from.

Freeman, appointed by the Kennedy administration, had the authority to nominate anyone at all, but, as Cliff recalled, Kennedy agreed to maintain the tradition of promotion from within the ranks. The choice for successors to McArdle actually came down to two: Edward Crafts or Edward Cliff, both major players in the 1950s.[5] Crafts had been Deputy Chief of Programs and Legislation. Considered a progressive at the time, Crafts believed recreation would play a greater role in the agency's future and he felt the agency needed to be more flexible, publicly responsive, and accommodating of nontimber multiple uses. Politically astute, Crafts was willing to gamble sometimes to move the Forest Service in new directions.[6] Cliff contrasted sharply with Crafts. He was the agency's point man for reducing tensions with graziers and its most visible advocate of maximum timber production during the Eisenhower years. An enthusiastic exponent of intensive management and a staunch defender of agency prerogative, Cliff was politically cautious and resisted the values changes promoted by the emerging environmental movement. (He had argued against equal treatment of multiple uses during early agency deliberations on the Multiple Use–Sustained Yield Act.)[7] Secretary Freeman chose Cliff. Freeman and Cliff shared a similar commodity-oriented perspective on resource development and established a close supportive relationship throughout the former's tenure.[8] Crafts left the Forest Service at that point to become the first director of the new Bureau of Outdoor Recreation, where he stayed until the arrival of the Nixon administration in 1969. He became an astute yet friendly outside critic of the agency during Cliff's tenure, and some tension between the two men remains evident in both their memoirs.

By the end of the 1960s, Cliff appeared not just cautious but downright reactionary to many observers. His appointment symbolized loyalty to the old status quo and initiated a period of unprecedented hostility between the Forest Service and environmentalists. Even old-guard conservationists criticized Cliff's reign as retrenchment rather than leadership. E. M. Sterling wrote a blistering critique of the Forest Service in *American Forests* in which he suggested that the agency suffered from "the greatest generation gap in history." Down to its lowest levels, he said, employees seemed to have "no concept at all of what the recreationists want, need, or even deserve." The Forest Service's "log-it-all philosophy," he said, had caused a situation in which the agency "no longer leads but is led." Significantly,

221

Sterling was no friend of the new wave of environmentalists. He characterized them as too uncompromising to provide leadership, and he praised the timber industry for proposing the so-called High-Yield Forestry Bill (the National Timber Supply Bill of 1969 that environmentalists pulled out all stops to defeat).[9] By the end of Cliff's tenure, such criticisms were ubiquitous. Even the consummately defensive Cliff finally agreed that he had made some mistakes. Reflecting after retirement on his period as chief, he admitted:

> Edward C. Crafts has said that the Forest Service was slow and insensitive to the wakening national awareness of our environment, and I don't disagree entirely with that. I think many people, including Dr. Crafts, didn't fully recognize the snowballing effect with which this movement grew. . . . I can admit, in my own reactions I didn't fully or quickly recognize the total potential impact or the strength of the opposition that was developing against such things as clearcutting.[10]

In September 1961, the Forest Service dusted off its two-year-old Operation Multiple Use and reissued it as the Kennedy administration's "Development Program for the National Forests." The only significant changes from the 1959 version were a one-third increase in estimated recreation use by 1972, a 20 percent increase in the timber harvest target for the same year, and an acceleration of the roads and trails construction program to achieve these increased forest development goals. The rest of the development program simply repeated the ambitious proposals of Operation Multiple Use and reiterated the truly staggering amount of soil, watershed, and vegetation rehabilitation projects needed to support the proposed higher levels of production on a sustained yield basis.[11]

Besides this national development program, the Forest Service initiated multiple use planning at the forest and district levels in 1961 as a direct response to the passage of the Multiple Use–Sustained Yield Act (MUSY). This planning effort began with the ten regional offices establishing overall management and development goals for their regions based on the types of resources within the region and, of course, based on overall expectations from Washington regarding regional contributions to the production targets. Then, within the guidelines set by the regional offices, each forest supervisor's office (the next rung down on the organizational ladder) developed a comprehensive multiple use plan in tandem with a series of ranger district multiple use plans (the bottom of the organizational ladder). This represented mostly top-down planning.[12] While these forest and district plans theoretically provided a reality check for the development programs articulated at higher levels of the agency, the ideal bottom-up integration of knowledge from the ground level into planning at the top usually floundered on organizational and fiscal realities. Since performance ratings and promotion were based on successful accomplishment of assigned resource production targets, there was a built-in incentive to "get out the cut."[13] And since Forest Service funding was tied to resource output expectations in Congress, the upper echelons of the agency felt pressed to ensure that targets were met.[14] Such incentives and pressures did not exist for soil, water, and wildlife conservation.

These organizational and political pressures had an obvious impact on multiple use planning. Timber production bias was evident everywhere, as exemplified in the 1961 Multiple Use Plan for the Canyon Creek Ranger District of the Gifford Pinchot National Forest. The entire Canyon Creek Ranger District fell into two timber "working circles": the Canyon Creek Working Circle encompassed 85 percent of the ranger district while the Spirit Lake Working Circle made up the remainder. The multiple use plan divided the land base of each working circle into "dominant use" areas. For Canyon Creek, timber production was assigned as the dominant use on 91 percent of the working circle, with recreation dominant on about 7.5 percent, and soil protection dominant on about 1.5 percent. For the Spirit Lake Working Circle, approximately 93 percent was assigned to timber production, 4.5 percent to soil protection, and 2.5 percent to recreation. No lands in either district were dedicated to wildlife as the dominant use. Lands assigned to recreation, furthermore, did not preclude logging; in fact, salvage logging was planned for most recreation areas.[15]

Timber production on the district was climbing rapidly. An annual allowable cut of 22 mmbf had been established in 1943 for the Canyon Creek Working Circle. The actual harvest in 1956 exceeded that limit by 30 percent, so in 1957 a new timber management plan raised the ceiling to 38 mmbf. Just three years later, the harvest was again bumping up against the new limit. With these pressures as a context, timber production objectives drove the multiple use plan. Regarding road construction, the stated goal of the plan was "rapid and full development of the transportation system on the District to permit intensive forest management and allow greater access and use of all resources." Use of the phrase "transportation system" was misleading, however, because as the plan admitted, "roads are gradually replacing trails . . . [especially] the better trails."[16] Recreationists not only lost their hiking trails to roads, but were excluded from the forest by administrative closure from July 10 to September 30 as a fire prevention measure. In the Northwest, summer is the dry season, so these months were popular for outdoor recreation as well as susceptible to forest fires. Of course logging activities and associated slash burning caused a large percentage of human-generated wildfires, but the agency did not consider the timber program expendable like recreation.

For recreation facilities the district at the time had only one "improved campsite." A five-year plan for developing three new campsites constituted the district's only goals for recreation. The district ranger seemed to consider recreation management a simple process of identifying a few popular vehicular destination spots (for berry-pickers mainly) where facilities might be built to serve that use. Consequently, the plan counted logging-road construction as a benefit to recreationists since it provided motorists more access to the forest.[17]

The plan's discussion of "Wildlife and Wildlife Habitat" also clearly evidenced a timber bias. Only "game" and "fur-bearing" animals were targeted for management and all wildlife decisions were to be "consistent with the requirements for other uses," meaning timber production. Although the plan stated that logging had increased winter browse for deer, it also mentioned that "browsing damage to plantations" had occurred and had to be controlled.[18]

The most revealing section of the plan dealt with watershed management. Agency regulations have always emphasized that areas with unstable soils that cannot be effectively protected from erosion during logging should be excluded from the commercial timberland base. But as the demand to increase harvests pressed upon allowable cut ceilings, foresters and engineers raised their tolerance level for erosion and adopted optimistic assumptions about their ability to engineer safe roads in just about any soil type. Soil classifications became not constraints but simply challenges that required more technical skill and capital. The Canyon Creek multiple use plan exemplified this. Due to steep terrain and loose pumice souls, Forest Service soil scientists had classified 74 percent of the district as "poor" or "very poor" in terms of soil stability. Only 7 percent of soils were rated "excellent" or "good." Acknowledging that "soil erosion has been severe," the agency planners still identified timber production as the "dominant use" for over 90 percent of the district with no recognition of irony or inconsistency.[19]

The second half of this multiple use plan described policies and priorities for *coordinating* multiple uses – the crucial task of national forest managers. Under a section on coordinating timber with watershed protection, the plan stated that logging would conform to "special requirements" when "critical soil" conditions existed. These special requirements remained largely discretionary but included promises of "prompt reforestation" and prohibitions against tractor logging in wet weather and wetlands. Also among the mitigations was a requirement for logging by cable rather than by tractor in slopes over 20 percent. (Public highways by law rarely exceed 6 or 8 percent slope at their steepest.) Under a section on coordinating recreation and timber, the plan called for retaining one-hundred- and two-hundred-foot-wide buffers of uncut forest along roadsides (now termed "beauty strips") and similar thin buffers along streams and lakes to give motorists and campers at least the illusion of a forest experience. The entire text of the section on coordinating wildlife with timber concentrated on two courses of action: (1) reducing damage to tree plantations from game (deer, elk, and bear) by negotiating with state game managers to increase hunting permits for the offending animals; and (2) reducing plantation damage by small mammals through the use of "rodenticides or other special measures."[20]

These multiple use plans were supposed to reflect the balanced management ideals espoused in MUSY, but in most cases they simply reflected a continued concentration on timber production with added promises to more fully consider the effects of logging on other resources. Conservation groups, especially those oriented toward wildlife and recreation, reacted to the plans with anger and frustration. Such groups had become especially strong and active in the Northwest in the early 1960s, particularly the Sierra Club, the Federation of Western Outdoor Clubs (a newly formed coalition of organizations), and the Mazamas (a hiking club turned politically active).

225

Logging on the national forests and national park advocacy became perhaps the key issues of concern to them in the 1960s. These interest groups had furthermore garnered powerful allies in the Senate (which had gone over-whelmingly Democratic in the 1960 election), including senators Henry "Scoop" Jackson (D-WA), Warren Magnuson (D-WA), Maurine Neuberger (D-OR), and Wayne Morse (D-OR), as well as the influential support of United States Supreme Court Justice William O. Douglas — also from Washington.

So much conservationist and political opposition to the district multiple use plans welled up in the Northwest that the Secretary of Agriculture finally asked the Forest Service to put the plans on hold temporarily while it developed a new comprehensive policy statement for forest management in the region.[21] The Forest Service Northwest Regional Office in response drafted a paper titled, "Long-Range Management Policy and Objectives for the High Mountain Areas of the Region" in October 1961. The use of the phrase "high mountains" reflected the fact that the current controversies centered on development proposals for previously undeveloped areas in the higher elevations of the national forests. The agency had formerly considered these areas to be of marginal commercial value and generally consigned them to custodial management for watershed, wildlife, and primitive recreation values. Conservationists wanted the traditional laissez-faire management of these areas continued and even endorsed as formal policy. The Forest Service wanted to be able to extend its "management" — which always meant roads and timber harvests — wherever feasible. Combining the desire to open these contended areas up for development with a desire to mollify the new wave of conservationists, the High Mountain Policy promoted "full use and development" while at the same time expressing support for nontimber values. The policy established a new management category called "Land-scape Management Areas," where exceptional scenic and recreational values required special sensitivity on the part of managers. Unfortunately, that sensitivity only meant smaller clearcuts, more selective cutting, and more beauty strips in areas designated for landscape management. Essentially, the Forest Service expected to go forward with its timber production plans even in scenic areas by adjusting logging activities to make them less disturbing esthetically. It fundamentally was unwilling to forgo development and fought tooth and nail to keep silvicultural options open.[22]

With the new High Mountains Policy approved and formally in place in March 1962, the Forest Service felt justified in moving forward with development plans. Northwest Regional Forester J. Herbert Stone submitted a proposal to the Washington Office of the Forest Service to declassify several "Limited Areas" (semiprotected Natural Areas) in order to accommodate expanded timber harvesting, an action he felt was fully consistent with the new High Mountain Policy. A memo from Neal Rahm of the Washington Office regarding Stone's proposal warned that such a move might better be delayed until after the elections that year, since declassifying protected areas "can be explosive." (Stone went ahead with the declassifications.) Rahm also warned Stone that traditional management discretion was under attack and to expect pressure for "urban planning" style land use allocations on the national forests: "A basic doctrine in our concept of multiple use is that *change is a constant,* so we design our plans to accommodate change [emphasis in original]. If there is one single feature in the tug-of-war today between the Forest Service and some recreation organizations, it is the desire to freeze our decisions and reduce management flexibility."[23] Again, the so-called recreation organizations did not like management flexibility because it rarely served their interests.

Several other undeveloped national forest areas slated for development — Waldo Lake and the Minam River valley in Oregon, and the North Cascades in Washington — had figured prominently in the environmentalist protests that originally led Secretary Freeman to ask the agency to reevaluate its policies. The protestors included all four Northwest senators mentioned above who had written to Secretary Freeman specifically asking him to halt development plans for these three areas pending a policy reevaluation. In a letter to Secretary Freeman transmitting the High Mountains Policy document, Chief Edward Cliff proudly announced his agency's more sensitive approach to the management of these remote wildlands and said he was prepared to put the management objectives of the new policy into effect. What did this new policy mean for the management of the three contested areas? Cliff explained in his letter to the secretary that he planned to "proceed with resource development . . . in Waldo Lake, Minam River, and North Cascades areas."[24] The outcry from those who had hoped for a change of heart in the Forest Service was both loud and predictable. This and Regional Forester Stone's decision to declassify Limited Areas seemed to validate the environmental lobby's worst fears about the agency's timber bias. Among other things, these two actions led to a vigorous agitation for the establishment of a North Cascades National Park to be carved out of national forest lands — a proposal which the Forest Service strenuously but unsuccessfully opposed. It also led to deteriorating relationships between the agency and many influential progressive politicians throughout the decade. One of those progressives who became extremely irritated with the Forest Service was Supreme Court Justice William O. Douglas. In a December 1961 polemic published in the Mazamas newsletter under the title "A Wilderness Bill of Rights," Douglas complained:

> There is hardly any place left in the country (outside Alaska) where one can get more than ten miles from a road. Roads, roads, roads — they seem to be the compulsion of state and federal officials. . . . The Forest Service is the main offender. In some states it is hardly more than the voice of the logging interests. . . . Those who are doubters should go to the Minam River in the Wallowas, hike its forty miles, and see what few trees Boise-Cascade Lumber Company would actually get out of the valley, and see what damage would be wrought with the millions of dollars of public money to be spent on a road up this, one of our last, roadless valley wilderness areas. The Forest Service calls this rape of the Minam an application of the principle of "multiple use." . . . Multiple-use in actual practice is a high-sounding term that means loggers and automobiles take over.[25]

Although the Forest Service moved aggressively in the 1960s to accommodate recreation as a major national forest use, it never satisfied the "recreation groups." That was because many of these so-called recreationists actually had a much larger agenda than securing campsites and hiking trails. To some degree Forest Service leaders misunderstood these groups and their values, but more often the agency accurately recognized that the new conservationists in fact opposed the centerpiece of national forest management: high-yield timber-farming. Accommodation was impossible under the circumstances. So, as an alternative, the agency sought to define this constituency as just another interest group demanding a product or service, which could then be satisfied through recreation facilities development. This approach had only limited success. The added emphasis on recreation actually exacerbated management conflicts. Most of the increase in recreation funds the agency received went to developing new campgrounds and picnic sites, which in turn generated greater public use of the national forests and more maintenance requirements. Because the agency had few people on staff in the early 1960s to deal with recreation management, the new recreation investments simply extended the old problems of overcrowding, inadequate sanitation, and facilities rehabilitation needs. Increased opportunities for national forest recreation also led to greater public expectations and thus greater disappointments in the face of perceived inadequacies. In this sense, the Forest Service repeated the same mistake it made with the timber industry: by making *demands* for goods and services rather than *environmental stewardship* the primary management guide, it encouraged user groups to think of the national forests as a sort of factory for generating products to meet their demands. A large segment of the recreating public held a narrow view of their interests and adopted this demand/supply attitude, but spokespersons for the new environmental movement turned to a critique of intensive management itself, challenging the privileged role of agency foresters to chart the course of national forest management.

Wilderness Legislation and Other Protective Zoning of the National Forests

Given the general enthusiasm of the Forest Service for maximum production and the failure of existing political institutions to ensure the protection of nonmarket values, environmentalists pursued a zoning strategy, seeking to legislatively restrict the activities of the Forest Service on special areas of the national forests. The wilderness preservation movement constitutes the prototype of this strategy. In lobbying for the Wilderness Act, environmentalists had three basic goals: (1) they wanted Congress to declare wilderness preservation a national policy; (2) they wanted legislative protection for agency designated wilderness areas to make it more difficult for the Forest Service to declassify those areas; and (3) they wanted a means whereby additional wilderness areas could be established. Each of these goals were met in the 1964 Wilderness Act. But the Act also contained a number of loopholes for development interests put in to help overcome opposition to the bill. While the Act prohibited roads, timber harvesting, and the use of motorized equipment, it allowed commercial livestock grazing (and its associated fences, stock tanks, and maintenance activities), water development, and mining on valid claims — as well as recreation associated activities such as camping, hunting, and fishing.[26] All these compromises developed over seven years of difficult negotiations. As historian Roderick Nash observed, "Congress lavished more time and effort on the wilderness bill than on any other measure in American conservation history. From June 1957 until May 1964 there were nine separate hearings on the proposal, collecting over six thousand pages of testimony. The bill itself was modified and rewritten or resubmitted sixty-six different times."[27] The resulting legislation cannot be called revolutionary, but it did indicate a crack in the ideological edifice of intensive management for maximum production.

The wilderness debate essentially represented a struggle between those seeking to define "conservation" as a combination of rational resource use along with deliberate nonuse, and those who sought to define conservation as wise use only.[28] The latter generally opposed wilderness preservation on principle, or supported it only when resource extraction was not a feasible option. One key congressional opponent of the many wilderness bills was Representative Wayne Aspinall (D-CO), who repeatedly stalled progress of the bills through his House Committee on Interior and Insular Affairs. At a White House Conference on Conservation in 1963, Aspinall had this to say about conservation and preservation: "Traditionally, conservation and wise use have been synonymous. To me this is what conservation has meant: Accepting all the material resources that nature is capable of providing, taking those natural resources where they are, and as they are, and developing them for the best use of the people as a whole. . . . I do not know when, where, or how the purist preservation group assumed the mantle of the conservationists."[29] A prominent wilderness bill opponent in the Senate, Gordon Allott, also from Colorado, argued that "the wilderness concept itself violates multiple use. Those areas in wilderness would be confined to wilderness use as the only use. So there would be no multiple use; the land could not be used for watershed protection or conservation or mining or forestry."[30] Often wilderness opponents invoked Gifford Pinchot as their guide and authority. William Welsh, a lobbyist for water development interests, proclaimed at an early hearing on the wilderness bill, "It is truly refreshing to note that neither Theodore Roosevelt nor Gifford Pinchot ever for a moment advanced the theory that conservation meant to set aside vast areas of a watershed where all of the natural resources should be bottled up and denied to the public except as something to look at."[31] This appropriation of Pinchot by lobbyists for the resource industries helps explain why environmental groups at that time turned to John Muir, Aldo Leopold, and others as their intellectual icons.

In the 1960s, the Kennedy and Johnson administrations lent support to the groups who felt conservation appropriately included both the production of market goods and the preservation of nonmarket values. Secretary of Interior Stewart Udall advocated a broadened concept of conservation in his widely read and influential 1963 book, *The Quiet Crisis,* in which he lamented how America had become "a land of vanishing beauty, of increasing ugliness, of shrinking open space, and of an overall environment that is diminished daily by pollution and noise and blight."[32] Early in his tenure as Secretary of the Interior, he wrote an article for the Wilderness Society's national magazine in which he stated, "Wilderness preservation is the first element in a sound national conservation policy."[33] President Johnson, whose wife "Lady Bird" initiated the "Keep America Beautiful" campaign, noted in a 1965 message to Congress transmitting the signed Wilderness Act: "What we have in woods and forest, valley and stream, in the gorges and the mountains and the hills, we must not destroy. The precious legacy of preservation of beauty will be our gift to posterity. . . . In the new conservation of this century, our concern is with the total relation between man and the world around him. Its object is not only man's material welfare but the dignity of man himself."[34] With administration support and backing from many prominent legislators, the zoning strategy for wilderness preservation had finally prevailed.

The Wilderness Act has been touted as a victory for preservationists and a defeat for advocates of total use, but this assessment can be overstated. As mentioned above, the Act was loaded with compromises. In fact, in the context of national forest management, the victors initially gained little and the defeated lost even less. As part of the Act, Congress established only 9 million acres of wilderness out of the 14 million acres the Forest Service had administratively categorized as wilderness, wild, and primitive. (A total of 186 million acres was then under Forest Service jurisdiction.) The Act mandated the agency review its remaining primitive areas and make a recommendation within ten years as to whether these areas should be added to the wilderness system. Furthermore, this 9 million acres of national forest wilderness contained very little commercial timber. In the Northwest, for example, out of 18 million acres of commercial timberland on the national forests, only 0.75 million acres were in wilderness.[35] The wilderness designations had virtually no effect on the accelerating timber harvest program. (Substantial additions to the national forest wilderness system did not come until the 1980s, when state-by-state wilderness bills provided a new context for the continuing struggle between development interests and environmentalists. Even then, the Forest Service continued to oppose wilderness designation for areas with commercial development potential.)[36]

Other successful legislative zoning-type proposals of the 1960s included the National Wild and Scenic Rivers Act and National Trails System Act passed in 1968, as well as the Endangered Species Acts of 1966, 1969, and 1973. Although promoted by recreation interests, the actual legislative proposals for the Wild Rivers and National Trails Acts were drafted by representatives of the Forest Service and other federal land agencies under the leadership of the Bureau of Outdoor Recreation, with Edward Crafts still at the helm. Limited in scope, the two laws permitted greater management flexibility than the Wilderness Act, but they still represented progress in zoning protection for nonmarket values in special areas.[37] The Endangered Species Acts of 1966 and 1969, took a few halting first steps toward the protection of habitat for wildlife species threatened with extinction. The 1973 act significantly extended those protections, allowing even more restrictive zoning regulations than the Wilderness Act.[38]

These laws clinched a trend toward greater congressional intervention in federal land management and decreasing agency autonomy and discretion. Edward Crafts noted in an oral interview in 1965 that in the early 1960s, "Congress exercised much more careful oversight control and spelled out the details of legislation a great deal more than they had twenty, thirty, and forty years before. In other words, the Congress gave much less discretion to the executive branch."[39] Public administration scholars, such as Frank Gregg (who served as director of the Bureau of Land Management under the Carter administration), later confirmed such observations: "the era of Forest Service discretion over major land use allocations ended with the Wilderness Act of 1964, which established the Congress as a direct decision maker on the uses to be permitted on millions of acres of national forests." Gregg further points out how additional laws passed in the 1960s and the legislative aftermath of clearcutting controversies of the 1970s further eroded professional discretion on multiple use lands.[40]

Controversy over Below-Cost Timber Sales

Besides pushing for legislative zoning, environmentalists in the 1960s stepped up their challenge of the ecological sustainability, social desirability, and economic rationality of certain forest management practices, particularly below-cost timber sales and large-scale clearcutting. The hugely expanded road construction program that supported these activities provided an obvious target. Forest development road system expansion in the 1960s (and 1970s) did not support a comparable increase in timber harvests, which meant the government was spending more money to access virtually the same amount of timber. In 1962, 9 billion board feet of timber were harvested off the national forests. The road budget that year was $49.5 million. In 1968, 12.1 bbf were harvested while the road budget had climbed to $124.3 million — almost a 300 percent increase in road funds for a 30 percent increase in harvests.[41] This invited questioning. Because the national consumption of domestic wood products in the 1960s failed to rise at the predicted rate, demand for national forest timber leveled off at 10–12 bbf annually from the mid-1960s until the 1980s. Why did road costs escalate so much if timber harvests were steady? One reason is that the declining supply of easily accessible, high quality national forest timber required construction of ever more costly roads into rugged and remote areas with lower valued timber. And those roads also entailed higher maintenance costs. Furthermore, as the cost of roads continued to escalate, the government lost some of its ability to pay for roads with timber purchaser credits and thus had to cough up more cash for road construction if it wanted to maintain the high harvest levels. Many, if not most, of these roads would never generate enough revenue from timber sales to recoup the costs of construction and subsequent maintenance (see fig. 11).

"Below-cost" timber sales consequently increased in number and extent. The Forest Service accordingly turned to increasingly complex economic rationales to justify its road construction/timber sale program. A favorite defense, one with a germ of truth to it, was the argument that timber roads subsequently provided access for recreationists and helped support fire and

233

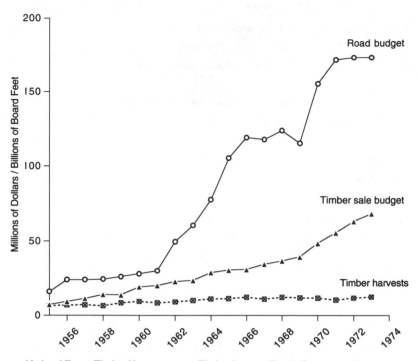

11. National Forest Timber Harvests versus Timber Program Funds. Source: timber harvest data from U.S. Forest Service, *Reports of the Chief of the Forest Service*; budget data from U.S. Forest Service, Budget Branch, "Budgets, 1961–1970, Composite Comparison" (Aug. 13, 1970), and "Timber Resource Management: Sales Administration and Management" (Feb. 21, 1973), both in Forest History Society archives, Western Timber Association records, box 31.

pest control, and thus ought to be considered "multiple use roads." Another was that road construction and forest access provided spin-off economic benefits to rural communities. The 1961 Development Program for the National Forests exhibited this rationale: "The existence of road systems permits an intensity of management and use for all National Forest purposes that is not otherwise possible. . . . Use of these roads by the public results in substantial benefits to the localities the roads serve."[42] While some indirect economic benefits certainly accrued, the argument was stretched. Critics pointed out that the dense pattern of roads associated with intensive forest management was unnecessary for anything but timber harvesting, and actually marred scenery, damaged wildlife habitat, and caused severe erosion.

The Forest Service routinely had to spend money to close and revegetate a significant portion of its timber access roads and skid roads each year to protect watersheds. If the timber removed on many such roads did not even cover the costs of building them — never mind the added costs of either maintaining or revegetating them — then why was the government so intent on logging the area? Recreationists and economists from the 1960s into the 1990s increasingly raised these questions.[43]

Along with the economic critique of the timber program came an ecological one. In the tradition popularized by Rachel Carson in *Silent Spring,* more and more biologists questioned the wisdom of aggressive chemical control of insects and diseases. (Aerial spraying of insecticides on the national forests increased 300 percent between 1950 and 1960 to over a million acres of treatment a year.)[44] Advanced research on the ecological role of fire also strengthened the minority of professional and lay persons questioning the wisdom of aggressive fire suppression.[45] Thus, as the timber program came under increasing scrutiny, the heretofore nearly unchallenged professional consensus on the desirability of intensive management for maximum production found itself on the defensive.

Continued Imbalance in Funding

During the 1950s, the Democrats had repeatedly criticized the Eisenhower administration for having abandoned conservation to curry favor with big business. In most cases, such charges were overstated political rhetoric, given that Democrats had controlled both houses of Congress and thus the government's purse strings for six of Ike's eight years in office. The Democrats deserved a large share of the blame for natural resource management failures in the 1950s. The problem was not partisan. In any case, the Kennedy administration presented Democrats a chance to showcase their own version of conservation. What did it look like? First, the overall Forest Service budget shot up dramatically under presidents Kennedy and Johnson. (The 1961 Development Program for the National Forests and the creation of the Bureau of Outdoor Recreation in 1962 provided organizational rationales and institutional support for this increase.)[46] But the agency's budget had also grown greatly under Eisenhower. What was the difference? The Democratic administrations supported greater boosts to recreational development. Demands to protect and enhance recreation resources became a populist chant: The national forests were "the people's forests." Advocates of recreation contrasted "public use" with "corporate abuse." Traditionally, Democrats rallied to the populist banner more often than Republicans. In the 1950s and 1960s, Democrats sensed the potential strength of this new, growing recreation constituency and artfully courted it by becoming more responsive than Republicans to requests for recreation oriented federal funding. The Forest Service's recreation budget jumped from approximately $15 million in FY 1961 to $35 million in FY 1968. This is about double the increase that occurred under Eisenhower's two terms in total dollars. For the first time, the recreation budget nearly equaled the timber sale budget. Even so, recreation facilities and maintenance capabilities had fallen so far behind existing needs during the previous two decades that these increases remained substantially below agency requests and kept the agency behind its implementation schedule.[47]

Failure to adequately support the Forest Service's reforestation and stand improvement program had provided another focus for Democratic criticism of the Eisenhower administration during the 1950s. As noted in the last chapter, however, the Democratic critics could not muster much more than rhetorical support from their own party for this program. This changed in 1961. Like recreation, the reforestation and timber stand improvement budget (referred to below as "reforestation" for brevity) rose dramatically. But unlike the recreation budget, increases for reforestation had no staying power. Congress approved nearly a threefold increase in the first year of the Kennedy administration — from $4.4 million in FY 1961 to $12.8 million in FY 1962, certainly due in part to leftover momentum from the Anderson-Mansfield Reforestation Act of 1960 — but funding then generally leveled off, with the agency receiving only about 60–70 percent of its requests between FY 1964 and 1968.

Thus, changes were made to the Forest Service budget that markedly improved the relative position of recreation, along with a brief flurry of support for reforestation; but beyond this, the status quo of the 1950s prevailed. Like the Eisenhower administration, the Democrats charged full speed ahead with a massive, subsidized, and environmentally destructive timber harvest program, while never extending adequate compensatory support for resource rehabilitation. Even Cliff, the consummate defender of maximized production, recalled after retirement, "We always, without ex-

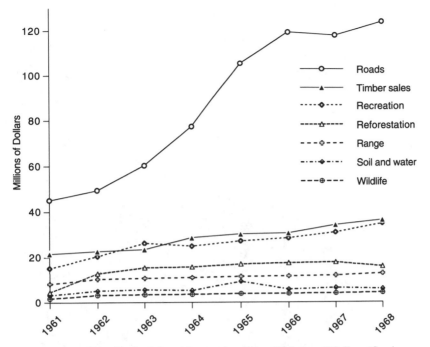

12. Comparison of Funding for Selected Programs, 1961–1968. Source: U.S. Forest Service, Washington Office, Budget Branch, "Budgets, 1961–1970, Composite Comparison" (Aug. 13, 1970), in Forest History Society archives, Western Timber Association records, box 31.

ception, were trying to get funded on a balanced basis, but were not successful in getting the recognition needed for the non-revenue-producing or low-revenue activities. Even in timber management it was out of balance. We could get money for timber sales, but money for reforestation and stand improvement was way behind, was under the recommended program level. This continued to be a problem during the period that I was chief."[48] Perhaps in bluff, certainly in frustration, Cliff went so far as to threaten to unilaterally reduce timber sales in 1970 if more balanced funding was not forthcoming. Issuing the warning in a pamphlet titled, "The Forest Service in the Seventies," he stated, "we can no longer afford to emphasize programs that produce revenues at the expense of others."[49] (See fig. 12 to compare the relative funding levels for selected forest management programs between 1961 and 1968. In figs. 13–15, compare the budget requests of the Forest Service, the Agriculture Department, and the Budget Bureau [shortly to

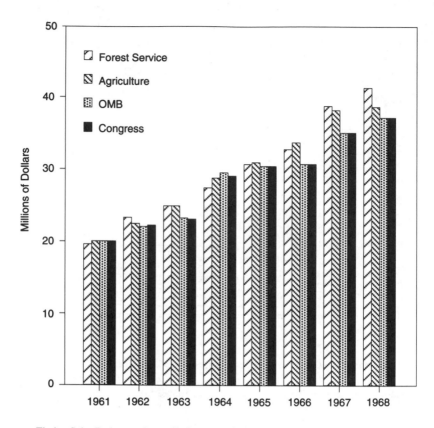

13. Timber Sales Budget, 1961–1968. Source: U.S. Forest Service, Washington Office, Budget Branch, "Budgets, 1961–1970, Composite Comparison" (Aug. 13, 1970), in Forest History Society archives, Western Timber Association records, box 31.

become the Office of Management and Budget, the OMB] with actual congressional appropriations for selected resource management programs for FYS 1961–68.)

It is important to remember that actual Forest Service budget requests did not reflect the agency's unconstrained assessment of its funding needs. At the local level, managers based their budget requests on the money they received the previous year slightly adjusted to their expectations of what they could ask for in the coming year based on the president's overall budget. Washington Office funding requests had to stay under an arbitrary overall ceiling imposed ahead of time by the Budget Bureau. Nor were Budget Bureau constraints distributed equitably across all resource pro-

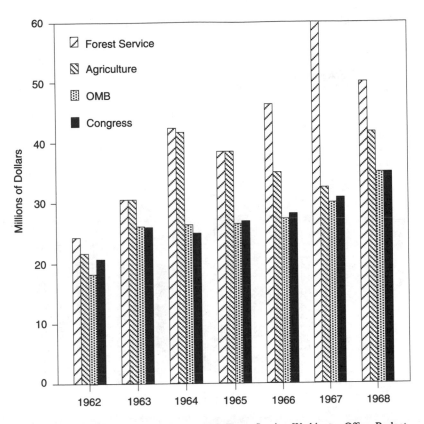

14. Recreation Budget, 1961–1968. Source: U.S. Forest Service, Washington Office, Budget Branch, "Budgets, 1961–1970, Composite Comparison" (Aug. 13, 1970), in Forest History Society archives, Western Timber Association records, box 31.

grams. As shown in earlier chapters, fiscal managers looked much more favorably upon immediate revenue generating activities, or management activities that at least stimulated economic development if revenues did not cover expenses. The agency thus knew it could push its timber sales and road construction requests to the practical limit without serious political repercussions. In contrast, requests for nonrevenue generating management activities met with resistance. The agency had to approach these budget items with a conservative pen. It reflected poorly on the administration, for example, when the agency asked for two or three times more for soil and water management than the partisan Agriculture Department or Budget Bureau were willing to approve. No president's handlers would tolerate this

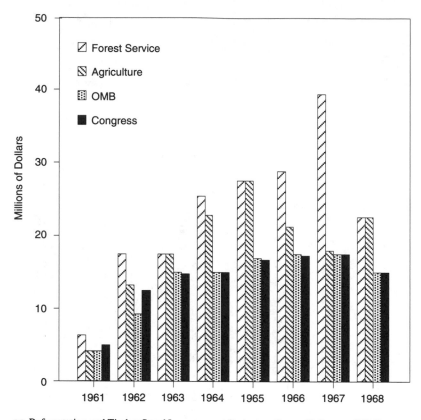

15. Reforestation and Timber Stand Improvement Budget, 1961–1968. Source: U.S. Forest Service, Washington Office, Budget Branch, "Budgets, 1961–1970, Composite Comparison" (Aug. 13, 1970), in Forest History Society archives, Western Timber Association records, box 31.

situation.[50] There was an identifiable pattern in which success in garnering a large budget increase for a program encouraged continued requests for large increases in that line item until the agency achieved its optimally desired funding level or until political support for the increases waned. Conversely, when a large requested increase was denied, the agency usually scaled back its requests in subsequent years until the political climate changed. (This pattern still inheres in budget politics today.) Only when the agency received permission to produce a long-range management plan with an attached unconstrained budget did it have greater latitude in funding requests. Until the 1970s, such wish list budgets appeared only in 1959 and in 1961 in the context of the long-range "Development Program for the National Forests." Otherwise annual budget requests generally remained subject to political constraints. (A new national forest planning act passed in 1974 — discussed in greater detail in Chapter 11 — attempted overtly but unsuccessfully to eliminate political constraints over Forest Service budget requests. The Reagan administration succeeded in firmly reestablishing political control.)

Conclusion

The eight-year reign of Democrats proved to be remarkably similar to the Eisenhower years regarding national forest management: intensive production of commodities with increased attention to recreation continued as the leitmotif of the 1960s. Recreation was popular and carried in its wake a form of indirect economic stimulation to rural communities that made it attractive to legislators. Because recreation fees generated little revenue, subsidies for recreational development (campgrounds, boat ramps, etc.) were substantial. Environmental groups and hunting and fishing organizations had gained clout in the political arena and successfully captured a share of the federal pie. This is not surprising. Recreation management is a form of development, requiring construction, maintenance, and federal expenditures in local economies. Recreationists liked it, local chambers of commerce grew to appreciate it, and the Forest Service fully supported it. Members of Congress could bring home the bacon and please a broad spectrum of constituents almost without negative repercussions (aside from the ecological ones, which did not much concern legislators), so long as recreation management did not interfere with other economically important resource development activities. The national forests were, after all, dedicated to "multiple use."

Accelerated recreation development coincided with an even more spectacular growth in the timber sales and road building budgets, however — despite the fact that the actual volume of timber harvested climbed at a slower rate. Thus, the rise of recreation did not initiate any real redistribution of priorities or funding; it instead reflected continued government efforts to expand the overall resource pie through more intensive management and capital investment. Congress, in fact, failed to recognize that recreational development has a significant impact on forest ecosystems too, requiring even more mitigation efforts. Resource management activities associated with the maintenance of forest health and productivity continued to receive short shrift. Reforestation constituted the only exception to this trend — a temporary and limited exception, as explained earlier. This represented an incremental improvement in efforts to get politicians to lend more than rhetorical support to the policy of sustained yield. But the funds were still significantly less than the agency needed to sustain the high volume of timber sales. Environmental policy innovations in the 1960s, such as the Wilderness Act, had relatively little effect on actual forest management, which remained wedded to the dream of maximizing all uses simultaneously and harmoniously. Environmentalists would try again to reform forest management in the 1970s. In the meantime, the conspiracy of optimism veiled from public view the general failure to implement the principles embodied in the Multiple Use–Sustained Yield Act.

II

From Gridlocked Conflict to Compromised
Policy Reform, 1969–1976

The Nixon administration came into office in 1969 at the beginning of a
major period of controversy over forest management. In some cases Nixon
exacerbated contention with his actions, while at other times his administration simply found itself caught in the crossfires of opposing interest groups.
Growing public opposition to clearcutting, increasing litigation by environmentalists, continuing logging pressure from the timber industry, lumber
supply anxieties, and congressional gridlock climaxed in the mid-1970s
with the enactment of two major laws that completely recast Forest Service
statutory authority: the 1974 Forest and Rangeland Renewable Resources
Planning Act (RPA) and the 1976 National Forest Management Act
(NFMA). The former was an ambitious but ineffective attempt to achieve
better integration of resource planning with budgeting. Building on the
agency's previous history with multiple use planning, RPA required the
Forest Service to develop comprehensive long-range multiple use management plans, updated every five years (subsequently called RPA Programs),
accompanied by a description of funds necessary to implement the plans.
Remarkably, this law also directed the executive branch to submit a budget
request consistent with the Forest Service's RPA driven budget or else
explain in detail why its budget deviated from the agency's. As with other
Forest Service long-range plans, the flurry of attention following each RPA
Program helped improve the relative balance of funding somewhat for a
year or two, but then the status quo generally returned.

The National Forest Management Act of 1976 continued this emphasis
on long-range planning but mandated individual forest plans to supplement

the national plan developed in Washington under RPA. Theoretically, the two types of planning — top down and bottom up — would be eventually integrated, although this integration has not yet effectively been achieved. NFMA, more than RPA, represented a curious bundle of compromises and inconsistencies. Enacted after a successful lawsuit by environmentalists that threatened to end clearcutting on the national forests, the NFMA legally authorized clearcutting and thereby preserved the silvicultural status quo on the national forests. The law also incorporated a number of clauses supported by environmental interests, including a mandate to maintain viable populations of native species of wildlife and preserve natural vegetation diversity. In practice, however, the environmental protection mandates in NFMA took a back seat to wood production in the first round of forest plans produced in the 1980s.

Events under the Nixon-Ford Administrations

In the name of balanced budget policy, Nixon's Office of Management and Budget (OMB) reverted ideologically to the Eisenhower years by emphasizing revenue generating programs while cutting nonrevenue generating ones. But unlike Eisenhower's Budget Bureau, Nixon's OMB applied its fiscal scalpel to the road budget too, incurring the wrath of the timber industry. In an attempt to reduce fiscal outlays, Nixon cut appropriated funds for road construction, forcing greater use of timber purchaser road credits for timber access. But, as explained earlier, many timber sales could not proceed without road subsidies, especially in regions like the Rocky Mountains, Great Basin, and Southwest. The entire industry pulled together and harangued the Nixon administration and Congress to restore funding to the maximum amount. Also angering industry, Nixon tried to cut funds for reforestation and timber stand improvement, which caused the Forest Service to threaten to freeze the allowable cut accordingly. In contrast to its insouciance during the Eisenhower years, industry in the 1970s lobbied assertively for reforestation and timber stand improvement funds. The Forest Service by then had sufficiently impressed upon timber purchasers the essential connection between more money for these activities and more timber sales for them.

Nixon's propensity to concentrate authority and discretion in the executive branch and his growing antagonism with Congress had additional repercussions on national forest management. As Congress continued to appropriate more money for programs that Nixon had tried to cut — which is their prerogative — Nixon finally responded by "impounding" appropriated funds, refusing to release selected portions of what Congress had approved. He did this for both road construction and reforestation funds for the national forests in 1973. A showdown appeared imminent about the time the Watergate scandal broke. Nixon's fall from power in 1974 precipitated a surge of legislative activism in which Congress greatly extended its influence over administrative matters and chastened the executive branch, especially OMB. In the next few years Congress passed the Resources Planning Act and the National Forest Management Act. Both were prescriptive legislation specifying in unprecedented detail the authorities and objectives of Forest Service management. During the House floor debate on RPA, Congressman Don H. Clausen of California summarized, "The intent of the legislation is to establish more congressional control over the management activities and appropriation processes of the national forest system lands."[1] And that it did.

But controversies specific to the national forests rather than generalized political battles between the Congress and the Executive really shaped events of the late 1960s and 1970s. Besides ubiquitous brush fires over wilderness designations, a related conflagration over clearcutting occupied the attentions and inflamed the passions of most everyone involved in national forest policy or management.

The Clearcutting Controversy

Until the 1950s, the Forest Service aggressively defended selective cutting of mature trees only, leaving younger trees and most of the forest ecosystem as intact as possible during the process of harvesting. But clearcutting was usually the most economically efficient method of harvesting. Furthermore, the vision of intensively managed wood fiber farms demanded replacement of the natural forest with homogeneous, even-aged stands of evenly spaced commercial species that would provide the greatest growth of the desired wood product in the least amount of time. Even-aged stands also facilitated efficient harvesting of the second crop of trees. As tree-farming technology advanced, and as the intensive management capabilities of the Forest Service expanded, clearcutting became the silvicultural method of choice.[2] The switch to clearcutting, accompanied by a plethora of experimental research defending its usefulness, met resistance.

In 1964, the banner year for wilderness advocates, Forest Service officials in West Virginia announced that henceforth "even-aged management" (clearcutting) would be practiced on the Monongahela National Forest. A few years later the effects of that decision caught up with the agency, with staggering repercussions. It began with a visit by some irate West Virginia turkey hunters to Chief Cliff in the early days of the Nixon administration. Cliff recalled: "They were very upset because there was some timber harvesting [clearcutting] in the area that they had been using for years for turkey hunting. They felt that the cutting that was being done was not compatible with hunting. They demanded that this be stopped." Cliff dismissed them as "a very self-centered protest from a very small segment of the population who wanted the national forest to be managed just for their own personal pleasure."[3] He failed to recognize that the hunters represented the tip of an iceberg of outrage over clearcutting which would shortly end the generally smooth sailing even-aged management had enjoyed on the national forests for the past decade or so. Cliff soon regretted having underestimated the resolve of the turkey hunters and the extent of grass-roots opposition to clearcutting.

The same year that the agency announced even-aged management for the Monongahela (1964), it was bulldozing terraces into steep, clearcut hillsides in Montana's Bitterroot National Forest, ostensibly to aid reforestation efforts, and it was preparing to offer an 8.75 *billion* board foot sale of timber in the Tongass National Forest of Alaska (a sale covering a million acres) in which clearcutting would be the primary harvesting method.[4] By 1970, grass-roots revolts against the Forest Service's timber program had erupted from New Hampshire to California, from Alaska to Georgia. Local efforts, as usual, presaged national campaigns by the organized environmental groups.

Because of the growing controversy, policy leaders in Washington initiated several studies of "the problem." Between 1969 and 1971, the Forest Service produced internal reviews of the Monongahela and Bitterroot forests, along with a report on four forests in northwestern Wyoming. In December 1969, Democratic Congressman Lee Metcalf of Montana asked the

School of Forestry at the University of Montana to analyze the Bitterroot controversy independently, while early in 1970 the West Virginia House of Delegates established a commission to study the Monongahela situation. Later that year, Senator Frank Church scheduled oversight hearings on clearcutting to take place early in the summer of 1971. Finally, Nixon established a President's Advisory Panel on Timber and the Environment (PAPTE) in September 1971. All of these panels, committees, commissions, and study groups submitted reports between 1969 and 1973, and all of them contained some criticism of Forest Service timber harvesting practices.[5] Even Ralph Nader's public interest warriors ("Nader's Raiders") got into the act, producing a book-length indictment alleging Forest Service mismanagement of the public trust.[6]

The Wyoming Forest Study Team, composed of six Forest Service researchers and managers, reported in 1971 that the Forest Service had indeed made some mistakes in timber management, which it now recognized and was attempting to correct. No crisis loomed, they said, but the agency urgently needed to emphasize nontimber values more in order to improve the quality of land management and recoup "public confidence and trust." "This will not be achieved by rhetoric," they said, "but will require repeated demonstration that declarations for quality in management are actually appearing as physical accomplishment on the ground."[7] On behalf of their agency, the reviewers accepted partial blame for management deficiencies: "It is apparent now that the estimates of allowable cut were partly based on over-optimistic assumptions." They criticized timber sale policies for encouraging harvests "without adequate provision for land restoration and regeneration," adding that the costs of regeneration sometimes exceeded the value of the timber sold. And regarding controversial programs of salvage logging for pest control, they acknowledged that "the use of timber cutting as a means of control of bark beetle infestation led to logging where no logging should have been done. The experience of the past 10 years has demonstrated that this logging was largely a vain effort but at one time it appeared to be a logical extension of Forest Service policies aimed at forest protection."[8] They defended clearcutting as appropriate silviculture under certain conditions, but judged the size, shape, and frequency of clearcuts to have been excessive. They feared that "past misuse of the technique might result in the loss of clearcutting as a silvicultural option."[9]

In addition to accepting blame, this Forest Service report also pointed to the external source of many of the problems: "the apparent overharvest of timber was partly a response to Federal law and USDA regulations that the Forest Service harvest timber to satisfy an obvious public need." In other words, higher-ups in the administration and Congress demanded certain outputs that were often incompatible with resource protection policies. The central source of management deficiencies, they concluded, involved "inadequacies and imbalance in manpower and money." Multiple use and sustained yield policies could not be implemented without adequate staffing and financing.[10] Although the authors of the report admitted that the agency's high-yield logging program had been based partly on unreliably optimistic assumptions, they still implied that more capital investments and labor could resolve the deficiencies and the public controversies.

Probably the most widely cited and influential of all the reports was that by the University of Montana's School of Forestry under the leadership of Professor Arnold Bolle. The "Bolle Report," as it came to be called, pulled no punches in its assessment of the clearcutting and terracing controversy on the Bitterroot National Forest. Published in December 1970, the report opened with a dramatic summary of its findings. The first of fifteen findings asserted, "Multiple use management, in fact, does not exist as the governing principle on the Bitterroot National Forest." Having disposed of that Forest Service policy cornerstone, a second finding suggested that the other cornerstone of national forests management — sustained yield — had also been abandoned: "The management sequence of clearcutting-terracing-planting cannot be justified as an investment for producing timber on the BNF. We doubt that the Bitterroot National Forest can continue to produce timber at the present harvest level." Another finding made a distinction between timber *management* and timber *mining*: "Timber *management,* i.e. continuous production of timber crops, is rational only on highly productive sites, where an appropriate rate of return on invested capital can be expected" (emphasis in original).[11] The report then accused the Forest Service of engaging in extractive, essentially nonrenewable timber mining. They did not recommend ending the practice of timber mining, but did argue that if timber mining continued, it must be under a closely regulated "single-tree selection cutting" regime, fully protecting nontimber values and minimizing disturbance to "residual" vegetation and scenic values. In other words,

248

no more clearcutting on marginally productive sites — which included most of the remaining unlogged national forest lands in Montana.

The Bolle Report went on to indict the political, bureaucratic, fiscal, and historical causes of this policy failure, an indictment that, in fact, neatly summarizes the thesis of this present book:

> In a federal agency which measures success primarily by the quantity of timber produced weekly, monthly, and annually, the staff of the Bitterroot National Forest finds itself unable to change its course, to give anything but token recognition to related values, or to involve most of the local public in any way but as antagonists.
>
> The heavy timber orientation is built in by legislative action and control, by executive direction and by budgetary restriction. It is further reinforced by the agency's own hiring and promotion policies and it is rationalized in the doctrines of its professional expertise.
>
> This rigid system developed during the expanded effort to meet national housing needs during the post-war boom. It continues to exist in the face of a considerable change in our value system — a rising public concern with environmental quality. While the national demand for timber has abated considerably, the major emphasis on timber production continues.[12]

Not all academic or professional foresters agreed with the Bolle Report's critical assessment, of course. The report of the PAPTE panel established by Nixon differed strikingly from the Bolle Report. Published in April 1973, it represented essentially a defense of the status quo. The report's summary outlined twenty recommendations. Number one asked for a presidential proclamation "emphasizing . . . the opportunities to improve substantially the productivity" of the national forests. Number two asked the president to require federal agencies to prepare a "nationwide program of forest development and timber supply." Number four recommended that all commercial forest lands not segregated for special protection (such as wilderness) "should be designated for commercial timber production," along with other "compatible" uses. Number six called for "retaining all proven and efficient methods of timber harvest, including clearcutting, under appropriate conditions."[13]

All of these recommendations contained qualifying statements about

The U.S. Forest Service resorted to radical measures such as clearcutting and terracing entire mountainsides on the Bitterroot and other national forests in the northern Rocky Mountains in the 1960s and early 1970s to maximize harvest levels. The terracing was designed to facilitate efficient replanting and future harvesting. A special tree-planting machine could drive along the terraces plugging seedlings into the ground. Decades later the terraces would allow easy access for logging machinery. A technological optimist would look at this scene and see order and productivity. Others see destruction and human arrogance. These two competing visions clashed in a bitter battle over national forest management policy in the early 1970s. *Photo: Bitterroot National Forest, Blue Joint drainage. © Dale A. Burk, 1971.*

preserving environmental quality and protecting soil, water, wildlife, and other nontimber values. Such statements were necessary to give the appearance of a balanced presentation. But the heart of Nixon's panel beat loudest for wood products — enhanced production of wood products, to be exact. Number eight stated, "The annual harvest on lands available for commercial timber production on western national forests can be increased substantially." It is important to recall here that the acreage defined as "commercial timberland" on the national forests had climbed steadily, from 78 million acres in 1946 to 96 million acres in 1968, the latter figure representing more than 50 percent of the total national forest land base.[14] Specifically, the Nixon panel report concluded, old-growth harvests could be raised from 50 to 100 percent above current levels. To encourage this accelerated cutting, the Forest Service should "promptly review and revise policies for allowable cut determinations."[15]

The terracing fiasco in Montana in fact resulted from efforts to raise the allowable cut. Commercially worthless lodgepole pine was clearcut and sold for pennies, after which the agency groomed the land so that machines could replant valuable ponderosa pine in neat rows. Natural forests that happened to be commercially "unproductive" were thus transformed into "timber crop." This permitted agency timber managers to raise their estimates of future lumber supply which, in turn, permitted them to increase the current allowable cut.[16] This kind of intensive management on marginally productive forests represented the worst form of subsidized timber exploitation. "The only way to justify the practice," the Bolle Report stated, "is to *ignore* economic analysis as a tool of decision-making."[17] Unfazed by such objections, Nixon's panel sought to reinforce the 1950s cornucopian ideology, calling for more timber production *and* more protection of nontimber values simultaneously. However, the preachers of this faith were losing much of their flock. To many observers, terracing on the Bitterroot belied noble promises. More and more, dissenters from the old status quo demanded reform rather than optimistic platitudes.

The Forest Service Environmental Program for the Future
In the face of these challenges, the Washington Office of the Forest Service drafted a new comprehensive plan for national forest management to replace the 1961 Program for the National Forests released under the Kennedy

administration. But instead of reform, the agency offered a simple reconstruction of the ideology of intensive management for maximum production
recast into 1970s jargon. Called "The Forest Service Environmental Program for the Future," this national multiple use management plan epito-
mized the conspiracy of optimism. Produced, like its predecessor, in response to a party change in administration, the plan attempted to respond to
the policy preferences of the Nixon White House as well as the personal
preferences of Chief Edward Cliff. Page 2 described two 1970 executive
directives by Nixon, the first one requiring the agency to find ways to
increase softwood lumber production and the second one requiring it to take
"environmental considerations . . . into account at the earliest possible stage
of the decisionmaking process." Predictably, the former directive dealing
with commodity production mandated a concrete objective, while the latter
directive dealing with environmental protection called only for the agency
to "consider" environmental values.[18]

At the same time that internal and external national forest management
reviews were claiming that the logging program had violated multiple use
principles, overreached biological capabilities, and exceeded social acceptability, the Nixon administration and the Forest Service Washington Office
were promoting a dramatic escalation in timber production, to be achieved,
of course, in full compliance with other multiple use and environmental
quality objectives. The Environmental Program's timber management objectives fully reveal the Washington Office's dissociation from reality:
Within ten years the allowable cut would be increased by 70 percent, from
13.6 bbf to 21 bbf (the same target, incidentally, aimed for in the agency's
1958 Timber Resources Review). To accomplish this goal, the Forest Service explained that it would have to (1) dedicate at least 97 million acres of
the national forests to commercial timber production — meaning no more
wilderness or other withdrawals for watershed, recreation, or wildlife in
areas considered to have commercial logging potential; (2) make "timely,
adequate, and successful investments in reforestation and intensive silviculture to result in added growth of 3.4 billion board feet" — meaning spend
vast sums of money to artificially maximize growth of usable wood fiber;
and (3) achieve "an additional 1.8 billion board feet of harvest from areas
and species not included in current harvesting plans" — that is, squeeze
every last potential board foot out of the forests whether there is a market for

it or not. An even more untenable expression of production-optimism followed these objectives. Near the end of the timber management section, the agency announced that along with this 70 percent increase in logging, it would develop "publicly acceptable timber harvesting and access practices [road construction] which are compatible with scenic beauty, water quality, and other intangible environmental values; and . . . [develop] a technology that will permit harvesting timber from fragile areas without environmental degradation and within the range of economic feasibility."[19]

This Environmental Program for the Future simply represented a recycled version of the grand development schemes of the 1950s and 1960s accompanied by glib promises to make that development socially acceptable, environmentally benign, and economically reasonable. To achieve social and environmental acceptability, the agency proposed to invest equally exorbitant funds on recreation development, wildlife habitat improvements, and soil erosion control. But these investments would not satisfy those who opposed intensive timber production on the national forests as a matter of principle nor would they likely mitigate the environmental damages of this extravagant logging program to a socially acceptable level. Nor would such extensive investments in either silviculture or the other multiple uses ever become cost-effective. The law of diminishing returns would compound the already existing deficits to astronomical proportions. This pie-in-the-sky management proposal had only two functions: to keep the agency busy and its budget fat, and to deflect political pressure.

Environmental groups, in pursuit of real change and convinced it was unlikely to come from the executive or legislative branches, increasingly turned to the courts to defend nontimber multiple use values and to attempt to block timber sales in remaining roadless areas. The judicial branch soon proved to be an effective forum for advancing environmental goals. Litigation proliferated. A representative of the Western Lumber Manufacturers wrote to a colleague in November 1969, warning:

Since J. Michael McCloskey became chief of staff of the Sierra Club earlier this year, George Craig and I have noticed increasing reference to legal procedures being tested and contemplated by the Club. This same interest in resolving public land use issues in the courtroom is being displayed by a number of other preservationist organizations.

... At the WLM annual meeting ... the Regional Forester warned our membership to expect future legal moves to block timber sales in presently unroaded national forest areas which groups hope to have classified as wilderness.[20]

Environmentalists' ability to sue the Forest Service over management decisions received a boost with the passage of the National Environmental Policy Act of 1969.[21] NEPA required agencies of the federal government to prepare environmental impact statements before undertaking significant actions affecting the human environment. Other lawsuits sought to enforce the Multiple Use–Sustained Yield Act.[22] The most influential of all, the anti-clearcutting lawsuit which the West Virginia turkey hunters initiated with the Izaak Walton League, utilized an old, almost forgotten dinosaur of a law: the 1897 National Forest Organic Act. Before reviewing that lawsuit and its results, however, two important legislative initiatives, in 1969 and 1974, must be discussed.

The National Timber Supply Bill of 1969

In 1967 and 1968, wholesale lumber prices unexpectedly went through the roof, rising 37 percent in just eighteen months. Housing prices escalated accordingly. Congress had been considering legislative means to improve opportunities for every American family to own their own home, and coincidentally passed the 1968 Housing and Urban Development Act, which established unrealistically high goals for new housing starts. Nearly one-fourth of the new homes were to be priced for low to moderate income families. The rise in lumber prices threatened these goals. At the same time, purchasers of federal timber paying these higher prices felt disadvantaged in the competition against companies that owned their own timber supplies. They advocated increased harvests from national forests to saturate the market enough to bring prices back down.[23] Consequently, an odd coalition of industry, pro-business congressmen, and pro–social welfare congressmen joined to support new legislation in 1969 facilitating increased logging of the national forests.

A series of congressional hearings and committee reports on lumber prices, most notably that of the Senate Banking Committee in March 1969, repeatedly urged an increase in the sale of federal timber as the appropriate response to rising prices and a fear of softwood lumber shortages. The fear of a lumber shortage was exacerbated in 1969 with the publication of the Forest Service's *Douglas-fir Supply Study,* which concluded that timber production from national forests in the coastal Northwest had already exceeded sustained yield and would inevitably decline in coming decades — especially supplies of softwood sawtimber (large conifers valuable for lumber). Those faithful to sustained yield policy suggested minor reductions in timber sales in the short term in order to avoid a crash in the future. Those who wanted to keep production at current levels had at least four counterarguments: (1) sustained yield should be waived until after the old-growth liquidation phase; (2) other timber supplies from Canada or from second- and third-growth forests elsewhere in the United States would make up for shortfalls in the future; (3) technological innovation would enhance the timber supply and moot current assumptions; and (4) sustained yield was an outmoded, unnecessary policy. The first two arguments ignored the issue of local community stability in favor of a national or international perspective on timber supply. While corporate executives in New York or Seattle could talk easily about the industry migrating to new regions, most people working in rural logging towns felt differently about the issue. The third argument involving the technological fix was a familiar keystone in the conspiracy of optimism. But public confidence in techno-fixes had substantially eroded during the 1960s. It would be a hard sell. The fourth argument to abandon sustained yield was contrary to established policy and the chances of repealing federal commitment to it seemed remote. Most importantly, all of the arguments ignored the fact that many Americans, including many foresters, valued other characteristics of the national forests besides board feet of lumber.

Chief Edward Cliff strongly encouraged the calls for increased production, but with a caveat: allowable cuts should only be raised "when we earn the right to do so" by performing intensive reforestation of nonstocked lands, cultivation of poorly stocked lands, thinning, and more complete protection from fire and pests.[24] Industry lobbyists saw that the agency could essentially be bribed to increase harvesting by pouring funds into intensive timber management to assuage theoretical concerns for sustained yield. To achieve their goals, then, industry searched for a way to get more funds for intensive silviculture. Ironically, their solution lay in abandonment of their previous opposition to earmarked funds. The National Forest Products Association (NFPA, formerly the NLMA) helped draft a bill that would set up a "high yield timber fund" into which virtually all nondedicated receipts from the sale of national forest logs would go for intensive timber management. The bill also proposed that all national forest lands with marketable timber not previously reserved for wilderness preservation be dedicated to intensive timber production, with other uses subordinate. It further provided for rapid liquidation of old-growth forests in the Pacific Northwest, allowing a balloon of unsustainably high timber yields for a couple of decades during the process of converting old natural forests to young timber plantations. Widespread bipartisan support quickly developed in both the House and Senate.[25]

The Nixon administration supported the bill in principle but requested a few amendments, which were accommodated in a new House bill designated H.R. 12025 and favorably reported out of committee (with nearly unanimous endorsement) in September 1969. It looked like industry's day in the sun. Environmentalists mobilized. In their view, the bill repudiated the Multiple Use–Sustained Yield Act. Even Edward Crafts agreed with that assessment.[26] The Sierra Club argued that the bill would expand subsidies for destructive silvicultural practices, close options for additional wilderness designations in forested areas, and jeopardize funding for nontimber resource management programs. Increasingly sympathetic, the media aided the environmentalists' campaign with dramatic editorials, such as the *New York Times*'s "Raid on the Forests" and the *Louisville Courier Journal*'s "License to Pillage and Plunder."[27] Support for the bill steadily eroded between September, when the committee had favorably reported the bill, and February 1970, when the House had scheduled a vote on it. Sensing possible defeat, the bill's sponsors delayed the vote for a few weeks to allow time for them to recoup a majority. In the end, a majority could not be mustered so the bill's sponsors tabled it. During this battle, environmental and timber lobbies escalated their activities to a frenetic pitch, cementing the politics of confrontation. Other substitute bills were introduced, but the lack of consensus made legislation at the time impossible.[28]

The Areas of Agreement Committee and the 1974 Resources Planning Act

Seeking a constructive middle ground to relieve tensions and break the congressional deadlock, Bill Towell of the American Forestry Association

(AFA) invited representatives of the opposing groups to come together informally in May 1970 to search for areas of agreement. For the next six years, this committee of odd bedfellows met to hammer out joint positions on forestry matters, especially those related to the national forests.[29] Although the committee commanded respect from congressmen and the Forest Service, it could resolve no real issues. As might have been expected, the only way agreement among the opposing interests could be achieved was to readopt the old utopian conspiracy, which they essentially did. The committee's fundamental recommendation was to promote full funding for all Forest Service activities, assuming that if the agency received all the money it asked for it could both vastly increase *and* make compatible all resource outputs and services without environmental degradation. Year after year the committee lobbied OMB and presented testimony to congressional appropriations committees supporting increased funding across the board.[30] As we can see from the data in figure 16, however, the general imbalance established decades earlier remained intact, with two new trends particular to the Nixon administration: (1) a sudden jump in reforestation funds in FY 1972 (like that of FY 1962), which followed on the heels of the Forest Service's *Douglas-fir Supply Study* and its Environmental Program for the Future and a 1970 national timber supply survey;[31] and (2) the near parity in funding between timber sales and recreation that the Kennedy and Johnson administrations achieved ended under Nixon, as the timber sales budget climbed steadily while the recreation budget leveled off.

Although Towell's hope to reduce interest-group conflict remained unfulfilled, his objective of reopening the possibility of legislation did make headway. Partly as a result of the committee's work, Hubert Humphrey introduced a natural resources planning and development bill that quickly gained momentum. According to Robert Wolf, a forester working for the Congressional Research Service, Senator Humphrey had asked him in 1972 to draft a bill providing: (1) statutory guidance for long-range forest planning; (2) provisions designed to reduce conflict between interest groups and the Forest Service; and (3) a method for curtailing the power of OMB over federal programs endorsed by Congress. At the time, the struggle between the "imperial presidency" of Nixon and Democrats in Congress reached full steam. Humphrey introduced Robert Wolf's draft as S. 2296 on July 3, 1973. Hoping to develop support for the bill, Humphrey's staff asked Towell to

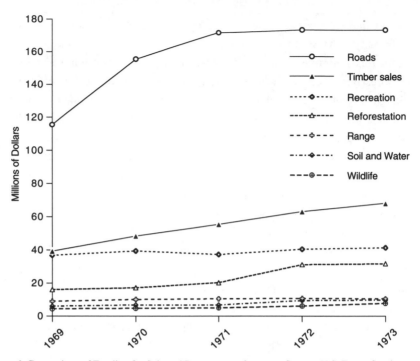

16. Comparison of Funding for Selected Programs, 1969–1973. Source: U.S. Forest Service, Washington Office, Budget Branch, "Timber Resource Management: Sales Administration and Management" (Feb. 21, 1973), in Forest History Society archives, Western Timber Association records, box 31.

gather together key members of his Areas of Agreement Committee to rework the draft into something acceptable to the majority. Towell cautiously invited only those members of his committee whom he considered to be "moderates." During September and October they drafted a new bill and submitted it to Humphrey. Humphrey and Congressman John R. Rarick (D-LA) then introduced new bills on November 7, 1973 (S. 2296, again, and H.R. 11320), with a collection of cosponsors that read like a Who's Who of Democratic leadership. After nine months of finagling, Congress passed the Forest and Rangeland Renewable Resources Planning Act 1974 (RPA). Although it had bipartisan support, the law was primarily a product of the Democratic leadership and reflected an attempt to circumscribe the powers of the executive. Many strategists expected a veto; at least OMB strongly recommended one. But as the bill went before the president for a signature, the president was going before the press protesting his innocence in the crimes of conspiracy and coverup. Nixon's resignation on August 9, 1974, left a number of bills unsigned, including RPA. Thus, one of Gerald Ford's first decisions in office was whether to veto RPA or not. Considering the extreme tension between Congress and the administration at the time, Ford evidently decided not to start off his tenure with an act of defiance.[32]

Primarily a policy for long-range planning, RPA required the Forest Service to periodically prepare three documents: (1) an assessment of the forest and rangeland situation in the United States; (2) a long-term program for national forest management with specific objectives along with budget estimates for all the resources, updated every five years and prepared with public participation; and (3) an annual report comparing agency accomplishments with the objectives of the RPA Program. Obviously these requirements endorsed standard operating procedures for the most part. Reform would be incremental. RPA also required the president to submit two documents: (1) a statement of policy to accompany each five-year RPA Program and to serve as the basis for annual budget requests; and (2) an explanation for any budget request that failed to provide the funds necessary to achieve the goals of the policy statement.[33] The Humphrey bill originally had *Congress* establishing the statement of policy every five years, but a compromise with House opponents gave that authority back to the president, with the caveat that Congress could amend the president's statement of policy or could reject it by a simple resolution of either the House or Senate. The requirement for an explanation of deviating budget requests was a slap at OMB. Congressional sponsors of RPA hoped that providing a mechanism for the Forest Service to release its own cost estimates would enable Congress to make better funding decisions. Similarly, Congress hoped that subjecting the executive to the indignity of explaining its deviations from the statement of policy might chasten efforts by OMB to manipulate the budget for fiscal or partisan reasons. The next chapter demonstrates how these hopes went unrealized.

RPA is an example of how natural resources legislation is not so much a product of rational goal-oriented decision making, as it is a product of considerations of political feasibility.[34] In the case of RPA, contending interest groups demanded inconsistent responses from government. When decision makers satisfied one group, they increased the dissatisfaction of another.

Dissatisfaction, when strong enough and widespread enough, paralyzes legislative action. To emerge from the post–National Timber Supply bill impasse, then, Congress had to find a course of action that would minimize dissatisfaction. First, RPA avoided making any specific resource allocations, since these were the crux of the dissatisfactions. Second, RPA constructed a policy framework that provided interest groups more access to Forest Service decision making. The legislators hoped this would not simply deflect controversy from them onto the agency but would actually reduce tensions by providing opportunities for meaningful public participation. Third, RPA promised each major interest group more of what they wanted through a budget reform mechanism designed to make it easier for the Forest Service to make full funding requests for full multiple use–sustained yield development. In other words, RPA endorsed the proven emollient that had served the agency so well for so many years: maximum accommodation of all uses. But it was precisely this ideology that environmentalists criticized and opposed: more intensive management with promises that it would be done better. This solution could not postpone conflict for long.

The Monongahela Lawsuit and the 1976 National Forest Management Act

The hoped-for truce in the battle over national forest management never materialized. Timber industry lobbyists continued to support reincarnated versions of the 1969 National Timber Supply bill, while opponents of intensive management continued to challenge specific development plans, below-cost timber sales, and clearcutting. One lawsuit, noted earlier in this chapter, adopted a novel approach. Looking for a handle with which to challenge clearcutting on the Monongahela, the West Virginia Division of the Izaak Walton League discovered language in the 1897 Organic Act related to timber harvesting that seemed perfectly suited to their purposes.

The 1897 Organic Act permitted the Secretary to sell only "dead, matured or large growth of trees" after individually marking and designating them.[35] Obviously, clearcutting violated these strictures. The law was written when selective cutting was considered the only acceptable form of sustainable silviculture. Foresters had abandoned that premise after World War Two, although clearcutting on the scale practiced by industry and the Forest Service still generated a great deal of professional debate. The 1897

Act also predated conditions in which the sheer scale and pace of harvesting rendered individual marking of trees impracticable. Enforcing this old statute would compel the agency to return to selective cutting and slow down the pace of harvesting. This is exactly what the Izaak Walton League wanted. (Industry apologists often accused environmental groups of trying to end timber harvesting. In fact, they only wanted to limit its extent and style of application on the national forests. The Sierra Club's official position papers opposing the National Timber Supply bill only opposed the liquidation of remaining old-growth forests in the Pacific Northwest. The club supported continued industrial forestry on roaded national forest lands.)[36] The language in the 1897 law was so clear and unequivocal that the League expected victory. Yet the established precedent for clearcutting and the monumental implications of a ban on clearcutting were so equally obvious that Forest Service lawyers likewise expected victory.[37]

Initiated on May 14, 1973, *Izaak Walton League v. Butz*[38] came to a swift conclusion. On November 6 of that year the District Court ruled in favor of the plaintiffs. Surprised but not yet panicking, the Forest Service appealed the decision to the Fourth Circuit Court of Appeals. On August 21, 1975, the Appeals Court upheld the lower court's decision.[39] Now the Forest Service panicked. The Appeals Court stated in its decision, "We are not insensitive to the fact that our reading of the Act will have serious and far reaching consequences, and it may well be that this legislation enacted over seventy-five years ago is an anachronism which no longer serves the public interest. However, the appropriate forum to resolve this complex and controversial issue is not the courts, but the Congress."

Immediately, the Forest Service, the timber industry, and their congressional allies began drafting legislation to repeal or revise the 1897 Act. On the other side, the large national environmental groups, somewhat stunned by this unmitigated triumph, began plotting a strategy to preserve their victory. Grass-roots organizations, such as the Texas Committee on Natural Resources headed by environmental lawyer Ned Fritz, pursued the Izaak Walton League's successful strategy only to find themselves opposed by the national groups who feared that additional favorable rulings would strengthen the hand of those mobilizing to repeal the 1897 Act. The prime strategy of the Sierra Club was to retain the old law by any means possible. In case that strategy failed, with the aid of other groups and congressional allies, they had drafted a substitute bill that compromised with the forces of industrial forestry while still retaining an emphasis on selective logging and environmental protection.[40] Senator Jennings Randolph (D-WV) went to bat for the reformers, introducing a bill based on negotiations with Professor Arnold Bolle, Edward Crafts, the Sierra Club's Gordon Robinson, and others. He dubbed his bill "the National Forest Timber Reform Act of 1976."[41] As "prescriptive" legislation, it would have established significant restrictions on forestry practices.

The timber industry, still pushing for a bill that would prioritize timber production wherever possible, hoped to exploit this window of opportunity presented by the Monongahela lawsuit and reassert a new version of the failed 1969 Timber Supply bill. The Forest Service itself hoped for a quick fix in the form of a simple repeal of the 1897 Act that left them maximum discretion. But as Chief John McGuire (who replaced Cliff in 1972) later recalled, "there was no chance of getting such a bill through Congress, because there were so many interests contending to put other things into the law."[42] Humphrey once more sponsored the compromise bill (with Robert Wolf again drafting it). The bill resulted from a search for the middle ground, again, but was primarily motivated by the perceived need to legalize clearcutting so that the Forest Service could get back to its task of rapidly liquidating its native forests and substituting even-aged forests of commercial species.

With the hope of broadening its support, Humphrey added numerous revisions to his bill, picking up some features supported by environmental groups in the Randolph bill. The legislative counterpart to Humphrey's bill on the House side, H.R. 15069, did not adopt as many of the environmentalist-backed restrictions as the Humphrey bill; environmental groups were unhappy with it. The conference committee, as usual, struck a compromise between the two. As a result, the conservation community split over whether or not to support the final version. Most of the wildlife groups and the AFA and SAF backed it, while the Sierra Club, Wilderness Society, Izaak Walton League, Natural Resources Defense Council, and Audubon Society opposed it. The lumber lobby had supported the House bill but opposed the Humphrey bill and the final version because it curbed rather than enhanced opportunities to maximize timber production. Not surprisingly, Towell's Areas of Agreement committee splintered and disintegrated in this atmosphere. The Ford administration throughout all this wrangling had tried to draft a bill of its own, but irresolvable differences between the agency, the Agriculture Department, and OMB soon consigned the administration to a role of commenting on congressional drafts. The Forest Service supported the Humphrey bill with a few reservations. With a slight majority of support, and in a very contentious atmosphere, the National Forest Management Act (NFMA) became law on October 22, 1976.[43]

The NFMA repealed the 1897 Organic Act. It adopted the clearcutting guidelines proposed by Senator Frank Church's committee (after extensive hearings on the controversy in 1971). These "Church guidelines" were supported by the Forest Service, and had been partly drafted by Edward Crafts. They kept Forest Service discretion intact with loopholes large enough to drive logging trucks through, and they applied mainly visual restrictions on clearcutting — such as the recommendation to hire more landscape architects to design smaller clearcuts with irregular boundaries conforming to landscape contours rather than large square blocks.[44] The law also required the Forest Service to preserve minimum viable populations of native wildlife (along with some nonnatives), and to protect multiple use values and environmental quality. It further expanded requirements for national forest management planning and provided additional opportunities for public involvement in that planning.

How the law dealt with the issue of sustained yield, however, is perhaps the most interesting and telling aspect of this so-called reform legislation. On the reform side, NFMA adopted a restrictive definition of sustained yield called "non-declining even-flow": a forest's output of timber must be capable of being sustained perpetually without declines (sec. 11). This may not sound new or different, but in fact it was a victory for environmentalists over the proponents of the timber supply bill who supported rapid old-growth liquidation. The western lumber industry strongly objected to the nondeclining even-flow clause because of its potential restriction of their access to old growth on the national forests. Timber purchasers preferred to quickly harvest the old-growth forests with the higher wood values to benefit the present generation. For example, George Craig of the Western Timber Association proposed departures from sustained yield before a subcommittee of the Senate Banking Committee in 1973, ostensibly to help lower lumber prices for the short term. He said the government should "increase offerings of

Federal timber for the next two or three decades with a clearly stated announcement that annual offerings from public lands in future decades may have to be reduced."[45] The nondeclining even-flow provision threatened to reduce national forest timber offerings because, as most knowledgeable observers then recognized, the supply of old growth was running low and second growth would not be available in time to make up the shortfall. Thus, either sustained yield policy had to be abandoned or else current harvests had to be slightly reduced to avoid a larger crash in the future. The nondeclining even-flow (NDEF) policy in NFMA reaffirmed agency commitment to sustained yield.

But as it turned out, NDEF did not result in immediately reduced harvests. The Forest Service and timber industry allies in Congress placed loophole language in the NFMA that allowed departures from NDEF under special circumstances, such as in the case of "salvage" logging (sec. 11[a] and 11[b]). More importantly, they also included language that allowed the agency to "earn" higher harvest levels through additional investments in intensive management. The latter loophole, a provision called "earned harvest effect" (sec. 6[g][3][D]), clearly reflected the continued dominance of techno-optimism and endorsed the very same management orientation that had led to the early 1970s forest management controversies. The earned harvest effect provision allowed the Forest Service to "permit increases in harvest levels based on intensified management practices, such as reforestation, thinning, and tree improvement."[46] In fact, it let forest managers increase current harvest levels (or maintain excessively high ones) entirely on the *expectation* of success for intensive management practices and the *expectation* of getting adequate funds for that intensive management, instead of making the agency actually "earn" the increased harvests through documented successes. This provision, however, included a mild safety stipulation: managers had to have a reasonable expectation that proposed intensive management practices would be successful and would be funded. If, at the end of a ten-year planning cycle, success or funding did not meet expectations, then NFMA managers were supposed to reduce the allowable harvest level.

The earned harvest effect (previously called the "allowable cut effect" by the Forest Service) proved to be quite a financial boon to the Forest Service timber program in many areas: wherever pressure to increase harvests existed, Congress could essentially buy the higher harvests from the Forest Service through increased funding for reforestation, thinning, fertilizing, or pest control. In turn, the forest managers could proclaim their continued dedication to sustained yield by promising higher future volumes through the earned harvest effect. The status quo had been maintained.

Conclusion

Despite NFMA's adoption of the more restrictive definition of sustained yield, unsustainable harvest levels and accelerated old-growth liquidation continued through the late 1970s and on into the 1980s, partly through the auspices of the earned harvest effect. Even the supposedly pro-environmental Carter administration pressed the Forest Service to purposefully depart temporarily from nondeclining even-flow near the end of its term in order to flood the timber market to bring down housing prices to fight inflation and recession.[47] As we will see in the next chapter, the first generation of forest plans developed under NFMA and released between 1982 and 1992 uniformly adopted unjustifiably optimistic assumptions to support high timber harvest targets. Technological optimism, administration pressure, and high timber quotas set in the annual appropriations acts remained the order of the day. The commitment to future generations implicit in the policy of sustained yield seemed always to yield to the demands of economic interests of the current generation.

Real reform would be postponed until the early 1990s when forest management monitoring showed that intensive silviculture was not as successful as predicted and that its negative impacts exceeded minimum legal standards of environmental protection. Simultaneously, many members of Congress began to feel that the financial costs of "earned" incremental increases to allowable harvests greatly exceeded their benefits. A revolution growing out of the collapse of the conspiracy of optimism was on the way.

12

Retrenchment and Revolt, 1977–1992

The short-lived Carter administration gained a reputation for being sympathetic to environmentalism, although this was only true in a limited sense. Many of Carter's environmental initiatives self-destructed for lack of political finesse or fell victim to congressional opposition, as in the case of Carter's western water project "hit list."[1] Carter's four years did not represent a golden age of environmental politics. In fact, the New Right political resurgence that came to be known in 1981 as the "Reagan revolution" had actually become quite well established in many ways by the late 1970s. Carter's environmental initiatives, though blunted, served to galvanize a pro-business, anti-regulatory, conservative backlash; just as the Reagan administration in turn energized an environmental opposition. With the aid of a slight conservative majority in a polarized Congress, the Reagan administration made an all-out effort to turn back the tide of environmental reform that had been building for two decades and sided unabashedly with the lobbyists for the business interests. Reasserting wildly optimistic goals for timber production (the old figure of 20 bbf surfaced again), the Reagan team in the Agriculture Department took specific, short-term steps to block environmental protection initiatives, such as ordering the Forest Service to increase road construction in roadless areas in order to eliminate the possibility of their being considered for wilderness at a future date, and ordering the relaxing of environmental protection standards in forest plans. Because of expanded requirements for public access to government information and decision making (greatly extended by RPA and NFMA), these top-down imposed initiatives could be easily brought into the light of day and criticized by opponents. But the business interests and the environmentalists mostly stalemated each other, as they had a decade and a half earlier during the clearcutting crisis.

The manifestations of political stalemate were varied and sometimes curious. While Congress blocked many of Carter's environmental initiatives, it also later blocked many of Reagan's anti-environmental initiatives. Often one house of Congress would block the other, or one legislative committee would work at cross purposes to another, depending on who chaired the respective committees. For example, while powerful pro-industry legislators in the appropriations committees set high timber harvest targets in Appropriation bills during the Reagan administration, their equally powerful colleagues in the Interior and Agriculture Committees held oversight hearings on national forest mismanagement and harangued the administration for its unbalanced priorities. This polarization rubbed off on the Forest Service, as lower level agency decision makers began openly criticizing and resisting what they felt were unrealistic mandates from Washington, D.C.

Like the stalemate of the 1960s that led to policy reform in the mid-1970s, the stalemate of the Reagan years led to a flood of reform initiatives in the late 1980s and early 1990s. But this time the reformers welled up from the grass roots — from the public and agency employees themselves — rather than from the halls of power in Washington, D.C. And this time the reform impulse took sharp aim at the ideology of intensive management, the whole style and philosophy of national forest management, with support from a new generation of foresters rebelling against tradition in their own discipline and agreeing that the old agronomic, techno-optimist model was dysfunctional. This reform movement, which ironically became firmly established during the time the Forest Service was celebrating the centennial of the national forest system, shook the conspiracy of optimism to its core.

The Continued Disjunction between Planning and Funding

The fundamental purpose of RPA and a major purpose of NFMA was to improve the quality of multiple use management planning on the national forests and to achieve better integration of management needs with funding. What happened in the relationship between planning and funding in the decade following these laws? Natural resource economist V. Alaric Sample thoroughly and masterfully analyzed that question in his 1990 monograph,

267

The Impact of the Federal Budget Process on National Forest Planning.
While RPA and NFMA immediately generated increased overall funds to
the agency and eventually led to improved resource inventories, better interdisciplinary planning, and more public participation, Sample nevertheless
found no evidence of any significant long-term improvement in the integration of program planning with program funding nor any long-term change in
the relative balance of program emphases during his study period of 1977–
86. For example, he cited a Forest Service study of 1985 which revealed that
accomplishment of individual RPA management objectives varied among
resource programs from 21 percent to 119 percent, with timber and roads at
the top and noncommodity programs at the bottom. "If the budget and
planning processes are indeed linked, the fact is not apparent from these
outcomes," he concluded.[2] Following is a summary of Sample's findings.

In late 1975, the Forest Service produced its first long-range comprehensive land management program under RPA guidelines. Fiscal year 1977 was
technically the first budget year reflecting RPA influences. Not coincidentally, the Forest Service budget for FY 1977 shot up higher than any other
single year since then. The RPA Program outlined budget requests totaling a
50 percent increase over FY 1976 levels and Congress approved 80 percent
of that increase. Throughout the Carter administration, Congress approved
an average increase of 6.5 percent annually in *real dollars*. This 6.5 percent
real growth substantially exceeded the real growth of the federal budget as a
whole. This picture contrasts sharply with the 1981–86 period. The Reagan
administration favored programs boosting economic growth while deem-
phasizing environmental protection and amenity programs. It accordingly
froze or reduced most noncommodity program budgets, and correspondingly tried but failed to increase the timber sale program. Economic recession in the early 1980s caused the lumber market to take such a dive that the
government ended up buying back timber sale contracts in the mid-1980s to
avoid contract defaults by timber purchasers. Thus, the overall Forest Service budget remained stagnant or suffered *real declines* during Reagan's
tenure.[3] But, importantly, the declines were not shared equally across the
board. As always, relative funding levels tell the real story — as does the
comparison of RPA budget targets to actual funding levels for each program.

Timber: Sample found that funding for timber programs remained quite generous throughout the years 1977–86 and came much closer to the RPA targets than any other resource program. Carter's Agriculture Department and OMB budget requests during these years consistently fell just slightly below the Forest Service's desired optimum budget targets. Also during the Carter years Congress approved more money for the timber program than either Agriculture or OMB asked for. This congressional generosity reflected continuing efforts to lower lumber prices, stimulate the housing industry, and boost the ailing economy in general. Under Reagan, between FYS 1982–86 the Agriculture Department and OMB requests were even closer to the RPA timber targets than under Carter, and in two of those years they actually exceeded the RPA target. Congress, however, was slightly less generous because of the early 1980s timber glut and later contract bailouts.

Recreation: A popular program, recreation received significant budgetary support under the Democratic administration between FY 1977 and FY 1981. Under Reagan, recreation funding declined. Even during the Carter administration, however, Agriculture, OMB, and Congress approved only half the RPA budget target for recreation. Under pressure from the higher-ups in the Carter administration, the Forest Service cut back its RPA budget targets for recreation in 1980 by nearly one-half. Yet during the Reagan years, Agriculture, OMB, and Congress still allocated budgets at only one-half to two-thirds of these reduced RPA targets.

Fish and Wildlife: This program followed the same pattern as the recreation program: substantial increases in FYS 1977–81 and then a leveling off or decline. With the exception of FYS 1977 and 1981, Agriculture, OMB, and Congress generally approved only about half the RPA target.

Soil and Water: Partly due to new Clean Water Act responsibilities, the soil and water budget shot way up in FY 1978, significantly above even the RPA target. Although declining somewhat in FYS 1979–81, it still remained high, just below the RPA target level. Then, from FY 1982 to FY 1986 the soil and water budget declined and the gap between the RPA target and actual funding widened steadily, until in FY 1985 actual funds were at half the targeted level.

Range management/livestock grazing: Although aimed at commodity production, this program fared little better than the noncommodity programs, indicating once again that the Forest Service tended to treat the livestock industry as a second-class constituency compared to the timber

269

industry. The pattern of relationships between RPA targets, Forest Service requests, Agriculture and OMB allowances, and congressional appropriations for the grazing program are nearly identical to that of the wildlife program.

Summary: Under Carter, all multiple uses received a boost in funding traceable to the influence of the first RPA Program. The relative balance between timber and nontimber programs, however, changed little. Timber related activities still received nearly the maximum amount targeted in RPA (and sometimes more) while nontimber programs got funded often at half the targeted levels. Under the Carter administration, the mechanism developed by RPA for displaying these discrepancies remained intact; that is, the Forest Service had a relatively free hand in determining RPA goals and budget targets, except that Carter's OMB fought successfully to have its own more conservative budget alternative inserted into the 1980 RPA Program alongside the agency's more liberal budget targets. This created an "RPA high-bound" budget and an "RPA low-bound" budget. Everyone, of course, knew that the high-bound budget targets represented the Forest Service proposal, while the lower figures represented OMB's perspective, so the discrepancies between OMB and the agency remained obvious.[4]

The Reagan administration, on the other hand, successfully regained control over the Forest Service and reined in RPA targets so that discrepancies were not so obvious. Assistant Secretary of Agriculture John Crowell established strict ceilings on Forest Service budget requests, demanding prior approval before the agency committed anything to writing. This enabled him to eliminate the obvious discrepancies between Forest Service and OMB budget requests. Crowell forced the Forest Service to conform its RPA targets to the OMB low-bound targets. On paper, it looked as though all the political players generally agreed with each other and with the natural resource professionals in the Forest Service. By 1986, the Reagan administration had successfully reestablished the pre-RPA status quo. More than that, it had erased most of the gains made during the Carter administration. National forest planning and funding had become wholly politicized again and consequently embroiled in unprecedented controversy.

Due to controversy over the forest plans being prepared under RPA and the National Forest Management Act (NFMA), Congress asked its Office of Technology Assessment (OTA) to analyze the strengths and weaknesses of

the forest planning process. The report, published in February 1992, concluded that (1) the development of forest plans emphasized timber and other
commodities while giving little attention to sustaining ecosystems; (2) the
monitoring and evaluation of forest management activities had been inadequate; (3) budget decisions overwhelmed planning decisions; and (4) output
targets imposed at the national level often nullified local management decisions.[5] These conclusions would have been valid had they been written at
any time since World War Two. Clearly the status quo established four
decades ago has been remarkably persistent.

A Renewed Wave of Opposition to the Forest Service's Timber Program

Timber management and its effect on other resources was the focus of a
major public debate in the 1980s. Timber production objectives continued to
drive decision making to the detriment of sustained yield and multiple use
policies. Jeff DeBonis, founder of the Association of Forest Service Employees for Environmental Ethics (AFSEEE), told *Common Cause* magazine in 1990, "There is tremendous pressure on timber planners, wildlife
biologists, hydrologists and others to suppress their professional expertise
and modify their documentation to ensure that short-term political expedi-
encies ... are met."[6] Forest management planning in Idaho in the mid-1980s
provides a case in point. Of Idaho's ten national forests, six draft forest plans
developed by the Forest Service had been rejected in 1986 by the U.S.
Environmental Protection Agency (EPA) for failing to protect minimum
standards of water quality. Only two other forest plans in the entire nation
had received an objectionable rating from the EPA at that time. Because of
those ratings, the Boise National Forest, which was still drafting its first
plan, adopted water quality protection standards acceptable to the EPA. But
before the plan could be released, the Intermountain Forest Industries Association complained to Douglas MacCleery, a political appointee in Reagan's
Agriculture Department, that the Boise Forest standards were too strict and
would result in a reduction of about 10 percent in the annual timber harvest
levels. MacCleery had come to the Reagan administration in 1981 from the
National Forest Products Association, the nation's leading lumber lobby. He
encouraged the Chief of the Forest Service to tell the Boise Forest to loosen
its tough water quality standards. The forest planners complied.[7]

In the mid-1980s, Congress also actively imposed timber harvest targets on the Forest Service. Two powerful congressmen from the timber state of Oregon, Republican Senator Mark Hatfield and Democratic Representative Les Aucoin, succeeded in attaching amendments to various bills — mostly appropriations bills — directing the Forest Service to increase the harvest levels in Washington and Oregon forests *above the already high targets set by the Reagan administration.* By legislative amendment, the two congressmen boosted timber harvests in the Pacific Northwest 10–30 percent between 1986 and 1989. This pattern continued into the Bush administration, though to a lesser extent.[8] The Forest Service was caught in the middle. R. Max Peterson, Chief of the Forest Service from 1979 to 1987, acknowledged to agency employees in Washington's Wenatchee National Forest in 1989 that "Anybody — on the back of an envelope — could have figured out that the rate of harvest cannot be sustained."[9] Proceedings from a convention of Forest Supervisors in 1989 included a strong complaint that the allowable sale quantities of timber (previously called allowable cut) for most forests were "unrealistically high even with full funding."[10] Despite this widespread internal recognition that timber targets were unrealistic, the Washington Office continued to promise the political establishment that indeed the high harvests could be achieved under multiple use, sustained yield principles if the agency received the proper fiscal and institutional support. An organizational gap between the Washington Office and many forest supervisors and district rangers, who opposed the high harvest levels, widened.

Throughout most of the Reagan administration, forest managers generally found ways to rationalize the higher timber targets, but they became increasingly difficult to defend. Public disclosure requirements exposed managers' rationales to scrutiny and often harsh criticism. As a result, it became harder for managers to avoid accountability for unrealistic assumptions or flawed data. Forest economist Randal O'Toole spent most of the decade of the 1980s exposing problems in forest planning, publicized through his private organization's journal *Forest Planning* (changed to *Forest Watch* in 1986). His 1986 analysis of the timber yield tables used for seven of California's national forest plans found that the timber yield model developed by the California Regional Office in 1977 for use in forest planning had overestimated growth rates for existing California forests by approximately one-third, and underestimated the time it would take for second-growth forests to reach desirable harvest age (called "Culmination of Mean Annual Increment," CMAI). Such errors resulted in higher estimates of future timber volume, which made the currently excessive harvest levels seem sustainable. O'Toole concluded that these flawed timber yield tables served as a hidden method for departing from NFMA's requirement of nondeclining even-flow.[11] In response to this criticism, the Regional Office reviewed its timber yield tables, acknowledged problems with them, and held up release of the California forest plans pending revisions.[12] California was not alone in this problem. Faulty yield tables and erroneous inventories showed up all over the country. A critical journalistic account of national forest management controversies by Grace Herndon, called *Cut and Run,* revealed numerous instances of these problems, including overestimated growth and yield assumptions by the Coconino National Forest in Arizona; lands added to the "suitable" commercial timber base on the Apache-Sitgreaves forest (also in Arizona) that should have been designated "unsuitable" under NFMA regulations, and a 45 percent overestimation of existing timber volume on the Rio Grande National Forest in New Mexico.[13]

While many agency employees dutifully developed data sets and assumptions tailored in part to comport with centrally driven management objectives, others grew frustrated with the unrealistic production goals handed down to them. As a result, some tension developed within the agency between reformers and those comfortable with the status quo. Banding together for solidarity, increasing numbers of forest supervisors began resisting the Reagan era timber targets after the 1988 elections and initiating or at least promoting reductions in annual timber sale levels in order to better achieve multiple use and sustained yield objectives. While the timber industry decried the reductions, environmentalists complained that timber harvests were still too high and stepped up their appeals and lawsuits to force even more substantial cutbacks. In many cases the courts sided with the environmental litigants, because the agency often had to violate administrative procedures or environmental protection laws to achieve the timber targets. In the midst of this battle, as mentioned in the Introduction, several endangered species became magnets of controversy because the measures required to protect them from extinction involved substantial logging reductions in many remaining old-growth forests in the Northwest and northern

Rockies. The most prominent of these endangered species were the northern spotted owl, the grizzly bear, and several populations of salmon. Escalating controversy over the declining timber supply in these regions focused almost exclusively on the endangered species angle, ignoring the larger and more important causes for the decline in national forest harvests. Forest supervisors in the Northern Region were among the most prominent in the reformist faction, and they developed extensive explanations of why their Reagan era forest plan timber targets could not be implemented. Of seven major reasons forest supervisors in the Northern Region gave in the early 1990s for the reduction in timber sales, only one was related to legal requirements to protect endangered species; four of them traced to Forest Service flaws in management, planning, data, and assumptions; one was related to the activities of private timber companies adjacent to the national forests; and one was related to general "public pressures." These factors are common to national forests across the country. Following is an explanation of each.

Past management problems: Many forest supervisors admitted that their national forests were overcut in previous decades or that resource rehabilitation efforts had been unsuccessful or inadequate. For example, a 1990 memo to the Regional Forester from the supervisor of the Clearwater National Forest in northern Idaho stated that the forest's "front country [was] exhausted," adding that "our currently developed lands are, in general, highly developed. The watershed and wildlife habitat conditions have been pushed to the limit by past activities. The same is true for the visual resource. Without what I believe to be substantial investments in major rehabilitation efforts in the very near future, I fear . . . we will be facing significant shortfalls below our historic trends until recovery occurs."[14] Other forests in the region echoed similar sentiments.[15]

Flaws in planning procedures: The methods and computer models used by the Forest Service to develop its forest plans often had built-in flaws that inflated allowable harvest levels. In addition to the problems mentioned above in connection with the faulty California timber yield tables, FORPLAN, the forest planning computer model used by the Forest Service to project future values and impacts of management, had several internal design characteristics that tended to inflate timber production capability assumptions. For example, FORPLAN scheduled management activities by acre and assumed that each acre of a forest is independent of every other acre. Nature, however, is not so independent; usually activities in one area affect ecological functioning in another. FORPLAN is a linear program that does not effectively accommodate ecological connections across acres of a forest.[16] Other more blatant computer modeling flaws were built in to the program by forest planners. In a 1991 analysis of why the Flathead National Forest in Montana had failed to meet its timber targets, the U.S. General Accounting Office found that the forest planners had modified the computer model used to develop the forest plan in 1986 by arbitrarily constraining it to establish a minimum allowable sale quantity (ASQ) of 100 mmbf per year in anticipation of the needs of the local timber industry. When this "floor constraint" of 100 mmbf was eliminated from the model, the computer generated an ASQ of 78 mmbf per year. Nevertheless, the planners stuck with the higher number. The environmental effects of this modification, however, were not taken into account in the computer model. Later, while implementing the plan, the foresters found they could not achieve the higher harvest level while simultaneously meeting minimum standards for environmental protection.[17] The Clearwater and Lolo national forests identified other flaws in the computer modeling process that similarly inflated their potential harvest level.[18]

Faulty data: Many forest plans contained exaggerated estimates of the amount of old-growth timber that remained on the forest. The Lolo National Forest discovered in 1990 and 1991 that 110,000 acres deemed "suitable" for harvesting in the 1986 forest plan had actually been logged already. They also discovered an additional 280,000 scattered acres thought to be mature forest but actually covered by young growth because of fires that had burned these areas between 1910 and 1935.[19] In its 1987 forest plan, the Kootenai National Forest in the northwest corner of Montana apparently overestimated by 40 percent the amount of old growth available for harvesting and underestimated by 500 percent the areas of the forest that had been clear-cut.[20] Private analysts have also found faulty timber yield tables in forest plans outside of California that exaggerate post-harvest regrowth rates and regrowth volumes.[21]

Flawed assumptions: In monitoring the effects of timber harvesting on the Clearwater National Forest, managers discovered that they had overestimated their ability to mitigate impacts to soil, water, and fisheries. They found that even at a 30 percent reduction of the harvest level, they were "consistently bumping up against the watershed and fisheries thresholds established in the forest plan." Interestingly, they also discovered that meeting just the minimum environmental protection standards often rendered timber sales economically nonviable, something not considered in the forest plan.[22] The Kootenai National Forest, which wanted to reduce its ASQ by approximately 30 percent in 1991, identified at least seven reasons for the reduction, three of which are traceable to faulty assumptions: (1) a slower than anticipated rate of recovery of wildlife habitat cover; (2) less than expected improvements in efficiency for industrial utilization of logs; and (3) a faster than anticipated rate of logging on intermingled private lands.[23]

Overcutting on private lands adjacent to national forests: Many national forests have large areas in "checkerboard" patterns of land ownership: every other square mile remaining in private ownership. This is a legacy from the nineteenth century, when the federal government gave alternating square mile land grants to railroads as an incentive to build the transcontinentals. In land management planning, the agency makes assumptions about the rate and style of management on these intermingled private lands. If these assumptions prove wrong, then the Forest Service may face unexpected changes in environmental conditions, to which it must then respond. Among the largest timber corporations in the West are Champion International and Plum Creek, both of which own substantial tracts of checkerboard land intermingled with national forests in Montana, Idaho, and elsewhere. In the 1970s and 1980s, both companies began to dramatically accelerate logging of their remaining timber in the northern Rockies, and Champion is now selling off its holdings. (The problem is just as acute on the Pacific Coast where 1980s hostile buyouts of Crown-Zellerbach Corporation and Pacific Lumber Company, among others, led to rapid logging by the corporate raiders to generate capital to pay off the debts incurred in the buyout. The companies were subsequently dismantled and sold off at a profit.)[24] This accelerated logging pushed soil, water, and wildlife protection standards in affected watersheds to the limit and beyond. The Kootenai, Clearwater, and Lolo national forests cited this problem as a major reason for their reduced harvests, arguing that any additional logging on intermingled national forest lands would exacerbate an already critical level of resource damage. In the case of the Lolo, a total of 400,000 acres of private checkerboard lands experienced "higher than anticipated" rates of logging, temporarily prompting the Lolo to prohibit cutting on 289,000 acres of its adjacent intermingled lands.[25]

Endangered species: Spotted owls and Pacific salmon in the Northwest, grizzly bears and bull trout in the northern Rockies, goshawks in the Southwest, red-cockaded woodpeckers in the Southeast — all are threatened or endangered species that are affecting timber harvesting or other commercial activities on the national forests. All were once relatively abundant (some like the salmon were superabundant) and all are now on the brink of extinction because of human-caused modifications of their habitat. Each species listed above, except the salmon and trout, is to a greater or lesser extent dependent on old-growth forest habitats. The fish are affected by sedimentation and water temperature changes caused by logging — and, of course, they are adversely affected by dams. Traditional intensive silviculture called for the liquidation of all "overmature" forests and their replacement with fast growing commercial plantations, leading to the current situation in which old growth has become very scarce and/or fragmented. If the Forest Service had not subordinated other uses and resource values so completely to intensive timber production since World War Two, many of these species may not have become endangered. It took a court injunction to finally force the agency to take steps to reduce logging in its remaining patches of old-growth forest along the Pacific Coast. Although the spotted owl was the focal species in this legal battle, it was in fact an "indicator species" of old growth, and thus its decline represented the plight of many other species associated with that increasingly rare habitat.[26]

Public pressures: National forest managers have often pointed to "changing public values" or "increasing public pressures" as one of their reasons for reducing timber harvests. Specifically, they meant pressures to keep roadless areas undeveloped and remaining old-growth forests intact. But conservationists had opposed the Forest Service's aggressive road construction and logging program for decades. These issues were not new. Public values did not suddenly change in the late 1980s. What changed was public *awareness* of the extent and the impact of industrial logging on the national forests and the public's ability to scrutinize and challenge agency decisions. Nontimber interest groups made limited but notable gains since the 1970s in weakening the grip of the old "Timber Triangle" that presided over the liquidation of most national forest old growth after World War Two. With the supply of marketable "mature" timber on the national forests waning, and with Congress's willingness to subsidize uneconomic timber sales similarly declining, more and more forest managers at the local level have simply chosen to bolt from the old conspiracy of optimism, reject the ethos of maximum production, and diversify their loyalties to nontimber interest groups.[27]

To sum up, the dramatic decline in national forest harvests recently (and the general decline since the 1970s in regions 1 and 6) is a legacy of organizational and political pressures to maximize timber production from the 1940s through the 1980s beyond sustainable levels and at the expense of resource protection mandates. These pressures created incentives for managers to make overoptimistic assumptions, to use faulty data bases and skewed planning procedures, and to place unjustified faith in intensive management solutions to resource problems. Despite managerial warnings of failures and environmental deterioration, high-level bureaucratic and political efforts to maintain an optimistic view of timber production potential continued in the 1980s. Counterpressures to reform national forest management increased simultaneously, however. Amidst the swelling controversy, ground level managers of the national forests came to a growing sense by the end of the decade of the 1980s that their capabilities and the ecological capabilities of the national forests were overstretched.

Below-Cost Timber Sales Controversies

Besides the controversy over timber targets, critical attention also focused on the issue of below-cost timber sales. The Natural Resources Defense Council initiated public attention to this issue in 1980 with a report titled "Giving Away the National Forests." A U.S. General Accounting Office investigation followed up on the NRDC report with its own critical analysis. After that a veritable flood of reports streamed out of public and private agencies and organizations and were still coming in the early 1990s.[28] The details of below-cost sales were in many cases quite dramatic, so the media picked up on the issue readily and hungrily. A 1983 article by Dennis Hanson in *Wilderness* magazine recounted details of the timber sale program for the San Juan National Forest in southwestern Colorado. The San Juans, a mountain range widely referred to as the "America Alps," are a rugged mass of rock, ice, lakes, streams, and alpine meadows, with some beautiful but commercially marginal stands of spruce, fir, and aspen holding on precariously to shallow, rocky soil. In the San Juan National Forest, Hanson related, "the government spent $3,479,595 in 1981 for timber sale management. It received for the timber involved total revenues of $461,158. In short, for the sale of this San Juan timber — this public resource — the Forest Service *lost* $3,018,437. One is moved to wonder what it would have cost us if we had simply abandoned timber management in the San Juans altogether."[29]

The 1984 General Accounting Office report mentioned above found that in 1981 and 1982, 96 percent of timber sales in the Forest Service's Rocky Mountain Region (mainly Colorado, South Dakota, and portions of Wyoming) lost money; while 93 percent in the Intermountain Region (Nevada, Utah, and portions of Wyoming and Idaho) lost money; and 60 percent in the Northern Region (Montana, Idaho Panhandle, and North Dakota) lost money.[30] A *Denver Post* article, following a few months after the GAO report, opened with the following jab at the agency: "The Forest Service, which spends a dollar for every dime it receives from the sale of timber in the Rockies, is under pressure to justify its plans for a vast expansion in logging operations." After reviewing the controversy and implying that the agency displayed the biases of an engineer (the chief then, Max Peterson, was an engineer), the article concluded that the Forest Service "would be wise to rethink its priorities."[31]

Another controversy erupted in New Mexico's Santa Fe National Forest in early 1990 when it became known that more than twice the authorized amount of timber had been cut from the "Los Utes" timber sale. Loggers had also crushed young groves of aspen in the sale area and used a stream and steep, unstable slopes for skid trails and logging roads. The Santa Fe *New Mexican* ran a blistering editorial, demanding that "before another inch of land is ravaged, the Forest Service must be held accountable for what was allowed to happen at Los Utes." The editorial writer suggested that the Forest Service's motto, "Caring for the Land, Serving the People," might appropriately be rephrased "careless with land, serving loggers." Worse yet, the writer continued, "under the Santa Fe National Forest's current operating plan, 348,000 acres — 22 percent of the total forest area in the state — are allocated to the timber business. Yet the timber program is losing money here to the tune of nearly a million and a half dollars over the last two years. If it makes neither financial nor environmental sense, why does the Forest Service permit loggers to denude our precious forests? Who stands to gain?"[32]

One of the most thorough and devastating journalistic attacks on the Forest Service timber program came from Perri Knize in a 1991 *Atlantic Monthly* article titled, "The Mismanagement of the National Forests." Knize argued that "pork barrel politics" had led to "forty years of forest devastation," hidden from public scrutiny by an elaborate charade of scientific management and "imaginative bookkeeping." One creative accounting procedure used by the Forest Service to help justify its timber sales in the 1980s was to amortize the cost of roads over an average of 240 years! (The life span of a typical road is twenty-five years.) Knize cited an instance in which the agency amortized the cost of one road in Alaska's Chugach National Forest over an 1,800 year period. Robert Wolf, Senator Humphrey's RPA and NFMA bill drafter mentioned earlier, studied the Forest Service's accounting procedures in the late 1980s with the intent of defending the agency against its critics. Shocked at what he found, he told Knize that in his opinion the timber program was "a fraud." Wolf has since embarked on a crusade of reform, publishing lengthy analyses and testifying before Congress.[33] Even the London *Economist* observed, "The Forest Service is a nationalised industry encouraged by federal budget habits to lose money by clear-cutting forests that almost everybody would prefer to leave standing for owls to live in. Change is imminent."[34]

Bolstered by these criticisms and by growing public concern over the huge federal budget deficit in the 1980s, many members of Congress, conservative as well as liberal, began speaking out against this pork barrel. One of the prominent congressional critics of the late 1980s was Democratic Senator Wyche Fowler of Georgia, who made strenuous but largely unsuccessful attempts to slash the Forest Service road construction budget. Georgians had reason to be concerned. An article in the *Atlanta Journal/Atlanta Constitution* in 1989 noted that the Forest Service had lost $1.2 million on timber sales in the Chatahoochie National Forest of northern Georgia the prior year; yet the Chatahoochie Forest Plan proposed adding approximately 1,000 miles of new roads over the next fifty years to open up three-quarters of the forest to logging. Reviewing several of Georgia's national forest plans, the editorial staff of the newspaper suggested, "Save the Forests, Ax the Game Plan."[35] Reinforced by such sentiments, Fowler, chairman of the Senate Subcommittee on Forestry and Conservation, held oversight hearings in 1989 and 1991 on national forest management and below-cost sales. Citing the estimate that below-cost timber sales would lose as much as $2 billion in the next decade — in the process degrading water quality, wildlife habitat, and environmental amenities — Fowler exclaimed in 1989, "To be absolutely candid, I cannot for the life of me figure out exactly why this controversy exists, why our Forest Service is not at the forefront of the fight to protect our forests from excessive timbering."[36] These sentiments were shared by many, both outside and within the Forest Service.

The timber harvesting costs-benefits issue has been and remains confusingly complex. The interconnection between the various resource programs and their budgets makes it impossible to achieve consensus on identifying timber-specific costs and related benefits. What percentage of fire control and pest control costs, for example, should be considered a timber management expense? If hunters use a timber access road seven years after the harvest, how much of the cost of that road should be written off as a recreation benefit? How should soil erosion be monetized as an additional "cost" of road construction? No one questions the existence of below-cost sales, but their extent and significance engenders heated debate. The Forest Service naturally takes advantage of this confusion in defending its expenditures. Disgusted with Forest Service accounting procedures, Senator William Proxmire (D-WI) recently quipped, "the Forest Service never met a number it could not twist."[37] Nevertheless, in 1990 the Forest Service began an "experimental" program to reduce below-cost sales, initiated by the Bush administration under great pressure from environmentalists, some economists, and an odd coalition of environmental liberals and fiscal conservatives within Congress.[38] Even some lumber industry representatives, such as Walter Minnick, head of Trus Joist Corporation of Idaho, had joined the voices of reform. Minnick told Congress in 1987 that below-cost timber sales were "the height of fiscal mismanagement," and scolded his own industry, saying, "It is more than a little inconsistent for industry leaders and conservative timber state legislators to advocate federal spending cutbacks for everyone else while simultaneously promoting more and more below-cost timber subsidies for themselves."[39]

Unrest within the Agency on the Eve of the Centennial

A poll of Forest Service employees conducted in 1988–89 by Jim Kennedy and Tom Quigley of Utah State University uncovered the remnants of the agency's incentive system for achieving timber targets. Polling a broad selection of employees from heads in the Washington Office to entry level folks at the district level, the researchers asked subjects to identify from a list of values those which they felt the Forest Service rewarded most and those which they felt the agency *ought to reward* the most. According to the survey, the five most rewarded Forest Service values were these:

1. Loyalty to the agency
2. Meeting timber and other commodity targets
3. Promoting a good USFS image
4. Following rules and regulations
5. Teamwork.

The five values that respondents felt *should* be rewarded most were these:

1. Professional competence
   (only 47% said the agency *did* reward this most)
2. Caring for healthy ecosystems
   (7% said the agency *did* reward this most)
3. Caring for future generations
   (4% said the agency *did* reward this most)
4. Innovation and risk-taking
   (13% said the agency *did* reward this most)
5. Caring for the welfare of others
   (8% said the agency *did* reward this most).[40]

This poll indicated that efforts to maintain timber production and to enforce compliance still remained central to the agency's bureaucratic ethos in 1989: employees ranked "independence" as the least rewarded value and "loyalty to the agency" as the most rewarded value. Thus the Forest Service rewarded those who served the organization rather than those who protected ecosystems and served people.

A number of other studies of changing Forest Service values in the early 1990s arrived at similar findings. One particularly comprehensive study by researchers at the University of California, Davis, interviewed over 1,000 Forest Service employees in 1989–92 and compared their findings with those of several previous studies dating back to the 1950s. They concluded that there had been significant change in attitudes among Forest Service personnel, accelerated during the 1980s. In particular, they found a marked decline in support for increased timber harvesting, from 62 percent of respondents in a 1981 study to 7 percent of respondents in their 1989–92 survey. The causes for the change in attitude included personnel turnover, an increase in the hiring of professionals trained in noncommodity disciplines, broader exposure of employees to other professions because of NFMA's requirement for interdisciplinary planning, and actual changes in individual attitudes of long-term employees.[41]

Another survey of Forest Service employees conducted in 1992 by researchers at the University of Michigan came up with these interesting results: When asked to rank in order of importance the five major multiple uses (timber, range, wildlife and fish, water, and recreation), 70 percent of respondents chose wildlife and fish or water or recreation as the most important use. Then, when asked which multiple uses seemed most important to the Forest Service as an organization, almost the same number identified timber alone as most important. Three-quarters of respondents said that some below-cost sales were justifiable, but over half of all respondents added that there were too many of these sales overall. Nearly three-quarters also said clearcutting was an acceptable management practice, but just as many added that the use of clearcutting was too frequent or extensive.[42] A third study conducted by researchers at the University of Idaho, Moscow, compared the values of members of the Association of Forest Service Employees for Environmental Ethics with the range of values held by employees in general and hypothesized that the former group embodied a "new resource management paradigm" toward which the agency as a whole seemed to be incrementally moving. Quoting forestry professor Richard Behan of Northern Arizona University, the two researchers concluded that "the timber management bias in professional forestry has been scrutinized, found wanting, and is now in the process of fundamental change."[43]

A national Forest Supervisors conference held in Tucson, Arizona, on November 14–16, 1989, ("Sunbird") provided a springboard for the reformers within the agency to network with each other and express their concerns in an organized manner. A remarkable memo to the Chief of the Forest Service emerged from the conference participants, criticizing the status quo and calling for substantial changes in management and policy. The memo included such statements as: "Public values and personal values of Forest Service employees, including Forest Supervisors, are changing. . . . Many members of the public and many of our employees no longer view us as leaders in environmental conservation. . . . There is a growing concern that we have become an agency 'out of control'. . . change must come faster." It went on to assert that the Forest Service cut too much timber, while soil, water, wildlife, and recreation received too little attention. Rejecting the traditional agency response to criticisms of its logging activities, the memo explained, "Public challenges to the timber program cannot be overcome by additional funding to timber management, nor by simply improving documentation of the NEPA [environmental impact statement] process"; charging that the "allowable sale quantities" of timber for many forests were too high, they suggested the agency simply cut fewer trees. Signed by the supervisors of sixty-three national forests in the northern and central Rockies, the Great Basin, and the Southwest, the memo also noted that the supervisors of national forests on the west coast from California to Alaska generally agreed with their sentiments.[44]

In an interesting social commentary, the conference memo also noted that "during the first half of this century, we operated in an environment of rural values. We are now operating in an environment where about 5 percent of the population relates to a rural setting" — an implication that the agency held outdated values and served a small portion of the American public. The conference participants also noted a major turnover of supervisors in the last five years and projected *70 percent retirement* in the following five to eight years. With this change in leadership, the conferees felt that significant bureaucratic reforms were possible. Remarkably, they recommended slashing the Washington Office staff, redefining and redirecting the "middle management positions," and pumping more of the budget into the district offices, where management actually takes place.[45]

Responding to pressure from the public and from its own employees at the grass roots, the Washington Office of the Forest Service began emphasizing commitment to a new direction in 1989. "There's a change going on in society," said Chief Dale Robertson, "and the Forest Service can't just ignore that. We intend to be more environmentally responsible."[46] A public information pamphlet accompanying the 1989 Resources Planning Act (RPA) Assessment promised, "The Forest Service will increase the environmental sensitivity of commodity production on National Forest System lands. The level of commodity production will be adjusted downward where commodity production cannot be accomplished in an environmentally acceptable manner."[47] Fine words, but ambiguous. The crux of the debate has always been and remains: Who defines what is "environmentally acceptable"? And *how well are these promises kept?*

In early 1990, the Washington Office of the Forest Service designated wildlife biologist Hal Salwasser as director of a "New Perspectives" initiative to promote this desired new "environmental sensitivity."[48] Salwasser subsequently toured the regional and field offices, giving workshops on New Perspectives. Jeff DeBonis, founder of AFSEEE, attended one of Salwasser's workshops held on the Tongass National Forest in Alaska and afterward remarked that agency personnel attending the meeting were "cynically optimistic," hoping amid a lingering pessimism that this initiative might become more than the usual "smoke and mirrors public relations games typical of past Forest Service responses to the public's calls for reform."[49] Norman Peck, a surveyor on the Six Rivers National Forest in California, echoed this cynicism with the following observation: "Salwasser all but admits that current practices are destructive to forest ecosystems. Now, for reasons unrevealed, he claims the Forest Service wants to reverse these practices, yet all the agency presents us is a vaguely worded, non-binding, self-enacted decree promising conscientious land stewardship from now on. Are we to believe this is something new?"[50]

The test of commitment comes in action, but here again the record remained ambiguous. In a congressional hearing on national forest management in April 1991, Senator Patrick Leahy (D-VT), chairman of the Senate Agriculture Committee, questioned the agency's commitment to New Perspectives. He said he had been encouraged by recent agency efforts to broaden its view of environmental stewardship, but the newly released Green Mountain National Forest Plan (from his home state of Vermont), which called for greatly increased logging to help meet national timber targets, dampened his optimism. Angrily, he told Forest Service representatives at the hearing, "You cannot have 'New Perspectives' and at the same time have a 66 percent increase in the Green Mountain's timber sale program. That is contradictory and it has to stop."[51]

But contradictions continued to mount. As mentioned above, forest supervisors in Montana had begun calling for lower harvest levels in the late 1980s in order to meet environmental protection laws and achieve a more sustainable yield. But under pressure from Congress and agency heads in

Washington, D.C., Northern Regional Forester John Mumma directed forest supervisors in Montana to increase their timber sales in 1990, saying, "Forests should set as a first priority the needed timber support levels to accomplish the timber targets."[52] This memo came half a year after the New Perspectives program had been launched. Undaunted, the forest supervisors intensified their documentation of the need for reduced harvests, and asked again for lower timber targets the following year. Mumma then reversed himself, and told the supervisors that if they had to choose between implementing environmental protection standards in their forest plan or implementing the timber harvest targets set by Congress, they should choose the former. Emboldened, many of the supervisors then wrote a joint memo to Dale Robertson, Chief of the Forest Service, in September 1991, explaining that they could not meet the Bush administration timber sale goal for region 1 of 940 million board feet and that the target should be reduced to no more than 590 million board feet. Under pressure from pro-timber western states senators and representatives, Robertson instead promised Congress that the Northern Region would deliver at least 664 million board feet and that it would strive for 750 million. Indicative of the political pressure being applied, Senator Larry Craig (R-ID) had written to the Chief in May 1991 saying, "Dale, I am very disappointed with the Forest Service's accomplishment and accountability for timber outputs in Idaho and the Nation as a whole. You have serious management problems that must be addressed. It is my hope you will move to assure targets are met and line officers are held accountable for targets."[53] The *New York Times* covered the story with the headline, "Forest Supervisors Say Politicians Are Asking Them to Cut Too Much."[54] Shortly thereafter, Robertson told Mumma to accept a transfer to an unspecified job in Washington, D.C., citing "poor performance ratings" as a reason. In fact, Mumma had met or exceeded all his targets for other renewable resources (recreation, fish and wildlife, watershed protection, etc.) and had received numerous awards over the years from the agency for outstanding service. In protest, Mumma chose to retire rather than accept transfer.

A nationwide storm of protest erupted against the "ouster" of Mumma, with supporters inside and outside the agency calling his forced retirement a "coup by hardliners," and "retrenchment" in the Forest Service.[55] At a press conference held in Missoula, Montana, after Mumma's ouster, four of the forest supervisors who had worked for Mumma expressed support for him, saying they would continue to implement his land stewardship policies and resist unsustainable timber harvest targets. The supervisor of the Clearwater National Forest, Win Green, flatly asserted, "Right now we have a timber target that is unrealistic and I don't hold my people accountable for something that is unattainable." Citing past overcutting, watershed damage, degradation of fish and wildlife habitat, and marred scenic views, Lolo National Forest Supervisor Orville Daniels announced that he would only allow a timber harvest level at 50 percent of his assigned target. Reformers within the agency wondered whether these forest supervisors would be next in line for transfers.[56]

The media, which had been intermittently covering this revolt of conscience within the Forest Service since 1989, recognized the controversy as seminal. *High Country News,* a biweekly newspaper covering environmental issues in the West, immediately featured a front page spread on Mumma's ouster and also covered the congressional hearings subsequently held by the House Civil Service Subcommittee to determine whether civil service guidelines had been violated in forcing Mumma out.[57] At the hearings, the disgruntled head of the Forest Service's "whistle-blower" review program, John McCormick, testified that harassment and transfer of employees who bucked the status quo was commonplace. The *New York Times* published an editorial by him in January 1992 (the month he retired), titled, "Can't See the Forest for the Sleaze." In it, McCormick hammered his former employer: "The Forest Service simply does not tolerate freedom of dissent. . . . The agency has become comfortable with lying to the public, ignoring longfestering problems and serving the timber industry as Government agents of environmental destruction rather than environmental protection."[58] This highly visible episode was only one of a number of instances where agency employees were transferred or otherwise punished for failing to support the timber targets.[59]

In an ironic postscript to the Mumma controversy, Chief Robertson announced a few months later that the New Perspectives program was being adopted as official Forest Service policy under the new title of "Ecosystem Management." He explained: "we have been courting the ecosystem approach for 3 years and we like the relationship and results. Today, I am announcing the marriage and that the Forest Service is committed to using an ecological approach in the future management of the national forests and grasslands."[60] Again, many forest managers had trouble locating the reality behind the rhetoric. Lee Coonce, retiring supervisor of Oregon's Umpqua National Forest, wrote a blistering memo to the Pacific Northwest Regional Forester John Lowe in December 1992, expressing his frustration with the high timber targets assigned to his forest and the associated budget constraints that locked in funding for timber production but left nontimber programs out in the cold. "The facade is we're giving lip service to Ecosystem Management, operations and maintenance of recreation facilities, anadromous fisheries . . . etc., but in the budget realm it's business as usual and that spells timber production."[61] Some other forests, in contrast, seem to have successfully downscaled timber management programs, such as the San Juan National Forest in Colorado, which reduced its ASQ by 41 percent and its "suitable" timber base by 21 percent in forest plan amendments in 1992.[62]

Building on this reform mood, the Clinton administration in its first few months promised significant change in national forest management. Yet its actions portrayed a mixed message. Early in his term, Clinton called a Northwest Forest Conference, or "timber summit," in Portland, Oregon, to seek a solution to what he called the "gridlock" that had developed over national forest logging, old-growth protection, and endangered species. Popularly conceived of as a conflict between environmentalists and loggers (or between owls and jobs), the so-called gridlock actually represented an impasse that had developed between branches of the federal government and between different departments within the executive branch. The National Forest Management Act included clear mandates regarding environmental protection. Other laws, such as the Clean Water Act and the Endangered Species Act, provide additional minimum standards for water quality and wildlife protection, all of which are supposed to constrain production activities. After decades of unbalanced, commodity-oriented management, however, ecosystem deterioration in the Northwest reached calamity proportions — or so claimed environmentalists and many scientists. Conservation groups then accelerated their legal challenges to Forest Service management plans and timber sales. They had been suing for decades, but in the late 1980s they started winning big. These "wins" in fact indicated that the federal judicial branch found substantial merit in environmentalists' claims that the Forest Service had been systematically and deliberately violating environmental protection laws to get out the cut. It was the federal courts, not environmental protestors, that shut down logging of most national forest old growth in 1989. It was a federal judge who told the Forest Service to go back to square one and draw up a "scientifically credible" plan to protect minimum viable populations of native wildlife as the National Forest Management Act requires. The Forest Service timber program also ran into trouble with other agencies within the executive branch, including the U.S. Fish and Wildlife Service, which implements the Endangered Species Act, and the Environmental Protection Agency, which administers the Clean Water Act. Both began citing the Forest Service for violations of these laws. State and tribal fish and game agencies were also causing trouble. This unusual state of affairs posed a serious problem for the Clinton administration, which is why Clinton brought his vice-president and several other members of his cabinet to Portland for a timber summit. As Clinton acknowledged then, "It is true that I was mortified when I began to review the legal documents surrounding this controversy to see that six different departments of the government were at odds with each other; so that there was no voice of the United States. I want each of the cabinet members to talk to each other to try to bring these conflicts to an end."[63]

Bringing these conflicts to an end will be easier said than done, however. The fundamental problem is that past logging levels in the Northwest (and most of the West) depended on the liquidation of old growth that contained high timber volumes. But old growth in the Northwest is almost gone and along with it may go as many as 480 species of plants and animals (at last count) that depend on old growth for their continued existence. Many of these species are now listed as threatened or endangered but many are being studied for possible listing. Every new endangered species is another potential lawsuit and an obstacle to further logging in old growth. As Charles Meslow, director of the U.S. Fish and Wildlife Service's Corvallis, Oregon, Research Station, said at the timber summit, "Mr. President, we look forward to having you visit the Pacific Northwest again; but not 480 times on contentious endangered species issues like this one [the spotted owl]."[64] He and the other biologists speaking at the summit called for the protection of remaining unfragmented old-growth ecosystems and the restoration of other forest areas that could eventually function as old-growth habitat in the future, as well as the adoption of "ecosystem management" principles on the huge estate of nonreserved forest lands that would continue to be managed for timber production.

Again, however, the basic obstacle to satisfying scientists, environmentalists, loggers, fishing interests, and the many others invested in this problem is that forest and related aquatic ecosystems are in such dire need of rehabilitation and old growth is so scarce that getting out even the bare minimum timber volume that industry needs is still likely to violate environmental laws. There is the rub. Clinton has three choices: he has to accept a dramatic long-term reduction in national forest timber harvests in the Northwest until the forests logged since the 1950s begin to provide a "second crop," or he has to get Congress to relax environmental protection laws, or he has to come up with a compromise that satisfies environmentalists enough to get them to drop their lawsuits. Environmentalists, for their part, have been complaining for years that environmental protection laws are too weak already, that crisis management is the unfortunate order of the day. They want no more cutting in national forest old growth, restrictions on exports of whole, unprocessed logs, subsidies for ecosystem restoration, and job retraining for surplus loggers. Industry and labor will not accept such a platform. But the best scientific minds agree that what industry and labor want in terms of a minimum, guaranteed annual harvest level will significantly increase the risk of extinction of many old-growth-dependent species, which is against the law. This is not an enviable position for a president to be in.

The mixed messages coming from the Clinton administration during and after the timber summit kept all the various interest groups wondering where he stood. At the summit he repeatedly reiterated his concerns for unemployed loggers, failing companies, and economically strapped rural communities. The guiding principles for any plan to resolve the gridlock, he said, must address "the needs of loggers and timber communities," and must provide "a sustainable and predictable level of timber." But in the next breath he stated unequivocally that the timber frontier had ended and that loggers and mill-workers faced a new future; "I can't repeal the laws of change," he concluded. Still, Clinton's fundamental contribution to the summit was a hopeful "win-win" message reflecting the same old conspiracy of optimism that led to the impasse in the first place. "This is not about choosing between jobs and the environment," he offered in his opening statement, "but about recognizing the importance of both." We can achieve "a balanced policy," he said in his closing remarks, "that promotes the economy, provides jobs, and protects the environment."[65] Neither Clinton nor anyone else offered a clear explanation for why previous administrations had failed to deliver on similar promises in the past. And just like in the 1950s and 1960s, when the phrase "intensive management" was invoked as the solution to land use conflicts, participants at the conference repeatedly invoked the new shiboleth "ecosystem management" as a panacea for today's problems. Of course, today's solution is significantly different from that of the 1950s in many ways. But whether our course of action will differ remains to be seen.

The mixed messages continued after the summit. Forest Service senior wildlife research biologist Jack Ward Thomas, chairman or member of at least four blue-ribbon scientific committees assigned to report on old-growth and endangered species issues for the government, was appointed Chief of the Forest Service late in 1993, despite a storm of protest from industry and from timber-allied staff people in the Forest Service. This is the first time ever that a non-forester, non-engineer has been appointed head of the Forest Service. At the summit, Thomas had told the president that his own definition of "balance" in resolving the logging impasse meant "obey the law with a high probability of success. And then minimize the social and economic costs."[66] Obeying the law, of course, meant observing wildlife protection laws. A high probability of success meant successful recovery of endangered species, including owls, marbled murrelets, numerous runs of salmon, grizzly bears, and many other species.

Notwithstanding Thomas's clear preferences, Clinton's post-summit plan and policy statement (based in part on a series of options developed by a scientific committee that included Thomas) staked out a middle road that would *not* satisfy environmental laws and would therefore require special exempting legislation or an agreement by environmental plaintiffs to drop their lawsuits. "Option Nine," as the Clinton plan was called, would allow full-scale logging of one-fifth of the remnant old growth. The rest would be put into old growth reserves, but thinning and salvage logging would still be allowed in them. Outside of old growth reserves, the fisheries protection measures recommended by the committee of scientists would be cut in half.

The probability of successful recovery for many keystone endangered species would *not* be "high." Just as alarming, forests on the east side of the Cascade Mountains (outside spotted owl and marbled murrelet habitat), which have suffered from the same overcutting problems as the west side forests, would experience accelerated logging to make up for some of the shortfall from the west side.

The Clinton administration then played hardball with environmental leaders to get them to support this plan. Hardball included threats to support legislation that would enact the plan and shield it and other timber sales in the Northwest from judicial review. Since this would throw environmentalists out of court and off the playing field, many of them compromised. Others rebelled.[67] Interestingly, the timber industry seemed even more disappointed with Option Nine than the environmentalists. Over time, political allies of the industry may succeed in further weakening environmental protection laws and the environmentalists' bargaining position. Only time will tell. Despite some encouraging signs of pending reform, such as ecosystem management and the appointment of a wildlife biologist as chief, it is not yet clear whether the agency over the long term will take the path of reform or the path of retrenchment.

Conclusion

On the centennial anniversary of the national forests (1991), the Forest Service was intensively reevaluating itself and its mission, trying painfully to contend with internal revolt, demands for change from progressive sectors of the forestry profession, pressure from lumbermen who warned of imminent economic collapse in the industry without accelerated harvesting on the national forests, and increasingly radical grass-roots environmental opposition to its management activities (Earth First! road blockades, tree-sitting, and other forms of civil disobedience). Congress, too, had a half dozen bills pending in 1991 designed to restructure national forest policy and delimit Forest Service management discretion.[68] Unlike other periods of crisis, however, the two factors that previously sustained intensive management solutions to national forest conflicts — perceptions of abundance and public faith in technologically enhanced forest production — had all but disappeared. Whether or not a false optimism promoting maximum and harmonious development of all resources can again overcome conflicts seems doubtful.

13

Conclusion

In the annals of Forest Service history, 1991 will be remembered as the year the manure hit the ventilator. The unstoppable force and the immovable object finally met. Region 6 [the Pacific Northwest], for the first time in history, will not even come close to meeting our timber sale target. Even though field foresters have known since the mid-1970s that this day was coming, it still represents a major shock to our bureaucratic system.

Tim Foss, Region 6 timber sale planner

World War Two initiated a new era in Forest Service history, an era of full-scale industrial production and an outdoor recreation boom that flooded the national forests with new and competing classes of users. The agency met these challenges with enthusiasm after four decades of mainly custodial management. But accelerated production forced the Service to face new challenges to its central policy of sustainability. As timber demands in particular exceeded earlier determinations of sustainable yield, the agency adopted the ideology of intensive management to justify increasing the allowable cut, believing that its foresters could greatly enhance forest productivity on a permanent basis. While a certain amount of artificial enhancement was achievable, environmental, political, fiscal, and technical constraints limited the success of intensive management so that sustainable levels of resource extraction were quickly exceeded. But rather than scale back development, denying forest users the full measure of their demands, agency leaders and politicians adopted a conspiracy of optimism, asserting that more infusions of technology, labor, and capital would keep artificially high levels of production sustainable and protect forest ecosystems. When technology failed, the merchants of optimism blamed it on flawed application that could be corrected with better training or more research. When the administration or Congress failed to fully support intensive management in the budget process, politics could be blamed. When nature failed to respond as expected, no one was to blame. In all cases, advocates of intensive management found ways to dodge responsibility and maintain the overoptimistic assumptions essential to continuing the high-yield status quo. Now the proverbial chickens have come home to roost. As Patricia Limerick noted in her book, *The Legacy of Conquest*, "postponements and evasions catch up with people." This is, she added, a "cruel but common lesson of western history."[1]

What explains this curious twist of fate in which America's historic architect of sustainable forestry — the U.S. Forest Service — now stands accused of presiding over an orgy of unsustainable logging of the public's forests? Did agency foresters cynically collaborate in irresponsible exploitation? Not usually. The faith in the technological fix was genuine. And most Americans shared it between the 1940s and 1960s. Foresters' psychological investment in the efficacy of intensive management was so powerful that it filtered every assumption and perception. Furthermore, enough science backed the faith in technological mastery over nature that foresters could assert an empirical foundation — and therefore unquestioned legitimacy — to their beliefs. But forest researchers for the most part were only asking the kinds of questions that would advance the conspiracy of optimism. Agency leaders consigned to marginality research that pointed to the flaws in the faith, or else they deferred judgment on problems until "additional studies" could be made.

If foresters were not cynical collaborators, then were they innocent victims of political manipulation? Once again, not usually. As Limerick artfully pointed out, one of the central ideologies of the American West has been a "myth of innocence." Westerners never blamed themselves for failures in achieving their visions of wealth, she argued. Instead, they invented a pantheon of antagonists to shift culpability to, including Easterners, the federal government, Indians, nature, and foreigners. It is an article of faith to assert in the face of any problem that some external force has made an innocent victim of the well-meaning western entrepreneur. This psychology is not, of course, confined to Westerners. The same charge applies to those at the top of the Forest Service's organizational pyramid. Foresters were painfully aware of the fact that budgets did not conform to budget requests, and that actual management did not conform to planned management. They also knew that forest ecosystems were not responding to intensive management as expected. Other than periodic complaints to political superiors, however, agency decision makers continued to endorse maximum production and defend the faith. They even glossed over their own failures and sought to discredit critics. Agency foresters were concertedly defensive. When conservationists split into two divergent wings in the 1960s, environmentalists on the one hand and defenders of the old maximum production ethos on the other, the Forest Service sided with the latter. When criticism of the timber program escalated in the 1970s (e.g., the clearcutting controversy), agency leaders stepped up their self-justification. These decisions came mainly from the upper echelons of the agency, the segment of the Forest Service most closely associated with the centers of power and capital. These elite decision makers considered themselves to be realists, effective organizational lobbyists fighting for a piece of the pie in a world of politics largely beyond their control. Those who did not share this politically pragmatic perspective did not get promoted to the pinnacles of authority.

But even if the agency had stood up for limits and demanded equitable treatment of the multiple forest values, its success would have been blunted by the realities of political economy. To a large degree, the agency is a pawn in a chess game presided over by organized special interest groups and their political allies. Realizing their limited bargaining power, agency leaders often resorted to a pragmatic acceptance of the status quo. Things might have been a little different if Edward Cliff (or some other chief) had followed through on his threat to reduce timber harvests until Congress approved a more balanced budget. But no one in Washington, D.C., did this. When a range manager in Colorado (Earl Sandvig) in the 1950s decided to implement needed grazing reductions despite opposition from the cattle industry, he was transferred. When a regional forester in the Northern Rockies (John Mumma) in 1991 refused to require his forest supervisors to meet unsustainable, environmentally destructive timber targets, he was removed. If lower echelon land managers make life difficult for upper echelon agency heads, they risk losing their jobs. Agency heads, in turn, must conform to the direction given them by political superiors or risk losing their jobs, or worse, damaging the bargaining power of their agency in the political arena. In reality, the agency is a tool of the federal government used to implement federal policy, and the majority of government policymakers apparently respect sustainable forestry only insofar as it does not conflict with economic development objectives. This will remain so until Americans elect representatives with different values and find a way to keep the representatives responsive to those alternative values once elected.

•   •   •

It is possible that the national forest centennial marked a third major watershed in the history of public forestry in America: the first being the founding of the national forests in 1891, and the second being the advent of an era of intensive management beginning in the 1940s. Perhaps the 1990s will be counted as the end of the intensive management era, the end of the conspiracy of optimism. At least three major episodes of widespread dissent against the post–World War Two high-yield timber production status quo have occurred in the last four decades. The first, between 1956 and 1964, centered on attempts by the newly emergent "environmental" organizations to get permanent zoning status for particularly valued wildlands, in order to make them off limits to intensive management. Environmentalists were trying to curb the power of the commodity-oriented elite. Defenders of maximum production fought the wilderness movement but failed to overcome it. They did maintain the status quo, however. The Wilderness Act at the time simply placed in a protective status a portion of those national forest lands already in an administrative category of protection. Environmentalists simply succeeded in making it more difficult to open up these protected areas to commercial development. This was a holding pattern, of sorts, but a step forward that provided an important new policy tool — zoning — for expanding protected areas in the future. But the Wilderness Act did not really get at the heart of the problem. It left open the vast majority of the national forests to an intensive form of management that threatened to violate sustained yield, multiple use, and ecosystem integrity.

A second period of attempted reform came between 1968 and 1976 in a major battle over intensive silviculture practices, especially clearcutting. The outcome was again the maintenance of the status quo under a facade of reform. In the Resources Planning Act (1974) and the National Forest Management Act (1976), Congress endorsed environmental protection *policies* and established resource planning *procedures* that were more responsive to public input and that incorporated action plans and specific budget needs. But, intensive silvicultural practices, which formed the heart of the controversy, were endorsed by Congress; the status quo of technologically enhanced maximum production received a solid legal foundation. Furthermore, the new environmental protection policies and the goal of conjoining planning with funding were ignored in the annual budgeting process whenever necessary to sustain the flow of timber to corporate mills.

The third period of attempted reform enlivened forest policy debates in the 1980s, and may have finally ushered in a new post–intensive management era in public forestry. Although the Reagan administration fought a no-holds-barred struggle to concentrate the Forest Service on industrial development, its efforts were blunted — not so much by conservationist opposition as by economic, political, and environmental realities. Political support for corporate welfare economics appears to be in decline since the federal budget deficit ballooned out of control in the 1980s and since America, for the first time in over one hundred years, has become a major debtor nation. Losing money while destroying national forest ecosystems in this economic climate seems increasingly irrational. In addition, and perhaps more importantly, the exploitable resource base of the national forests is in decline. Ironically, reform may now be feasible only because America's vast reservoir of valuable old-growth timber has been mostly liquidated. There is relatively little left of America's pre-Columbian forests to exploit. The government-sponsored "Great Barbecue" is over.

This sobering climate of greater resource scarcity, fiscal conservatism, management humility, and awareness of ecosystem degradation is driving the Forest Service into unfamiliar new territory. Many in the agency, fortunately, welcome the changes and look forward to the journey. As John Bedell, supervisor of the Apache-Sitgreaves National Forest, recently explained to journalist Grace Herndon, "there is a major change in the wind. I can tell you this is no fad. I expect more change [in the agency] in the next five years than in the last fifty years."[2] Let us hope he is right.

APPENDIX

Footpaths
through Forest History

This book is in many ways an extension of the work of others. Here I will discuss briefly where my analysis parallels and where it diverges from some of the more prominent scholars on this subject who have influenced my thinking. This is by no means intended to be a comprehensive review of the relevant literature. (See list of references for full citations of books cited below.)

Donald Worster (*Rivers of Empire,* 1985; *Dust Bowl,* 1979; *Nature's Economy,* 1977) has greatly influenced my thinking about science, economic systems and ideologies, and the moral dimensions of the relationship between humans and nature. The advanced industrial-capitalist state, argues Worster, is "Janus-faced," simultaneously bearing the visages of the private corporation and public government. Both work hand-in-hand to convert nature into capital in pursuit of the accumulation of wealth and social control. Under this mode of social organization, an elite of primary beneficiaries controls wealth, expertise, and political authority, and dominates a relatively dependent population. Individual liberty is increasingly circumscribed — traded off for a modicum of material comfort and security. In both *Dust Bowl* and *Rivers of Empire,* Worster further argues that this mode of production and social organization is unsustainable. Beyond his critique of political economy, his special contribution as an environmental historian has been to elucidate the ways in which the capitalist economy ignores "nature's economy" to its ultimate peril.

Worster's view that industrial capitalism is ultimately destructive of its own support systems is entirely, unequivocally applicable to the history of timber production on the national forests. His characterization of natural resource "development" as being accomplished by a dual-faced, public-private monopoly of wealth, expertise, and authority is also eerily accurate, although the monolithic or hegemonic character of this partnership can be exaggerated. The elite model is attractive but not wholly explanatory. Actual political economy is more complex than the model suggests. I have found the arena of political and economic decision making to be more a pluralistic conglomeration of contending interest groups than a hegemonic elite imposing control over a dependent population. The elite, in fact, is not united or self-conscious, nor is it unassailable. With that said, it is important to add, however, that the distribution of power among interest groups in the political decision making arena is *not equal*. Nor is *access* to the decision arena equally available to all social groups. Pluralism does not imply equal opportunity. One can speak of the dominance of certain interests and values. If there is such a thing as hegemony, it does not come in the form of personalized, self-interested wielders of power, but in the plain fact that over long periods of time certain values are consistently favored and benefits consistently flow to certain enterprises and social groups — as this case study in national forest management bears out. Even though multiple-use management itself is an expression of the recognition of pluralist values, and even though the relative balance of the various uses changed somewhat during the period 1945–93, one can still effectively argue, as I do, that certain interests and outcomes consistently remained dominant despite contending interest group pressures and "official" policies to redistribute the flow of costs and benefits. This has occurred partly as a result of social inertia, partly as a result of overt mechanisms of elite domination, and partly from mass attraction to the promised material and employment advantages of natural resource development. Worster himself acknowledges that the "elite" structure of power is upheld to a large degree by Americans' cultural complicity. The masses share an "instrumentalist" vision of nature as a material resource, and directly or indirectly condone the system of exploitation. Worster trenchantly explains:

> Accepting the authority of engineers, scientists, economists, and bureaucrats along with the power of capital, the common people become a herd. . . . Instead of maturing into autonomous, rational individuals

capable of deciding ultimate issues, as one side of the Enlightenment promised they would all do in the modern age, they instead become lifelong wards of the corporation and the state. Sensing their own impotence in the midst of so much general power, they may feel anger welling up inside them; but they do not know whom or what to blame, so thoroughly have they absorbed and internalized the ruling ideas, so completely have they lost the capacity for critical thought. (*Rivers of Empire*, pp. 57–58)

Historical consistency in the motives, methods, and consequences of the conquest of nature has been thoroughly elaborated by another historian of the American West: Patricia Limerick. Her book, *The Legacy of Conquest: The Unbroken Past of the American West* (1987), opens with a renewed offensive on the old Frederick Jackson Turner school of history, which posited that contact with the institutionless and materially abundant frontier had forged an individualistic, democratic, egalitarian society in America. The closing of the frontier (which Turner ceremoniously announced in 1893) meant the probable end, according to Turner, of America's individualistic, libertarian political culture. A half century later, Walter Prescott Webb's *The Great Frontier* (1951) reiterated these themes of an American golden age and the fear that scarcity would breed authoritarianism. The central feature of Webb's historical view was that things were better, more egalitarian, before the frontier closed and that since then we have experienced increasing inequities of wealth, class conflict, and government authoritarianism. Turner's thesis (which is actually more complex and interesting than I have allowed here) has spawned an entire cottage industry of critical analysis in the history profession. Patricia Limerick argues that there really was no Golden Age. Rather, the consistent realities of social hierarchy, western economic dependency, and the exploitation of nature in pursuit of wealth were simply veiled by Anglocentric and male-centric myths, like the Turner thesis. Limerick suggests that the "passion for profit" is much more central to explaining the settlement of the West than the passion for democracy; that westerners — those who forged the real character of the American West — were hell-bent on economic development and cloaked their dependence on eastern corporate investors and federal subsidies with showy rhetoric about home rule and their "colonial" status.

Limerick's analysis fits quite well with the realities and rhetoric of resource development on the national forests since 1945, especially the machinations of the livestock industry, which I discuss in chapters 3 and 4. In fact,
Limerick has a chapter in *The Legacy of Conquest* titled "Mankind the
Manager," in which she explores how Gifford Pinchot's philosophy of professional management for efficient use evolved into a controversial institution promoting corporate timber exploitation. Looking closely into the
efforts of timber industry lobbyists to influence national forest policy and
Forest Service funding, I have found the same demand for subsidies coupled
with demands for autonomy; the same quiet recognition of dependence on
federal road construction and reforestation dollars disguised alongside diatribes against the dictatorial impulses of national forest managers. And,
like Limerick, who argues in another chapter that westerners sustain themselves on a "myth of innocence," I have found a tendency on the part of
corporate beneficiaries of federal largesse to blame the government or some
other agency like nature (or environmentalists) for environmental and social
problems attributable to their own actions or negligence or lack of planning.
Claiming innocence, they lobby for subsidies and demand that taxpayers or
nature absorb the costs of environmental rehabilitation and social and economic welfare.

On the subject of industry motivations and actions in the political arena,
William Robbins has made a strong impression on my own analysis. His
recent *Hard Times in Paradise* (1988) traces the 100-year rise and fall of
Coos Bay, Oregon, a timber-dependent community that has suffered misera-
bly from the failure to develop a sustainable timber economy. Robbins
emphasizes the social and environmental repercussions of corporate concern for the "bottom line," and characterizes the lumber industry as primarily "migratory" and "extractive" rather than rooted and agricultural.
With a few notable exceptions, this assessment is basically correct, I believe. Social responsibility seems not to be a dependable characteristic of
timber corporations or a natural result of "free market" timber economies.

Robbins's most important work on the subject, *Lumberjacks and Legislators* (1982), deals with the period 1890–1941. In a sense, I pick up where
he left off. Like Robbins, I found a "shared ideological vision" among
foresters, whether in industry, government agencies, or academia — a mate-
rialist/technological dream of turning idle forests into wood fiber farms.

Additionally, like Robbins, I found that the private sector, with government cooperation, was successful in reconstructing "conservation" policy into an economic philosophy of production rather than a social philosophy of long-term sustainable development. In his treatment of the U.S. lumber industry, Robbins elucidates the government-industry partnership concept that was well-articulated earlier by Grant McConnell in *Private Power and American Democracy* (1966) and developed later by Donald Worster in *Rivers of Empire*. Timber leaders, Robbins says, sought and received government aid in creating an economic climate favorable to their interests, even to the point of violating biological sustained yield on the national forests and pushing aside commitments to protect nonmarket forest values. Of course, government favors to the timber industry were often blunted by competing political and economic agendas, and so lumbermen never expressed full satisfaction with the results of their lobbying. This dissatisfaction with government policy can be mistakenly interpreted as evidence that government and industry were hostile rather than cooperative. But if one looks beneath the ubiquitous rhetoric of antagonism that has marked industry-government relations, one finds an uneasy but mutualistic relationship — something akin to bickering siblings rather than irreconcilable enemies.

Although McConnell brilliantly analyzed the impact on democracy of this symbiotic relationship between industry and government — the iron triangle of Congress/resource agency/industry — his interpretation of the Progressive conservation movement in *Private Power and American Democracy* is now outdated. Ignoring tendencies toward economic nationalism and elitism, McConnell characterized Progressivism as generally hostile to big business and viewed conservationism as a democratic movement. On the democratic impulse of conservationism, see also his essay, "The Conservation Movement — Past and Present." McConnell's contemporaries, Samuel Hays (*Conservation and the Gospel of Efficiency,* 1959) and Robert Weibe (*The Search for Order, 1877–1920,* 1967), hit closer to the mark in interpreting the Progressive era and conservation movement.

Unlike Robbins, I do not delve into the organization of the industry itself. Instead, I focus entirely on its lobbying activities in regard to national forest management. Consequently, the sector of the timber industry that appears in this narrative as "the industry" is really only one, albeit large, component of a more extensive and rather diverse lumber, pulp, and paper industry. This should be kept in mind. The timber associations that appear here are those which have been most concerned with getting access to national forests — i.e., those with operations primarily in the West and especially those engaged in lumber production. This is because most of the national forests are in the West and, by World War Two, most of the trees suitable for lumber (what foresters call "sawtimber") were in the West. That is why the West Coast lumber industries became particularly active in timber lobbying activities in Washington, D.C., after World War Two. Their strong influence is manifest in my analysis. Most of my archival research concentrated on the National Lumber Manufacturers Association (which became the National Forest Products Association) and the Western Timber Association.

This book has an evident western bias. This is unfortunate in the sense that most analysts of the national forests have also concentrated on the West. Eastern national forests have been generally neglected by scholars (a reversal of the usual eastern cultural bias of historians). This tendency among forest historians to focus westward is easy to understand. In the decades after mid-century, the greatest pressures for timber harvesting on the national forests were in the West. Most of the public land livestock grazing and virtually all of the grazing controversies centered in the West. Population growth in the nation after mid-century conspicuously shifted southward and westward. Perceptions of water scarcity were most acute in the West, and most of the surface water in that region flowed off national forests. A majority of the nation's game fish and wildlife lived in the West. The West held virtually all of the remaining large-expanse virgin forests suitable for preservation as wilderness. In congressional records and in the archives of the Forest Service, the timber lobbyists, and the national conservation organizations, the West is simply dominant in national forest policy debates. Eastern national forests have experienced most of the same challenges and problems as western ones, especially since the 1960s, but the sheer scale and quantity of controversies in the West have overshadowed those in the East. For a history focusing especially on the 1945–60 period, as this one does, it is easy and perhaps appropriate to emphasize the West. I apologize to eastern readers for having listed westward in this narrative.

Another scholar whose analytical track runs parallel to mine is David A. Clary (*Timber and the Forest Service,* 1986). Clary argues that the Forest Service has been professionally absorbed with timber production for its entire history, becoming completely coopted by the private timber market after World War Two. The agency traditionally sees itself as being on a quasi-sacred mission to avert a national timber famine, he says, resulting in ever more obsessive quests to increase timber production. This organizational bias toward wood products eventually put the agency out of step with changing public values during the 1960s and 1970s. Clary wrote his book during the height of the Reagan era, at the end of his own term as the Forest Service's chief historian (1986). It is primarily a story of a stubborn, narrow-minded bureaucracy that fell behind the times and grew publicly unresponsive.

Agency apologists characterize Clary's critical analysis as the exaggerated product of a disgruntled ex-employee, but a review of its compellingly thorough corroborative documentation suggests otherwise. My own research of the years 1945–91 indicates that Clary was right on the money, with one exception: he attributes too much motive power to the timber famine ideology. The agency's obsession with timber production is more convincingly explained as resulting from larger institutional incentives to cooperate with the political economy of government-sponsored resource development (as Worster and Robbins show) than by reference to an ideological mission of providing wood to the world. By focusing so closely on the agency itself, Clary puts too much stock in its own bureaucratic rationales. I do agree with Clary, however, that timber has dominated the Forest Service's actions and imagination, and that its steadfast devotion to wood production has made it peculiarly inflexible when responding to environmental controversies such as the clearcutting brouhaha of 1969–76, the wilderness battles, and today's below-cost sales and old-growth forest preservation debates. My analysis here takes a magnifying glass to a portion of Clary's sweeping century-long review of the Forest Service. I pay greater attention to the other multiple uses while Clary focuses entirely on timber, plus I emphasize budget politics, a subject that he barely touches on.

Scholars have usually paid more attention to the Forest Service than to the national forests. In contrast, I have tried to ground my discussion of the agency and forest policy with reference to the actual lands and resources in question. Still, the bulk of my focus is institutional, not ecological. A number of other scholars besides Clary have provided an excellent foundation for research on the Forest Service. Harold Steen, the dean of Forest Service historians (*The U.S. Forest Service: A History,* 1976), sets the standard for research and comprehensiveness. His book, however, does not argue a particular thesis; it is compendious rather than interpretive. Unlike Steen, I am arguing a point. My history is not meant to be comprehensive or disinterested. Like Steen, however, I focus on the top of the organizational pyramid: agency heads and decision makers in Washington, D.C., for the most part. I am aware that in politically correct circles this approach is considered passé; nevertheless, I felt that another look at the centers of influence was warranted, especially today with the intense controversy over top-down imposed commodity output targets on the national forests. I argue that what happens on the ground is more influenced by decisions from the top than by any other single factor or multitude of factors, especially budget decisions that determine the organizational resources to accomplish management objectives. Local managers have discretion and their decision environment is important at the local level, but they work within a constrained institutional environment in which Washington, D.C., largely sets the boundaries of the choices available to them. The overall character and outcome of national forest management is very effectively directed by institutional inputs at the top of the pyramid. It is this centralized direction that I am interested in, not localized aberrations or questions of real or imagined autonomy at the bottom of the pyramid.

While I have not tried to further the debate between organizational theorists on the nature of the Forest Service as a policy implementing agent of the federal government, I have been influenced by several of them. Herbert Kaufman wrote an unsurpassed classic on how the agency elicits central policy compliance from its local rangers, *The Forest Ranger* (1960). The study is now outdated in the sense that some of the methods by which top-down compliance had been orchestrated have now been altered. For example, the policy of regularly reassigning rangers in order to loosen their ties to a community while strengthening their identification with the agency has been largely abandoned in many regions. Still, many other incentives to conform to central policy exist, most importantly, performance evaluations and promotions based on achieving assigned output targets. Kaufman is valuable for elucidating internal organizational means for compelling conformity, but he does not historically contextualize his discussion and he does not look outside the agency to larger forces that shape the organizational environment. His is an abstracted view of internal bureaucratic mechanisms of employee control.

Kaufman helped spur on a debate over whether the Forest Service had effectively insulated itself from external pressures. If an agency had established efficient internal mechanisms for achieving centralized policy compliance, then wouldn't it be more or less immune to pressure from special interests? Not if the special interest pressure is applied at the top where policy is constructed. In contrast to Kaufman, others have argued that the agency has been a hapless pawn of special interests, "captured" by its commercial constituencies. Classic exponents of the capture thesis are Philip Foss (*Politics and Grass,* 1960) and Grant McConnell (*Private Power and American Democracy,* 1966). Although Foss focuses on the Bureau of Land Management rather than the Forest Service, his rendition of how a natural resource managing agency of the federal government can be politically manipulated into catering to commercial beneficiaries (the graziers, in this case) is provocative. The difference between Kaufman, Foss, and McConnell is that the latter two looked at the political context within which the agency as a whole functioned. This is the tack I take. Kaufman's view is not incompatible with Foss's and McConnell's, however. There is still room within the capture thesis for a theory of how political mandates from above can be translated into conforming actions on the ground, even when those actions are contrary to other stated organizational policies.

A more recent variation on the capture debate is Paul Culhane's *Public Lands Politics* (1981), which argues that the Forest Service and the Bureau of Land Management play interest groups off each other to avoid being captured by them. At the local level this appears to have some validity, since all interest groups invariably criticize the agencies for not adequately accommodating their interests. But Culhane bases his assertion of bureaucratic independence on perceptions of local interest groups and local agency decision makers, as well as on a statistical survey of how often interest groups got what they wanted in particular resource decisions. This is an interesting methodology, but of limited value. Like Kaufman, Culhane fails to take into account the larger political, economic, and historical context of resource allocation. Furthermore, perceptions of individual participants at the local level are not particularly explanatory. First, most decision makers at least superficially perceive that they are masters of their own decision making, especially professional managers, so perceptions of independence among forest rangers are to be expected. Second, tallying pleasure or dissatisfaction with agency decisions among interest groups does not take into account differences in expectations or other tactical considerations on the part of the lobbyist. Finally, the fact that a set of specified interest groups each get something of what they want is not a qualitative indication of equity in resource allocation nor a measure of independence among bureaucrats. Nor does it have anything to do with managing for sustainability.

Ben W. Twight and Fremont J. Lyden offer a detailed critique of Culhane's thesis in their study of professional bias within the Forest Service ("Measuring Forest Service Bias," 1989, and "Constituency Bias in a Federal Career System," 1990). These authors surveyed 400 district rangers (compared to 28 studied by Culhane) regarding their values and preferences, and compared those responses to 565 responses from members of the public (half aligned with industry user groups and half identifying themselves as "environmentalists"). They found that the district rangers' values and preferences overlapped considerably with those of the industry groups but only a little with environmentalists. That substantial "bias," they argue, is reflected in their decision making.

"Capture" becomes a misleading term when describing the political/organizational theory of Twight and Lyden. It implies defeat and control of an unwilling group by another more powerful one. This is not what Twight and Lyden are arguing, however. Instead, they claim that the Forest Service does not need to be "captured" because it already shares fundamental values and preferences with industry groups. Clary, Robbins, and Worster essentially agree with this perspective, and I find it compelling, too. Any "capturing" taking place occurs only in a broader "market" sense, where commercial considerations take hold of the imaginations and objectives of forest managers or where production commitments and economic dependency become constraints on manager discretion.

There are those, too, who simultaneously find fault with and sympathize with the agency, offering another critical perspective that suggests the Service is neither captured nor autonomous nor a willing conspirator, but a pawn of politics and a victim of its own bureaucratic timidity. William Voigt takes this view in his analysis of Forest Service grazing management, *Public Grazing Lands* (1976). Michael Frome joins Voigt in pointing the finger at forces of conciliation within the agency that place organizational stability and security above sound management (*The Forest Service,* 2nd ed., 1984). In truth, all of these critiques are more or less accurate, depending on which angle of view you take and which agency spokespersons you choose to define as characteristic of the whole. It is best to remember that the capture versus autonomy debate is only a sidebar to the larger issue of how national forests are managed, how resources are allocated, how competing public values are negotiated, and how resultant policies are implemented.

Another group of scholars upon whose work I build focus on national forest policy development. In the same sense that Steen's work offers a comprehensive overview of Forest Service history, Samuel T. Dana and Sally K. Fairfax provide a compendium of forest policy evolution in *Forest and Range Policy* (2nd ed., 1980). But, like Steen, Dana and Fairfax offer less interpretation than narrative description. Like them, I am interested in policy development, although since I concentrate on only one agency and only the post–World War Two era, I am able to substitute detailed analysis for the rather curt summaries contained in their monograph. Also, I am less inclined to defend the agency perspective in the controversies of the 1960s and 1970s than Sally Fairfax (who wrote most of the material on that period).

A policy specialist to whom I am particularly indebted is Dennis C. LeMaster, author of *Decade of Change: The Remaking of Forest Service Statutory Authority during the 1970s* (1984). LeMaster was a participant in the policy debates of the 1960s and 1970s in Washington and put together a revealing and detailed analysis of the political maneuvering behind major national forest legislation between 1964 and 1976. I draw on his research extensively in chapters 10 and 11. In fact, my treatment of that period is condensed to avoid duplication of his work. In contrast, I spend considerable time on policy events between 1945 and 1960, offering a level of detail for this earlier period comparable to LeMaster's. Such extended treatment of national forest policy debates between 1945 and 1960 is not available anywhere else.

One policy scholar with whom I contrast greatly is Marion Clawson of Resources for the Future. Clawson holds the classic economist's view that trees are unused capital and that forests should be commodified. His philosophical orientation is similar to the school of "new resource economists" who believe in assigning dollar values to all forest uses, privatizing resource allocations whenever possible, and dedicating forests to their "highest" economic use. Clawson's specific viewpoint advanced in his book *Forests for Whom and for What?* (1975) is critiqued in Chapter 2, "Two Views of the Forest."

An economist who has positively influenced my thinking is Randall O'Toole (*Reforming the Forest Service*, 1988). With his prolific pen (O'Toole founded *Forest Watch* magazine out of Eugene, Oregon), he has compellingly exposed the economic and bureaucratic incentives for Forest Service mismanagement, and decimated agency rationales for its economically irrational road-building and below-cost timber sales programs. O'Toole's nonprofit consulting business, Cascade Holistic Economic Consultants, has critically analyzed dozens of forest plans and other Forest Service documents. While respecting his analytical skills, however, I diverge from his approach to solving forest management problems. O'Toole strongly adheres to the "free-market" faith. Trained in the neoclassical school of economics, O'Toole believes that marketizing forest resources would be the best way to eliminate pork barrel logging and to protect environmental amenities. To some degree, his proposals would improve national forest management; but markets are not a panacea. The failure of the market to protect amenities, nonpriceable values, and other "public goods" was one of the main reasons for establishing the national forests and for promoting "public forestry." Free-market resource economists advance their own conspiracy of optimism, dogmatically upholding the institutions of private property and unfettered market exchanges as the true source of liberty, equality, and justice. O'Toole and other adherents to the faith do not fully appreciate the fact that markets are constrained institutions that can *never* be "free," and that many values cannot be traded in a marketplace. (A valuable critique of the free-market faith is found in Frank Gregg's 1988 essay, "Public Land Policy: Controversial Beginnings for the Third Century.")

For my interpretation of conservationism and environmentalism as social phenomena, Samuel Hays has been influential. His *Conservation and the Gospel of Efficiency* (1959) characterized the Progressive era conservation movement, personified in Gifford Pinchot, as concerned primarily with efficiency of production, a mission that advocated elite, professional management by public spirited federal bureaucrats. The legacy of those ideals still permeated the Forest Service in the period following World War Two. Gifford Pinchot remains an agency icon today. But this ethos is partly what got the Forest Service in trouble in the 1960s. Hays's more recent monograph *Beauty, Health, and Permanence* (1987) analyzes the history of environmental politics from 1955 to the mid-1980s and argues that a watershed change in public values occurred sometime after World War Two. America switched from being a nation obsessed with production to a nation obsessed with concerns for "quality of life," including environmental amenities. The Forest Service was slow to change with the times, however, according to Hays, and remained doggedly wedded to maximizing production.

The watershed change in public values that Hays refers to, and its connection to a consumer culture, is reflected in my research. Those who opposed environmental protection policies after World War Two generally invoked the twin fears of economic depression and material scarcity as a rationale for defending less restrained economic development. By the mid-1950s, the spectacular economic growth initiated during the war and continuing in the postwar era made abundance so conspicuous and sustained prosperity so apparently dependable that old memories of the depression of the 1930s faded. A new ethos of optimism replaced the old gnawing economic insecurity. This allowed for the phenomenal growth of the new environmental movement, which depended on a materially satisfied and secure population willing to turn to questions of *quality* of life rather than quantity.

Probably the most unique angle to my analysis is the special focus on budget decisions. Forest Service funding is the channel through which the government distributes capital and other benefits to the private sector. It is the engine of corporate welfare. It is also the primary means through which forest policies are either implemented or shelved. Yet, oddly, most scholars avoid analyzing the budgeting and funding process. It is crucial, yet remarkably neglected. It is also, unfortunately, largely hidden from public view. Overt political manipulation of the Forest Service through the budget process during the Reagan Administration brought this issue into public consciousness. Beginning in the early 1980s, citizens had been asked to give formal input into lengthy, expensive, excruciatingly complex land management plans; but when annual congressional funding levels for the agency ended up facilitating certain outcomes while stymying others, without regard for what was written in the plans, the value of the planning process was called into question. Having experienced this first hand, I decided to explore the historical roots of this disjunction between planning and funding. That was the seed for this study.

Only two other scholars to my knowledge have rigorously analyzed this issue. One is Randal O'Toole, mentioned above (see his "Citizens' Guide to the Forest Service Budget," 1992, and his book, *Reforming the Forest Service,* 1988); the other is V. Alaric Sample (see his 1990 monograph, *The Impact of the Federal Budget Process on National Forest Planning*). Sample is an economist who traced with marvelous sophistication the flow of federal dollars to the various resource programs of the Forest Service between 1960 and 1986. He especially focused on the years 1977–86, for which he had data allowing him to compare agency budget requests with administration requests to Congress and actual congressional funding levels. He analyzed trends over the entire period and made case studies of several individual national forests for which he followed the budget process from the local level to Washington and back down to the forest, to compare how the various resource program requests were honored and what effect the assigned budgets had on the accomplishment of resource management objectives. The evidence unequivocally showed that funding was only tenuously tied to land management plans and that there was a *significant* timber bias in the agency.

My work here takes the assessment of this planning/funding disjunction back to 1945. I was also able to dig up specific budget data unavailable to Sample for the years 1955–73. Those data are reflected in the figures in chapters 9, 10, and 11. As an economist, Sample offers a more sophisticated fiscal analysis than I have been able to accomplish here (discounting for inflation, for example), but as a historian I have been able to more effectively weave my economic data into a human narrative. While Sample only touches on the political and social context of funding decisions, my treatment here elaborates them, at least for the period from 1945 to 1976. For the period after 1976, on the subject of planning and funding, I rely on Sample's findings (Chap. 11).

There are some differences between my presentation of budget data and Sample's which require explanation. Sample uses a discount rate to display budget data in "constant" dollars. This is necessary for comparing budgets in the 1970s and 1980s, when inflation rates took an unprecedented jump upward. It is less necessary for the 1950s and 1960s, when inflation was lower, especially when comparing budgets for only one or two presidential terms at a time as I do. Consequently, I have presented the budget figures exactly as they appear in government documents. We also differ on our specific budget categories. While I again display the data for the various resource management programs exactly as they appear in the federal budget, Sample merges all or portions of several budget line items to come up with new budget categories. For example, he merges timber sales, reforestation and stand improvement, and the bulk of the road budget together to make up the "timber program." This is a sensible approach, but does not allow him to distinguish between timber harvesting budgets and forest regeneration budgets, as I do (the former maximized and the latter minimized). Finally, Sample has included money made available by the 1930 Knutsen-Vandenberg Act (K-V funds), while I left them out. Although it is appropriate that Sample incorporates K-V funds into his budget figures, I omitted them for several reasons: First, in the 1940s and 1950s, where I concentrate my economic analysis, and to a lesser degree in the 1960s, K-V funds remained a minor source of supplementary financing. Second, because records have not been retained, these funds are hard to trace prior to the 1970s. Third, they are one-shot discretionary mitigations applied at the local level and do not represent long-term political commitment to balanced management. It should be realized, however, that K-V funds can only be used where timber sale activities have occurred; thus, they tend to function as an incentive to engage in timber sales, reinforcing the handmaiden status of nontimber resources.

Although there are other scholarly works that could be mentioned here, these have been the most influential on my analysis. Additional references to these and other scholars are found throughout the book.

Notes

Introduction: An Overview of the Issues

1. A few of the more prominent recent critiques of national forest management in the popular press include the following: Perri Knize, "The Mismanagement of the National Forests," *Atlantic Monthly* (Oct. 1991), pp. 98–112; Michael D. Lemonick, "Whose Woods Are These?" *Time* (Dec. 9, 1991), pp. 70–75; "Time for a Little Perestroika," *Economist* (March 10, 1990), p. 28; John McCormick, "Can't See the Forest for the Sleaze," *New York Times* (Jan. 29, 1992), p. A21; "Two Say Politics Rules Their Agencies," *High Country News* 23, no. 18 (Oct. 7, 1991): 1, 10–13; Brad Knickerbocker, "Fight for Federal Lands Spreads," *Christian Science Monitor* (March 14, 1990), p. 7; the special supplement to the Portland, Ore., newspaper, the *Oregonian,* by Kathie Durban and Paul Koberstein, "Forests in Distress" (Oct. 15, 1990); and the special supplements to the Spokane, Wash., newspaper, the *Spokesman Review,* by Jim Lynch, J. Todd Foster, and Julie Titone, "Our Failing Forests" (Nov. 21, 25, and 28, 1993).

2. "Feedback to the Chief from the Forest Supervisors of Regions 1, 2, 3, and 4," in the "Sunbird Proceedings": 2nd National Forest Supervisors' Conference, Tucson, Arizona, November 13–16, 1989, reprinted in *Inner Voice* 2 (Winter 1990): 7, 11.

3. The two most prominent pieces of evidence of this internal rebellion are the "Sunbird" Forest Supervisors' Conference (ibid.) and the establishment of the Association of Forest Service Employees for Environmental Ethics (AFSEEE), founded in 1989. AFSEEE has a nationally distributed bimonthly newspaper called the *Inner Voice* which serves as a forum for those promoting reform of the agency (P.O. Box 11615, Eugene, Oregon 97440). AFSEEE has been widely discussed in the popular press. For one example, see Timothy Egan, "Forest Service Abusing Role, Dissidents Say," *New York Times* (March 4, 1990). For an interesting sociological analysis of the Forest Service internal reform movement, see Greg Brown, "AFSEEE and Bottom-Up Change in the Forest Service," *Inner Voice* 5, no. 1 (Jan./Feb. 1993): 7,

10. Also see the extensive and valuable study by James J. Kennedy, Richard S. Krannich, Thomas M. Quigley, and Lori A. Cramer, *How Employees View the USDA: Forest Service Value and Reward System* (Logan, Utah: College of Natural Resources, March 1992); and the study by Paul Mohai and Phyllis Stillman, *Are We Heading in the Right Direction? A Survey of USDA Forest Service Employees* (Ann Arbor: School of Natural Resources and Environment, University of Michigan, October 1993). For a thoughtful insider's views of the tension between traditional foresters and those promoting change, see W. Dean Carrier, "The Forest Service: Divided against Itself," *High Country News* 24, no. 24 (Dec. 28, 1992): 20. Also see Forest Service historian Gerald Williams's unpublished essay, "Forest Service Leadership: Credibility Problems Facing Current and Future Leaders," Umpqua and Willamette National Forests, Roseburg and Eugene, Oregon, Feb. 1992. I discuss AFSEEE and the national forest reform movement at length in Chap. 12.

4. The classic exposition of the Forest Service as an efficient, respectable organization is Herbert Kaufman, *The Forest Ranger: A Study in Administrative Behavior* (Baltimore: Johns Hopkins Press, 1960).

5. "Time for a Little Perestroika," p. 28.

6. USDA Forest Service, *The Forest Service Program for Forest and Rangeland Resources* (Washington, D.C.: USDA Forest Service, 1990), pp. 5.10–5.12.

7. Much has been written about public land policy over the years by scholars in many different fields. In the field of history, the classic compendium is that written by Paul Gates for the Public Land Law Review Commission, *A History of Public Land Law Development* (Washington, D.C.: GPO, 1968).

8. USDA Forest Service, *The Forest Service Program,* p. 6.5.

9. *Report of the President's Advisory Panel on Timber and the Environment* (Washington, D.C.: GPO, April 1973), p. 34.

10. In 1952, the national forests contributed 10 percent of domestic timber production; by 1962 that amount had risen to 16 percent and stayed at that level until the 1980s. In 1986 it was 13 percent, and in 1992, 12 percent. These figures are derived from statistics found in USDA Forest Service, *Forest Statistics of the U.S., 1977* (Washington, D.C.: GPO, 1978), p. 80; and *Forest Statistics of the United States, 1987,* Forest Service Resource Bulletin PNW-168, p. 21. The 1992 percentage was derived from data in Keith Schneider, "U.S. Would End Cutting of Trees in Many Forests," *New York Times* (April 30, 1993), p. A1.

11. The issue of below-cost timber sales has a huge recent literature. The Natural Resources Defense Council initiated public attention to this issue in the 1980s with a report by Thomas J. Barlow, Gloria E. Helfland, Trent W. Orr, and Thomas B. Stoel, Jr., *Giving Away the National Forests: An Analysis of Forest Service Timber Sales Below Cost* (New York: NRDC, June 1980). A U.S. General Accounting Office

investigation followed up on the NRDC report: "Report to the Congress: Congress Needs Better Information on Forest Service's Below-Cost Timber Sales," GAO/RCED-84–96 (June 28, 1984). Contemporary with the GAO report was a strongly critical analysis by the Wilderness Society written by economist V. Alaric Sample, *Below-Cost Timber Sales on the National Forests* (Washington, D.C.: Wilderness Society, 1984). A rather defensive Forest Service response to the growing controversy is found in Ervin G. Schuster and J. Greg Jones, "Below-Cost Timber Sales: Analysis of a Forest Policy Issue," General Technical Report INT-183 (Ogden, Utah: USDA Forest Service, Intermountain Research Station, May 1985). Responding to a request from Congress, the Forest Service came up with a Timber Sale Program Information Reporting System (TSPIRS) in 1987 to compare costs and benefits. The best critical analyses of TSPIRS and timber program economics in general have been written by natural resource economists Robert Wolf and Randal O'Toole. See O'Toole's *A Critique of TSPIRS,* co-written with Randy Selig, Cascade Holistic Economic Consultants (CHEC) Research Paper #20 (Oak Grove, Oreg.: CHEC, November 1989), and *Growing Timber Deficits: Review of the Forest Service's 1990 Budget and Timber Sale Program,* CHEC Research Paper #23 (Oak Grove, Oreg.: CHEC, April 1991). Robert Wolf offers an equally detailed critique and a historical evaluation of the below-cost timber sales issue in "National Forest Timber Sales and the Legacy of Gifford Pinchot: Managing a Forest and Making It Pay," *University of Colorado Law Review* 60, no. 4 (1989): 1037–78.

12. Political sociologist Ben Twight has argued that the professional values of foresters in the Forest Service which trace from Prussian roots in the nineteenth century have forged a "closed system" organization largely unresponsive to constituencies that do not share its values orientation; see Twight, *Organizational Values and Political Power: The Forest Service Versus the Olympic National Park* (University Park: Pennsylvania State University Press, 1983), pp. 15–28. Twight's thesis applies well to the Forest Service prior to the 1970s, but it begins to break down after that time as the agency hired more and more nonforesters who began to challenge the hegemony of the old forestry paradigm.

13. For a historiographic discussion of forestry in the West in the twentieth century, see William G. Robbins, "The Western Lumber Industry," in Gerald D. Nash and Richard Etulain, eds., *The Twentieth-Century West* (Albuquerque: University of New Mexico Press, 1989), pp. 233–56. On the depletion of private timber on the Pacific coast specifically, see Robbins, pp. 242–46, and Michael Williams, *Americans and Their Forests: A Historical Geography* (Cambridge: Cambridge University Press, 1989), pp. 326–30.

14. The President's Materials Policy Commission, *Resources for Freedom,* vol. 1, *Foundations for Growth and Security* (Washington, D.C.: GPO, June 1952), p. 1.

15. An excellent exploration of the effects on natural resources development of this cultural dedication to economic growth in the Truman and Eisenhower years is Elmo Richardson's *Dams, Parks, and Politics* (Lexington: University Press of Kentucky, 1973). Richardson focuses on the Department of Interior, especially national park preservation versus water resource development, and so he does not cover the national forests, but his analysis of political culture in this postwar period is illuminating.

16. The quote is from resource economist John Baden, "Spare That Tree!" *Forbes* (Dec. 9, 1991), p. 230. On the currently existing national forest road system mileage, see USDA Forest Service, *The Forest Service Program for Forest and Rangeland Resources* (Washington, D.C., 1990), pp. 6–18. One example of high road densities is the Gifford Pinchot National Forest in Washington, which had an average of 2.4 miles of active roads per square mile of forest in the early 1980s. When wilderness areas are subtracted from the total forest acreage, the road density actually equals 3 miles per square mile; see USDA Forest Service, Pacific Northwest Region, *Analysis of the Management Situation, Gifford Pinchot National Forest* (Portland, Oregon, no date [1982?]), p. 119.

17. Methods and justifications for raising the allowable cut in the 1950s are discussed in Chapter 6.

18. USDA Forest Service, Lolo National Forest, *Report for 1955* (no date), p. 4. The harvest data cited for 1955 appear to refer to the calendar year rather than the fiscal year. Thus the data differ from official harvest figures reported in regional office records and used elsewhere in this book.

19. Harvest data from U.S. Forest Service, Region 1 Office (Missoula), "Timber Business" fiscal year reports and "Timber Cut and Sold" reports.

20. USDA Forest Service, Northern Regional Office, published as *Full Use and Development of Montana's Timber Resources,* Senate doc. #9, 86th Congress, 1st Sess. Jan. 27, 1959.

21. Gordon Robinson, a forester and lobbyist for the Sierra Club in the 1960s and 1970s, fought consistently for timber management reform to protect multiple use and biological sustainability. His book, *The Forest and the Trees: A Guide to Excellent Forestry* (Washington, D.C.: Island Press, 1988), is his manifesto.

22. Michael McCloskey, in the foreword to Gordon Robinson's *The Forest and the Trees,* p. v.

23. For an excellent introduction to the deleterious impacts of roads and logging on soil, water, and wildlife, see the Forest Service's 1980 series of research reports edited by William R. Meehan: *Influence of Forest and Rangeland Management on Anadromous Fish Habitat in Western North America,* especially Carlton S. Yee and Terry D. Roelofs, "Planning Forest Roads to Protect Salmonid Habitat," General Technical Report PNW-109 (July 1980).

24. Incredible ironies in the use of these "K-V funds" have become common-place. For example, one forest manager logged an area partly to get K-V money from the sale to help replant a clearcut nearby that had failed to regenerate. Another forest built roads and sold timber in one place to get money to close logging roads in another place, ostensibly to benefit wildlife. In a third instance, $2,000 in receipts from one timber sale was earmarked to pay for signs explaining to forest visitors why the forest was being clearcut. For a history and critique of the Knutson-Vandenberg Act, see Karen Knudsen and Randal O'Toole, *Good Intentions: The Case For Repealing the Knutson-Vandenberg Act,* CHEC Research Paper #24 (Sept. 1991); also see O'Toole's "The Citizens' Guide to the Forest Service Budget," *Forest Watch* 12, no. 9 (April 1992): 12–14. These examples of the use and misuse of K-V funds are cited in both the above documents, as well as Baden, "Spare That Tree!," pp. 229–30; and Stephen Budiansky, "Sawdust and Mirrors," *U.S. News and World Report* (July 1, 1991), pp. 55–57.

25. Randal O'Toole, *Reforming the Forest Service* (Washington, D.C.: Island Press, 1988).

26. The most complete assessment of the failure to integrate program funding with long-term planning is V. Alaric Sample's *The Impact of the Federal Budget Process on National Forest Planning* (New York: Greenwood Press, 1990). Sample focuses primarily on the period 1977–86, with some analysis of the years between 1960 and 1976. He offers a sophisticated economic critique amid a review of theories of organizational behavior. For a fuller discussion of his findings, see Chapter 12.

27. Koppes discusses corporate liberalism versus commonwealth liberalism as they developed between 1933 and 1953. The commonwealth advocates, including Harold Ickes, Henry Wallace, and Rexford Tugwell, among others, promoted national, long-term, comprehensive economic planning aimed at distributing benefits and wealth in the broadest, most equitable manner possible. The corporate liberals, according to Koppes, generally eschewed proposals to redistribute wealth and saw big business as a partner rather than a problem. They merged Keynesian governmental activism with the trickle-down theory of economic welfare. Clayton Koppes, "Environmental Policy and American Liberalism: The Department of the Interior, 1933–1953," in Kendall E. Bailes, ed., *Environmental History: Critical Issues in Comparative Perspective* (Lanham, Md.: University Press of America, 1985), pp. 437–75. Donald Worster also keenly analyzes the political economy of resource development in the American West in his book *Rivers of Empire* (New York: Pantheon Books, 1985). He discusses the "two faces" of the capitalist state — government and the private sector — united in the post–World War Two American West in pursuit of "total use for greater wealth." Under the illusory banner of technology and democracy, he argues, a state-sponsored empire of corporate wealth strove for do-

minion over nature and a corresponding dominion over a "large, anonymous, and dependent population" (p. 261).

28. Quoted by Jim Ludwig in his article, "Pin Arguments on Demand, Forest Researcher Advises," *Missoulian* (Sept. 13, 1991).

29. For a scholarly analysis from the 1960s that portrays the Forest Service as defensive and entrenched in a professional ideological straitjacket, see Ashley Schiff, "Innovation and Administrative Decision-Making: The Conservation of Land Resources," *Administrative Science Quarterly* 2, no. 1 (June 1966): 1–30. See also Twight, *Organizational Values and Political Power*.

30. USDA Forest Service, "Work Force Data Book, 1990–1991," (Washington, D.C.: Forest Service, 1991), pp. 28–30.

31. This issue of Forest Service bias toward timber has been widely debated and is discussed in more detail in the chapters that follow. The classic exposition of timber bias is historian David Clary's *Timber and the Forest Service* (Lawrence: University Press of Kansas, 1986). In contrast to Clary, political scientist Paul J. Culhane studied the impact of pressure groups on the Forest Service and Bureau of Land Management and concluded that the federal land managers occupied a middle ground between the user groups and environmentalists: *Public Land Politics* (Baltimore: Johns Hopkins University Press, 1981). Ben W. Twight and Fremont J. Lyden criticized Culhane's methodology and came to the conclusion that national forest managers held a value system much more closely allied with the user groups' values than with environmentalists, and that those values strongly biased decision making: "Measuring Forest Service Bias," *Journal of Forestry* 87, no. 5 (May 1989): 35–41. See also Twight, Lyden, and E. Thomas Tuchmann, "Constituency Bias in a Federal Career System? A Study of District Rangers of the U.S. Forest Service," *Administration and Society* 22, no. 3 (Nov. 1990): 358–89. In this latter article, Culhane responds. Most recently, this issue of agency bias was addressed in the U.S. Office of Technology Assessment report, *Forest Service Planning: Accommodating Uses, Producing Outputs, and Sustaining Ecosystems,* OTA-F-505 (Washington, D.C.: GPO, Feb. 1992). The report's first finding was this: "The Forest Service emphasizes allocating lands and producing physical outputs, especially timber, in forest planning and gives little attention to sustaining ecosystems" (p. 10).

32. Samuel P. Hays, *Beauty, Health, and Permanence: Environmental Politics in the United States, 1955–1985* (New York: Cambridge University Press, 1987), chap. 1, "From Conservation to Environment."

33. Susan R. Schrepfer traced the 1950s origins of the Sierra Club's effort to establish a formal role for conservationists to influence administrative decision-making in her essay, "Establishing Administrative 'Standing': The Sierra Club and the Forest Service," *Pacific Historical Review* 62 , no. 1 (Feb. 1989): 55–81. Samuel

Hays discussed the legislative and administrative reform initiatives of environmental groups in the 1960s and 1970s in *Beauty, Health, and Permanence,* pp. 458–79.

34. Crowell refused to send the Forest Service's 1985 Resources Planning Act (RPA) *Program for the National Forests* to the president for approval because it did not support his accelerated timber production goals. In a memo to the Chief of the Forest Service, R. Max Peterson, Crowell insisted that the fifty-year RPA program should steadily increase national forest logging from 11 billion board feet to 20 billion board feet by the year 2030; see the memo from John Crowell to Max Peterson, re: RPA Recommended Program (Jan. 7, 1985), available from CHEC Forest Planning Bibliography. Arnold Bolle, Dean Emeritus of the Montana School of Forestry, briefly discussed Crowell's drive to double national forest timber production and its effect on national forest planning in the 1980s. See Bolle's essay, "The Bitterroot Revisited: A University Re-view of the Forest Service," *Public Land Law Review* 10 (1989): 16–17. See also Tom Ribe, "To ASQ or Not to ASQ: Timber Targets vs. Environmental Protection," *Inner Voice* 2, no. 4 (Summer/Fall 1990): 1, 14.

35. AFSEEE, "Crisis on the Clearwater: The Mismanagement of a National Resource," (Eugene, Oreg.: AFSEEE, Nov. 22, 1992). See also Steve Hinchman, "Forest Service Can't Get the Cut Out," and Marcia Franklin, "An Idaho Forest Is Told: Log," both in *High Country News* (Dec. 14, 1992), pp. 12–13, 15.

36. USDA Forest Service, *Timber Sale Program Annual Report, Fiscal Year 1988 Test, National Summary* (Washington, D.C.: USDA Forest Service, 1989). Also Robert Wolf, "National Forest Timber Sales," for a historical analysis of the below-cost sales issue. And Wolf's important and remarkably detailed written testimony before the Subcommittee on Environment, Energy, and Natural Resources of the House Committee on Government Operations, "Review of the Forest Service's Timber Sale Program," 102nd Cong., 2nd Sess. (March 31, 1992), pp. 30–89.

37. Testimony of Dr. Richard E. Rice, Senior Resource Economist for the Wilderness Society, before the Subcommittee on Forests, Family Farms, and Energy of the House Committee on Agriculture Hearing on "Timber Sale Economics and Information Reporting System," 101st Cong., 1st Sess. (Nov. 21, 1989), pp. 332–42, 383–93. On pp. 390–93, Rice compiles the real costs and revenues for each national forest and lists amortization periods for roads and reforestation, based on Forest Service data.

38. Keith Schneider, "U.S. Would End Cutting of Trees in Many Forests," *New York Times* (April 30, 1993), pp. A1, A12.

39. The information on the Bighorn National Forest is found in an article by Michael Riley, "The Bighorn's Fatally Flawed Forest Plan," *High Country News* (Dec. 14, 1992), p. 15. For additional examples of public exposure of faulty data and

assumptions regarding timber sale levels, see U.S. General Accounting Office, *Forest Service: The Flathead National Forest Cannot Meet Its Timber Goal,* GAO/RCED-91–124 (Washington, D.C.: GPO, May 1991), pp. 14–16; testimony of Barry Flamm, Chief Forester for the Wilderness Society, before the Subcommittee on Forests, Family Farms, and Energy, House Committee on Agriculture, Hearing on "National Forest Timber Supply Outlook and Sustainable Timber Yield," 101st Cong., 2nd Sess. (March 6, 1990), pp. 540–41; Randal O'Toole, *Analysis of Region 5 Timber Yield Tables,* CHEC Research Paper #17 (Oak Grove, Oreg.: Cascade Holistic Economic Consultants, Sept. 1986), pp. 6–14; Grace Herndon, *Cut and Run: Saying Goodbye to the Last Great Forests in the West* (Telluride, Colo.: Western Eye Press, 1991), chaps. 4, 7. See also Chap. 12 here for a fuller discussion.

40. "Feedback to the Chief from the Forest Supervisors of Regions 1, 2, 3, and 4," in the "Sunbird Proceedings," p. 3.

41. U.S. General Accounting Office, "Public Land Management: Attention to Wildlife is Limited," GAO/RCED-91–64 (Washington, D.C.: GPO, March 1991), p. 3. The GAO also reviewed management of riparian areas on federal lands and concluded that conditions were degraded from overuse and rehabilitation was inadequate. General Accounting Office, "Some Riparian Areas Restored but Widespread Improvement Will Be Slow," GAO/RCED-88–105 (Washington, D.C.: GPO, June 1988).

42. USDA Forest Service, *Douglas-fir Supply Study: Alternative Programs for Increasing Timber Supplies from the National Forests* (Portland, Oreg.: Pacific Northwest Forest and Range Experiment Station, 1969), pp. 14–16.

43. For a detailed, journalistic narrative of the biological, political, and social dimensions of the spotted owl controversy, see William Dietrich, *The Final Forest: The Battle for the Last Great Trees of the Pacific Northwest* (New York: Simon & Schuster, 1992), chaps. 2, 4, and 14.

44. Quoted by Bridgid Schulte, "Busted Timber Towns Seek New Economic Foundation," *High Country News* 24, no. 16 (Sept. 7, 1992): 4.

45. Ibid.

46. Tim Foss, "Seizing the Moment in 1993," *Inner Voice* 5, no. 1 (Jan./Feb. 1993): 1.

47. "Feedback to the Chief," in the "Sunbird Proceedings," pp. 2–3. See also Hinchman, "Forest Service Can't Get the Cut Out," pp. 12–13.

48. See Chap. 12 for an in-depth discussion of the causes for this crash in timber production and the attendant economic dislocations. For examples of communities suffering from recent declines in national forest harvests, see Dietrich, *The Final Forest,* chaps. 3, 5, and 15; Herndon, *Cut and Run,* chap. 7, "Wyoming, flat run out of

trees . . . ." Also see William Robbins's excellent analysis, *Hard Times in Paradise: Coos Bay, Oregon, 1850–1986* (Seattle: University of Washington Press, 1988).

49. Worster, *Rivers of Empire*, p. 261.

50. On the growing involvement of environmentalists in administrative decision-making, see Hays, *Beauty, Health and Permanence*, pp. 473–79; also see Paul Mohai, "Public Participation and Natural Resource Decision-Making: The Case of the RARE II Decisions," *Natural Resources Journal* 27 (Winter 1987): 123–55. Legal "standing" to sue agency decisions has been a significant development, too; see Hays, pp. 479–90, and Schrepfer, "Establishing Administrative 'Standing.' " For a scholarly analysis of how the changing mix of resource professionals and the requirement for interdisciplinary planning have influenced changing attitudes in the Forest Service, see Catherine McCarthy, Paul Sabatier, and John Loomis, "Attitudinal Change in the Forest Service: 1960–1990" (forthcoming in *Society and Natural Resources*). Also see the important work being done at the University of Michigan, Ann Arbor, by Paul Mohai, Phyllis Stillman, Pamela Jakes, and Chris Liggett, "Assessing the Impacts of Gender, Race, and Professional Training on Forest Service Attitudes and Perceptions," paper presented at the meeting of the Society of American Foresters, Indianapolis, November 1993.

51. Donald Worster, *Dust Bowl: The Southern Plains in the 1930s* (New York: Oxford University Press, 1979), pp. 6, 8.

1. Two Views of the Forest

1. C. P. Snow, *The Two Cultures: And a Second Look* (London: Cambridge University Press, 1963). Cambridge Press first printed Snow's lecture in 1959 (he actually gave the address in 1956), and reprinted it ten times in the following three years. In 1963 a second edition came out with fifty pages of reflections by Snow over the unexpected and fairly overwhelming public response his ideas attracted at home in England and abroad. Part of the public response, a good deal of which was negative, was generated by literary critic F. R. Leavis, who publicly rebutted Snow *and* convinced many of his students to do likewise.

2. Ibid., pp. 9, 66–67.

3. Aldo Leopold, *A Sand County Almanac* (New York: Ballantine Books, 1966 [1949]), pp. 258–61.

4. Donald Worster, *Nature's Economy: A History of Ecological Ideas* (Cambridge: Cambridge University Press, 1985). Worster defined arcadian science as the pursuit of knowledge for enlightenment, as opposed to imperialist science, which pursued knowledge for the purposes of control over nature. Worster concluded that ecologists over time have straddled both ideological allegiances. Recognizing the

diversity within the field of ecology, I am sticking with an admittedly overgeneralized homogeneous interpretation of "ecologist" for the purposes of comparing and categorizing forestry paradigms.

5. Thomas G. Alexander, "Timber Management, Traditional Forestry, and Multiple-Use Stewardship: The Case of the Intermountain Region, 1950–85," *Journal of Forest History* 33, no. 1 (Jan. 1989): 21–34.

6. Tim Foss, "New Forestry — A State of Mind," *Inner Voice* 2, no. 1 (Winter 1990): 4–6; and Alan G. McQuillan, "New Perspectives: Forestry for a Postmodern Age," *Western Wildlands* (Winter 1992), pp. 13–20. For a discussion of the "new resource management paradigm" versus the "dominant resource management paradigm," see G. Brown and C. C. Harris, "U.S. Forest Service Resource Management," *Society and Natural Resources* 5 (July/Sept. 1992): 231–45.

7. Leopold, *A Sand County Almanac,* pp. 258–59.

8. Barry Commoner, in his book *Science and Survival* (New York: Viking Press, 1963, 1967) suggested that "the age of innocent faith in science and technology may be over" (p. 3). See also Rachel Carson, *Silent Spring* (Greenwich, Conn.: Fawcett Crest, 1962); Paul B. Sears, "Ecology — A Subversive Subject," *BioScience* 14, no. 7 (July 1964): 11–13; and R. Buckminster Fuller, *Operating Manual for Spaceship Earth* (Carbondale: Southern Illinois University Press, 1969). John Opie edited selections of several of these and other authors' writings for his *Americans and Environment: The Controversy over Ecology* (Lexington, Mass.: D. C. Heath, 1971).

9. Council on Environmental Quality, *Global 2000 Report* (Washington, D.C.: GPO, 1980); Donella H. Meadows et al., *The Limits of Growth* (New York: Universe Books, 1972).

10. George Perkins Marsh, *Man and Nature: The Earth as Modified by Human Action* (New York: Scribner, Armstrong, 1864); Paul B. Sears, *Deserts on the March* (Norman: University of Oklahoma Press, 1959 [first pub. 1935]); Fairfield Osborn, *Our Plundered Planet* (Boston: Little, Brown, 1948). Also see William Vogt, *Road to Survival* (New York: William Sloane, 1948). Vernon Gill Carter and Tom Dale offer a more recent version of this genre in *Topsoil and Civilization* (Norman: University of Oklahoma Press, 1974).

11. E. L. Stone, "Soil and Man's Use of Forest Land," *Forest Soils and Forest Land Management,* Proceedings of the Fourth North American Forest Soils Conference, ed. by B. Bernier and C. H. Winget (Quebec: Les Presses de L'Université Laval, 1975), p. 7.

12. Philip F. Hahn, quoted in Ray Raphael, *Tree Talk: The People and Politics of Timber* (Covelo, Calif.: Island Press, 1981), pp. 45–46. *Tree Talk* is an oral history of the opinions and perceptions of people involved in and affected by the Pacific coast timber economy.

13. I am indebted to E. L. Stone for his illuminating discussion of four professional perspectives on soil, "models" as he calls them. I have taken some liberty with his definitions and added my own interpretations, but his influence is manifest. Stone, "Soil and Man's Use of Forest Land," pp. 2–4.

14. Ibid., p. 3.

15. USDA, *Soils and Men: 1938 Yearbook of Agriculture* (Washington, D.C.: GPO, 1938), p. 940; quoted in Gordon Robinson, *The Forest and the Trees* (Washington, D.C.: Island Press, 1988), p. 86.

16. Mycorrhizae are fungi that attach themselves to tree roots, receiving food from the host plant and giving moisture and mineral nutrients in return. A brief, highly technical discussion of these symbiotic "mycorrhizal relationships" within forest soils is found in D. H. Marx and W. C. Bryan, "The Significance of Mycorrhizae to Forest Trees," *Forest Soils and Forest Land Management,* pp. 107–17. "The prevalence of mycorrhizal associations on roots of plants throughout the world is so widespread that a nonmicorrhizal plant is by far the exception rather than the rule," p. 107. Mycorrhizae are so important to root system physiology that trees, especially commercial species of conifers, are essentially incapable of feeding themselves without mycorrhizal relationships, pp. 110–11.

17. Paul Ehrlich, *The Machinery of Nature* (New York: Simon & Schuster, 1986), pp. 37–38.

18. Gordon Robinson, *The Forest and the Trees: A Guide to Excellent Forestry* (Washington, D.C.: Island Press, 1988); in chap. 5, "Care for the Soil," pp. 83–96, he discusses in detail the deleterious effects of common industrial forestry practices on soil. His references include numerous government research reports and an extensive annotated bibliography.

19. USDA Forest Service, *Report of the Chief of the Forest Service, 1963* (Washington, D.C.: GPO, 1964), p. 8.

20. In 1971 Oregon State University published *Proceedings of a Symposium, Forest Land Uses and Stream Environment,* ed. by J. T. Krygier and J. D. Hall (Corvallis: Oregon State University, 1971), which focused on the effects of forest development activities on waters and watersheds. See especially R. L. Fredriksen, "Comparative Water Quality — Natural and Disturbed Streams Following Logging and Slash Burning," and Jack Rothacher, "Regimes of Streamflow and Their Modification by Logging." Also valuable is A. R. Hibbert, "Forest Treatment Effects on Water Yield," *International Symposium on Forest Hydrology,* ed. by W. E. Sopper and H. W. Lull (New York: Pergamon Press), pp. 527–43.

21. See R. L. Fredriksen, D. G. Moore, and L. A. Norris, "The Impact of Timber Harvest, Fertilization, and Herbicide Treatment on Streamwater Quality in Western Oregon and Washington," *Forest Soils and Forest Land Management,* pp. 283–313.

The authors, all Forest Service researchers, offered only cautious and indirect criticism of their employer, but their message was nonetheless clear: "Timber harvest operations can seriously degrade the quality of streamwater. Soil disturbance by forest roads crossing steep slopes and unstable soils can markedly increase soil erosion and stream sedimentation." The authors went on to suggest the "need for a more equitable assignment of values among various resources of this land." Their point was that watershed values weighed too low on the scale of values driving national forest decision making.

22. Harold F. Heady, "The Rangeland System," in William A. Duerr, Dennis E. Teeguarden, Sam Guttenberg, and Neils B. Christiansen, eds., *Forest Resource Management: Decision Making Principles and Cases* (Corvallis: Oregon State University Book Stores, 1975), p. 21-1.

23. Donald Worster, *Dust Bowl: The Southern Plains in the 1930s* (New York: Oxford University Press, 1979), p. 72.

24. Worster, *Nature's Economy*, p. ix.

25. Heady, "The Rangeland System," p. 21-1.

26. The subject of vegetation change on the western grasslands and its causes is a fertile field of research, especially for southwestern arid rangelands. Major works on the Southwest include the following: James Rodney Hastings and Raymond M. Turner, *The Changing Mile* (Tucson: University of Arizona Press, 1965); Robert R. Humphrey, "The Desert Grassland: A History of Vegetational Changes and an Analysis of Causes," *Botanical Review* 24 (1958): 193–252; Clark S. Martin, *Ecology and Management of Southwestern Semi-Desert Grass-Shrub Ranges: The Status of Our Knowledge,* U.S.D.A. Forest Service Research Paper RM-156, Rocky Mountain Forest and Range Experiment Station, Ft. Collins, Colo. (Washington, D.C.: GPO, 1975); and the most recent monograph on the subject by Conrad J. Bahre, *A Legacy of Change: Historic Human Impact on Vegetation in the Arizona Borderlands* (Tucson: University of Arizona Press, 1991). For the conservationist's perspective on public land grazing, see George Wuerthner, "How the West Was Eaten," *Wilderness* 54 (Spring 1991): 28–37. For an unapologetic polemic on the history of rangeland abuse by the livestock industry, see Denzel and Nancy Ferguson, *Sacred Cows at the Public Trough* (Bend, Oreg.: Maverick Publications, 1983); and Lynn Jacobs, *Waste of the West: Public Lands Ranching* (Tucson, Ariz.: by the author, P.O. Box 5784, Tucson, 85704, 1991).

27. Phil R. Ogden, "Ramifications of Vegetation Manipulation, Positive and Negative Aspects," *Rangeland Policies for the Future, Proceedings of a Symposium, January 28–31, 1979, Tucson, Arizona* (Washington, D.C.: GPO, Oct. 1979), p. 88.

28. For a discussion of recent trends and controversies in national forest grazing management, see the "Change on the Range" special issue, *Inner Voice* 3, no. 3

(Summer 1991), and *Inner Voice* 5, no. 4 (July/Aug. 1993). See also Ed Marston, "Rocks and Hard Places," *Wilderness* 54 (Spring 1991): 38–45.

29. Lawrence S. Davis and Frederic Wagner, "Forest Wildlife," in *Forest Resource Management: Decision Making Principles and Cases,* pp. 22-1, 22-13, 22-18. For a philosophical critique of this positivistic, mathematical approach to forestry, see McQuillan, "New Perspectives: Forestry for a Postmodern Age," p. 16.

30. William D. Hagenstein, "Tree Farms — Greener Every Year," address delivered at the University of British Columbia, March 17, 1977 (Vancouver: University of British Columbia, 1977), p. 8.

31. Lolo National Forest, *Report for 1955,* Northern Regional Office historical records.

32. Aldo Leopold, "Wild Lifers vs. Game Farmers: A Plea for Democracy in Sport," originally published in the April 1919 issue of the *Bulletin of the American Game Protective Association,* reprinted in Dave E. Brown and Neil B. Carmony, eds., *Aldo Leopold's Wilderness* (Harrisburg, Pa.: Stackpole Books, 1990), pp. 54–60. Brown and Carmony have done a great service by rescuing from obscurity many of Leopold's early writings. The editors include an introduction and brief commentaries after each essay.

33. Aldo Leopold, *A Sand County Almanac,* pp. 138–39.

34. Thomas Dunlap has recently summarized this event and its historical significance in chap. 5 of his book, *Saving America's Wildlife* (Princeton: Princeton University Press, 1988).

35. From a table in Chris Maser, *The Redesigned Forest,* p. 53; adopted from R. H. Waring and J. F. Franklin, "Evergreen Coniferous Forests of the Pacific Northwest," *Science* 240 (1979): 1380–86.

36. I am indebted to Chris Maser, *The Redesigned Forest,* pp. 49–53, for this discussion of tree life cycles. Additional discussions of the role of the dead tree in Pacific Northwest forest ecology is found in Chris Maser, R. F. Tarrant, J. M. Trappe, and J. F. Franklin, *From the Forest to the Sea, A Story of Fallen Trees,* USDA Forest Service General Technical Report (Portland, Oreg.: Pacific Northwest Research Station, 1988); Chris Maser and J. M. Trappe, eds., *The Seen and Unseen World of the Fallen Tree,* USDA Forest Service General Technical Report PNW-164 (Portland, Oreg.: Pacific Northwest Research Station, 1984); and Elliot A. Norse, *Ancient Forests of the Pacific Northwest* (Washington, D.C.: Island Press, 1990).

37. "The Tree is Dead! Long Live the Tree!" *Audubon* 92, n. 6 (Nov. 1990): 100.

38. James L. Madden, *Proceedings of the Fourth American Forest Congress* (Washington, D.C.: American Forestry Association, 1953), p. 52.

39. Marion Clawson, *Forests For Whom and For What?* (Baltimore: Johns Hopkins University Press, 1975), p. ix (subsequent references in parentheses in the text).

40. "Those of us hired by industry used the tree farm program as a vehicle to get public support for good [fire and pest] protection, for reasonable taxation. At the time there was a drive on in the United States — a political drive by the Roosevelt Administration — to allege that a long-term crop like timber couldn't be handled by anyone except the government. The government either would have to grow timber on its own lands alone, or would have to regulate the private owners. And there was nobody in our industry who looked with favor upon the idea of the federal government coming in and telling us how to do it. So the tree farm program was in part a vehicle to build up some public confidence that here was an industry prepared to do the job of managing these lands." William Hagenstein, oral interview with Ray Raphael, *Tree Talk: The People and Politics of Timber,* p. 33.

41. William Robbins elaborates examples of shared leadership and professional symmetry among leaders of the timber industry and the Forest Service in his book *American Forestry: A History of National, State, and Private Cooperation* (Lincoln: University of Nebraska Press, 1985).

42. Lyle Watts, Chief, USDA Forest Service, *Report of the Chief of the Forest Service, 1948* (Washington, D.C.: GPO, 1949), p. 4.

43. Ezra Taft Benson, *Proceedings of the Fourth American Forest Congress,* p. 47.

44. Chris Maser, *The Redesigned Forest,* pp. vii–viii; Elliot Norse, *Ancient Forests of the Pacific Northwest,* pp. 161–219.

45. Although the Forest Service has been engaging in below-cost timber sales extensively since the 1950s, these sales did not become a major issue of contention in forest policy debates until the 1980s, partly because the public was generally unaware of the fact earlier, but also because there was a broad public consensus that the federal government should use its resources to ensure the general prosperity of the country — and this meant using national forest timber and tax dollars to stimulate economic development. For various reasons, which will be explained in later chapters, this tolerance for subsidized industrial development of the national forests began to break down in the 1970s. For a recent condensed view of the facts and the controversy over below-cost sales, see U.S. Congress, "Oversight Hearing on the Management Practices of the U.S. Forest Service and Below-Cost Timber Sales," Senate Hearing before the Subcommittee on Conservation and Forestry of the Committee on Agriculture, 101st Cong., 1st sess., Oct. 30, 1989; and a second hearing two years later by the same committee, "Oversight on Below-Cost Timber Sales and National Forest Management," 102 Cong., 1st sess., April 11, 1991.

46. USDA Forest Service, Region 1, memo to forest supervisors, "Revised Table/ Timber Suitability Test," Feb. 27, 1981; and USDA Forest Service, Region 1, "Timberland Suitability Criteria," March 1981. CHEC Forest Planning Bibliography.

47. Gordon Robinson, *The Forest and the Trees: A Guide to Excellent Forestry* (Washington, D.C.: Island Press, 1988), pp. 3–4.

48. Ibid., pp. 70–82.

49. Clawson, p. 166.

50. Cheri Brooks, "The Difference between Dead Trees and Dying Forests: Tree Farming Revisited," *Inner Voice* 3, no. 5 (Fall 1991): 10. For recent criticisms of industrial tree farming, see Sandra Postel and John C. Ryan, "Reforming Forestry," *State of the World 1991: A Worldwatch Institute Report on Progress toward a Sustainable Society,* ed. by Lester R. Brown et al. (New York: W. W. Norton, 1991), pp. 74–92; Elliot A. Norse, *Ancient Forests of the Pacific Northwest* (Washington, D.C.: Island Press, 1990); and three articles by Tim Foss in *Inner Voice:* "New Forestry: A State of Mind," vol. 2, no. 1 (Winter 1990): 4–6; "New Forestry: A Truly 'New Perspective,'" vol. 2, no. 2 (Spring 1990): 5; and "New Forestry: The Global Perspective," vol. 2, no. 4 (Summer/Fall 1990): 10.

51. Tim Foss, "New Forestry: A State of Mind," 4–5.

52. Ibid., p. 4.

53. Maser, *The Redesigned Forest,* pp. 96–98.

54. Ibid., pp. 4–5. See also Norse, *Ancient Forests of the Pacific Northwest,* chap. 8, "Sustainable Forestry for the Pacific Northwest," pp. 243–70.

55. On the "paradigm shift" taking place in forestry, see esp. Richard W. Behan, "Multiresource Forest Management: A Paradigmatic Challenge to Professional Forestry," *Journal of Forestry* 88, no. 4 (April 1990): 12–18. See also Jerry Franklin, "Toward a New Forestry," *American Forests* 95, no. 11/12 (Nov./Dec. 1989): 37–44; Hal Salwasser, "Gaining Perspective: Forestry for the Future," *Journal of Forestry* 88, no. 11 (Nov. 1990): 32–38; and Alan McQuillan, "From Pinchot to Post-Modern: The Circular Century of US Forestry," *Inner Voice* 4, no. 6 (Nov./Dec. 1992): 10–11.

56. See esp. the April, May, and September 1991 issues of the *Journal of Forestry.*

57. V. Alaric Sample for the Pinchot Institute for Conservation, *Land Stewardship in the Next Era of Conservation* (Milford, Pa.: Grey Towers Press, 1991), pp. vii–viii.

58. The relative insularity of the Forest Service and its bias toward timber production has been the subject of several interesting sociological analyses. Looking at the 1910s–1930s battle to establish Olympic National Park out of the Olympic National Forest, Ben W. Twight argued forcefully that the resistant Forest Service was a "closed" organization obsessed with silviculture and unresponsive to alternative public values; Twight, *Organizational Values and Political Power: The Forest Service versus the Olympic National Park* (University Park: Pennsylvania State University Press, 1983). David A. Clary has argued similarly, applying the "timber bias" thesis to the entire history of the agency from its origins to the 1980s; Clary, *Timber*

and the Forest Service (Lawrence: University Press of Kansas, 1986). In contrast, Paul Culhane studied the agency's relationship to various interest groups in the 1970s and argued that the Forest Service trod a middle path between its various constituencies and exhibited no clear bias; Culhane, *Public Lands Politics* (Baltimore: Johns Hopkins University Press, 1981). Twight came back with a rebuttal to Culhane in 1989, showing through values surveys that the agency in the 1980s was still ideologically aligned much more with industry groups than with environmentalists; Ben W. Twight and Fremont J. Lynden, "Measuring Forest Service Bias," *Journal of Forestry* 87, no. 5 (May 1989): 35–41. Paul Mohai and Paul Sabatier have advanced this debate with more sophisticated personnel surveys and they conclude that since the mid-1970s, the agency has been going through a slow revolution in values and management orientation; Paul Mohai, "Public Participation and Natural Resource Decision-Making: The Case of the RARE II Decisions," *Natural Resources Journal* 27 (Winter 1987): 123–55; and Mohai and Phyllis Stillman, *Are We Headed in the Right Direction? A Survey of USDA Forest Service Employees* (Ann Arbor: University of Michigan, School of Natural Resources and Environment, March 1993). Catherine McCarthy, Paul Sabatier, and John Loomis, "Attitudinal Change in the Forest Service: 1960–1990," (forthcoming in *Society and Natural Resources*).

59. On the attempt to integrate the ecological and agronomic orientations, see Thomas Bonnicksen, "Managing Biosocial Systems: A Framework to Organize Society-Environment Relationships," *Journal of Forestry* 89, no. 10 (Oct. 1991): 10–15.

2. Historical Antecedents

1. On the boom/bust timber economies of the nineteenth and early twentieth centuries, see Michael Williams's magisterial work, *Americans and Their Forests: A Historical Geography* (Cambridge: Cambridge University Press, 1989), chaps. 7, 8, and 9. See also Thomas R. Cox, Robert S. Maxwell, Phillip Drennon Thomas, and Joseph J. Malone, *This Well-Wooded Land: Americans and Their Forests from Colonial Times to the Present* (Lincoln: University of Nebraska Press, 1985), chaps. 9 and 10. Arthur McEvoy recently dissected a similar natural resource boom/bust phenomenon in his study of anadromous fisheries on the Pacific coast, *The Fisherman's Problem: Ecology and Law in the California Fisheries, 1850–1980* (Cambridge: Cambridge University Press, 1986); see esp. p. 6 and chap. 3.

2. Quoted by Williams, ibid., p. 230.

3. Ibid. Williams noted that "in the quest for immediate profits, the reckless and prodigal cutting of the better grades of white and jack pine had left a slash cover on the ground that caused devastating fires, which destroyed the humus in the already poor soil and any saplings that managed to grow. Only stunted bush grew to occupy the ground in time" (p. 234).

4. The best historical analysis of the role of "timber famine" ideology in national forest advocacy is David A. Clary, *Timber and the Forest Service* (Lawrence: University Press of Kansas, 1986). Clary argues that the Forest Service organizational psychology — its "timber production bias" — can be explained as a product of a professional obsession with averting a timber famine, an obsession with roots in these early years.

5. The standard history of the role of hunting groups in the forest conservation movement is John Reiger, *American Sportsmen and the Origins of Conservation* (New York: Winchester Press, 1975).

6. Historian Alfred Runte has recently argued that artists, writers, and others with a primarily esthetic sensibility played a significant role in forest reserve advocacy. Adapting themes he developed in his book *National Parks: The American Experience,* 2nd ed. (Lincoln: University of Nebraska Press, 1987), Runte claimed that national forests contributed to an "American sense of place," expressing values that transcended economic considerations; Runte, *Public Lands, Public Heritage: The National Forest Idea* (Niwot, Colo.: Roberts Rinehart Publishers, 1991), pp. 7, 12–16. Although Runte's claim that "the founders of the national forest idea . . . were consistent in their advocacy for landscape esthetics" (p. 7) is overstated, his contention that esthetics did play a role is supported by the evidence.

7. General Revision Act of 1891 (26 Stat. 1103). On the early agitation for a forest policy and federal forest reservations, see Wisconsin's 1867 "Report on the Disastrous Effects of the Destruction of Forest Trees Now Going On So Rapidly in the State of Wisconsin"; Franklin B. Hough's 1873 essay, "On the Duty of Governments in the Preservation of Forests"; and the U.S. Land Commissioner's report of 1877. Each of these, and other similar documents, are reprinted in Frank E. Smith's, *Conservation in the United States, A Documentary History: Land and Water,* vol. 1 (New York: Chelsea House, 1971). Old classic histories of the early forest conservation movement that contain valuable narratives of conservation politics in the late nineteenth century include John Ise, *United States Forest Policy* (New Haven: Yale University Press, 1920), and Jenks Cameron, *The Development of Governmental Forest Controls in the United States* (Baltimore: Johns Hopkins Press, 1928).

8. For the most detailed and dependable treatment of the early debate over forest reserve policy, see Harold K. Steen, *The Beginning of the National Forest System,* published by the Forest Service (Washington, D.C.: GPO, May, 1991), pp. 28–31; and the study by Paul W. Gates, written for the Public Land Law Review Commission, *A History of Public Land Law Development* (Washington, D.C.: GPO, 1968), pp. 563–71; and Charles F. Wilkinson and H. Michael Anderson, "Land and Resource Planning in the National Forests," *Oregon Law Review* 64, nos. 1 & 2 (1985): 46–52.

9. Gates, pp. 568–69.

10. "Pettigrew Act" of June 4, 1897, 30 Stat. 34–36; referred to today as the Organic Administration Act.

11. Gates, pp. 569–71, 585–91; and Ise, p. 139.

12. Still the best analysis of Progressive era conservation is Samuel P. Hays's *Conservation and the Gospel of Efficiency: The Progressive Conservation Movement, 1890–1920* (Cambridge, Mass.: Harvard University Press, 1959).

13. Gifford Pinchot, *The Fight for Conservation* (New York: Doubleday, 1910), pp. 48–49.

14. The Roosevelt speech is reprinted in Frank E. Smith, *Conservation in the United States,* 2:10–14.

15. See Michael Frome's discussion of Pinchot's philosophy of "preservation through use," *The Forest Service,* 2nd ed. (Boulder, Colo.: Westview Press, 1984), pp. 21–23. On Pinchot's opposition to preservation, see Hays, *Conservation and the Gospel of Efficiency,* pp. 40–42; on his support for logging Adirondack Park, see Hays, pp. 191–92, and Roderick Nash, *Wilderness and the American Mind,* 3rd ed. (New Haven: Yale University Press, 1982), pp. 116–21. Charles Wilkinson addresses the debate over Pinchot's utilitarianism in his book *Crossing the Next Meridian: Land, Water, and the Future of the West* (Washington, D.C.: Island Press, 1992), pp. 128–31.

16. Samuel Hays provides the classic interpretation of Pinchot's utilitarianism in chap. 3 of his *Conservation and the Gospel of Efficiency.* Patricia Limerick also offers a lively interpretation of this aspect of Pinchot's philosophy in "Mankind the Manager," chap. 9 of her recent book, *The Legacy of Conquest* (New York: W. W. Norton, 1987); see esp. pp. 297–300.

17. Letter of Secretary of Agriculture James Wilson to Chief Forester Gifford Pinchot, Feb. 1, 1905 (written by Pinchot); reprinted in full in Pinchot's *Breaking New Ground* (Harcourt, Brace, 1947), pp. 261–62; and in USDA Forest Service, *Report of the Chief of the Forest Service,* 1948, p. 3; and in Wilkinson's *Crossing the Next Meridian,* p. 128.

18. Ibid.

19. Pinchot, *The Fight for Conservation,* p. 45.

20. McGee, quoted in Ben W. Twight, *Organizational Values and Political Power: The Forest Service versus the Olympic National Park* (University Park: Pennsylvania State University Press, 1983), p. 24.

21. Ben W. Twight has recently explored this theme of Prussian intellectual influence on early American forestry, concentrating on Bernhard Fernow's contributions to the fight to establish federal forest reserves. Twight, "Bernhard Fernow and Prussian Forestry in America," *Journal of Forestry* 88, no. 2 (Feb. 1990): 21–25.

Char Miller, a recent biographer of Gifford Pinchot, has challenged Twight's assessment, arguing that American political and social institutions "muted" the influence of Prussian forestry, especially in the Forest Service. Miller, "The Prussians Are Coming! The Prussians Are Coming!: Bernhard Fernow and the Roots of the USDA Forest Service," *Journal of Forestry* 89, no. 3 (March 1991): 23–27, 42.

22. Herbert Croly, *The Promise of American Life* (New York: Macmillan, 1909, reprinted by Archon Books, 1963), pp. 246–54.

23. Teddy Roosevelt, reprinted in Smith, *Conservation in the United States,* v.1, pp. 10–14.

24. Roosevelt and Pinchot, quoted by Charles Wilkinson and H. Michael Anderson in their discussion of the history of wildlife and recreation planning on the national forests, "Land and Resource Planning in the National Forests," *Oregon Law Review,* 64:278, 313.

25. Statistics cited in Robert E. Wolf, "The Concept of Multiple Use: The Evolution of the Idea within the Forest Service and the Enactment of the Multiple-Use Sustained-Yield Act of 1960," written for the U.S. Office of Technology Assessment, Contract #N-3-2465.0 (unpublished, Washington, D.C., Office of Technology Assessment, Dec. 1990), p. 13.

26. USDA Forest Service, *A National Plan for American Forestry,* 2 vols., published as Senate Doc. 12, 73rd Cong., 1st Sess. The quotes are from pp. 89–90, 124.

27. Ibid., p. 90.

28. Wolf, pp. 3–4. Although a forester/economist himself, Wolf thoroughly critiques the Forest Service's "single-use" argument repeatedly in this essay and is one of many scholars who argue that the agency invented the multiple-use concept as a defensive measure against Park Service expansionism.

29. Carsten Lien, *Olympic Battleground: The Power Politics of Timber Preservation* (San Francisco: Sierra Club Books, 1991). See also Twight's *Organizational Values and Political Power,* chaps. 3–5. The narrative heart of Twight's book is a case study of the Olympic National Park battle. The analytical heart of his book is an analysis of Forest Service bureaucratic psychology and timber bias.

30. On the World War Two boundary reduction, see Lien, *Olympic Battleground,* chaps. 14–15. On the Municipal Watershed Act and the Port Angeles anecdote, see Wolf, pp. 30–31.

31. Wolf, ibid., p. 4.

32. David Jackson, professor of economics, School of Forestry, University of Montana, interview with the author, October 16, 1992, Missoula, Montana.

33. See Clary, *Timber and the Forest Service,* pp. 4, 34–35, for a discussion of how Pinchot defined sustained yield in 1910. I am also indebted to forestry professors B. Thomas Parry, Henry J. Vaux, and Nicholas Dennis for the following

discussion of the evolution of sustained-yield policy — although my interpretation of the social genesis and historical significance of definitions of sustained yield differs from theirs; see their "Changing Conceptions of Sustained Yield Policy on the National Forests," *Journal of Forestry* 81, no. 3 (March 1983): 150–54.

34. On Mason and the reinterpretation of sustained yield in the 1920s and 1930s, see Parry, Vaux, and Dennis, ibid. See also William G. Robbins, "Lumber Production and Community Stability: A View from the Pacific Northwest," *Journal of Forest History* 31 (1987): 187–96; Harold K. Steen, *The U.S. Forest Service: A History* (Seattle: University of Washington Press, 1976), pp. 225–28, 251. On David T. Mason in general, see Elmo Richardson, *David T. Mason: Forestry Advocate* (Santa Cruz, Calif.: Forest History Society, 1983), and Rodney C. Loehr, ed., *Forests for the Future: The Story of Sustained Yield as Told in the Diaries and Papers of David T. Mason, 1907–1950* (Saint Paul: Forest Products History Foundation, Minnesota Historical Society, 1952).

35. Sustained Yield Forest Management Act of March 29, 1944 (58 Stat. 132).

36. Clary, pp. 126–46.

37. The Pinchot literature is legion. For a sample of the debate over these questions, see Twight, "Bernhard Fernow and Prussian Forestry in America," and Miller, "The Prussians Are Coming! The Prussians Are Coming!" See also citations in notes 15 and 16 above.

38. The second Pinchot quotation is cited in Roy Keene, "Salvage Logging: Health or Hoax," *Inner Voice* 5, no. 2 (March/April 1993): 1.

39. Aldo Leopold, "A Biotic View of Land," *Journal of Forestry* 37, no. 9 (Sept. 1939): 730.

40. Ibid., p. 729.

3. The End of the Forest Service's Custodial Era

1. John R. McGuire, "An Interview with John R. McGuire, Forest Service Chief, 1972–79," conducted by Harold K. Steen (Durham: Forest History Society and U.S. Forest Service, 1988), p. 45.

2. The 1942, 1943, and 1944 *Reports of the Chief of the Forest Service* outlined the ways the agency contributed to the war effort, including performing natural resource inventories, increasing the production of timber and livestock, developing a rubber substitute from the desert guayule plant, opening Alaska's Tongass National Forest to old-growth sitka spruce harvesting for airplane construction, and making available to the military more than half a million acres of national forest land for military operations. On the agency's consultation with the War Department on fire, see Stephen Pyne, *Fire in America* (Princeton: Princeton University Press, 1982), pp. 394–95.

3. USDA Forest Service, *Washington Office Information Digest,* no. 3 (Jan. 5, 1944), p. 2.

4. USDA Forest Service, *Report of the Chief of the Forest Service, 1945,* p. 11 (hereafter cited as *Report of the Chief, 1945,* for example).

5. Ibid., *1942,* pp. 18, 19.

6. Ibid., *1943,* pp. 8–9; ibid., *1945,* p. 8.

7. Ibid., *1945,* p. 9.

8. Michael Williams, *Americans and Their Forests: A Historical Geography* (Cambridge: Cambridge University Press, 1989), pp. 326–30.

9. William D. Hagenstein, spokesman for the West Coast lumber industry since 1941, recently characterized the "tree farm" movement inaugurated in 1942 as a planned public relations effort by industry to build up support (and federal funding) for fire control and to "allay the threat . . . of our Federal government taking over control of private forests" through regulation. See his address, "Tree Farms: Greener Every Year," delivered at the University of British Columbia, March 17, 1977 (Vancouver: University of British Columbia, 1977), pp. 1, 18.

10. Stuart Moir to Senator Dennis Chavez, Sept. 14, 1945, FHS, NFPA Box 68, Forest Service Appropriations file.

11. David A. Clary, *Timber and the Forest Service* (Lawrence: University Press of Kansas, 1986), p. 94.

12. *Report of the Chief, 1946,* p. 1.

13. Ibid., p. 18.

14. Ibid., *1960,* p. 23.

15. Al Weiner, quoted in "Timber Management in the Pacific Northwest: Oral History of Five Region 6 Employees," interviews conducted by Dennis Roth and Jerry Williams (Washington: Forest Service, History Unit, 1986), pp. 22–26.

16. The information in this anecdote dealing with timber production in western Montana in 1946 is drawn from a series of letters between a logging company, Senator James E. Murray (D-Montana), and the Forest Service Regional Office in Missoula, Montana, located in the James E. Murray Papers, University of Montana Archives, Collection 91, Series I, Box 234.

17. Ibid., Dwight Seymour to Senator James E. Murray, Oct. 22, 1946.

18. Ibid., Senator James E. Murray to Mr. Percy D. Hanson, Nov. 14, 1946.

19. Ibid., L. A. Campbell (for P. D. Hanson) to Senator James E. Murray, Dec. 2, 1946.

20. USDA Forest Service, "Program for the National Forests," Miscellaneous Publication 794; reprinted in the *Congressional Record,* 86th Cong. 1st sess. (March 24, 1959), p. 5127.

21. For a recent discussion of the recreation impulse in the postwar period, see

Samuel P. Hays, *Beauty, Health, and Permanence* (Cambridge: Cambridge University Press, 1987), pp. 115–17.

22. Statistics and quote gleaned from the *Report of the Chief, 1960*, pp. 2, 19, 20; and ibid., *1955*, p. 5.

23. American Forestry Association, *Proceedings of the American Forest Congress* (1946). The full study appeared in print in 1948 under the title, *Forests and National Prosperity: A Reappraisal of the Forest Situation in the United States*, USDA Misc. Pub. no. 688.

24. For a brief, inside look at these two timber appraisals and the relationship between the Forest Service and AFA at the time, see Harold K. Steen, *The U.S. Forest Service: A History* (Seattle: University of Washington Press, 1976), pp. 256–57.

25. *Report of the Chief, 1946*, p. 5.

26. Ibid., pp. 10–13.

27. John B. Woods, "Report of the Forest Resource Appraisal," *American Forests* 52 (Sept. 1946): 414–28; and AFA, *Proceedings of the American Forest Congress* (1946).

28. Clapp and Watts quoted in Steen, *The U.S. Forest Service*, pp. 257–58.

29. Christopher M. Granger, "Forest Management in the United States Forest Service, 1907–1952," an oral history conducted in 1965 by Amelia Fry, Regional Oral History Office, Bancroft Library, University of California, Berkeley, 1965, p. 40. Courtesy of the Bancroft Library.

30. Cited in Clary, *Timber and the Forest Service*, p. 122.

31. *Report of the Chief, 1948*, p. 5. The same report offered a rather narrow interpretation of the policy of sustained yield: "Sustained-yield management of timber means that the forest is managed for maximum continuous production of timber of desired kinds" (p. 3).

32. Mason to Dana Parkinson, March 22, 1946, quoted in Clary, *Timber and the Forest Service*, p. 122.

33. Bernard Frank, "Forest Resource Evaluation in the Public Interest," *Proceedings: Society of American Foresters Meeting, Dec. 17–20, 1947* (Washington, D.C.: SAF, 1948), pp. 65, 66.

34. Richard G. Lillard, *The Great Forest* (New York: Alfred A. Knopf, 1947), p. 328.

35. H. Dean Cochran, "Future Trends in Federal Employment of Foresters," *Proceedings: Society of American Foresters Meeting, Dec. 17–20, 1947* (Washington, D.C.: SAF, 1948), pp. 43–45.

36. Walter Mulford, "The Decade 1948–1958 in the Forestry Schools of the United States," *Proceedings: Society of American Foresters Meeting, Dec. 17–20, 1947* (Washington, D.C.: SAF, 1948), pp. 59–63.

37. Lewis M. Turner, "Training Wildland Managers," *Journal of Forestry* 44, no. 7 (July 1946): 491–96.

38. USDA Forest Service, Washington Office news release, "Lloyd Swift Named Forest Service Wildlife Chief," April 12, 1944.

39. *Report of the Chief, 1944,* p. 15.

40. Ibid., *1948,* p. 9.

41. On the role of wildlife groups in the early conservation movement, see John Reiger, *American Sportsmen and the Origins of Conservation* (New York: Winchester Press, 1975).

42. Lloyd Swift, "Wildlife Policy and Administration in the U.S. Forest Service," an oral history conducted in 1964 by Amelia Fry, Regional Oral History Office, Bancroft Library, University of California, Berkeley, revised 1975, pp. 10–11. Courtesy of the Bancroft Library.

43. Ibid., p. 13.

44. Budget figures derived from U.S. Congress, House of Representatives, "Department of Agriculture Appropriations Bill, Fiscal Year 1949," Report no. 1571, 80th Cong., 2nd sess., March 16, 1948.

45. I am indebted to Thomas Dunlap, *Saving America's Wildlife* (Princeton: Princeton University Press, 1988), pp. 98–100, for pointing out some of the significant "firsts" occurring in 1948. Dunlap analyzes American attitudes toward wildlife, especially toward predators, and traces the influence of the science of ecology on public perceptions and public policy.

46. U.S. Congress, House of Representatives, "Department of Agriculture Appropriations Bill, Fiscal Year 1949," Report no. 1571, 80th Cong., 2nd sess., March 16, 1948.

47. *Report of the Chief, 1948,* p. 11.

48. Ibid., *1945,* p. 25.

49. Ibid., p. 24.

50. Ibid., p. 25, 49; ibid., *1947,* p. 29; ibid., *1948,* p. 13.

51. Ibid., *1948,* p. 13.

52. John W. Spencer, "The Place of Recreation in the Multiple-Use Management of the National Forests," *Proceedings: Society of American Foresters Meeting, Dec. 17–20, 1947* (Washington, D.C.: SAF, 1948), p. 180.

53. Ray E. Bassett, "Recreational Forest Management As a Part of the Forestry Profession," *Proceedings: Society of American Foresters Meeting, Dec. 17–20, 1947* (Washington: SAF, 1948), p. 153.

54. Ibid., p. 155.

55. Spencer, p. 181.

56. Ibid., p. 180; Bassett, pp. 155, 158.

57. Bassett, pp. 158, 155.

58. Spencer, p. 179.

59. Bassett, p. 156.

60. Spencer, pp. 178, 182.

61. For a full history of the early years of government attempts to impose grazing regulations on the forest reserves, later the national forests, see chaps. 2 and 3 of William D. Rowley, *U.S. Forest Service Grazing and Rangelands: A History* (College Station: Texas A & M University, 1985).

62. Ibid., pp. 173, 177; see also his discussion of World War One, pp. 112–18.

63. Quoted in Michael Frome, *The Forest Service,* 2nd ed. (Boulder: Westview Press, 1984), pp. 125–26; see also Rowley, pp. 179–80.

64. Frome, ibid.

65. Rowley, pp. 173–75; see also William Voigt, Jr., *Public Grazing Lands: Use and Misuse by Industry and Government* (New Brunswick: Rutgers University Press, 1976), pp. 264–66.

66. Edward P. Cliff, "Half a Century in Forest Conservation: A Biography and Oral History of Edward P. Cliff" (Washington, D.C.: USDA Forest Service, History Section, March 1981), pp. 141–51.

67. The *Proceedings* of the Society of American Foresters' annual meeting in 1947 included four papers by Forest Service personnel on range management problems in the Ozarks, the Southwest, California, and the Pacific Northwest. Each paper described deteriorated range conditions and damaged watersheds from overgrazing; and each recommended reductions in use, more intensive management, and better integration of grazing with other multiple uses.

68. The first issue of the *Journal of Range Management* (October 1948) recounted the society's beginnings in a short essay by Joseph Pechanec, "Our Range Society," pp. 1–2.

69. C. E. Fox to permittees, Routt National Forest, October 11, 1945, quoted in Rowley, p. 202.

70. There are essentially two views on how the agency handled grazing reductions at this time. Some, like William Voigt of the Izaak Walton League and Clarence Woods, claimed the agency suffered from a failure of nerve, caving in to political pressures at the expense of the health of the nation's resources. Others, like Ed Cliff and Walt Dutton (then head of Range Management in Washington), claimed the agency sought cooperation not conciliation and that hardliners like Woods and Earl Sandvig actually made progress more difficult. See William Voigt, *Public Grazing Lands,* pp. 151–70, for the former perspective, and Cliff, "Half a Century in Forest Conservation," pp. 167–70, for the latter viewpoint. In either case, however, all agreed that the reductions were needed; only tactics and politics were at issue.

71. Rowley, p. 205; Steen, pp. 272–73; Bernard DeVoto, "The West against Itself," *Harper's* (Jan. 1947), reprinted in *The Easy Chair* (Boston: Houghton Mifflin, 1955), p. 248. An editorial in the Feb. 1947 issue of *American Forests,* vol. 53, no. 2, criticized the Jan. 1947 resolution of the American Livestock Association.

72. S 33, S 1945, and HR 7638; see DeVoto, pp. 250–52, for a summary and critique of these bills.

73. The primary publicists against the "Land Grab" were DeVoto; Lester Velie of *Collier's* magazine; Arthur Carhart, who had worked in recreation management for the Forest Service for many years but was living and working in Denver as an outdoor writer; William Voigt of the Izaak Walton League; and Hoyt Wilson, editor of the *Denver Post.*

74. DeVoto, pp. 234–35.

75. Ibid., p. 245.

76. Ibid., pp. 245–46.

77. Rowley, p. 208; DeVoto, p. 277; *American Forests* 54, no. 2 (Feb. 1948): 61.

78. DeVoto, p. 277.

79. Quoted in DeVoto, p. 280.

80. DeVoto, p. 278; Steen, p. 275.

81. V. Alaric Sample and Randal O'Toole have comprehensively analyzed this relationship between budgets and policy implementation in recent national forest management. Sample's book, *The Impact of the Federal Budget Process on National Forest Planning* (New York: Greenwood Press, 1990) focuses mainly on the period 1977–86, with some additional data on the 1960–76 period (see Chap. 12 for a summary of Sample's findings). O'Toole's book, *Reforming the Forest Service* (Washington, D.C.: Island Press, 1988), concentrates on the 1980s and goes into great detail on how economic incentives drive the Forest Service rather than public interest oriented resource planning.

82. Budget figures derived from NLMA Forest Conservation Committee memo, "Forestry and Conservation in the 1946–1947 Budget," Jan. 29, 1946, FHS, NFPA box 68, Forest Service Appropriations file. Truman actually achieved balanced budgets during most of his eight years, despite the outbreak of the Korean War. He was the last president to do so.

83. Stuart Moir to G. Harris Collingwood, Feb. 28, 1946, FHS, NFPA box 68, Forest Service Appropriations file.

84. This excerpt and the following ones in the text are from a copy of Colgan's address to Congress, "Statement of Richard A. Colgan, Jr., Before the Senate Committee on Appropriations, Agriculture Subcommittee, June 24, 1947," FHS, NFPA box 68, Forest Service Appropriations file (with subsequent citations in parentheses). Colgan graduated from Michigan State in 1913 with a degree in forestry and subse-

quently spent four years with the Forest Service before going into work for private industry in 1920.

85. The majority of road mileage on the national forests since World War Two has been constructed via timber purchaser road credits. Thus, federal forest capital in the form of stumpage has been consumed to pay for a road system mainly to get out timber. Timber purchaser roads have often been used subsequently for other purposes, such as fire suppression, disease and insect control, and access for recreational use, while waiting for the hoped-for second crop of trees to mature. Because of this, the Forest Service defends such roads as materially contributing to the multiple use management of the forests.

86. "Van" to George Fuller, Feb. 13, 1948, including memo from Stuart Moir on 1948–49 Forest Service budget, FHS, NFPA box 68, Forest Service appropriations file.

87. "Statement of R. A. Colgan, Jr., Before the Sub-Committee on Agricultural Appropriations, House Appropriations Committee, Feb. 27, 1948," copy of statement in FHS, NFPA box 68, Forest Service appropriations file.

88. The Spring 1991 issue of *The Inner Voice* published by the Association of Forest Service Employees for Environmental Ethics (AFSEEE) featured a series of articles under the theme "Pressure from the Top," including an article by then editor Tom Ribe titled, "Rangering from Capitol Hill." Ribe explained that "[timber] cutting volume expectations are tied directly to the funding lifeline of the Forest Service. As a result of this top-down management (coming from Congress and the FS Washington Office), FS employees at the forest and district level are constantly looking for trees to cut in order to meet their 'timber targets.' The local resource staffer . . . who may wish to reduce logging or protect environmental qualities, has to confront his supervisors who are under the gun to produce volume and meet the expectations of specific people on Capitol Hill," *Inner Voice* 3, no. 2 (Spring 1991): 5, 7. See also his article "To ASQ or Not to ASQ: Timber Targets vs. Environmental Protection," *Inner Voice* 2, no. 4 (Summer/Fall 1990): 1, 14.

4. Forestry, Freedom, and Fiscal Conservatism

1. Chris Granger, "The National Forests Are in the Black," *American Forests* 58 (July 1952): 6–9. Granger's accounting procedures were rather loose, ignoring many capital improvements such as road construction (a substantial expense), and the congressionally mandated payments to counties of 25 percent of total revenues "in lieu of taxes." But Granger's point that (many) timber sales generated substantial revenue was not lost on revenue-conscious conservatives in industry and Congress.

2. Edward C. Crafts, "Forest Service Researcher and Congressional Liaison: An

Eye to Multiple Use," oral interview conducted by Susan Schrepfer, produced under cooperative agreement between the Forest Service and Forest History Society (Santa Cruz: Forest History Society, 1972), p. 37.

3. *Report of the Chief, 1946,* p. 19; *Report of the Chief, 1953,* p. 24.

4. Richard E. McArdle, "Dr. Richard E. McArdle: An Interview with the Former Chief, U.S. Forest Service, 1952–1962," (Santa Cruz: Forest History Society, 1975), p. 81.

5. Harry S. Truman, "State of the Union Message," January 1949; quoted in Forest Service, *Information Digest,* no. 2 (Jan. 7, 1949).

6. In his Budget Message to Congress, Truman stated: "In a period of high prosperity it is not sound public policy for the Government to operate at a deficit. . . . I am, therefore, recommending new tax legislation to raise revenues by 4 billion dollars"; *Information Digest,* no. 4 (Jan. 12, 1949).

7. Quoted in *Information Digest,* no. 3 (Jan. 11, 1949).

8. Elmo Richardson, *Dams, Parks, and Politics* (Lexington: University Press of Kentucky, 1973).

9. *Information Digest,* no. 4, (Jan. 12, 1949).

10. Ibid., no. 38 (April 21, 1949); no. 41 (May 6, 1949); no. 42 (May 10, 1949); no. 54 (June 13, 1949); and no. 60 (June 24, 1949).

11. Ibid., no. 10 (Feb. 1, 1950).

12. *Report of the Chief, 1949,* pp. 42–43.

13. Edward C. Crafts, "Public Forest Policy in a National Emergency," presented to Division of Economics, SAF annual meeting, Dec. 14, 1951, p. 7 of original paper; copy of paper in FHS, NFPA box 28, Forest Service file.

14. NLMA Advisory Committee memo to Executive Committee and members, regarding Forest Service participation in war mobilization, "Immediate Steps Needed to Increase the Contribution of Federal Forestry Agencies to Defense," second draft of policy statement for testimony on the Defense Production Act, Aug. 23, 1950, p. 2; FHS, NFPA box 28, Forest Service file.

15. Ibid., pp. 2, 6.

16. Ibid.

17. Crafts, "Public Forest Policy," pp. 1, 7.

18. "Statement of R. A. Colgan, Before the Agricultural Appropriations Sub-committee of the House Appropriations Committee," March 9, 1951, p. 2; copy in FHS, NFPA box 28, Forest Service file.

19. Ibid. Colgan told the committee that during World War Two, the timber industry felt, "and it still feels, that a larger share of the lumber supply burden should be placed on the federal timberlands." See also NLMA Advisory Committee memo

to Executive Committee and members, "Immediate Steps Needed to Increase the Contribution of Federal Forestry Agencies to Defense," Aug. 23, 1950, FHS, NFPA box 28, Forest Service file, p. 1.

20. Forest Industries Council, memo to members, June 15, 1951, FHS, NFPA box 18, forest policy file.

21. *Report of the Chief, 1948*, pp. 24–25.

22. Ibid., *1951*, pp. 39–40.

23. See Association of Forest Service Employees for Environmental Ethics (AFSEEE), "The Tongass National Forest: Under Siege," *Inner Voice* 2, no. 1 (Winter 1990). Also, David Katz, "Tongass at the Crossroads: Forest Service Mismanagement in the Wake of the Tongass Timber Reform Act" (Eugene, Oreg.: AFSEEE, 1993).

24. Figures derived from the 1949, 1951, and 1953 *Reports of the Chief*.

25. In 1952, U.S. wood harvest totalled 11.8 billion *cubic* feet while national forest harvest was at 1.1 billion *cubic* feet; USDA Forest Service, *Forest Statistics of the U.S., 1977* (Washington, D.C.: GPO, 1978), p. 80.

26. Crafts, "Public Forest Policy," p. 6.

27. Clary, *Timber and the Forest Service*, p. 125.

28. *Report of the Chief, 1951*, p. 51.

29. Ibid.

30. "More Funds for Logging Roads Urged," *San Francisco Chronicle* (Aug. 28, 1950).

31. *Report of the Chief, 1949*, p. 55. The following year, the annual report repeated this suggestion for a $100 million log-haul road investment, adding, "with a continuing program of lateral road construction thereafter, much of which is done by the timber operators, the timber could be harvested at this rate [6 bbf per year] indefinitely." To underscore the revenue generation possibilities of this investment, the report ended with the statement, "At current prices this would bring into the Federal Treasury about $45,000,000 annually"; *Report of the Chief, 1950*, p. 50.

32. These figures include both direct appropriations and the additional 10 percent of receipts kicked back to the Service for roads and trails made available each year from the so-called "10-percent fund" authorized by Congress March 4, 1913. The data were derived from the annual *Reports of the Chief, 1950*, p. 50; *1951*, p. 51; *1952*, p. 33; *1953*, pp. 30–31.

33. Ibid., *1951*, p. 52; *1953*, p. 31.

34. "More Funds for Logging Roads Urged."

35. Earl H. Clapp, "Public Forest Regulation," *Journal of Forestry* 47, no. 7 (July 1949): 528–29.

36. *Report of the Chief, 1950*, p. 40; ibid., *1949*, p. 46.

37. P.L. 81-348, Oct. 11, 1949. Anderson's Senate Joint Resolution 53 introduced on Feb. 14, 1949, was reported favorably out of the Agriculture Committee three weeks later without a hearing and passed by the full Senate a month later (April 11) without amendment. An identical bill, House Joint Resolution 167 introduced by Representative Mansfield of Montana, similarly encountered no opposition.

38. *Information Digest*, no. 24 (March 22, 1950); no. 63 (July 10, 1950).

39. *Information Digest*, no. 66 (July 21, 1950); no. 71 (Aug. 4, 1950); no. 79 (Aug. 25, 1950); and no. 83 (Sept. 1, 1950).

40. *Report of the Chief, 1951*, p. 41.

41. Ibid., *1950*, p. 41.

42. William Rowley, in his *U.S. Forest Service Grazing and Rangelands* history, discusses major grazing fee controversies that occurred in 1905–11 (pp. 60–68); 1916–19 (pp. 118–28); and 1932 (pp. 149–51); and he ends his book identifying the issue as a major source of controversy in the 1960s and 1970s. There have been numerous government studies, including the 1953 *Report of the Chief;* a study by the U.S. Department of the Interior and U.S. Department of Agriculture, *Study of Fees for Grazing Livestock on Federal Lands* (Washington, D.C.: GPO, Oct. 21, 1977); and a Forest Service and Bureau of Land Management *1985 Grazing Fee Review and Evaluation Draft Report* (Washington, D.C.: 680, 1985).

43. Bernard DeVoto, "Two-Gun Desmond is Back," *Harper's* (March 1951), reprinted in *The Easy Chair* (Boston: Houghton Mifflin, 1955), p. 295.

44. *Information Digest*, no. 63 (July 10, 1950); *Report of the Chief, 1950*, p. 69.

45. Recently, the U.S. General Accounting Office prepared an analysis of the grazing fee controversy for Congressman Mike Synar. The report has no title but takes the form of a letter to Synar dated June 11, 1991. It is signed by James Duffus III and is numbered B-24430. The report analyzes the dimensions, causes, and consequences of the below–fair market value grazing fee. Synar was deeply involved in unsuccessful congressional efforts to raise grazing fees to fair market value in the late 1980s and early 1990s.

46. *Report of the Chief, 1951*, p. 43.

47. Cliff, "Half a Century in Forest Conservation," p. 171.

48. *Information Digest*, no. 100 (Nov. 8, 1950).

49. Cliff, "Half a Century in Forest Conservation," pp. 167–69.

50. Rowley, *U.S. Forest Service Grazing and Rangelands*, discusses at length the Sandvig controversy, pp. 212–17. Showing that he was still sensitive about the issue thirty years later, Ed Cliff devoted nine full pages of densely packed text to this controversy in his oral history/biography, "Half a Century in Forest Conservation,"

pp. 167–75. William Voigt, *Public Grazing Lands,* dedicates an entire chapter to the Sandvig controversy (chap. 14, pp. 171–88), which he titles, "Hide on a Corral Fence."

51. *Report of the Chief, 1947,* p. 9.

52. *Information Digest,* no. 83 (Sept. 13, 1950).

5. Transition to the "Businessman's Administration"

1. Ike's coattails, like Truman's in 1948, did not stretch very far. Both the House and Senate were recaptured by Democrats two years later, although conservatives continued to dominate both houses of Congress for most of Eisenhower's eight years in office.

2. Quoted in the *New York Times* (Oct. 8, 1952), cited in Harold Steen, *The U.S. Forest Service: A History* (Seattle: University of Washington Press, 1976), p. 269.

3. Edward C. Crafts, "Congress and the Forest Service, 1950–1962," an oral history conducted in 1965 by Amelia Fry, Regional Oral History Office, Bancroft Library, University of California, Berkeley, 1975, p. 5. Courtesy of the Bancroft Library.

4. "Adams Gets Top Policy Post," *American Forests* 59, no. 1 (Jan. 1953): 9, 30; Sherman Adams, "People and Conservation," *American Forests* 57, no. 11 (Nov. 1951): 25–29.

5. Douglas McKay, "Oregon States Its Case against Socialized Forestry," *American Forests* 57, no. 1 (Jan. 1951), quoted in "Meet Douglas McKay," *American Forests* 59, no. 1 (Jan. 1953): 9.

6. See William Robbins, *Hard Times in Paradise: Coos Bay, Oregon, 1850–1986* (Seattle: University of Washington Press, 1988), for a social history of Coos Bay as a boom-bust lumber town in the twentieth century.

7. Harold K. Steen, *The U.S. Forest Service: A History* (Seattle: University of Washington Press, 1976) pp. 270–71.

8. This perspective can be traced back to the origins of American forestry. Gifford Pinchot, in his book *The Fight for Conservation* (New York: Doubleday, 1910), stated, "The first principle of Conservation is development, the use of natural resources on this continent for the benefit of the people who live here now. There may be just as much waste in neglecting the development and use of certain natural resources as there is in their destruction"; quoted in *Americans and Environment,* ed. by John Opie (Lexington, Mass.: D. C. Heath, 1971), p. 41.

9. Ezra Taft Benson, *Proceedings of the Fourth American Forest Congress,* Oct. 29, 30, 31, 1953 (Washington, D.C.: American Forestry Association, 1953), pp. 46–47. Benson was flexible in his opposition to some kinds of nonuse. He supported the "soil bank" program in which the government paid farmers to retire lands from agricultural production in an effort to keep farm surpluses down and farm prices up.

Conservation benefits came out of this program, too, because the government placed a high priority on retiring lands prone to erosion or easily depleted of nutrients.

10. L. G. Hines, "The Myth of Idle Resources: A Reconsideration of the Concept of Nonuse in Conservation," *Transactions of the Eighteenth North American Wildlife Conference* (Washington, D.C.: Wildlife Management Institute, 1953), pp. 28–35.

11. Ibid.

12. Forest Industries Council, "Growing Trees in a Free Country," Fourth (final) Draft, Aug. 14, 1953; Forest History Society (FHS), NFPA box 18, Forest Industry Council Forest Policy file. This "fourth draft" had been approved by the American Pulpwood Association and the American Pulp and Paper Association and awaited only final approval from the NLMA before being printed.

13. See esp. Gordon Robinson, *The Forest and the Trees: A Guide to Excellent Forestry* (Washington, D.C.: Island Press, 1988), pp. 3–4.

14. "Dr. Richard E. McArdle: An Interview with the Former Chief, U.S. Forest Service, 1952–1962," interviewed by Elwood Maunder (Santa Cruz: Forest History Society, 1975), p. 69.

15. H.R. 5603 and S. 2069, 83rd Cong., 1st sess.; P.L. 83-285. Stuart Moir, "Timber as Collateral," *Proceedings of the Fourth American Forest Congress,* pp. 227–29.

16. To avoid such corporate raiding in the early 1980s, the Plum Creek timber company in Roslyn, Washington, began raiding its own timber reserves, clearcutting blocks as a large as a square mile and exporting up to half its logs to Japan to generate liquid assets. An official for the company explained to Timothy Egan of the *New York Times,* "Let's face it, the market forces and the threat of stock market takeover won't let us do otherwise. If you keep a lot of this timber on the books, you're undervalued and you become an easy takeover target"; Timothy Egan, "Where Have All the Forests Gone?" *New York Times* (Feb. 15, 1989); reprinted in *Inner Voice* 1, no. 1 (Summer 1989): 3.

17. Edward Cliff, testimony before the Appropriations Committee, Subcommittee on Agricultural Appropriations, 83rd Cong., 1st sess., April 22, 1953, pp. 360, 413–14.

18. Crafts, "Congress and the Forest Service," pp. 43–44.

19. *Report of the Chief, 1953,* p. 22.

20. Budget information from: NLMA memos to Committee on Forest Conservation, "Revised Forest Service Budget for Fiscal Year 1954," March 31, 1953; and "House Approved Federal Forestry Appropriations for the Fiscal Year 1954," May 27, 1953; both in FHS, NFPA box 8, Forest Service Appropriations file; plus Albert Hall, "Washington Lookout," *American Forests* 59, no. 2 (Feb. 1953): 5.

21. NLMA memos to committee on Forest Conservation.

22. Ellsworth's bill is mentioned in Albert Hall's "Washington Lookout," *American Forests* 59, no. 7 (July 1953): 6.

23. Cliff, testimony before the Senate Appropriations Committee, Subcommittee on Agricultural Appropriations, Hearings on H.R. 5227, April 22, 1953, pp. 411–13.

24. Ibid.

25. USDA Forest Service, Lolo National Forest, *Report for 1955* (n.d.), p. 6; in author's possession.

26. Robert D. Baker, Robert S Maxwell, Victor H. Treat, and Henry C. Dethloff, *Timeless Heritage: A History of the Forest Service in the Southwest,* FS-409 (Washington, D.C.: USDA Forest Service, Aug. 1988), pp. 61–63.

27. Edward P. Cliff, "Half a Century in Forest Conservation," (Washington, D.C.: USDA Forest Service, Washington Office, History Unit, 1981), pp. 176–78.

28. Forest Service, Wyoming Forest Study Team, "Forest Management in Wyoming," 1971, p. 9. See also Arnold Bolle, "The Bitterroot Revisited: A University Re-View of the Forest Service," *Public Land Law Review* 10 (1989): 1–18, for a continuation of the 1971 critical analysis. For an example of the general public acceptability of these salvage sales, even among conservationists, see Bernard Frank, *Our National Forests* (Norman: University of Oklahoma Press, 1955), pp. 33–34. In this selection, Frank, who is cited later in this chapter as a defender of wilderness and esthetic values, praises two very large salvage sales on the Olympic and Willamette National Forests of Washington and Oregon in 1952. Regarding the Willamette sale, he said, "It included two areas of wind-thrown timber, which, unless quickly salvaged, will invite insect pests and increase the threat of serious fires." Regarding the Olympic sale, he added that the salvage operation would "help nature create a new forest." Of course wind-throw, insects, and disease have always been a part of forest ecology and are only "destructive" from a narrow economic point of view.

29. Bolle, "The Bitterroot Revisited," pp. 3–4.

30. Albert Hall, "Washington Lookout," *American Forests* 59, no. 7 (July 1953): 5.

31. Senate Appropriations Committee, Subcommittee on Agricultural Appropriations, Hearings on H.R. 5227, April 22, 1953, pp. 348, 365.

32. Chief McArdle later recalled that Forest Service plans to maximize timber harvests through intensive management required "prompt and vigorous attention to improvement of the one-third of the national forest acreage that was in immature stands. Yet little or no money of this kind was being spent on these forests. . . . Such funds requests were consistently cut out by the Budget Bureau"; "Dr. Richard E. McArdle: An Interview with the Former Chief," p. 69.

33. Senate Hearings on H.R. 5227, April 22, 1953, pp. 348, 365.

34. Crafts, "Congress and the Forest Service," p. 24.

35. "Challenge at Higgins Lake," *American Forests* 59, no. 6 (June 1953): 7; see also "Forestry Primed for Higgins Lake," same issue, pp. 4, 40, and "Higgins Lake — 1953," *American Forest* 59, no. 8 (Aug. 1953): 7.

36. E. R. Aston, "Multiple Use of Forest Lands in Western Pine Region," *Proceedings of the Fourth American Forest Congress,* p. 177.

37. "Challenge at Higgins Lake," p. 7.

38. Aston, "Multiple Use of Forest Lands," p. 177.

39. "A Proposed Program for American Forestry," *American Forests* 59, no. 8 (Aug. 1953): 30.

40. Aston, "Multiple Use of Forest Lands," p. 176.

41. Benson, *Proceedings of the Fourth American Forest Congress,* p. 47.

42. Robert Sawyer, "The Whole Story," *American Forests* 59, no. 3 (March 1953): 10–12, 39.

43. Benson, *Proceedings of the Fourth American Forest Congress,* p. 48.

44. Editorial, *American Forests* 59, no. 3 (March 1953).

45. Chris Granger, "Comments on AFA's Forest Survey Resolution," *American Forests* 59, no. 4 (April 1953): 4, 46; Granger, "Federal Forest Landownership," *Proceeding of the Fourth American Forest Congress,* pp. 296–99. See also Steen, *The U.S. Forest Service,* pp. 291–93.

46. Editorial, *American Forests* 59, no. 3 (March 1953).

47. William Voigt, Jr., "Multiple Use," *Proceedings of the Fourth American Forest Congress,* p. 179.

48. Albert Hall, "Washington Lookout," *American Forests* 59, no. 10 (Oct. 1953): 4.

49. Steen, *The U.S. Forest Service,* pp. 293–94.

50. Crafts, "Congress and the Forest Service," p. 27.

51. "The Uniform Federal Grazing Land Act," H.R. 4023 and S. 1491, 83rd Cong., 1st sess., April 1953.

52. Arthur Carhart, "They Still Covet Our Lands," *American Forests* 59, no. 4 (April 1953): 11; editorial, "Stockmen's Bill Challenged," *American Forests* 59, no. 6 (June 1953): 6; Chris Granger, "A 'Square Deal' for Half a Century," *American Forests* 59, no. 6 (June 1953): 19, 47–51.

53. Crafts, "Congress and the Forest Service," p. 34.

54. Carl Shoemaker, "Status of Some Pending Bills in Congress," *Proceedings of the Thirty-Third Annual Conference of Western Association of State Game and Fish Commissioners,* Long Beach, Calif., June 1953, p. 8.

55. Cliff, testimony before Senate Appropriations Committee, Hearings on H.R. 5227, pp. 361–63.

56. Bernard Frank, "The Value of Standing Primeval Forests," *Proceedings* of the Fourth American Forest Congress, pp. 160–61.

57. Paul A. Herbert, "Multiple Use of Forest Land," *Proceedings* of the Fourth American Forest Congress, pp. 169–71.

58. Edward Cliff, "Multiple Uses on National Forests," *Proceedings* of the Fourth American Forest Congress, pp. 161–62.

59. Howard Zahniser, "Wilderness in a Multiple Use Forestry Program," *Proceedings* of the Fourth American Forest Congress, p. 171.

60. Edward Crafts, "Forest Service Researcher and Congressional Liaison: An Eye to Multiple Use," interview with Susan Schrepfer (Santa Cruz: Forest History Society, 1972), p. 38.

6. Getting Out the Cut

1. Percentages derived from USDA Forest Service, *Forest Statistics of the U.S., 1977* (Washington, D.C.: GPO, 1978), p. 80.

2. Ibid., for data through 1977. For 1980s harvest figures, see USDA Forest Service, *An Analysis of the Timber Situation in the United States: 1989–2040,* General Technical Report RM-199 (Fort Collins, Colo.: Rocky Mountain Forest and Range Experiment Station, Dec. 1990), p. 55.

3. Edward P. Cliff, "Half A Century in Forest Conservation: A Biography and Oral History of Edward P. Cliff" (Washington, D.C.: Forest Service, History Section, March 1981), p. 230.

4. In a 1953 pamphlet, the FIC said "Currently . . . the cut from federal lands is far less than the allowable annual harvest on a sustained yield basis. . . . This can be corrected by the application of more intensive forest practices and increasing the cuts to the amounts required to put national forests on a truly sustained yield basis"; FIC, "Growing Trees in a Free Country," fourth draft, Aug. 14, 1953, p. 13.

5. Edward Crafts, "Congress and the Forest Service, 1950–1962," an oral history conducted in 1965 by Amelia Fry, Regional Oral History Office, Bancroft Library, University of California, Berkeley, 1975, p. 23. Courtesy of the Bancroft Library.

6. *Report of the Chief, 1951,* p. 38.

7. Richard McArdle, "Dr. Richard E. McArdle: An Interview with the Former Chief, U.S. Forest Service, 1952–1962," interviewed by Elwood Maunder (Santa Cruz: Forest History Society, 1975), pp. 68–69.

8. Ed Cliff, testimony before Senate Appropriations Committee, Subcommittee on Agricultural Appropriations, Hearings on H.R. 5227, 83rd Cong., 1st Sess., April 22, 1953, p. 360; *Report of the Chief, 1953,* p. 22; *Report of the Chief, 1955,* p. 2; *Report of the Chief, 1961,* pp. 12, 35.

9. USDA Forest Service, press release, "Gifford Pinchot National Forest to be Dedicated October 15," Sept. 19, 1949 (for Sept. 26, release), USDA 1993–49.

10. In 1956, at the request of the NLMA, the Forest Service began compiling annual timber statistics in booklet form organized by region and forest. Titled "Report on National Forest Timber Resource Operations," the booklets covering the years 1956–65 can be found in FHS, NFPA box 54. Timber production statistics for the years 1963–75 can also be found in the Gifford Pinchot National Forest's *Final Environmental Statement, Timber Management Plan, 1975–1984* (Feb. 1975), p. 5.

11. According to the Gifford Pinchot National Forest annual *Multiple Use Reports*, 7,000 acres were logged in 1962, 12,000 in 1965, and 13,500 each in 1966 and 1967 (640 acres equals 1 square mile). The annual cut for those years ranged from 430 million board feet (mmbf) to 510 mmbf. This harvest level remained consistent for the next 20 years, and so it can be assumed that the area logged similarly remained in that range. The *Multiple Use Reports* are located at the Forest Service Region 6 historical records warehouse in Portland, Oregon.

12. Peter Morrison, *Old Growth in the Pacific Northwest: A Status Report* (Washington, D.C.: Wilderness Society, 1988), pp. 27–28.

13. Thomas G. Alexander, "Timber Management, Traditional Forestry, and Multiple-Use Stewardship: The Case of the Intermountain Region, 1950–85," *Journal of Forest History* 33, no. 1 (Jan. 1989): 23–25. See also Alexander's *The Rise of Multiple Use Management in the Intermountain West: A History of Region 4 of the Forest Service,* FS-399 (Washington, D.C.: Forest Service, May 1987), chap. 8, on the decade of the 1950s.

14. Alexander, "Timber Management, Traditional Forestry, and Multiple-Use Stewardship," p. 24.

15. George W. Craddock, "Watershed Management Problems of the Intermountain West," *Proceedings: Society of American Foresters Meeting, 1958* (Washington, D.C.: SAF, 1959), p. 32.

16. Ibid., pp. 31–32.

17. John Keats, *The Crack in the Picture Window* (Boston: Houghton Mifflin, 1956), pp. xi–xvii. In that same year, a more sophisticated critique of mass organization and social engineering appeared in William H. Whyte, Jr.'s popular and influential book, *The Organization Man* (New York: Doubleday, 1956).

18. Crafts, "Congress and the Forest Service," pp. 20–21. See also Steen, pp. 285–90; and "Forests and Facts," editorial, *American Forests,* v. 59, no. 1, p. 7.

19. Richard McArdle gave a lengthy, formal summary of the TRR in October 1955 at the Society of American Foresters annual Meeting, *Proceedings: Society of American Foresters Meeting, 1955* (Washington, D.C.: SAF, 1956), pp. 11–16. See also USDA Forest Service, *Timber Resources for America's Future,* Forest Resource Report no. 14 (Washington, D.C.: GPO, Jan. 1958).

20. NLMA news release, "Special to Trade Press," Portland, Oregon, Sept. 14,

1956; includes Alf Z. Nelson, "The Great Guessing Game," speech before the Western Pine Association annual meeting, Sept. 14, 1956; FHS, NFPA box 28. Sixty years earlier John Wesley Powell had similarly been accused by land speculators, resource developers, and Western politicians of promoting creeping socialism through his Irrigation Survey under the U.S. Geological Survey. Powell had suggested that federal guidance and intervention in the development of the arid West would ensure greater economic stability and less human misery. His views on the matter eventually led to the fiscal emasculation of the Irrigation Survey by hostile congressmen on the appropriations committees and to Powell's resignation. Wallace Stegner, *Beyond the Hundredth Meridian* (Boston: Houghton Mifflin, 1953), pp. 316–38.

21. Richard McArdle, foreword to *Timber Resources for America's Future,* p. iii.

22. Forest Service, *Timber Resources for America's Future,* p. 108.

23. A. W. Greeley, "Protecting the Public's Interest in Converting the Old Forest to New," SAF *Proceedings* (1955), pp. 2–3.

24. Forest Service, "The Care and Use of National Forests," quoted in David Clary, *Timber and the Forest Service* (Lawrence: University Press of Kansas, 1986), pp. 165–66.

25. E. P. Stamm, "Converting the Old Growth Forest: Utilization and Road Problems," SAF *Proceedings* (1955), pp. 5, 6.

26. Ibid., pp. 6, 7.

27. Justin Leonard, "People and the Land," *Pennsylvania Angler* 25, no. 3 (1956): 6–9.

28. W. Winston Mair, "Toward an Ecological Conscience," *Proceedings of the Thirty-Sixth Annual Conference of the Western Association of State Game and Fish Commissioners* (June 1956), pp. 14–17.

29. Ibid., pp. 14, 15.

30. "Statement of H. Robert Hansen, Jr., Before the Senate Appropriations Subcommittee for the Department of the Interior and Related Agencies," 86th Cong., 1st sess., May 20, 1959; copy in FHS, WTA box 31, file 2.411.

31. Ibid.

32. *Report of the Chief, 1958,* statistical tables, pp. 28, 31. On total revenues and expenses, see Forest Service, "Report on National Forest Timber Resource Operations Fiscal Year 1958." These reports were compiled by the Forest Service at the request of the National Lumber Manufacturers Association. Reports covering the years 1956–65 and are found in FHS, NFPA box 54.

33. Ibid., "Report on National Forest Timber Resource Operations."

34. David Clary characterized the Forest Service as religiously holding to "a sacred mission to provide wood to the world in order to avert the evils of a 'timber famine' "; *Timber and the Forest Service,* p. xi.

35. Forest Service, "Report on National Forest Timber Resource Operations," 1956–65.

36. *Report of the Chief, 1958*, pp. 28, 31.

37. The U.S. General Accounting Office analysts in 1984 tested the agency argument that road and reforestation costs would be recouped in the second harvest. Analyzing eight "below-cost" sales in different regions, the GAO concluded that the Forest Service's hypothesis "was not valid." Not only were road costs unlikely to be recouped, but it appeared that the second stand of timber would likewise show a loss. GAO, "Congress Needs Better Information on Forest Service's Below-Cost Timber Sales," GAO/RCED-84–96, June 28, 1984, pp. 20–21 and appendix IV.

38. Willis A. Evans, "The Effect of Current West Coast Logging Practices upon Fisheries Resources," *Proceedings: Society of American Foresters Meeting, Nov. 15–19, 1959* (Washington, D.C.: SAF, 1960), pp. 106–7.

39. R. L. Fredriksen, "Erosion and Sedimentation following Road Construction and Timber Harvest on Unstable Soils in Three Small Western Oregon Watersheds," Pacific Northwest Forest and Range Experiment Station Research Paper PNW-104, 1970, pp. 8–11.

40. E. C. Steinbrenner and S. P. Gessel, "Effect of Tractor Logging on Soils and Regeneration in the Douglas-Fir Region of Southwestern Washington," SAF *Proceedings, 1955*, pp. 77–80.

41. Evans, "The Effect of Current West Coast Logging Practices," p. 107.

42. The theory of externalities, developed around the turn of the century by such economists as A. C. Pigou, is an important though often neglected aspect of any analysis of costs and benefits. See Pigou, *Wealth and Welfare* (London: Macmillan, 1912). See also Marshall I. Goldman, *Ecology and Economics: Controlling Pollution in the 1970s* (Englewood Cliffs, N.J.: Prentice Hall, 1972).

43. Evans, p. 107.

7. The Fight to Protect Nontimber Values

1. Earmarked revenue disbursements worked as follows: (1) 10 percent of gross Forest Service receipts automatically returned for road work, as authorized by an act of March 4, 1913. (2) A variable percentage of the money paid to the agency by timber purchasers could be used directly for reforestation and other improvements in the vicinity of the sale area, as authorized by the June 9, 1930 Knutson-Vandenberg Act — and called "K-V funds." (3) Because states had no authority to tax agents of the federal government, Congress authorized 25 percent of gross receipts to be disbursed back to the states and counties where the revenues had been generated as payments "in lieu of taxes," authorized by an act of May 23, 1908.

2. Howard Baker, testimony on H.R. 1972, Hearings before the Committee on

Agriculture, "Disposition of Moneys from the National Forests," 83rd Cong., 1st sess. (March 11, 12, 1953), pp. 4–5.

3. Ibid., p. 25.

4. Ibid., p. 129.

5. Ibid., Chester Wilson, p. 6; William Voigt, Izaak Walton League, p. 21.

6. Ibid., George M. Fuller, p. 123.

7. Ibid., William Voigt, p. 25.

8. The NLMA's George Fuller wrote to Jude White of the Long-Bell Lumber Company in California on April 16, 1953, explaining, "the Bureau of the Budget originally did not seem to understand this legislation and did not make their position clearly understood to the interested agencies such as the Department of Agriculture. However, subsequently, when this matter was called to their attention, they took a position in opposition. Consequently, the Senate Committee have advised us that they will not even hold hearings." FHS, NFPA box 105.

9. George Fuller to National Affairs Committee, re: H.R. 8225, April 6, 1954; FHS, NFPA box 105.

10. Stuart Moir to Alf Z. Nelson, April 6, 1954; FHS, NFPA box 105.

11. Nelson to Moir, April 15, 1953; and Clarence Miles, Chamber of Commerce of the United States, to Clifford Hope, Chairman of the House Agriculture Committee, opposing H.R. 8225; FHS, NFPA box 105.

12. A. Z. Nelson to Emanuel Fritz, June 30, 1954; FHS, NFPA box 105.

13. Lee Metcalf, "Extension of Remarks," *Congressional Record,* 84th Cong., 2nd sess., Jan. 5, 1956.

14. Ibid. Metcalf included a copy of the Outdoor Writers Association resolution in his *Congressional Record* remarks. Also, see John H. Sieker, "Recreation Policy and Administration in the U.S. Forest Service," interview conducted by Amelia Fry in 1964 (Berkeley: Bancroft Library, University of California Regional Oral History Office, 1968), p. 11, on public support for recreation on the national forests.

15. USDA press release, "Bumper Crop of Vacationists Expected to Head for National Forests," Washington, D.C., June 13, 1956; FHS, NFPA box 105.

16. Edward C. Crafts, testimony on H.R. 1823 before the House Subcommittee on Forestry of the Committee on Agriculture, 84th Cong., 2nd sess., June 26, 1956, p. 8.

17. USDA Forest Service, press release, "Operation Outdoors Designed to Double National Forest Recreation Facilities," Washington, D.C., Jan. 15, 1957 (for morning release, Jan. 17).

18. Recreation Division Chief John Sieker recalled in 1964, "The Chief of the Forest Service would not have had the authority to publish 'Operation Outdoors' as it was published because it had an outline of appropriations needed to implement it. That very fact would have made it improper, because this was not, at that time, part

of the President's budget. So the Chief of the Forest Service took the Operation Outdoors program to the Secretary of Agriculture. The Secretary cleared it with the Budget Bureau and published it." John H. Sieker, "Recreation Policy and Administration in the U.S. Forest Service," in John H. Sieker and Lloyd Swift, "U.S. Forest Service: Recreation and Wildlife," an oral history conducted in 1964 by Amelia Fry, Regional Oral History Office, Bancroft Library, University of California, Berkeley, 1968, p. 41. Courtesy of the Bancroft Library.

19. Ibid., p. 11.

20. Competition between the Park Service and Forest Service was so long-standing and acrimonious, at least between the 1910s and 1960s, that all the standard histories of the agencies mention it. One lesser known but interesting treatment of this is Ben Twight's *Organizational Values and Political Power: The Forest Service versus Olympic National Park* (University Park: Pennsylvania State University Press, 1983).

21. Sieker, p. 15.

22. Brower had called for a "Scenic Resources Review" in the Spring 1956 issue of the Wilderness Society's magazine, *The Living Wilderness,* vol. 21, no. 56, p. ii, starting the momentum. Ed Crafts also recalled, "I remember one day, shortly after completion of the Timber Resources Review, Joe Penfold of the Izaak Walton League and I sat in my office and pretty well roughed out the bill that ultimately passed and set up the Outdoor Recreation Resources Review Commission. This I think is a fact that is not generally known." Crafts, "Congress and the Forest Service, 1950–1962," an oral history conducted in 1965 by Amelia Fry, Regional Oral History Office, Bancroft Library, University of California, Berkeley, 1975, p. 30. Courtesy of the Bancroft Library.

23. S. 846, 85th Cong, 2nd sess. See Anderson's remarks in the *Congressional Record,* Jan. 25, 1957. The Senate Interior Committee held hearings May 15, 1957, and the Senate passed the bill shortly thereafter. The House Interior Committee made some changes and then reported the bill favorably on Feb. 25, 1958. The bill became law on June 28, 1958 (72 Stat. 328).

24. U.S. House of Representatives, Committee on Interior and Insular Affairs, Report no. 1386, to accompany S. 846, 85th Cong., 2nd sess., Feb. 25, 1958, pp. 4–5.

25. Michael Bean traces the development of federal-state legal relationships and authorities regarding wildlife in chapter 2 of his book, *The Evolution of National Wildlife Law,* Report to the Council on Environmental Quality (Washington, D.C.: GPO, 1977).

26. *Proceedings: Society of American Foresters Meeting, Oct. 16–21, 1955* (Washington, D.C.: SAF, 1956): Donald A. Spencer, "The Effects of Rodents on Reforestation," pp. 125–28; J. Burton Lauckhart, "The Effect of Logging Old

Growth Timber on Bear," pp. 128–30; Casey E. Westell, Jr., "Ecological Relationships between Deer and Forests in Lower Michigan," pp. 130–32; Kramer A. Adams, "The Effects of Logging Old-Growth Timber on Landowner-Sportsman Relationships," pp. 133–36.

27. P. W. Schneider, "The Effects of Logging Old-Growth Timber on Fish Management," SAF *Proceedings, 1955,* p. 121.

28. *Report of the Chief, 1961,* p. 14.

29. Interview with Dave Foreman, Southwest representative for the Wilderness Society in New Mexico in the 1970s, Sept. 4, 1991.

30. Reflecting on the wilderness debate of the late 1950s, Chief McArdle said, "At one of the Senate hearings on wilderness legislation I had to defend our policy for setting aside enormous areas which were or could be used by so few people. My personal feeling then and now, and it is a strong one, is that these large areas should be preserved as wilderness even if no one uses them." Richard McArdle, "An Interview with the Former Chief, U.S. Forest Service, 1952–1962" (Santa Cruz: Forest History Society, 1975), p. 149.

31. Henry Harrison, Forest Service Assistant Director of Recreation and Land Uses, Washington, D.C., "How Much Land for Forest Recreation?" SAF *Proceedings, 1958,* p. 97.

32. H. H. Chapman, "Shall Trees Be Cut within National Parks, Wilderness or Natural Areas?" *American Forests* 64, no. 2 (Feb. 1958).

33. Zahniser explained in some detail his organization's multiple rationales for supporting both wilderness and a congressionally designated national wilderness system in a speech to the Society of American Foresters in 1958 titled, "The Case for Wilderness Preservation Legislation," SAF *Proceedings, 1958,* pp. 104–10.

34. This anecdote is recounted in detail by Susan R. Schrepfer in "Establishing Administrative 'Standing': The Sierra Club and the Forest Service," *Pacific Historical Review* 58, no. 1 (Feb. 1989): 68–78.

35. Grant McConnell, "The Conservation Movement — Past and Present," *Western Political Quarterly* 7, no. 3 (Sept. 1954): 474–78.

36. Kramer Adams, "The Effects of Logging Old-Growth Timber on Landowner-Sportsman Relationships," SAF *Proceedings, 1955,* p. 135.

37. American Forest Products Industries, Inc., "Hiawatha Never Had It So Good," *Story Tips for Outdoor Writers,* bulletin no. 1 (Feb. 1955); FHS, NFPA box 105.

38. Ibid., "Youth Learns about Logging," *Story Tips for Outdoor Writers,* bulletin no. 2 (May 1955); FHS, NFPA box 105.

39. Ibid., "A New Kind of Management For Recreational Forests," *Story Tips for Outdoor Writers,* bulletin no. 2 (May 1955); FHS, NFPA box 105.

40. John J. Abele, "Welcome Mats in Timberlands Replace No-Trespassing Signs," *New York Times* (Oct. 8, 1956).

41. Hansen to Connaughton, June 1, 1959; FHS, WTA box 31, file 2.411.

8. Multiple Use and Sustained Yield

1. See the bibliographic essay for a discussion of this capture versus autonomy debate.

2. Chief McArdle briefly explained why he chose to push for legislation in "Why We Needed the Multiple Use Bill," *American Forests* 76, no. 6 (June 1970): 10, 59. Edward Crafts explained in intimate detail the agency's rationale and its political negotiations in "Saga of a Law," in two parts, *American Forests* 76, nos. 6 & 7 (June and July 1970).

3. Granger-Thye Act of April 24, 1950 (64 Stat 82).

4. The bill's sponsors, Clifford Hope and George Aiken, were both liberal Republicans, by 1950s standards, and were considered prominent conservationists. *American Forests* featured a biographical spread on both men in its March 1953 issue, pp. 13, 44–45. George Aiken (Vermont) was one of the few members of Congress who signed Senator Margaret Chase Smith's "Declaration of Conscience" against Joseph McCarthy's red-baiting excesses.

5. Hugh Woodward explained this chain of events and argued for support of the amended Aiken Grazing Bill in a piece titled, "In Defense of the Aiken Grazing Bill," *American Forests* 60, no. 7 (July 1954): 34–36.

6. S.2548, Sec. 12, as passed by the Senate March 8, 1954, 83rd Cong., 2nd sess.

7. Susan Schrepfer discusses this effort to establish citizen advisory councils in her essay, "Establishing Administrative 'Standing': The Sierra Club and the Forest Service," *Pacific Historical Review* 58 (Feb. 1989): 78–79.

8. Hugh Woodward and Elliot Barker, quoted by Albert Hall in his "Washington Lookout" column of *American Forests* 60, no. 12 (Dec. 1954): 6.

9. H.R. 6347 by John P. Miller (D-Calif.), May 18, 1955, 84th Cong., 1st sess.; also in the same session: H.R. 6290 by John Blatnik (D-Minn.), and H.R. 6200 by Lester Johnson (D-Wisc.). The Forest Service's Washington Office *Information Digest* reported on May 26, 1955, that these bills had been introduced and summarized their provisions, but added no commentary.

10. Carl Shoemaker, "Report on Conservation Pending in Congress," *Proceedings of the Thirty-Fifth Annual Conference of Western Association of State Game and Fish Commissioners, June 16, 17, 18, 1955,* pp. 12, 15.

11. S. T. Dana and Sally Fairfax (citing Bergoffen) attributed the drive for multiple use legislation entirely to agency initiative and flatly stated, "The Forest Service wrote the bill and lobbied for it"; *Forest and Range Policy* (New York: McGraw-

Hill, 1980), p. 201. Gene S. Bergoffen, whose father worked for the agency, wrote a master's thesis in 1962, titled "The Multiple Use–Sustained Yield Law: A Case Study of Administrative Initiative in the Legislation Policy-Forming Process" (Syracuse: State University College of Forestry, Syracuse University, June 1962). While Bergoffen mentioned the series of bills introduced in 1955–56, he characterized them as unimportant and argued that the Forest Service was the crucial initiator of multiple use legislation (pp. 63–73). Harold Steen cited the 1956 Humphrey multiple use bill as the initial event leading ultimately to the passage of MUSY; Steen, *The U.S. Forest Service,* pp. 304–5. Robert E. Wolf, who worked for several government agencies and congressional committees on natural resource issues from 1954 until the 1980s, drafted a lengthy, as yet unpublished report in 1990 for the U.S. Office of Technology Assessment, titled "The Concept of Multiple Use: The Evolution of the Idea within the Forest Service and the Enactment of the Multiple-Use Sustained-Yield Act of 1960," contract N-3–2465.0 (Washington, D.C., Dec. 30, 1990), in which he claims repeatedly (pp. 35–40) that unnamed people in the agency "drafted" all of the early bills, including the Hope-Aiken bill and Clem Miller's bill. Unfortunately he offers no evidence beyond personal recollections. While it is likely that someone from the agency was involved informally in many of the negotiations, Wolf exaggerates the agency role when he credits it with drafting the bills. First, the bills were widely inconsistent in emphasis and language, and most contained clauses the agency unequivocally opposed. Second, as Wolf admits, agency leaders disagreed on how to approach the multiple use bills and took no formal position until 1958. Until then they were mainly reactive.

12. Alf Z. Nelson to Leo V. Bodine, "Report on Conference with Messrs. McArdle and Mason on February 17, 1955" (Feb. 21, 1955), FHS, NFPA box 28, "Department of Agriculture/Forest Service" file.

13. Bergoffen, pp. 73–77.

14. S. 3615, 84th Cong., 2nd sess., April 11, 1956. See also *Information Digest,* no. 28 (April 13, 1956). Wolf (p. 40) again claimed that an unnamed Forest Service staff person unofficially initiated and drafted the 1956 Humphrey bill. This is curious, because the bill contained the conservationists' pet provision for an advisory council, which agency leaders opposed, and it did not mention sustained yield, which agency leaders considered most important. Wolf did, however, acknowledge that McArdle was "luke-warm" about the idea and the Budget Bureau opposed the legislation.

15. More so than today, political lobbying in the 1950s involved one or two key individuals from each organization establishing close relationships with supportive representatives and senators. Recreation and wildlife groups, in fact, had only recently started setting up permanent offices and lobbying capabilities in Washington, D.C., in the 1950s. Conservation politics then involved personalities more than

institutions. Today, although personalities are still central to political negotiations, environmental groups have mushroomed into great bureaucracies with large and changing staffs running efficient lobbying machines in the nation's capital.

16. Crafts, "Saga of a Law, Part 1," p. 16; Steen, *The U.S. Forest Service,* p. 304–6; Dana and Fairfax, pp. 200–201.

17. Crafts, "Saga of a Law, Part 1," p. 17.

18. On this demographic and economic growth of the West during and after World War Two, see Gerald D. Nash, *World War II and the West: Reshaping the Economy* (Lincoln: University of Nebraska Press, 1990).

19. Donald E. Clark, "Management Planning for Future Multiple-Use Forestry on Western National Forests," SAF *Proceedings, 1958,* pp. 2–3.

20. Steele Barnett, "Logging — The Key to Forest Management," *Proceedings: Society of American Foresters Meeting, 1958* (Washington, D.C.: SAF, 1959), p. 62.

21. Ibid.

22. Ibid., p. 64.

23. Ibid., pp. 63, 64, 65.

24. Fred J. Sandoz, "Our Citizens among Our Trees," SAF *Proceedings, 1958,* p. 10.

25. Howard Zahniser, "The Case for Wilderness Preservation Legislation," SAF *Proceedings, 1958,* pp. 106, 109.

26. Clark, "Management Planning."

27. Charles A. Connaughton, "Multiple Use of Forest Land," USDA Forest Service, 1959; copy in FHS, NFPA box 28.

28. Ibid., pp. 1, 3.

29. Ervin L. Peterson and Richard McArdle, testimony on H.R. 10572 before the Subcommittee on Forests of the Committee on Agriculture, House of Representatives, 86th Cong., 2nd sess., March 16, 1960, pp. 3–4, 36–39.

30. Peterson, ibid., p. 3.

31. Act of June 12, 1960, "The Multiple Use–Sustained Yield Act," P.L. 86-517, sec. 4(b).

32. Edward P. Cliff, "Half a Century in Forest Conservation: A Biography and Oral History of Edward P. Cliff" (Washington, D.C.: USDA Forest Service, March 1981), p. 205.

33. H. R. Glascock, testimony on H.R. 10572, before the Subcommittee on Forests of the Committee on Agriculture, House of Representatives, 86th Cong., 2nd sess., March 16, 1960, p. 56.

34. Ralph D. Hodges, ibid., pp. 62–66.

35. Louis Horrell of the American National Cattlemen's Association and Edwin E. Marsh of the National Woolgrowers Association, ibid., pp. 51–53, 82–83.

36. William E. Welsh, Secretary-Manager of the National Reclamation Association in Washington, D.C., ibid., pp. 75–77.

37. Stephen Fox calls the battle over Echo Park Dam in Dinosaur National Monument a "second Hetch-Hetchy" and engagingly recounts the story in *The American Conservation Movement: John Muir and His Legacy* (Madison: University of Wisconsin Press, 1985), pp. 281–86. Forthcoming in the fall of 1994 from the University of New Mexico Press is a book by Mark W. T. Harvey, *A Symbol of Wilderness: Echo Park and the American Conservation Movement.*

38. See Louis Clapper's testimony for the National Wildlife Federation on pp. 61–62 of the House Agriculture Committee hearing record; Spencer Smith's testimony for the Citizen's Committee on Natural Resources, p. 110; and C. R. Gutermuth of the Wildlife Management Institute, p. 111.

39. Penfold, ibid., p. 79.

40. Ibid., pp. 80–81.

41. J. Edgar Chenoweth, Henry Aldous Dixon, and Robert Sikes, ibid., pp. 22, 5, and 7–8, respectively.

42. U.S. Congress, House Report 1551, H.R. 10572, 86th Cong. 2nd sess., April 25, 1960; Senate Report 1407, S. 3044, May 23, 1960.

43. Multiple Use–Sustained Yield Act, P.L. 86-517, June 12, 1960, sec. 4(a).

44. USDA Forest Service, *Report of the Chief of the Forest Service, 1960,* p. 1.

45. J. Michael McCloskey, "Natural Resources — National Forests — The Multiple Use–Sustained Yield Act of 1960," *Oregon Law Review* 41, no. 1 (Dec. 1961): 49–77.

46. Alf Nelson, "Minutes of the Meeting of the Committee on Forest Management and the Forest Advisory Committee, Fairmont Hotel, San Francisco, California, April 30, 1960," reproduced for a meeting of the two committees six months later in San Francisco, Nov. 5–6, 1960. FHS, NFPA box 120.

47. Ibid.

48. Edward C. Crafts, "Congress and the Forest Service, 1950–1962," an oral history conducted in 1965 by Amelia Fry, Regional Oral History Office, Bancroft Library, University of California, Berkeley, 1975, p. 49. Courtesy of the Bancroft Library.

49. *Congressional Record,* 86th Cong., 2nd sess. (June 2, 1960), pp. 11700–22. Representative Barry may have spoken with tongue in cheek, since he had just been elected to the 86th Congress and thus had served only about a year and a half.

50. Staggers, Testimony on HR 10572, before the subcommittee on forests of the House Committee on Agriculture, p. 20.

51. Walter Prescott Webb, *The Great Frontier* (Austin: University of Texas Press, 1951), pp. 103–39, 191–202.

52. Samuel Hays dedicated an entire, voluminous monograph to describing and explaining this evolution of public consciousness, this rise of concern for "quality of life," between World War Two and the 1980s: *Beauty, Health, and Permanence* (Cambridge: Cambridge University Press, 1987).

9. "Operation Multiple Use"

1. U.S. Congress, hearings before the House Committee on Agriculture, "Long-Range Program for the National Forests," 86th Cong., 1st sess. (May 14 & 15, 1959), vol. 3, Serial Y, pp. 108, 110.

2. *Congressional Record,* 86th Cong., 1st sess. (March 24, 1959), p. 5127.

3. E. L. Peterson, hearings before the House Committee on Agriculture, "Long-Range Program for the National Forests," p. 6.

4. Ibid., pp. 103–5.

5. Ibid., pp. 31–32.

6. Ibid., pp. 26, 32.

7. Ibid., p. 26.

8. Ibid., p. 109.

9. *Congressional Record,* 86th Cong., 1st sess. (March 24, 1959), p. 5129.

10. Ibid., pp. 5129–30; see sections entitled "Protection," and "Administrative Structures and Equipment."

11. Ibid., p. 5130.

12. USDA Forest Service, *The Forest Service Program for Forest and Rangeland Resources* (Washington, D.C., 1990), p. 6.18.

13. *Congressional Record,* 86th Cong., 1st sess. (March 24, 1959), p. 5130.

14. Ibid., pp. 5128–29. See the section entitled "Water Resources."

15. Walt Hopkins, J. D. Sinclair, and P. B. Rowe, "From Forest Influences to Applied Watershed Management in Southern California," *Proceedings, Society of American Foresters Meeting, 1958* (Washington, D.C.: SAF, 1959), pp. 36–38.

16. *Congressional Record,* 86th Cong., 1st sess. (March 24, 1959), pp. 5128–29.

17. "Over many years the Forest Service has attempted to bring livestock numbers into balance with available forage"; *Congressional Record,* 86th Cong., 1st sess. (March 24, 1959), p. 5129.

18. Ibid.

19. Ibid.

20. Act of March 1, 1911, Weeks Law (36 Stat. 961). Clarke-McNary Act of June 7, 1924 (43 Stat. 653). For a discussion of the acquisition program in 1937 and 1938, see the *Report of the Chief, 1937,* pp. 14–15; and *Report of the Chief, 1938,* pp. 27–28, 33–35.

21. *Report of the Chief, 1945,* p. 12.

22. Senate Interior Committee hearing record on S. J. 95 "Acceleration of the Reforestation Programs," 86th Cong., 2nd sess. (April 22, 1960).

23. These and the following figures on the number of years required to complete the reforestation task were supplied by the Forest Service to the Senate Interior Committee in a letter dated Jan. 29, 1960. That letter and accompanying tables are found on pp. 10–15 of the Senate Interior Committee hearing record on S. J. 95, "Acceleration of the Reforestation Programs," 86th Cong., 2nd sess. (April 22, 1960).

24. Chief McArdle, ibid., p. 11.

25. Senator Wayne Morse, ibid., pp. 17–23.

26. Representative Lee Metcalf, ibid., pp. 28–29.

27. Senator Mike Mansfield, ibid., pp. 23, 30. Elected as Senate majority leader in 1961, Mansfield's influence was considerable.

28. Ibid., pp. 7–8.

29. The budget figures were gleaned from two sources, both originating with the Forest Service: Senate Interior Committee hearing on Senate Joint Resolution 95 (ibid.), pp. 18, 26; and *Congressional Record,* 86th Cong. 2nd sess. (June 8, 1960), pp. 12080–81. There are some minor unexplained discrepancies in the two sets of budget statistics. For example, the table on p. 26 of the Senate Interior Committee hearing cites $3,015,000 as the congressional appropriation figure for national forest reforestation, while the table on p. 12081 of the *Congressional Record* cites $3,162,000 as the congressional appropriation. Note: Knutson-Vandenberg Act funds authorizing the reuse of portions of national forest timber sale receipts for reforestation and "stand improvement" in the vicinity of timber harvests are not included in the reforestation budget figures here for three reasons: first, the Forest Service did not include them when presenting Congress with reforestation expenditure records in appropriations hearings; second, these funds are earmarked and thus exempt from political negotiation; third, their significance as a source of funding remained minor during the 1950s. They do, however, become important in later decades.

30. Spencer Smith and Joseph Penfold, testimony before the House Agriculture Committee hearing on the "Long Range Program for the National Forests," pp. 143–46.

31. Senate Committee on Appropriations, Hearing on Interior and Related Agencies Appropriations for Fiscal Year 1960, 86th Cong. 1st sess. (May 18, 1959), pp. 735–37. The Forest Service had indicated that it needed an annual increase of approximately $40 million a year for the next five years to reach a budget plateau of $320 million to implement the first, "short-term" phase of Operation Multiple Use (see p. 747). Senator Murray asked which programs the Forest Service would concentrate on if the Congress allowed them about half of the $40 million increase.

32. House Committee on Appropriations, Hearings on Department of Interior and Related Agencies Appropriations for 1960, 86th Cong. 1st sess. (Feb. 5, 1959), pp. 923, 926–28; and Senate Committee on Appropriations, Hearing on Interior and Related Agencies Appropriations, 86th Cong. 1st sess. (May 18, 1959), p. 755.

33. Senate Committee on Appropriations, Hearing on Interior and Related Agencies Appropriations for Fiscal Year 1960, 86th Cong. 1st sess. (May 18, 1959), pp. 750–52.

34. *Congressional Record,* 86th Cong., 1st sess. (Aug. 5, 1959), pp. 15138–39.

35. See budget tables printed in *Congressional Record,* 86th Cong., 2nd sess. (June 8, 1960), v. 106, pp. 12079–81.

36. *Report of the Chief, 1958,* p. 18.

37. House Appropriations Committee, Hearings on Interior and Related Agencies Appropriations for 1960, 86th Cong. 1st sess. (Feb. 5, 1959), pp. 934, 937, 966.

38. *Congressional Record,* 86th Cong. 1st sess. (May 14, 1959), pp. 8179–80.

39. Assistant Secretary Ervin Peterson offered this $10 million revenue generation statistic in his testimony before the House Appropriations Committee, Hearings on Interior and Related Agencies Appropriations for 1960, 86th Cong. 1st sess. (Feb. 5, 1959), p. 933.

40. Statement of Senator Hubert Humphrey, Senate Committee on Appropriations, Hearing on Interior and Related Agencies Appropriations for Fiscal Year 1960, 86th Cong. 1st sess. (May 18, 1959), p. 760.

41. Senator Robert Byrd, ibid., p. 748.

42. Testimony of Don Magnuson, House Appropriations Committee, Hearings on Interior and Related Agencies Appropriations for 1960, 86th Cong. 1st sess. (Feb. 5, 1959), p. 1039. Congressman Don Magnuson is not to be confused with Senator Warren Magnuson, also a Democrat from Washington.

43. Published by the Forest Service in May 1959, the pamphlet is titled, "Program for the National Forests: Estimates of Work Needed and Costs by States for the Short Term — Initial 12 Years." The Eisenhower administration, concerned about keeping federal expenditures down, actually blocked the agency from developing these cost estimates earlier. This pamphlet resulted from a request from Congress for a full accounting of costs prior to a House Agriculture Committee hearing on the 1959 Program scheduled for May.

44. The appropriation act figures for 1961 are found in the *Congressional Record,* 86th Cong., 2nd sess. (June 8, 1960), pp. 12079–82.

10. Patterns of the Fifties Repeated in the Sixties

1. Samuel P. Hays, *Beauty, Health, and Permanence: Environmental Politics in the United States, 1955–1985* (Cambridge: Cambridge University Press, 1987),

p. 13. The entirety of Hays's chapter 1 is devoted to a discussion titled, "From Conservation to Environment." Stephen Fox, *The American Conservation Movement* (Madison: University of Wisconsin Press, 1985), p. 315, includes figures on membership growth between 1966 and 1975 for the Sierra Club, National Wildlife Federation, Audubon Society, and Wilderness Society, plus the record of membership decline for the Izaak Walton League in the same period. Fox also provides a complex yet engaging analysis of the evolution of the conservation/environmental movement in this period in chapter 9 of his book. His discussion of the factions and disagreements *within* the movement is especially valuable for countering assumptions that the environmental movement was monolithic. See also Laura and Guy Waterman, *Forest and Crag* (Boston: Appalachian Mountain Club, 1989), pp. 627–37, for an interesting discussion of how the Appalachian Mountain Club debated the pros and cons of its own membership growth in the 1970s.

2. Hays, ibid.

3. Fox, *The American Conservation Movement,* chap. 10, "The Amateur Tradition: People and Politics"; Dave Foreman, "The New Conservation Movement," *Wild Earth* 1, no. 2 (Summer 1991): 6–12.

4. E. B. White, quoted by Rachel Carson in *Silent Spring* (Greenwich, Conn.: Fawcett Crest, 1962), p. 12.

5. Edward Cliff discussed the transition from McArdle's tenure in detail in his oral history. The third candidate, Arthur Greeley, apparently was more of a backup candidate in case both Cliff and Crafts proved unacceptable to the Kennedy administration. Edward P. Cliff, "Half a Century in Forest Conservation" (Washington, D.C.: USDA Forest Service, March 1981), pp. 209–13.

6. In Crafts's 1965 oral history, he stated, "You never get things done if you are not willing to take risks." His rules for lobbying were: (1) don't worry about personal risks, and (2) don't jeopardize the organization. Edward C. Crafts, "Congress and the Forest Service, 1950–1962," an oral history conducted in 1965 by Amelia Fry, Regional Oral History Office, Bancroft Library, University of California, Berkeley, 1975, p. 61. Courtesy of the Bancroft Library. The fact that he was relatively "progressive" did not necessarily make him a friend of environmentalists. He still accused the Sierra Club of being "militant and overly aggressive" and of alienating people in Washington.

7. Crafts, ibid., p. 54.

8. Cliff, "Half a Century in Forest Conservation," pp. 217–18.

9. E. M. Sterling, "The Myth of Multiple Use," *American Forests* 76, no. 6 (June 1970): 24–27.

10. Cliff, "Half a Century in Forest Conservation," p. 230.

11. USDA Forest Service, "A Development Program for the National Forests" (Washington, D.C.: GPO, Sept. 1961), pp. 8, 13, 14.

12. Hamilton K. Pyles, "Multiple Use of the National Forests," oral history interview conducted by Susan R. Schrepfer (Santa Cruz: Forest History Society, 1972), p. 112. During the 1950s, Pyles had been Assistant Regional Forester and Director of Information and Education for Lake States Region with headquarters in Milwaukee, Wisconsin, and Regional Forester for the Eastern Region. In 1962 he took Crafts's job in Programs and Legislation until his retirement in 1966.

13. Herbert Kaufman, in his 1960 book *The Forest Ranger: A Study in Administrative Behavior* (Baltimore: Johns Hopkins Press, 1960), detailed the many organizational checks and incentives used by the agency to promote desired behavior from lower levels of the agency, including: (1) the pre-forming of forest ranger decisions by centralized authorizations, prohibitions, and directives; (2) procedures for detecting and discouraging deviance from central policy directives through requirements for ranger diaries and other reports, inspections, performance evaluations and employee transfers; and (3) procedures for recruiting employees likely to develop a voluntary will to conform to central policy directives. All of these characteristics applied to the Forest Service of the 1960s.

14. Financial management records from the 1960s for national forests in the Pacific Northwest indicate that the individual forests received a lump sum each year for "national forest protection and management" — i.e., for multiple use management — allocated to them by the regional office, with timber sale and reforestation targets attached. Only timber sales and reforestation activities were "hard-wired" into the budget allocations; everything else was secondary and expendable. (The main exceptions were special projects that received special funding — almost always construction projects.) This budget practice evolved naturally from the fact that the Washington Office backed its funding requests with promises to achieve a certain output of timber and a certain amount of replanting. The Washington Office then passed both the funds and the management targets on to the regional offices, which in turn allocated money and targets to the forests. Historical financial management files from northwestern national forests contain numerous memos to the forests from the regional office on the importance of accomplishing the timber and reforestation targets within the allotted budget. Neither large deficits nor large surpluses in end of the year accounting were tolerated. (Although financial management files for individual national forests are not scheduled for permanent retention, some are still available at Federal Records Centers.)

15. Forest Service, Gifford Pinchot National Forest, *Canyon Creek Ranger District Multiple Use Plan*, April 28, 1961, p. 41. (Copy of plan in the author's pos-

session. Available at Gifford Pinchot National Forest Supervisor's Office storage warehouse.)

16. Ibid., pp. 9, 38 for allowable cut and harvest data; and p. 16 on the transportation system.

17. Ibid., pp. 5–6, 34.

18. Ibid., pp. 7–8, 35.

19. Ibid., pp. 4, 32.

20. Ibid., pp. 22–23, 26–29.

21. The decision to develop a regional policy statement in response to communications from several senators is recounted in a letter from Secretary of Agriculture Orville Freeman to Maurine Neuberger, March 30, 1962, Seattle FRC, Acc. #66-A236, box 81175, folder 2150.

22. Forest Service, Northwest Regional Office, *Long-Range Management Policy and Objectives for the High Mountain Areas of the Region,* October 20, 1961, Seattle FRC, Acc. #66-A236, box 81175, folder 2150.

23. Neal M. Rahm for The Record (Attn: Messrs. Payne and Greeley), July 12, 1962, in reference to J. Herbert Stone's memorandum of June 1, 1962, Forest Service, Washington Office; in Seattle FRC, Acc. #67-A309, box 63993, folder 2320.

24. Edward Cliff to Orville Freeman, March 26, 1962, Seattle FRC, Acc. #66-A236, box 81175, folder 2150.

25. Justice William O. Douglas, from *Mazama* vol. 43, no. 13 (Dec. 1961), copy of article in Seattle FRC, Acc. #66-A236, box 81175, folder 2140.

26. The Wilderness Act, P.L. 88-577, Sept. 3, 1964.

27. Roderick Nash, *Wilderness and the American Mind,* 2nd ed. (New Haven: Yale University Press, 1973), p. 222. The literature on the Wilderness Act and its implementation is voluminous. Besides Nash, see Michael Frome, *Battle for the Wilderness* (New York: Praeger, 1974); Craig Allin, *The Politics of Wilderness Preservation* (Westport, Conn.: Greenwood Press, 1982); William L. Graf, *Wilderness Preservation and the Sagebrush Rebellions* (Savage, Md.: Rowan & Littlefield, 1990); J. Michael McCloskey, "The Wilderness Act of 1964: Its Background and Meaning," *Oregon Law Review* 45 (June 1966): 288–321; Dennis Roth, *The Wilderness Movement and the National Forests: 1964–1980* (USDA Forest Service, Dec. 1984), and *The Wilderness Movement and the National Forests: 1980–1984* (Forest Service, Aug. 1988); and Mark Harvey, "Echo Park, Glen Canyon, and the Post-War Wilderness Movement," *Pacific Historical Review* 60, no. 1 (1991): 43–67.

28. I am indebted to Peter M. Zmyj, a graduate student in history at the University of Arizona, for his thoughts on the struggle to redefine "conservation" in the context of the wilderness debate and for his original spade work on opposition to the wilder-

ness act contained in his unpublished paper, " 'Wise Use or No Use': Opposition against the Wilderness Act, 1957–1964," Dec. 10, 1992.

29. *White House Conference on Conservation: Official Proceedings* (Washington, D.C.: GPO, 1963), pp. 61–62.

30. Senator Gordon Allott, U.S. Congress, *Congressional Record* 107 (Sept. 5, 1961): 18085.

31. William Welsh, Secretary-Manager of the National Reclamation Association, testimony before the Senate Committee on Interior and Insular Affairs, *National Wilderness Preservation Act, Hearings on S. 1176,* 85th Cong., 1st sess., June 19–20, 1957, p. 329.

32. Stewart Udall, *The Quiet Crisis* (New York: Holt, Rinehart & Winston, 1963), p. viii.

33. Stewart Udall, "Wilderness," *Living Wilderness* 80 (Spring/Summer 1962): 4.

34. U.S. Congress, House, *Message from the President of the United States Transmitting the National Wilderness Preservation System,* House doc. 79, 89th Cong., 1st sess., Feb. 8, 1965.

35. Forest Service, Northwest Regional Office, *Long-Range Management Policy and Objectives for the High Mountain Areas of the Region,* p. xxii.

36. On the attitude of the Forest Service toward additional wilderness designations in the late 1970s, see Paul Mohai, "Public Participation and Natural Resource Decision-Making: The Case of the RARE II Decisions," *Natural Resources Journal* 27 (Winter 1987): 123–55.

37. The National Wild and Scenic Rivers Act, P.L. 90-542, Oct. 2, 1968; and the National Trails System Act, P.L. 90-543, Oct. 2, 1968. For a discussion of these laws from the Forest Service perspective, see Hamilton K. Pyles, "Multiple Use of the National Forests," pp. 128–29; and Ed Cliff, "Half a Century in Forest Conservation," pp. 226–27.

38. Michael J. Bean, *The Evolution of National Wildlife Law,* Report to the Council on Environmental Quality, (Washington, D.C.: GPO, 1977), pp. 370–417.

39. Crafts, "Congress and the Forest Service," p. 65.

40. Frank Gregg, "Public Land Policy: Controversial Beginnings for the Third Century," *Government and Environmental Politics,* ed. by Michael Lacey (Washington, D.C.: Smithsonian Institution, 1988), pp. 158–59.

41. *Report of the Chief, 1962,* pp. 39; *Report of the Chief, 1968,* pp. 48; budget figures from Forest Service, Budget Branch, "Budgets 1961–1970 Composite Comparison," dated Aug. 13, 1970; FHS: WTA box 31, Forest Service Budget file no. 2.411.

42. Forest Service, "A Development Program for the National Forests," p. 13.

43. John McGuire, who became Forest Service Chief in 1972 after Cliff retired, recalled in a later interview that the Natural Resources Defense Council challenged below-cost sales as a tactic in their campaign to keep roadless lands undeveloped. "An Interview with John R. McGuire, Forest Service Chief, 1972–79," interviewed by Harold K. Steen (Durham: Forest History Society, 1988), pp. 67–68. In 1978 the U. S. General Accounting Office published a critique of below-cost sales suggesting that the Forest Service should concentrate its efforts in regions where timber sales where profitable: GAO, *Need to Concentrate Intensive Timber Management on High Productive Lands* (Washington, D.C.: GPO, 1978). The GAO again criticized below-cost sales in 1984, "Congress Needs Better Information on Forest Service's Below-Cost Timber Sales," GAO/RCED-84-96, June 28, 1984.

44. USDA Forest Service, *National Forest Wildlife: Operation Outdoors, Part Two* (Washington, D.C.: GPO, Feb. 1961), p. 9.

45. Stephen Pyne, *Fire in America: A Cultural History of Wildland and Rural Fire* (Princeton: Princeton University Press, 1982), pp. 490–96. In these pages, Pyne discusses the change in thinking that evolved between the mid-1960s and the mid-1970s regarding wildfire and its potential use as a *tool* of management. The change resulted partly from the necessity of dealing with the issue of managing fires in wilderness after the passage of the Wilderness Act in 1964. The Tall Timbers Research Station in Tallahassee, Fla., began a series of annual conferences on fire ecology in 1962 aimed at understanding and working with fire in a natural environment.

46. The Bureau of Outdoor Recreation was a product of recommendations by the Outdoor Recreation Resources Review Commission established in 1958, which finally reported its findings in 1962. S. T. Dana and Sally K. Fairfax review both organizations in *Forest and Range Policy* (New York: McGraw Hill, 1980), pp. 196–97 and 209–13.

47. Budget figures supplied by the Forest Service, Budget Branch, in a document titled, "Budgets 1961–1970 Composite Comparison," dated Aug. 13, 1970; FHS: WTA box 31, Forest Service Budget file no. 2.411.

48. Cliff, "Half a Century in Forest Conservation," p. 190.

49. Ibid., pp. 25–26.

50. Both Edward Cliff and John McGuire, who was Deputy Chief of Programs and Legislation in the Washington Office from 1967 to 1971 and Chief of the agency from 1972 to 1979, explained in detail these budget politics, including attempts by OMB to force the Forest Service to defend the president's budget and not embarrass the administration by revealing its original requests. Both recounted how members of the congressional appropriations committees often made direct requests for this information, which the agency was then obliged to provide. McGuire explained,

"Then the [committee] chairman would put a table in the hearing record saying here's what the agency wanted and here's what OMB put in the president's budget. Look at that; big difference! That would justify giving the agency more than the president wanted us to get." "An Interview with John R. McGuire," by Harold K. Steen (Durham: Forest History Society, 1988), pp. 83, 98–99. Cliff, "Half a Century in Forest Conservation," pp. 186–91. An example of this struggle by administration personnel to control Forest Service budget requests at this time is a memo from Secretary Freeman to the Forest Service Chief in which Freeman complained that "employees in various agencies of the Department have been . . . divulging to unauthorized personnel entirely too much information as to agency budget requests and departmental requests to the Bureau of the Budget. This practice must stop immediately"; memorandum of Orville Freeman to Richard McArdle, March 9, 1962. Edward Cliff, who became chief shortly after this order was issued, accordingly forwarded a memo to all major Washington Office and Regional Office personnel reiterating Freeman's concerns; Cliff to Regional Foresters, Directors, and Washington Office Staff, April 2, 1962; both memos in Seattle FRC, Acc. #66-A236, box 81173, folder 6510.

11. From Gridlocked Conflict to Compromised Policy Reform

1. Rep. Don H. Clausen, quoted in Dennis C. LeMaster, *Decade of Change: The Remaking of Forest Service Statutory Authority during the 1970s* (Westport, Conn.: Greenwood Press, sponsored by the Forest History Society, 1984), p. 40.

2. A very uncritical history of federal forest management in the southern Appalachians, sponsored by the Forest Service but written by Shelly Smith Mastran and Nan Lowerre, *Mountaineers and Rangers* (Washington, D.C.: USDA Forest Service, 1983), FS-380, offers these telling comments about the switch to clearcutting: "In the early 1960s — under policy directives to increase National Forest timber production, with the support of long-awaited new silvicultural research findings, a more stringent need for economy and efficiency in harvesting, and with demand increasing from the region's pulpwood industry — clearcutting in patches (called even-aged management by foresters) became a more prominent practice." Clearcutting accounted for 50 percent of timber harvest volume in the East in 1969 (more in the West); p. 144.

3. Cliff, "Half a Century in Forest Conservation," pp. 230–31.

4. LeMaster, *Decade of Change*, p. 17.

5. Dennis LeMaster discusses these clearcutting studies as well as subsequent events in chap. 2 of his *Decade of Change*. Charles Wilkinson and H. Michael Anderson also discuss them in "Land and Resource Planning in the National Forests," *Oregon Law Review* 64, nos. 1 and 2 (1985): 139–51. My summary of these events is partly based on these accounts.

6. Daniel R. Barney, *The Last Stand: Ralph Nader's Study Group Report on the National Forests* (New York: Grossman Publishers, 1974). Chapter titles include "Clearcutting: Technology and Turmoil," "The Forest Service Mandate: Cut at Will," and " 'Bureaucracy Running Wild.' "

7. USDA Forest Service, Wyoming Forest Study Team, *Forest Management in Wyoming,* p. 9; reprinted in hearings on "Clearcutting" Practices on the National Timberlands, Senate Committee on Interior and Insular Affairs, 92nd Cong., 1st sess., May 7, 1971, pp. 1116–1201.

8. Ibid., p. 8 (p. 1128).

9. Ibid., p. 12 (p. 1132).

10. Ibid., pp. 8, 71–72 (pp. 1128, 1191–92).

11. "A University View of the Forest Service," prepared for the Committee on Interior and Insular Affairs, U.S. Senate, by a select committee of the University of Montana, 91st Cong, 2nd sess., Dec. 1, 1970, Senate Document no. 91–115, pp. 13–14.

12. Ibid., p. 14.

13. *Report of the President's Advisory Panel on Timber and the Environment* (Washington, D.C.: GPO, April 1973). Brief biographies of the panel members are found on pp. 121–22.

14. USDA Forest Service, testimony before the Senate Committee on Interior and Insular Affairs, hearings on "Clearcutting" Practices on the National Timberlands, 92nd Cong., 1st sess., May 7, 1971, p. 839, table 1.

15. Ibid., p. 4.

16. "Gordon Robinson: Forestry Consultant to the Sierra Club," an interview conducted by Harold K. Steen (San Francisco: Sierra Club History Committee, 1979), pp. 74–75.

17. "A University View of the Forest Service," p. 22.

18. USDA Forest Service, Washington Office, "A Forest Service Environmental Program for the Future," draft, April 1971; first produced as "A Forest Service Environmental Program for the 1970s," draft, Sept. 25, 1970. Controversy over the program kept it from being formally released in final form as an approved administration document. Available at Forest Service Region 6 storage warehouse, historical files, box F32.

19. Ibid., p. 10.

20. John T. Keane to Richard L. Ocheltree, Nov. 4, 1969; FHS, WTA box 14, Forest Legislation file.

21. P.L. 91-190 (83 Stat. 852). The precedent-setting judicial interpretation of NEPA occurred in *Calvert Cliffs' Coordinating Committee v. Atomic Energy Commission,* D.C. District Court, 449 F. 2nd 1109 (1971). Scholarly analysis of NEPA

exceeds even that of the Wilderness Act. Two valuable works include: Lettie McSpadden-Wenner, "The Misuse and Abuse of NEPA," *Environmental [History] Review* 7, no. 3 (Fall 1983): 229–54; and Richard Mott, "NEPA Violations and Equitable Discretion," *Oregon Law Review* 64, no. 3 (1986): 497–512.

22. Dennis LeMaster briefly discusses four especially influential lawsuits won by environmentalists between 1969 and 1973 in *Decade of Change*, p. 34. See also the important work by Richard Stewart, "The Reformation of American Administrative Law," *Harvard Law Review* 88 (1975): 1667–1813.

23. LeMaster, pp. 19–20.

24. Ibid., p. 21.

25. S. 1832, introduced by Senator John Sparkman (D-Alabama), April 18, 1969 and H.R. 10344, introduced by Rep. John L. McMillan, April 21, 1969, 91st Cong., 1st sess. See especially Sparkman's testimony on his bill in the *Congressional Record*, April 18, 1969, pp. S3083–86. Also, LeMaster, pp. 21–22.

26. Edward C. Crafts, "Forest Service Researcher and Congressional Liaison: An Eye to Multiple Use," an interview conducted by Susan Schrepfer (Santa Cruz: Forest History Society, 1972), pp. 113–14.

27. Sierra Club, San Francisco Office, "National Timber Supply Act-Summary of the Problem" and "Environmental Impacts of the 'National Timber Supply Act' "; *New York Times* (May 13, 1969), *Louisville Courier Journal* (Nov. 4, 1969); Denver Public Library, Western History Branch, Wilderness Society Files, box 74, file 8.

28. LeMaster, pp. 25–26.

29. Towell recounts in detail the formation and function of his Areas of Agreement Committee in "An Interview with William E. Towell," pp. 101–8.

30. Congressional testimony from the Areas of Agreement Committee and minutes of some of its meetings are available in the Forest History Society's Western Timber Association records, box 31.

31. USDA Forest Service, "The Outlook for Timber in the United States: A Preliminary Summary of the 1970 Timber Review" (Washington, D.C.: Forest Service, Dec. 1972). This document strongly emphasized the appalling lack of funding for reforestation, stand improvement, and other activities necessary to sustain high harvest levels, and predicted that the timber supply from national forests would have to be adjusted accordingly. With fresh data in hand and a document to circulate in Congress, the agency was able to secure a temporary boost in reforestation funds.

32. LeMaster recounts in intricate detail the progress of RPA, from Humphrey's conversation with Robert Wolf to the signature of Gerald Ford, pp. 37–50. For Wolf's personal recollections, see the series of interviews of him produced by the University of Montana School of Forestry and housed in the archives section of the University of Montana Library.

33. For this summary of RPA I am indebted to Charles F. Wilkinson and H. Michael Anderson, "Land and Resource Planning in the National Forests," *Oregon Law Review* 64, nos. 1 & 2 (1985): 39–40.

34. V. Alaric Sample, in chap. 4 of *The Impact of the Federal Budget Process on National Forest Planning,* compares three conceptual models of the policy process: (1) the rational actor model, (2) the organizational process model, and (3) the bureaucratic politics model. He discusses where they fit and where they fall short in the context of national forest management. He concludes that each has strengths and weaknesses in explanatory power, depending on the context in which it is applied. Wisdom concedes that all three perspectives should inform any analysis. RPA justifies this assessment.

35. Act of June 4, 1897 (30 Stat. 34).

36. Sierra Club, Washington Office, "Environmental Impacts of the 'National Timber Supply Act,'" Denver Public Library, Wilderness Society records, box 74, file 8.

37. Again, I am indebted to LeMaster, *Decade of Change,* and Wilkinson and Anderson, "Land and Resource Planning on the National Forests," for much of the basic information on the Monongahela lawsuit and the development of the National Forest Management Act.

38. *Izaak Walton League v. Butz,* 367 F. Supp. 422 (N.D. W. Va. 1973).

39. *Izaak Walton League v. Butz,* 522 F. 2d 945 (4th Circuit 1975).

40. A key lobbyist for the Sierra Club on forestry matters at this time was Gordon Robinson, who had been head of forestry for Southern Pacific of California for twenty-seven years. After retiring (under pressure) he became a consultant to the Club. He discussed the lobbying politics surrounding NFMA in "Gordon Robinson: Forestry Consultant to the Sierra Club," pp. 121–22.

41. S. 2926, 94th Cong., 2nd sess., Feb. 4, 1976.

42. John R. McGuire, "An Interview with John R. McGuire, Forest Service Chief, 1972–79," conducted by Harold K. Steen (Durham: Forest History Society and U.S. Forest Service, 1988), p. 122.

43. National Forest Management Act, P.L. 94-588, Oct. 22, 1976. See LeMaster, pp. 63–79; Wilkinson and Anderson, p. 42; and Towell, "An Interview with William E. Towell," p. 111.

44. NFMA sec. 6(g)(3)(F) contains the clearcutting guidelines.

45. George Craig, statement to Subcommittee on Housing and Urban Affairs, Senate Committee on Banking, Housing and Urban Affairs, March 27, 1973; FHS, WTA box 31, file 2.411.

46. The earned harvest effect provision and its legislative history is discussed in Wilkinson and Anderson, pp. 125–28, 151–54, and 184–86.

47. Conversation with Frank Gregg, Director of the Bureau of Land Management under the Carter administration, March 1990.

12. Retrenchment and Revolt

1. An excellent journalistic account of Carter's water project "hit list" fiasco is contained in Marc Reisner's *Cadillac Desert* (New York: Penguin, 1986). See the chapter titled "The Peanut Farmer and the Pork Barrel." This chapter also illuminates the unsteady relationship between the Carter White House and the environmental lobby.

2. *Report of the Chief, 1985,* p. 80; cited in V. Alaric Sample, *The Impact of the Federal Budget Process on National Forest Planning* (New York: Greenwood Press, 1990), p. 8.

3. Sample, ibid., pp. 18–21.

4. Ibid., pp. 21–30.

5. U.S. Office of Technology Assessment, "Forest Service Planning: Accommodating Uses, Producing Outputs, and Sustaining Ecosystems," GPO Stock #052-003-01264-2 (Washington, D.C.: GPO, 1992).

6. Quoted by Peter Montgomery, "Science Friction," *Common Cause* 16, no. 5 (Nov./Dec., 1990), p. 26.

7. Andrew Garber, "Rules to Protect Fish Delay 50-Year Plan for Boise Forest," *Idaho Statesman* (Dec. 28, 1986).

8. See articles in *Forest Voice* 4, no. 1 (Spring 1991). *Forest Voice* is published by a private conservation organization at P.O. Box 2171, Eugene, Oregon 97402. Also see Jeff DeBonis, "Timber Industry Wins Again, Congress Sets Dangerously High Timber Cut for '91," *Inner Voice* 3, no. 1 (Winter 1991): 11.

9. R. Max Peterson, quoted in Perri Knize, "The Mismanagement of the National Forests," *Atlantic Monthly* (Oct. 1991), p. 107.

10. "Feedback to the Chief," in the "Sunbird Proceedings," 1989.

11. Randal O'Toole, "Analysis of Region 5 Timber Yield Tables," CHEC Research Paper #17, (Oak Grove, Oreg.: Cascade Holistic Economic Consultants, Sept. 1986), pp. 14–15.

12. Conversation with Randal O'Toole and Jeff St. Clair, *Forest Watch* staff, February 1993.

13. Grace Herndon, *Cut and Run: Saying Goodbye to the Last Great Forests in the West* (Telluride, Colo.: Western Eye Press, 1991), pp. 113–34.

14. Fred L. Trevey, Clearwater National Forest Supervisor, to John Mumma, Regional Forester, "Timber Resource Strategy Update," Feb. 29, 1990; in the author's possession.

15. See, e.g., the Lolo National Forest letter to "concerned citizens" from forest

supervisor Orville Daniels, dated Sept. 11, 1991, p. 1; in the author's possession. Daniels indicates that the Lolo NF had been "intensively logged" during the 1960s and 1970s at levels exceeding what forest managers now believe to have been prudent, and that as a result "many of these areas cannot be re-entered yet because more cutting would violate standards" established in the forest plan for resource protection.

16. Klaus H. Barber and Susan A. Rodman, "FORPLAN: The Marvelous Toy," *Western Wildlands* 15, no. 4 (Winter 1990): 18–22.

17. US General Accounting Office, *Forest Service: The Flathead National Forest Cannot Meet Its Timber Goal,* GAO/RCED-91–124 (Washington, D.C.: GPO, May 1991), p. 14.

18. See citations in notes 14 and 15 above.

19. Daniels's letter, note 15 above.

20. "Critics Say Forest Service Scapegoats Grizzlies," *High Country News* 24 (Sept. 21, 1992). Liz Sedler et al., "A Report on Kootenai National Forest Timber Inventory Data Used for FORPLAN and Forest Plan Projections for Future Harvest," prepared for Congress and Kootenai National Forest planners by the Inventory Inquiry Project, P.O. Box 1203, Sand Point, Idaho 83864 (Aug. 1992).

21. Testimony of Barry Flamm, Chief Forester for the Wilderness Society, before the House Subcommittee on Forests, Family Farms, and Energy, Committee on Agriculture, Hearing on "National Forest Timber Supply Outlook and Sustainable Timber Yield," 101st Cong., 2nd sess., March 6, 1990, pp. 540–41.

22. Trevey's letter, note 14 above.

23. Letter from Robert Schrenk, Kootenai National Forest Supervisor, to Liz Sedler, Inventory Inquiry Project, Aug. 31, 1992; in the author's possession. Also see Kootenai National Forest, "1991 Monitoring Report," p. 19.

24. For a book-length exposé of private forest liquidation in Montana in the 1980s, see Richard Manning, *Last Stand: Logging, Journalism, and the Case for Humility* (Salt Lake City: Peregrine Smith Books, 1991). Manning was a journalist for the *Missoulian* newspaper during this period, and his book is based an a series of investigative reports he wrote for the newspaper, which won him a national journalism prize. See also Alan McQuillan, "Accelerated Cutting on Private Industrial Timberlands," *Missoula Independent* (Nov. 7, 1991), pp. 19–20. McQuillan is a professor of forestry at the University of Montana who worked for the Forest Service and for Champion International in the late 1970s and early 1980s. See also the in-depth articles by Paul Koberstein, "Plum Creek Timber Leaves Its Mark on Montana" and "Private Forests Face Critical Log Shortages," *The Oregonian* (Oct. 15, 1990, special supplement: "Northwest Forests: Day of Reckoning"), pp. 2–6. Also, Sherry Devlin, "Eco-battle Looms for Champion," *Missoulian* (May 21, 1992), pp.

B-1, B-3. An article in *Forbes* magazine reported on how Champion International accumulated a great deal of debt during an aggressive expansion program in the late 1970s, for which it had to radically accelerate logging on its vast holdings to service that debt: Jean A. Briggs, "Full Speed Ahead, Damn the Recession!" *Forbes* (March 5, 1979), pp. 61, 64. Another critical review of Champion's legacy in Montana is Tim Egan, "Land Deal Leaves Montana Logged and Hurt," *New York Times* (Oct. 19, 1993), A1, A7. On the Pacific Coast aspect of this problem, see Casey Bukro, "Environmentalists Side with Loggers: Threat of Raisers Brings Foes Together," *Washington Post* (May 29, 1990), pp. E1, E6.

25. Letter cited in notes 14 and 15 above.

26. For a detailed, journalistic narrative of the biological, political, and social dimensions of the spotted owl controversy, see William Dietrich, *The Final Forest: The Battle for the Last Great Trees of the Pacific Northwest* (New York: Simon & Schuster, 1992), chaps. 2, 4, and 14. Specifically regarding the Seattle Federal District Court injunction against logging in spotted owl habitat and its effect on timber harvests in the Northwest, see "Judge Dwyer Does It Again: Opinion Rebukes Forest Service for 'Remarkable Series of Violations,' " *Forest Watch* 11, no. 10 (May 1991): 10–12. For popular press coverage of the role of endangered species in the larger fight over the fate of remaining old growth on national forests, see Ted Gup, "Owl vs. Man," *Time* (June 25, 1990), pp. 56–65; and Michael D. Lemonick, "Whose Woods Are These?" *Time* (Dec. 9, 1991), pp. 70–75.

27. For an example of one national forest's recent shift toward a broader alliance with nontimber interest groups, see the article by Jim Doherty, "When Folks Say 'Cutting Edge' at the Nez, They Don't Mean Saws," *Smithsonian* 23, no. 6 (Sept. 1992): 33–44.

28. Barlow et al., *Giving Away the National Forests;* U.S. General Accounting Office, "Report to the Congress: Congress Needs Better Information on Forest Service's Below-Cost Timber Sales"; Sample, *Below-Cost Timber Sales on the National Forests;* Schuster and Jones, "Below-Cost Timber Sales"; O'Toole, *Growing Timber Deficits;* Wolf, "National Forest Timber Sales and the Legacy of Gifford Pinchot."

29. Dennis Hanson, "The Aspect of the Tally Sheet: Some Notes on the Business of Trees," *Wilderness* 47, no. 161 (Summer 1983): 24–31.

30. GAO, "Report to the Congress: Congress Needs Better Information on Forest Service's Below-Cost Timber Sales," p. 11. The Forest Service began publishing its own timber sale cost-revenue accounting during the Bush administration and even this self-appraisal showed that most timber sales lost money. In 1990, for example, their figures showed that only two out of twenty-four forests in Arizona, New Mexico, Colorado, and Utah returned had revenues beyond expenses. The government—

the taxpayers — lost $14.7 million on logging programs in the Southwest and central Rockies. USDA Forest Service, Washington Office, "Timber Sale Program Annual Report, Fiscal Year 1990."

31. "Forest Service out on a Limb on Timber Sales," *Denver Post* (Sept. 23, 1984).

32. "Careless with Land, Serving the Loggers," (Santa Fe) *New Mexican* (March 18, 1990).

33. Perri Knize, "The Mismanagement of the National Forests," *Atlantic Monthly* (Oct. 1991), pp. 98–112. Wolf is quoted on p. 103. On Wolf's reform crusade, see his articles criticizing agency implementation of RPA and NFMA in *Inner Voice* 1, no. 2 (Fall 1989): 9–11 (reprinted from *Forest Watch* magazine); his essay "National Forest Timber Sales and the Legacy of Gifford Pinchot," cited above; and his written testimony submitted to the House Subcommittee on Forests, Family Farms, and Energy, Committee on Agriculture and Forestry, Hearing on Below-Cost Timber Sales, 102nd Cong., 1st sess., Oct. 30, 1991 (original copy of testimony in author's possession).

34. "Time for a Little Perestroika," *Economist* (March 10, 1990), p. 28.

35. John Harmon, "Fowler Trying to Cut Federal Funds for Logging Roads," *Atlanta Journal/Atlanta Constitution* (Sept. 3, 1989), pp. C1, C9; editorial, "Save the Forests, Ax the Game Plan," *Atlanta Journal/Atlanta Constitution* (Feb. 18, 1989), p. 22A.

36. US Senate, Subcommittee on Conservation and Forestry of the Committee on Agriculture, "Oversight Hearing on the Management Practices of the U.S. Forest Service and Below-Cost Timber Sales," 101st Cong., 1st sess., Oct. 30, 1989, pp. 1–2. See also Senate Subcommittee on Conservation and Forestry of the Committee on Agriculture, "Oversight on Below-Cost Timber Sales and National Forest Management," 102nd Cong., 1st sess., April 11, 1991.

37. Senator William Proxmire, *Congressional Record* (Sept. 9, 1986), quoted by John Teare of Gannett News Service in his article, "Timber Sales Losses Curtail Roadbuilding," reprinted in "Our National Forests: A Time of Turmoil," Gannett News Service Special Reprint, Washington, D.C., 1987.

38. USDA Forest Service, *The Forest Service Program for Forest and Rangeland Resources: A Long-Term Strategic Plan* (Washington, D.C.: GPO, May 1990), pp. 5.27–5.28.

39. Walter Minnick, in testimony before the House Subcommittee on Conservation and Forestry, quoted by the Associated Press, *Lewiston Tribune* (Idaho), June 18, 1987.

40. Jim Kennedy and Tom Quigley summarized the findings of their poll at the

"Sunbird" conference, in the "Sunbird Proceedings," 1989. The full report on their research appeared several years later as: James J. Kennedy, Richard S. Krannich, Thomas M. Quigley, and Lori A. Cramer, *How Employees View the USDA: Forest Service Value and Reward System* (Logan, Utah: College of Natural Resources, March 1992).

41. Catherine McCarthy, Paul Sabatier, and John Loomis, "Attitudinal Change in the Forest Service: 1960–1990," forthcoming in *Society and Natural Resources*. See also the pioneering work being done at the University of Michigan, Ann Arbor, by Paul Mohai and colleagues, especially "Assessing the Impacts of Gender, Race, and Professional Training on Forest Service Attitudes and Perceptions," by Mohai, Phyllis Stillman, Pamela Jakes, and Chris Liggett. Summaries of this paper and other related research were presented at the 1993 Society of American Foresters' Convention, Indianapolis, November 1993, and are available in the conference proceedings.

42. Paul Mohai and Phyllis Stillman, *Are We Heading in the Right Direction? A Survey of USDA Forest Service Employees* (Ann Arbor: School of Natural Resources and Environment, University of Michigan, March 1993).

43. Greg Brown and Charles C. Harris, "The U.S. Forest Service: Toward the New Resource Management Paradigm?" *Society and Natural Resources* 5 (July/ Sept. 1992): 231–45. The Behan quote is from Behan's essay "The RPA/NFMA: Solution to a Nonexistent Problem," *Western Wildlands* 15 (1990): 35. See also Behan's essay, "Multiresource Forest Management: A Paradigmatic Challenge to Professional Forestry," *Journal of Forestry* 88, no. 4 (April 1990): 12–18.

44. "Feedback to the Chief from the Forest Supervisors of Regions 1, 2, 3, and 4," in the "Sunbird Proceedings," 1989.

45. U.S. Forest Service, "Sunbird Proceedings."

46. *New York Times* (March 4, 1990).

47. USDA Forest Service, "The Forest Service Pathway into the 90s and Beyond," *Resources Planning Act 1989 Assessment: Fact Kit,* FS-430 (Washington, D.C.: GPO, May 1989), p. 3.

48. Salwasser discusses the New Perspectives initiative in "Gaining Perspective: Forestry for the Future," *Journal of Forestry* 88, no. 11 (Nov. 1990); 32–38.

49. Jeff DeBonis, "New Perspectives," *Inner Voice* 2, no. 4 (Summer/Fall 1990): 8–9.

50. Norman Peck, "On Organizational Models . . . ," *Inner Voice* 5, no. 1 (Jan./ Feb. 1993): 14. For another critique of New Perspectives, see Tim Foss, "New Perspectives, Old Interpretation?" *Inner Voice* 3, no. 3 (Summer 1991): 13.

51. Senator Patrick J. Leahy, hearing before the Subcommittee on Conservation

375

and Forestry, Senate Committee on Agriculture, "Oversight on Below-Cost Timber Sales and National Forest Management," 102nd Cong., 1st sess., April 11, 1991, p. 33.

52. "Mumma Orders Higher Timber Goals for Forests," *Daily Interlake* (Great Falls, Idaho, Nov. 30, 1990), citing a Nov. 6, 1990, letter sent to the forest supervisors by Deputy Regional Forester John Hughes for Mumma.

53. Larry Craig's letter to Chief Robertson reprinted with article by Jeff DeBonis, "Retrenchment in the Forest Service: Hardliners Oust Mumma in the Northern Rockies," *Inner Voice* 3, no. 5 (Fall 1991): 1–2.

54. Timothy Egan, "Forest Supervisors Say Politicians Are Asking Them to Cut Too Much," *New York Times* (Sept. 16, 1991), pp. A1, A12. Also, see the thorough historical analysis by University of Montana professor Alan McQuillan, "Inside Mumma-Gate," *Missoula Independent* (Oct. 31, 1991), pp. 18–19.

55. See articles in the *Missoulian*: "Mumma Fight Shifts to Congress" (Sept. 7, 1991), p. A-1; "Dissenters' Fate Turns Focus on FS" (Sept. 8, 1991), p. B-1; "Foresters Cry Coup in Mumma Ouster" (Sept. 12, 1991), p. A-1; and "A Return to McCarthyism," editorial (Dec. 30, 1990); and McQuillan, "Inside Mumma-Gate," pp. 18–19. Also, Sherry Devlin, "Biologists' Union Throws Its Weight behind Mumma," *Missoulian* (Sept. 19, 1991).

56. *Inner Voice* 3, no. 5 (Fall 1991), "Retrenchment in the Forest Service," p. 1, and "The Crumbling of the Coup," p. 3.

57. "Two Say Politics Rules Their Agencies," *High Country News* 23, no. 18 (Oct. 7, 1991): 1, 10–13.

58. John McCormick, "Can't See the Forest for the Sleaze," *New York Times* (Jan. 29, 1992), p. A21.

59. Speaking at a federal "whistle-blowers" conference in Washington, D.C., in March 1992, Jeff DeBonis of AFSEEE observed: "We federal employees are here because it hurts. It hurts to work for once proud agencies that no longer meet the public trust . . . these agencies have literally been turned into instruments of mismanagement, instruments of political pork barrels, instruments of environmental destruction and, worst of all, instruments of repression against ethical employees." His statement along with others on this topic is reprinted in the proceedings of a conference sponsored by the Government Accountability Project and AFSEEE, "Protecting Integrity and Ethics: A Conference for Government Employees of Environmental, Wildlife, and Natural Resource Agencies" (Eugene, Oreg.: AFSEEE, March 1992). For congressional testimony on alleged harassment and repression of employees, see statements of Jeff DeBonis, Marynell Oechsner, and John McCormick before the Subcommittee on Environment, Energy, and Natural Resources of

the House Committee on Government Operations, 102nd Cong., 2nd sess., March 31, 1992, pp. 180–97. See also the editorial by the John McCormick, "Can't See the Forest for the Sleaze," and articles by Don Schwennesen, "Forest biologist Cites Pressure to Sell," *Missoulian* (March 31, 1992), p. A-1; J. Todd Foster, "Critics Say Agency Is Eating Its Young," *High Country News* 25, no. 1 (Jan. 25, 1993): 2; and "A Combat Biologist Calls It Quits," *Inner Voice* 5, no. 1 (Jan./Feb. 1993): 5.

60. F. Dale Robertson to Regional Foresters and Station Directors, "Ecosystem Management of the National Forests and Grasslands" (June 4, 1992), p. 1. For an academic analysis of the Ecosystem Management initiative, see Hanna J. Cortner and Margaret Ann Moote, "Ecosystem Management: It's Not Only about Getting the Science Right," *Inner Voice* 5, no. 1 (Jan./Feb. 1993): 1, 6.

61. Lee F. Coonce to John Lowe, Umpqua National Forest, Dec. 14, 1992. Reprinted in *Inner Voice* 5, no. 1 (Jan./Feb. 1993): 13.

62. USDA Forest Service, San Juan National Forest, *San Juan National Forest Newsletter: 1992 Year in Review,* Durango, Colorado (Feb. 1993), p. 4.

63. An analysis of the timber summit and partial transcripts of it can be found in *Forest Watch* 13, no. 9 (April/May 1993). The Clinton quotation is on p. 30.

64. Ibid., pp. 5, 26; quotation by Charles Meslow, p. 26.

65. Ibid., pp. 10, 17, 30.

66. Ibid., p. 28.

67. Extensive analysis of Option Nine and the political deal-making between the administration and the Sierra Club Legal Defense Fund handling the main lawsuits is covered in *Forest Watch* 14, no. 2 (Aug. 1993), esp. the article by Jeffrey St. Clair, "Dealing away Dwyer," pp. 9–12. *Forest Watch* ended publication after that issue and reconstituted itself as a new journal, *Wild Forest Review,* which continued this analysis in vol. 1, no. 1 (Nov. 1993), in another essay by Jeffrey St. Clair, "Meditations on a Done Deal," pp. 7–14. One of the most vocal dissenting groups against Option Nine and the Sierra Club capitulation is the Oregon Natural Resources Council. See its journal, *Wild Oregon* 19, no. 3 (Fall 1993), for a series of articles criticizing Option Nine.

68. Among the bills in the congressional hopper in 1991 were these: H.R. 2501, "The National Forest Timber Sale Cost Recovery Act," introduced by Rep. Jim Jontz (D-Indiana); H.R. 842, "The Ancient Forest Protection Act," also by Rep. Jontz; H.R. 1590, another "Ancient Forest Protection Act" introduced by Rep. Bruce Vento (D-Minn.); and the "Forest Biodiversity and Clearcutting Prohibition Act of 1991," introduced by Rep. John Bryant (D-Texas). In addition to these pro-environment national forest reform bills were several contrary bills promoted by timber industry allies, including, H.R. 2463 and S. 1156, "The Forests and Families Protec-

tion Act of 1991," introduced by Rep. Jerry Huckaby (D-Louisiana) and Senator Bob Packwood (R-Oregon). Most of these bills are summarized and critiqued in the Sierra Club's *Public Lands Activist,* no. 31 (March 22, 1991); and the AFSEEE's *AFSEEE Activist* 1, no. 2 (June 1991).

13. Conclusion

1. Patricia Limerick, *The Legacy of Conquest* (New York: Norton, 1987).
2. John Bedell, quoted in Grace Herndon, *Cut and Run,* p. 124.

References

Order of Sections:

Books, Conference Proceedings, Theses and Dissertations

Oral Histories

Articles, Essays, Reports, Speeches

Unpublished Archival Collections

Government Documents (arranged by date)

    Congressional Publications, Hearings, Records

    Forest Service Publications

    Miscellaneous Government Documents

Books, Conference Proceedings, Theses and Dissertations

Allin, Craig W. *The Politics of Wilderness Preservation*. Westport, Conn.: Greenwood Press, 1982.

American Forestry Association. *Proceedings of the American Forest Congress, 1946*. Washington, D.C.: American Forestry Association, 1946.

——. *Proceedings of the Fourth American Forest Congress, Oct. 29–31, 1953*. Washington, D.C.: American Forestry Association, 1953.

Bahre, Conrad J. *A Legacy of Change: Historic Human Impact on Vegetation in the Arizona Borderlands*. Tucson: University of Arizona Press, 1991.

Barlow, Thomas J., Gloria E. Helfland, Trent W. Orr, and Thomas B. Stoel, Jr. *Giving Away the National Forests: An Analysis of Forest Service Timber Sales below Cost*. New York: Natural Resources Defense Council, June 1980.

Barney, Daniel R. *The Last Stand: Ralph Nader's Study Group Report on the National Forests*. New York: Grossman Publishers, 1974.

Bergoffen, Gene S. "The Multiple Use–Sustained Yield Law: A Case Study of Administrative Initiative in the Legislation Policy-Forming Process." Master's thesis. Syracuse: State University College of Forestry, Syracuse University, June 1962.

Brown, David E., and Neil B. Carmony, eds. *Aldo Leopold's Wilderness.* Harrisburg, Pa.: Stackpole Books, 1990. (Selected early essays of Aldo Leopold. Annotated.)

Cameron, Jenks. *The Development of Governmental Forest Controls in the United States.* Baltimore: Johns Hopkins Press, 1928.

Carson, Rachel. *Silent Spring.* Greenwich, Conn.: Fawcett Crest, 1962.

Carter, Vernon Gill, and Tom Dale. *Topsoil and Civilization.* Norman, Okla.: University of Oklahoma Press, 1974.

Catton, William R., Jr. *Overshoot: The Ecological Basis of Revolutionary Change.* Urbana: University of Illinois Press, 1980.

Clary, David A. *Timber and the Forest Service.* Lawrence: University Press of Kansas, 1986.

Clawson, Marion. *Forests for Whom and for What?* Baltimore: Johns Hopkins University Press, 1975.

Commoner, Barry. *Science and Survival.* New York: Viking Press, 1963, 1967.

Cox, Thomas R., Robert S. Maxwell, Phillip Drennon Thomas, and Joseph J. Malone. *This Well-Wooded Land: Americans and Their Forests from Colonial Times to the Present.* Lincoln: University of Nebraska Press, 1985.

Croly, Herbert. *The Promise of American Life.* New York: Archon Books, 1963 [orig. pub.: Macmillan, 1909].

Culhane, Paul J. *Public Lands Politics: Interest Group Influence on the Forest Service and the Bureau of Land Management.* Baltimore: Johns Hopkins University Press, 1981.

Dana, Samuel T,. and Sally K. Fairfax. *Forest and Range Policy: Its Development in the United States.* 2nd ed. New York: McGraw-Hill, 1980.

Dietrich, William. *The Final Forest: The Battle for the Last Great Trees of the Pacific Northwest.* New York: Simon & Schuster, 1992.

DeVoto, Bernard. *The Easy Chair.* Boston: Houghton Mifflin, 1955. (Reprinted editorial essays from *Harper's* magazine, 1940s and 1950s.)

Duerr, William A., Dennis E. Teeguarden, Sam Guttenberg, and Neils B. Christiansen, eds. *Forest Resource Management: Decision Making Principles and Cases.* Corvallis: Oregon State University Book Stores, 1975.

Dunlap, Thomas. *Saving America's Wildlife.* Princeton: Princeton University Press, 1988.

Ehrlich, Paul. *The Machinery of Nature.* New York: Simon & Schuster, 1986.

Ferguson, Denzel, and Nancy Ferguson. *Sacred Cows at the Public Trough.* Bend, Oreg.: Maverick Publications, 1983.

Foss, Philip. *Politics and Grass.* Seattle: University of Washington Press, 1960.

Fox, Stephen. *The American Conservation Movement: John Muir and His Legacy.* Madison: University of Wisconsin Press, 1985.

Frank, Bernard. *Our National Forests*. Norman: University of Oklahoma Press, 1955.

Frome, Michael. *Battle for the Wilderness*. New York: Praeger Publishers, 1974.

———. *The Forest Service*. 2nd ed. Boulder, Colo.: Westview Press, 1984.

Fuller, R. Buckminster. *Operating Manual for Spaceship Earth*. Carbondale: Southern Illinois University Press, 1969.

Gates, Paul W. (See Public Land Law Review Commission under "Government Documents")

Government Accountability Project and AFSEEE. *Protecting Integrity and Ethics: A Conference for Government Employees of Environmental, Wildlife, and Natural Resource Agencies*. Eugene, Oreg.: AFSEEE, March 1992.

Graf, William L. *Wilderness Preservation and the Sagebrush Rebellions*. Savage, Md.: Rowan & Littlefield, 1990.

Harvey, Mark W. T. *A Symbol of Wilderness: Echo Park and the American Conservation Movement*. Albuquerque: University of New Mexico Press, 1994.

Hastings, James Rodney, and Raymond M. Turner. *The Changing Mile*. Tucson: University of Arizona Press, 1965.

Hays, Samuel P. *Conservation and the Gospel of Efficiency: The Progressive Conservation Movement, 1890–1920*. Cambridge, Mass.: Harvard University Press, 1959.

———. *Beauty, Health, and Permanence*. Cambridge: Cambridge University Press, 1987.

Herndon, Grace. *Cut and Run: Saying Goodbye to the Last Great Forests in the West*. Telluride, Colo.: Western Eye Press, 1991.

Ise, John. *United States Forest Policy*. New Haven: Yale University Press, 1920.

Jacobs, Lynn. *Waste of the West: Public Lands Ranching*. Tucson, Ariz.: By the author, P.O. Box 5784, Tucson, 85704, 1991.

Kaufman, Herbert. *The Forest Ranger: A Study in Administrative Behavior*. Baltimore: Johns Hopkins Press, 1960.

Keats, John. *The Crack in the Picture Window*. Boston: Houghton Mifflin, 1956.

Kennedy, James J., Richard S. Krannich, Thomas M. Quigley, and Lori A. Cramer. *How Employees View the USDA: Forest Service Value and Reward System*. Logan, Utah: College of Natural Resources, March 1992.

Krygier, J. T., and J. D. Hall, eds. *Proceedings of a Symposium: Forest Land Uses and Stream Environment*. Corvallis: Oregon State University, 1971.

LeMaster, Dennis C. *Decade of Change: The Remaking of Forest Service Statutory Authority during the 1970s*. Westport, Conn.: Greenwood Press, 1984.

Leopold, Aldo. *A Sand County Almanac*. Oxford: Oxford University Press, 1949.

Lien, Carsten. *Olympic Battleground: The Power Politics of Timber Preservation*. San Francisco: Sierra Club Books, 1991.

Lillard, Richard G. *The Great Forest*. New York: Alfred A. Knopf, 1947.

Limerick, Patricia. *The Legacy of Conquest: The Unbroken Past of the American West*. New York: W. W. Norton, 1987.

Loehr, Rodney C., ed. *Forests for the Future: The Story of Sustained Yield as Told in the Diaries and Papers of David T. Mason, 1907–1950*. Saint Paul: Forest Products History Foundation, Minnesota Historical Society, 1952.

Manning, Richard. *Last Stand: Logging, Journalism, and the Case for Humility*. Salt Lake City: Peregrine Smith Books, 1991.

Marsh, George Perkins. *Man and Nature: The Earth as Modified by Human Action*. Cambridge: Cambridge University Press, 1965 [first published in 1864].

Maser, Chris. *The Redesigned Forest*. San Pedro, Calif.: R. and E. Miles, 1988.

McConnell, Grant. *Private Power and American Democracy*. New York: Alfred A. Knopf, 1966.

McEvoy, Arthur. *The Fisherman's Problem: Ecology and Law in the California Fisheries, 1850–1980*. Cambridge: Cambridge University Press, 1986.

Meadows, Donella H., et al. *The Limits of Growth*. New York: Universe Books, 1972.

Mohai, Paul, and Phyllis Stillman. *Are We Heading in the Right Direction? A Survey of USDA Forest Service Employees, Executive Summary*. Ann Arbor: School of Natural Resources and Environment, University of Michigan, March 1993.

Morrison, Peter. *Old Growth in the Pacific Northwest: A Status Report*. Washington, D.C.: Wilderness Society, 1988.

Nash, Gerald D. *World War II and the West: Reshaping the Economy*. Lincoln: University of Nebraska Press, 1990.

Nash, Roderick. *Wilderness and the American Mind*. 3rd ed. New Haven: Yale University Press, 1982.

Norse, Elliot A. *Ancient Forests of the Pacific Northwest*. Washington, D.C.: Island Press, 1990.

Opie, John, ed. *Americans and Environment: The Controversy over Ecology*. Lexington, Mass.: D. C. Heath, 1971.

Odum, Eugene P. *Ecology and Our Endangered Life Support Systems*. Sunderland, Mass.: Sinauer Assoc., 1989.

Osborn, Fairfield. *Our Plundered Planet*. Boston: Little, Brown, 1948.

O'Toole, Randal. *Analysis of Region 5 Timber Yield Tables*. CHEC Research Paper no. 17. Oak Grove, Oreg.: Cascade Holistic Economic Consultants, September 1986.

————. *Reforming the Forest Service*. Washington, D.C.: Island Press, 1988.

O'Toole, Randal, and Karen Knudsen. *Growing Timber Deficits: Review of the Forest Service's 1990 Budget and Timber Sale Program*, CHEC Research Paper no. 23. Oak Grove, Oreg.: Cascade Holistic Economic Consultants, April 1991.

————. *Good Intentions: The Case For Repealing the Knutson-Vandenberg Act.*

CHEC Research Paper no. 24. Oak Grove, Oreg.: Cascade Holistic Economic Consultants, September 1991.

O'Toole, Randal, and Randy Selig. *A Critique of TSPIRS*. CHEC Research Paper no. 20. Oak Grove, Oreg.: Cascade Holistic Economic Consultants, November 1989.

Pinchot, Gifford. *The Fight for Conservation*. New York: Doubleday, 1910.

——. *Breaking New Ground*. New York: Harcourt, Brace, 1947.

Postel, Sandra, and John C. Ryan. "Reforming Forestry." Pp. 74–92 in *State of the World 1991: A Worldwatch Institute Report on Progress toward a Sustainable Society*, ed. by Lester R. Brown et al. New York: W. W. Norton, 1991.

Pyne, Stephen. *Fire in America: A Cultural History of Wildland and Rural Fire*. Princeton: Princeton University Press, 1982.

Raphael, Ray. *Tree Talk: The People and Politics of Timber*. Covelo, Calif.: Island Press, 1981.

Reiger, John. *American Sportsmen and the Origins of Conservation*. New York: Winchester Press, 1975.

Reisner, Marc. *Cadillac Desert*. New York: Penguin, 1986.

Richardson, Elmo. *Dams, Parks, and Politics*. Lexington: University Press of Kentucky, 1973.

——. *David T. Mason: Forestry Advocate*. Santa Cruz, Calif.: Forest History Society, 1983.

Robbins, William. *Lumberjacks and Legislators: Political Economy of the U.S. Lumber Industry, 1890–1941*. College Station: Texas A & M University, 1982.

——. *American Forestry: A History of National, State, and Private Cooperation*. Lincoln: University of Nebraska Press, 1985.

——. *Hard Times in Paradise: Coos Bay, Oregon, 1850–1986*. Seattle: University of Washington Press, 1988.

Robinson, Gordon. *The Forest and the Trees: A Guide to Excellent Forestry*. Washington, D.C.: Island Press, 1988.

Rowley, William D. *U.S. Forest Service Grazing and Rangelands: A History*. College Station: Texas A & M University, 1985.

Runte, Alfred. *National Parks: The American Experience*. 2nd ed. Lincoln: University of Nebraska Press, 1987.

——. *Public Lands, Public Heritage: The National Forest Idea*. Niwot, Colo.: Roberts Rinehart Publishers, 1991.

Sample, V. Alaric. *Below-Cost Timber Sales on the National Forests*. Washington, D.C.: Wilderness Society, 1984.

——. *The Impact of the Federal Budget Process on National Forest Planning*. New York: Greenwood Press, 1990.

——. *Land Stewardship in the Next Era of Conservation*. Milford, Pa.: Pinchot Institute for Conservation, Grey Towers Press, 1991.

Sears, Paul B. *Deserts on the March*. Norman: University of Oklahoma Press, 1959 [orig. pub. in 1935].

Sheperd, Jack. *The Forest Killers*. New York: Weybright & Talley, 1975.

Smith, Frank E. *Conservation in the United States, A Documentary History: Land and Water*. 2 vols. New York: Chelsea House, 1971.

Snow, C. P. *The Two Cultures: And a Second Look*. London: Cambridge University Press, 1964.

Society of American Foresters. *Proceedings of the Society of American Foresters*. (Annual meeting proceedings from the 1940s to the 1960s consulted.)

Steen, Harold. *The U.S. Forest Service: A History*. Seattle: University of Washington Press, 1976.

Twight, Ben W. *Organizational Values and Political Power: The Forest Service Versus the Olympic National Park*. University Park: Pennsylvania State University Press, 1983.

Udall, Stewart. *The Quiet Crisis*. New York: Holt, Rinehart & Winston, 1963.

Voigt, William, Jr. *Public Grazing Lands: Use and Misuse by Industry and Government*. New Brunswick: Rutgers University Press, 1976.

Vogt, William. *Road to Survival*. New York: William Sloane, 1948.

Waterman, Laura, and Guy Waterman. *Forest and Crag*. Boston: Appalachian Mountain Club, 1989.

Webb, Walter Prescott. *The Great Frontier*. Austin: University of Texas Press, 1951.

Weibe, Robert H. *The Search for Order, 1877–1920*. New York: Hill & Wang, 1967.

Western Association of State Game and Fish Commissioners. *Proceedings of the Thirty-Third Annual Conference of Western Association of State Game and Fish Commissioners*. Long Beach, Calif., June 1953.

Whyte, William H., Jr. *The Organization Man*. New York: Doubleday, 1956.

Wilkinson, Charles. *Crossing the Next Meridian: Land, Water, and the Future of the West*. Washington, D.C.: Island Press, 1992.

Williams, Michael. *Americans and Their Forests: A Historical Geography*. Cambridge: Cambridge University Press, 1989.

Worster, Donald. *Dust Bowl: The Southern Plains in the 1930s*. New York: Oxford University Press, 1979.

———. *Nature's Economy: A History of Ecological Ideas*. Cambridge: Cambridge University Press, 1985.

———. *Rivers of Empire*. New York: Pantheon Books, 1985.

Oral Histories

Cliff, Edward P. "Half a Century in Forest Conservation." USDA Forest Service, Washington Office, History Unit, 1981.

Crafts, Edward C. "Forest Service Researcher and Congressional Liaison: An Eye to Multiple Use." Interview with Susan Schrepfer. Santa Cruz: Forest History Society, 1972.

——. "Congress and the Forest Service, 1950–1962." An oral history conducted in 1965 by Amelia Fry. Regional Oral History Office, Bancroft Library, University of California, Berkeley, 1975.

Granger, Christopher M. "Forest Management in the United States Forest Service, 1907–1952." An oral history conducted in 1965 by Amelia Fry. Regional Oral History Office, Bancroft Library, University of California, Berkeley, 1965.

McArdle, Richard E. "Dr. Richard E. McArdle: An Interview with the Former Chief, U.S. Forest Service, 1952–1962." Interviewed by Elwood Maunder. Santa Cruz: Forest History Society, 1975.

McGuire, John R. "An Interview with John R. McGuire, Forest Service Chief, 1972–79." Conducted by Harold K. Steen. Durham, N.C.: Forest History Society and U.S. Forest Service, 1988.

Pyles, Hamilton K. "Multiple Use of the National Forests." Interview conducted by Susan R. Schrepfer. Santa Cruz: Forest History Society, 1972.

Robinson, Gordon. "Gordon Robinson: Forestry Consultant to the Sierra Club." Interview conducted by Harold K. Steen. San Francisco: Sierra Club History Committee, 1979.

Sieker, John H. "Recreation Policy and Administration in the U.S. Forest Service." In John H. Sieker and Lloyd Swift, "U.S. Forest Service, Recreation and Wildlife." An oral history conducted in 1964 by Amelia Fry. Regional Oral History Office, Bancroft Library, University of California, Berkeley, 1968.

Swift, Lloyd. "Wildlife Policy and Administration in the U.S. Forest Service." In John H. Sieker and Lloyd Swift, "U.S. Forest Service, Recreation and Wildlife." An oral history conducted in 1964 by Amelia Fry. Regional Oral History Office, Bancroft Library, University of California, Berkeley, revised 1975.

"Timber Management in the Pacific Northwest: Oral History of Five Region 6 Employees." Interviews by Dennis Roth and Jerry Williams. Washington, D.C.: USDA Forest Service, History Unit, 1986.

Towell, William E. "An Interview with William E. Towell." Interview conducted by Harold K. Steen. Durham, N.C.: Forest History Society, 1989.

Articles, Essays, Reports, Speeches

Adams, Kramer. "The Effects of Logging Old-Growth Timber on Landowner-Sportsman Relationships." *Proceedings: Society of American Foresters Meeting, 1955.* Washington, D.C.: SAF, 1956.

Adams, Sherman. "People and Conservation." *American Forests* 57 (Nov. 1951): 25–26.

AFSEEE. "Crisis on the Clearwater: The Mismanagement of a National Resource." Eugene, Oreg.: AFSEEE, Nov. 22, 1992.

Alexander, Thomas G. "Timber Management, Traditional Forestry, and Multiple-Use Stewardship: The Case of the Intermountain Region, 1950–85." *Journal of Forest History* 33 (Jan. 1989): 21–34.

Andrews, Richard N. L. "Class Politics or Democratic Reform: Environmentalism and American Political Institutions." *Natural Resources Journal* 20 (April 1980): 221–41.

Aston, E. R. "Multiple Use of Forest Lands in Western Pine Region." *Proceedings of the Fourth American Forest Congress, 1953,* pp. 176–78. Washington, D.C.: American Forestry Association, 1953.

Audubon Staff. "The Tree is Dead! Long Live the Tree!" *Audubon* 92 (Nov. 1990): 100.

Baden, John. "Spare That Tree!" *Forbes* (Dec. 9, 1991): 229–33.

Barber, Klaus H., and Susan A. Rodman. "FORPLAN: The Marvelous Toy." *Western Wildlands* 15 (Winter 1990): 18–22.

Barnett, Steele. "Logging — The Key to Forest Management." *Proceedings: Society of American Foresters Meeting, 1958,* pp. 62–65. Washington, D.C.: SAF, 1959.

Bassett, Ray E. "Recreational Forest Management as a Part of the Forestry Profession." *Proceedings: Society of American Foresters Meeting, Dec. 17–20, 1947,* pp. 153–58. Washington, D.C.: Society of American Foresters, 1948.

Behan, Richard W. "Multiresource Forest Management: A Paradigmatic Challenge to Professional Forestry." *Journal of Forestry* 88 (April 1990): 12–18.

——. "The RPA/NFMA: Solution to a Nonexistent Problem." *Western Wildlands* 15 (1990): 32–36.

Bodine, Leo V. "Comments on AFA's Forest Survey Resolution." *American Forests* 59 (April 1953): 4, 46.

Bolle, Arnold. "The Bitterroot Revisited: A University Re-View of the Forest Service." *Public Land Law Review* 10 (1989): 1–18.

Bonnicksen, Thomas. "Managing Biosocial Systems: A Framework to Organize Society-Environment Relationships." *Journal of Forestry* 89 (Oct. 1991): 10–15.

Briggs, Jean A. "Full Speed Ahead, Damn the Recession!" *Forbes* (March 5, 1979): 61, 64.

Brooks, Cheri. "The Difference between Dead Trees and Dying Forests: Tree Farming Revisited." *Inner Voice* 3 (Fall 1991): 5, 10.

Brown, Greg, and Charles C. Harris. "The U.S. Forest Service: Toward the New

Resource Management Paradigm?" *Society and Natural Resources* 5 (July/Sept. 1992): 231–45.

Budiansky, Stephen. "Sawdust and Mirrors." *U.S. News and World Report* (July 1, 1991): 55–57.

Carhart, Arthur. "Our Public Lands in Jeopardy." *Journal of Forestry* 46 (June 1948): 409–15.

———. "They Still Covet Our Lands." *American Forests* 59 (April 1953): 10.

Carrier, W. Dean. "The Forest Service: Divided against Itself." *High Country News* 24 (Dec. 28, 1992): 20.

Chapman, Herman H. "A Showdown on Federal Forest Regulation." *Journal of Forestry* 47 (Sept. 1949): 746–48.

———. "Scientific Forestry in National Parks and Wilderness Areas." *American Forests* 64 (Feb. 1958): 18–19, 39–41.

Clapp, Earl H. "Public Forest Regulation." *Journal of Forestry* 47 (July 1949): 528–29.

Clark, Donald E. "Management Planning for Future Multiple-Use Forestry on Western National Forests." *Proceedings: Society of American Foresters Meeting, 1958,* pp. 2–3. Washington, D.C.: SAF, 1959.

Cliff, Edward P. "Multiple Uses on National Forests." *Proceedings of the Fourth American Forest Congress, 1953,* pp. 161–65. Washington, D.C.: American Forestry Association, 1953.

Cochran, H. Dean. "Future Trends in Federal Employment of Foresters." *Proceedings: Society of American Foresters Meeting, Dec. 17–20, 1947,* pp. 43–45. Washington, D.C.: SAF, 1948.

Cortner, Hanna J., and Margaret Ann Moote. "Ecosystem Management: It's Not Only about Getting the Science Right. *Inner Voice* 5 (Jan./Feb. 1993): 1, 6.

Craddock, George W. "Watershed Management Problems of the Intermountain West." *Proceedings: Society of American Foresters Meeting, 1958.* Washington, D.C.: SAF, 1959.

Crafts, Edward C. "Public Forest Policy in a National Emergency." *Proceedings: Society of American Foresters Meeting, Dec. 14, 1951.* Washington, D.C.: SAF, 1951.

———. "Saga of a Law." In 2 parts. *American Forests* 76 (June and July 1970).

Davis, Lawrence S., and Frederic Wagner. "Forest Wildlife." In William A. Duerr, Dennis E. Teeguarden, Sam Guttenberg, and Neils B. Christiansen, eds. *Forest Resource Management: Decision Making Principles and Cases.* Corvallis: Oregon State University Book Stores, 1975.

DeBonis, Jeff. "New Perspectives." *Inner Voice* 2 (Summer/Fall 1990): 8–9.

———. "Retrenchment in the Forest Service: Hardliners Oust Mumma in the Northern Rockies." *Inner Voice* 3 (Fall 1991): 1–2.

———. "Timber Industry Wins Again, Congress Sets Dangerously High Timber Cut for '91." *Inner Voice* 3 (Winter 1991): 11.

Doherty, Jim. "When Folks Say 'Cutting Edge' at the Nez, They Don't Mean Saws." *Smithsonian* 23, no. 6 (Sept. 1992): 33–44.

Egan, Timothy. "Where Have All the Forests Gone?" *New York Times* (Feb. 15, 1989).

———. "Forest Service Abusing Role, Dissidents Say." *New York Times* (March 4, 1990).

———. "Forest Supervisors Say Politicians Are Asking Them to Cut Too Much." *New York Times* (Sept. 16, 1991), A1, A12.

———. "Land Deal Leaves Montana Logged and Hurt." *New York Times* (Oct. 19, 1993), A1, A7.

Evans, Willis A. "The Effect of Current West Coast Logging Practices upon Fisheries Resources." *Proceedings: Society of American Foresters Meeting, Nov. 15–19, 1959,* pp. 106–7. Washington, D.C.: SAF, 1960.

Foreman, Dave. "The New Conservation Movement." *Wild Earth* 1 (Summer 1991): 6–12.

Foss, Tim. "New Forestry: A State of Mind." *Inner Voice* 2 (Winter 1990): 4–6.

———. "New Perspectives, Old Interpretation?" *Inner Voice* 3 (Summer 1991): 13.

———. "Seizing the Moment in 1993." *Inner Voice* 5 (Jan./Feb. 1993): 1, 6.

Foster, J. Todd. "Critics Say Agency Is Eating Its Young." *High Country News* 25 (Jan. 25, 1993): 2.

Frank, Bernard. "Forest Resource Evaluation in the Public Interest." In *Proceedings: Society of American Foresters Meeting, Dec. 17–20, 1947,* pp. 65–75. Washington, D.C.: SAF, 1948.

Franklin, Jerry. "Toward a New Forestry." *American Forests* 95 (Nov./Dec. 1989): 37–44.

Franklin, Marcia. "An Idaho Forest Is Told: Log." *High Country News* 24 (Dec. 14, 1992): 15.

Fredriksen, R. L. "Comparative Water Quality-Natural and Disturbed Streams Following Logging and Slash Burning." *Proceedings of a Symposium, Forest Land Uses and Stream Environment,* ed. by J. T. Krygier and J. D. Hall. Corvallis: Oregon State University, 1971.

Fredriksen, R. L., D. G. Moore, and L. A. Norris. "The Impact of Timber Harvest, Fertilization, and Herbicide Treatment on Streamwater Quality in Western Oregon and Washington." *Forest Soils and Forest Land Management,* Proceedings of the Fourth North American Forest Soils Conference, ed. by B. Bernier and C. H. Winget, pp. 283–313. Quebec: Les Presses de L'Université Laval, 1975.

Granger, Chris. "The National Forests Are in the Black," *American Forests* 58 (July 1952): 6–9.

———. "Comments on AFA's Forest Survey Resolution." *American Forests* 59 (April 1953): 4, 46.

———. "Federal Forest Landownership." *Proceedings of the Fourth American Forest Congress, 1953*, pp. 296–300. Washington, D.C.: American Forestry Association, 1953.

———. "A 'Square Deal' for Half a Century." *American Forests* 59 (June 1953): 19, 47–51.

Greeley, Arthur W. "Protecting the Public's Interest in Converting the Old Forest to New." *Proceedings: Society of American Foresters Meeting, 1955*, pp. 1–4. Washington, D.C.: SAF, 1956.

Gregg, Frank. "Public Land Policy: Controversial Beginnings for the Third Century." *Government and Environmental Politics*, ed. by Michael Lacey, pp. 141–81. Washington, D.C.: Smithsonian Institution, 1988.

Hagenstein, William D. "Tree Farms: Greener Every Year." An address delivered at the University of British Columbia, Vancouver, March 17, 1977.

Hall, Albert. "Washington Lookout." *American Forests*. (Monthly column reviewing political activity regarding forestry matters, throughout 1950s.)

Hanson, Dennis. "The Aspect of the Tally Sheet: Some Notes on the Business of Trees." *Wilderness* 47 (Summer 1983): 24–31.

Harrison, Henry. "How Much Land for Forest Recreation?" *Proceedings, Society of American Foresters Meeting, 1958*. Washington, D.C.: SAF, 1959.

Harvey, Mark. "Echo Park, Glen Canyon, and the Post-War Wilderness Movement." *Pacific Historical Review* 60 (1991): 43–67.

Heady, Harold F. "The Rangeland System." In William A. Duerr, Dennis E. Teeguarden, Sam Guttenberg, and Neils B. Christiansen, eds., *Forest Resource Management: Decision Making Principles and Cases*. Corvallis: Oregon State University Book Stores, 1975.

Herbert, Paul A. "Multiple Use of Forest Land." *American Forest Congress Proceedings, 1953*, pp. 169–71. Washington, D.C.: American Forestry Association, 1953.

Hibbert, A. R. "Forest Treatment Effects on Water Yield." *International Symposium on Forest Hydrology*, ed. by W. E. Sopper and H. W. Lull, pp. 527–43. New York: Pergamon Press.

High Country News (staff). "Two Say Politics Rules Their Agencies." *High Country News* 23 (Oct. 7, 1991): 1, 10–13.

Hinchman, Steve. "Forest Service Can't Get the Cut Out." *High Country News* 24 (Dec. 14, 1992): 12–13.

Hines, L. G. "The Myth of Idle Resources: A Reconsideration of the Concept of Nonuse in Conservation." *Transactions of the Eighteenth North American Wildlife Conference,* pp. 28–35. Washington, D.C.: Wildlife Management Institute, 1953.

Hopkins, Walt, J. D. Sinclair, and P. B. Rowe. "From Forest Influences to Applied Watershed Management in Southern California." *Proceedings: Society of American Foresters Meeting, 1958,* pp. 36–38. Washington, D.C.: SAF, 1959.

Humphrey, Robert R. "The Desert Grassland: A History of Vegetational Changes and an Analysis of Causes." *Botanical Review* 24 (1958): 193–252.

Keene, Roy. "Salvage Logging: Health or Hoax." *Inner Voice* 5 (March/April 1993): 1, 4.

Koppes, Clayton. "Environmental Policy and American Liberalism: The Department of the Interior, 1933–1953." In Kendall E. Bailes, ed., *Environmental History: Critical Issues in Comparative Perspective,* pp. 437–75. Lanham, Md.: University Press of America, 1985.

Knickerbocker, Brad. "Fight for Federal Lands Spreads." *Christian Science Monitor* (March 14, 1990): 7.

Knize, Perri. "The Mismanagement of the National Forests." *Atlantic Monthly* (Oct. 1991): 98–112.

Lemonick, Michael D. "Whose Woods Are These?" *Time* (Dec. 9, 1991): 70–75.

Leonard, Justin. "People and the Land." *Pennsylvania Angler* 25 (1956): 6–9.

Leopold, Aldo. "Wild Lifers vs. Game Farmers: A Plea for Democracy in Sport." *Bulletin of the American Game Protective Association* (April 1919). Reprinted in Dave E. Brown and Neil B. Carmony, eds., *Aldo Leopold's Wilderness.* Harrisburg, Pa.: Stackpole Books, 1990.

———. "A Biotic View of Land." *Journal of Forestry* 37, no. 9 (Sept. 1939): 730.

Ludwig, Jim. "Pin Arguments on Demand, Forest Researcher Advises." *Missoulian* (Sept. 13, 1991).

Lynch, Jim, J. Todd Foster, and Julie Titone. "Our Failing Forests." Special supplements to *Spokesman Review* (Nov. 21, 1993), H1–H10; (Nov. 25, 1993), A1, A6–A7; and (Nov. 28, 1993), H1–H6 (Spokane, Wash.).

Mair, W. Winston. "Toward an Ecological Conscience." *Proceedings of the Thirty-Sixth Annual Conference of the Western Association of State Game and Fish Commissioners,* June 1956, pp. 14–17.

Marston, Ed. "Rocks and Hard Places." *Wilderness* 54 (Spring 1991): 38–45.

Marx, D. H., and W. C. Bryan. "The Significance of Mycorrhizae to Forest Trees." *Forest Soils and Forest Land Management.* Proceedings of the Fourth North American Forest Soils Conference. Ed. by B. Bernier and C. H. Winget, pp. 107–17. Quebec: Les Presses de L'Université Laval, 1975.

McArdle, Richard A. "Why We Needed the Multiple Use Bill." *American Forests* 76 (June 1970): 10, 59.

McCarthy, Catherine, Paul Sabatier, and John Loomis. "Attitudinal Change in the Forest Service: 1960–1990." Forthcoming in *Society and Natural Resources*.

McCloskey, J. Michael. "Natural Resources — National Forests: The Multiple Use–Sustained Yield Act of 1960." *Oregon Law Review* 41 (Dec. 1961): 49–77.

———. "The Wilderness Act of 1964: Its Background and Meaning." *Oregon Law Review* 45 (June 1966): 288–321.

McConnell, Grant. "The Conservation Movement — Past and Present." *Western Political Quarterly* 7 (September 1954): 463–78.

McCormick, John. "Can't See the Forest for the Sleaze." *New York Times* (Jan. 29, 1992): A21.

McKay, Douglas. "Oregon States Its Case against Socialized Forestry." *American Forests* 57 (Jan. 1951).

McQuillan, Alan. "Inside Mumma-Gate." *Missoula Independent* (Oct. 31, 1991): 18–19.

———. "Accelerated Cutting on Private Industrial Timberlands." *Missoula Independent* (Nov. 7, 1991): 19–20.

———. "From Pinchot to Post-Modern: The Circular Century of U.S. Forestry." *Inner Voice* 4 (Nov./Dec. 1992): 10–11.

———. "New Perspectives: Forestry for a Postmodern Age." *Western Wildlands* (Winter 1992): 13–20.

McSpadden-Wenner, Lettie. "The Misuse and Abuse of NEPA." *Environmental [History] Review* 7, no. 3 (Fall 1983): 229–54.

Miller, Char. "The Prussians Are Coming! The Prussians Are Coming!: Bernhard Fernow and the Roots of the USDA Forest Service." *Journal of Forestry* 89 (March 1991): 23–27, 42.

Mohai, Paul. "Public Participation and Natural Resource Decision-Making: The Case of the RARE II Decisions." *Natural Resources Journal* 27 (Winter 1987): 123–55.

Mohai, Paul, and Phyllis Stillman. "Are We Headed in the Right Direction? A Survey of USDA Forest Service Employees." Ann Arbor: University of Michigan, School of Natural Resources and Environment, October 1993.

Mohai, Paul, Phyllis Stillman, Pamela Jakes, and Chris Liggett. "Assessing the Impacts of Gender, Race, and Professional Training on Forest Service Attitudes and Perceptions." Paper presented at the meeting of the Society of American Foresters, Indianapolis, November 1993.

Moir, Stuart. "Timber as Collateral." *Proceedings of the Fourth American Forest Congress, 1953*, pp. 227–29. Washington, D.C.: American Forestry Association, 1953.

Montgomery, Peter. "Science Friction." *Common Cause* 16 (Nov./Dec. 1990): 24–29.

Mott, Richard. "NEPA Violations and Equitable Discretion." *Oregon Law Review* 64, no. 3 (1986): 497–512.

Mulford, Walter. "The Decade 1948–1958 in the Forestry Schools of the United States." *Proceedings: Society of American Foresters Meeting, Dec. 17–20, 1947*, pp. 59–63. Washington, D.C.: SAF, 1948.

National Wildlife Federation. *Conservation Report.* (Semiweekly political reports; 1950s reports issued by Carl Shoemaker, NWF Conservation Director, primarily consulted.)

Native Forest Council. *Forest Voice.* P.O. Box 2171, Eugene Oregon, 97402. (Environmental journal of the Pacific Northwest, founded 1989.)

"Northwest Forests: Day of Reckoning." Special Supplement to the *Oregonian* (Portland, Oct. 15, 1990).

Ogden, Phil R. "Ramifications of Vegetation Manipulation, Positive and Negative Aspects." *Rangeland Policies for the Future, Proceedings of a Symposium, January 28–31, 1979, Tucson, Arizona.* Washington, D.C.: GPO, Oct. 1979.

O'Toole, Randal. "The Knutson-Vandenberg Act: National Forest Enemy Number One." *Reform!* 1 (March–April 1989). Oak Grove, OR: Cascade Holistic Economic Consultants.

———. "Citizens' Guide to the Forest Service Budget." *Forest Watch* 12 (April 1992): 1–38.

Parke, William. "Recent Experiments in Administering and Charging for Camping and Picnicking Privileges on the National Forests." *Journal of Forestry* 48 (April 1950): 275–77.

Parry, B. Thomas, Vaux, Henry J., and Dennis, Nicholas. "Changing Conceptions of Sustained Yield Policy on the National Forests." *Journal of Forestry* 81 (March 1983): 150–54.

Pechanec, Joseph. "Our Range Society." *Journal of Range Management* 1 (October 1948): 1–2.

Peck, Norman. "On Organizational Models . . ." *Inner Voice* 5 (Jan./Feb. 1993): 14.

Ribe, Tom. "To ASQ or Not to ASQ: Timber Targets vs. Environmental Protection." *Inner Voice* 2 (Summer/Fall 1990): 1, 14.

———. "Rangering from Capitol Hill." *Inner Voice* 3 (Spring 1991): 5, 7.

Riley, Michael. "The Bighorn's Fatally Flawed Forest Plan." *High Country News* (Dec. 14, 1992): 15.

Robbins, William G. "Lumber Production and Community Stability: A View from the Pacific Northwest." *Journal of Forest History* 31 (1987): 187–96.

———. "The Western Lumber Industry." In Gerald D. Nash and Richard Etulain, eds.

The Twentieth-Century West. Albuquerque: University of New Mexico Press, 1989.

Rothacher, Jack. "Regimes of Streamflow and Their Modification by Logging." *Proceedings of a Symposium, Forest Land Uses and Stream Environment,* ed. by J. T. Krygier and J. D. Hall. Corvallis: Oregon State University, 1971.

Salwasser, Hal. "Gaining Perspective: Forestry for the Future." *Journal of Forestry* 88 (Nov. 1990): 32–38.

Sandoz, Fred J. "Our Citizens among Our Trees." *Proceedings: Society of American Foresters Meeting, 1958,* pp. 7–11. Washington, D.C.: SAF, 1959.

Sawyer, Robert. "The Whole Story." *American Forests* 59 (March 1953): 10.

Schiff, Ashley. "Innovation and Administrative Decision-Making: The Conservation of Land Resources." *Administrative Science Quarterly* 2 (June 1966): 1–30.

Schneider, Keith. "U.S. Would End Cutting of Trees in Many Forests." *New York Times* (April 30, 1993), A1, A12.

Schneider, P. W. "The Effects of Logging Old-Growth Timber on Fish Management." *Proceedings, Society of American Foresters Meeting, 1955.* Washington, D.C.: SAF, 1956.

Schrepfer, Susan R. "Establishing Administrative 'Standing': The Sierra Club and the Forest Service." *Pacific Historical Review* 58 (Feb. 1989): 55–81.

Schulte, Bridgid. "Busted Timber Towns Seek New Economic Foundation." *High Country News* 24 (Sept. 7, 1992): 4.

Schwennesen, Don. "Forest Biologist Cites Pressure to Sell." *Missoulian* (March 31, 1992): A-1.

Sears, Paul B. "Ecology — A Subversive Subject." *BioScience* 14 (July 1964): 11–13.

Shoemaker, Carl. "Status of Some Pending Bills in Congress." *Proceedings of the Thirty-Third Annual Conference of Western Association of State Game and Fish Commissioners.* Pp. 8–9. Long Beach, Calif., 1953.

Sierra Club. *Public Lands Activist.* (Semimonthly national Sierra Club Public Lands Committee newsletter.)

Spencer, John W. "The Place of Recreation in the Multiple-Use Management of the National Forests." *Proceedings: Society of American Foresters Meeting, Dec. 17–20, 1947,* pp. 179–82. Washington, D.C.: SAF, 1948.

Stamm, E. P. "Converting the Old Growth Forest: Utilization and Road Problems." *Proceedings: Society of American Foresters Meeting, 1955,* pp. 5–7. Washington, D.C.: SAF, 1956.

Steinbrenner, E. C., and S. P. Gessel. "Effect of Tractor Logging on Soils and Regeneration in the Douglas-Fir Region of Southwestern Washington." *Proceedings: Society of American Foresters Meeting, 1955,* pp. 77–80. Washington, D.C.: SAF, 1956.

Sterling, E. M. "The Myth of Multiple Use." *American Forests* 76 (June 1970): 24–27.

Stewart, Richard. "The Reformation of American Administrative Law." *Harvard Law Review* 88 (1975): 1667–1813.

Stone, E. L. "Soil and Man's Use of Forest Land." *Forest Soils and Forest Land Management.* Proceedings of the Fourth North American Forest Soils Conference. Ed. by B. Bernier and C. H. Winget. Quebec: Les Presses de L'Université Laval, 1975.

Turner, Lewis M. "Training Wildland Managers." *Journal of Forestry* 44 (July 1946): 491–96.

Twight, Ben W. "Bernhard Fernow and Prussian Forestry in America." *Journal of Forestry* 88 (Feb. 1990): 21–25.

Twight, Ben W., and Fremont J. Lyden. "Measuring Forest Service Bias." *Journal of Forestry* 87 (May 1989): 35–41.

Twight, Ben W., Fremont J. Lyden, and E. Thomas Tuchmann. "Constituency Bias in a Federal Career System? A Study of District Rangers of the U.S. Forest Service." *Administration and Society* 22 (Nov. 1990): 358–89.

Udall, Stewart. "Wilderness." *Living Wilderness* 80 (Spring/Summer 1962): 4.

Waring, R. H., and J. F. Franklin. "Evergreen Coniferous Forests of the Pacific Northwest." *Science* 240 (1979): 1380–86.

Wilkinson, Charles F., and H. Michael Anderson. "Land and Resource Planning in the National Forests." *Oregon Law Review* 64 (1985): 1–373.

Williams, C. S. "Integration of Agricultural Herbicide Methods for Vegetation Management on Rangelands." *Rangeland Policies for the Future, Proceedings of a Symposium, January 28–31, 1979, Tucson, Arizona.* Washington, D.C.: GPO, Oct. 1979.

Wolf, Robert E. "National Forest Timber Sales and the Legacy of Gifford Pinchot: Managing a Forest and Making It Pay." *University of Colorado Law Review* 60 (1989): 1037–78.

———. "The Concept of Multiple Use: The Evolution of the Idea within the Forest Service and the Enactment of the Multiple-Use Sustained-Yield Act of 1960." Written for the U.S. Office of Technology Assessment, Contract no. N-3-2465.0. Unpublished. Washington, D.C., Dec. 1990.

Woods, John B. "Report of the Forest Resource Appraisal." *American Forests* 52 (Sept. 1946): 414–28.

Woodward, Hugh. "In Defense of the Aiken Grazing Bill." *American Forests* 60 (July 1954): 34–36.

Wuerthner, George. "The Price Is Wrong." *Sierra* 75 (Sept.–Oct. 1990): 38–43.

———. "How the West Was Eaten." *Wilderness* 54 (Spring 1991): 28–37.

Voigt, William, Jr. "Can We Beat Back the Attack on the Public Lands." *Transactions of the Fourteenth North American Wildlife Conference,* pp. 136–42. Washington, D.C.: Wildlife Management Institute, 1949.

——. "Multiple Use." *Proceedings of the Fourth American Forest Congress, 1953,* pp. 178–80. Washington, D.C.: American Forestry Association, 1953.

Zahniser, Howard. "Wilderness in a Multiple Use Forestry Program." *Proceedings of the Fourth American Forest Congress, 1953,* pp. 171–73. Washington, D.C.: American Forestry Association, 1953.

——. "The Case for Wilderness Preservation Legislation." *Proceedings: Society of American Foresters Meeting, 1958,* pp. 104–10. Washington, D.C.: SAF, 1959.

Unpublished Archival Collections

CHEC (Cascade Holistic Economic Consultants) Forest Planning Bibliography (Oak Grove, Oregon)

Federal Records Center (FRC) of Seattle

Forest History Society (FHS) archives:

    National Forest Products Association (NFPA)/National Lumber Manufacturers Association (NLMA)

    Society of American Foresters (SAF)

    Western Timber Association (WTA)

    Oral Histories

University of Montana Archives (Missoula):

    Senator James E. Murray Papers

    Robert Wolf Papers

    Oral Histories

USDA Forest Service, Washington Office, History Unit collections

USDA Forest Service, Pacific Northwest Regional Office, Portland, Oregon, historical records

USDA Forest Service, Northern Regional Office, Missoula, Montana, historical records

USDA Forest Service, historical records from various national forest supervisors' offices

Wilderness Society records, Denver Public Library, Western History Branch.

Government Documents

CONGRESSIONAL PUBLICATIONS, HEARINGS, RECORDS
(PARTIAL LISTING BY DATE)

U.S. Congress. Senate. *A National Plan for American Forestry,* 2 vols. Senate Doc. 12. 73rd Cong., 1st sess., March 27, 1933.

U.S. Congress. House and Senate Committees on Appropriations, Subcommittees on Agricultural Appropriations and Interior Appropriations. (Annual federal budget hearings related to the Forest Service, 1945–1961, consulted.)

U.S. Congress. House of Representatives Committee on Agriculture. Hearing on HR 1972. "Disposition of Moneys from the National Forests." 83rd Cong., 1st sess., March 11, 12, 1953.

U.S. Congress. Senate. Committee on Interior and Insular Affairs. *National Wilderness Preservation Act.* Hearings on S. 1176. 85th Cong., 1st sess., June 19–20, 1957.

U.S. Congress. House of Representatives. Committee on Agriculture. Hearings on "Long-Range Program for the National Forests." 86th Cong., 1st sess., May 14–15, 1959.

U.S. Congress. House of Representatives. Committee on Agriculture. Subcommittee on Forests. Hearings on H.R. 10572, "The Multiple Use–Sustained Yield Act of 1960." 86th Cong., 2nd sess., March 16, 1960.

U.S. Congress. Senate Interior Committee. Hearing on S. J. 95. "Acceleration of the Reforestation Programs." 86th Cong., 2nd sess., April 22, 1960.

U.S. Congress. House of Representatives. *Message from the President of the United States Transmitting the National Wilderness Preservation System.* House Doc. 79. 89th Cong., 1st sess., Feb. 8, 1965.

U.S. Congress. Public Land Law Review Commission (Paul W. Gates). *A History of Public Land Law Development.* Washington, D.C.: GPO, 1968.

U.S. Congress. Senate Banking Committee. "Problems in Lumber Pricing and Production." 91st Cong., 1st sess., 1969.

U.S. Congress. Senate Committee on Interior and Insular Affairs. "A University View of the Forest Service." 91st Cong., 2nd sess., 1970. Sen. Doc. 91–115. Prepared by a Select Committee of the University of Montana. ("The Bolle Report.")

U.S. Congress. Senate Subcommittee on Public Lands of the Committee on Interior and Insular Affairs. *"Clearcutting" Practices on National Timberlands,* 3 vols. 92nd Cong., 1st sess., 1971.

U.S. Congress. Senate Subcommittee on Conservation and Forestry of the Committee on Agriculture. "Review the Sustainabiity of Forest Resources." 101st Cong., 1st sess., June 21, 1989.

U.S. Congress. Senate Subcommittee on Conservation and Forestry of the Committee on Agriculture, "Oversight Hearing on the Management Practices of the U.S. Forest Service and Below-Cost Timber Sales." 101st Cong., 1st sess., Oct. 30, 1989.

U.S. Congress. House Subcommittee on Forests, Family Farms, and Energy of the

House Committee on Agriculture. "Timber Sale Economics and Information Reporting System." 101st Cong., 1st sess., Nov. 21, 1989.

U.S. Congress. House Subcommittee on Forests, Family Farms, and Energy, Committee on Agriculture. "National Forest Timber Supply Outlook and Sustainable Timber Yield." 101st Cong., 2nd sess., March 6, 1990.

U.S. Congress. Senate Subcommittee on Conservation and Forestry of the Committee on Agriculture, "Oversight on Below-Cost Timber Sales and National Forest Management." 102nd Cong., 1st sess., April 11, 1991.

U.S. Congress. Subcommittee on Environment, Energy, and Natural Resources of the House Committee on Government Operations. "Review of the Forest Service's Timber Sale Program." 102nd Cong., 2nd sess., March 31, 1992.

FOREST SERVICE PUBLICATIONS

USDA Forest Service. *Washington Office Information Digest.* (Periodic newsletter, consulted for 1940s and 1950s. Housed in Washington Office Forest Service History Unit. Contact: Dr. Terry West.)

USDA Forest Service. *Reports of the Chief of the Forest Service.* (Annual reports, 1930s–1980s.)

USDA Forest Service. *Forests and National Prosperity: A Reappraisal of the Forest Situation in the United States.* USDA Misc. Pub. no. 688. Washington, D.C., GPO, 1948.

USDA Forest Service, Lolo National Forest. *Report for 1955* (no date).

USDA Forest Service. *Timber Resources for America's Future.* Forest Resource Report no. 14. Washington, D.C.: GPO, Jan. 1958. [Often referred to as the Timber Resources Review.]

USDA Forest Service, Northern Regional Office. *Full Use and Development of Montana's Timber Resources.* Also published as Senate Doc. 9, 86th Congress, 1st sess., Jan. 27, 1959.

Connaughton, Charles A. "Multiple Use of Forest Land." USDA Forest Service publication, 1959.

USDA Forest Service. "Program for the National Forests." Miscellaneous Publication 794. Washington, D.C.: GPO, 1959. Reprinted in the *Congressional Record,* 86th Cong. 1st sess. (March 24, 1959).

USDA Forest Service. "Program for the National Forests: Estimates of Work Needed and Costs by States for the Short Term — Initial 12 Years." Washington, D.C.: GPO, May 1959.

USDA Forest Service. *National Forest Wildlife: Operation Outdoors, Part Two.* Washington, D.C.: GPO, Feb. 1961.

USDA Forest Service. Northwest Regional Office. *Long-Range Management Policy and Objectives for the High Mountain Areas of the Region.* Portland, Oreg., Oct. 20, 1961.

USDA Forest Service. "Report on National Forest Timber Resource Operations." Washington, D.C., 1956–65. (Located in NFPA records box 54, Forest History Society Archives.)

USDA Forest Service. *Douglas-fir Supply Study.* Portland, Oreg.: Pacific Northwest Forest and Range Experiment Station, 1969.

USDA Forest Service. Budget Branch. "Budgets 1961–1970 Composite Comparison." Aug. 13, 1970. "Budgets 1963–1973." Feb. 21, 1973. (Located in Western Timber Association box 31, Forest Service Budget file no. 2.411.)

USDA Forest Service: Fredriksen, R. L. "Erosion and Sedimentation following Road Construction and Timber Harvest on Unstable Soils in Three Small Western Oregon Watersheds." Pacific Northwest Forest and Range Experiment Station. Research Paper PNW-104, 1970.

USDA Forest Service, Washington Office. "A Forest Service Environmental Program for the Future," draft, April 1971. (First produced as "A Forest Service Environmental Program for the 1970s," draft, Sept. 25, 1970.)

USDA Forest Service, Wyoming Forest Study Team. "Forest Management in Wyoming," 1971.

USDA Forest Service. Washington Office. "The Outlook for Timber in the United States: A Preliminary Summary of the 1970 Timber Review." Dec. 1972.

Martin, Clark S. "Ecology and Management of Southwestern Semi-Desert Grass-Shrub Ranges: The Status of Our Knowledge." U.S.D.A. Forest Service Research Paper RM-156. Rocky Mountain Forest and Range Experiment Station, Ft. Collins, Colo., 1975.

USDA Forest Service. *Forest Statistics of the U.S., 1977.* Washington, D.C.: GPO, 1978.

USDA Forest Service, Pacific Northwest Region. *Analysis of the Management Situation, Gifford Pinchot National Forest.* Portland, Oreg., no date (1982?).

Mastran, Shelly Smith, and Nan Lowerre. *Mountaineers and Rangers: A History of Federal Forest Management in the Southern Appalachians, 1900–1981.* FS-380. Washington, D.C.: USDA Forest Service, 1983.

Maser, Chris, and J. M. Trappe, eds. "The Seen and Unseen World of the Fallen Tree." USDA Forest Service General Technical Report, PNW-164. Portland, Oreg.: Pacific Northwest Research Station, 1984.

Roth, Dennis. *The Wilderness Movement and the National Forests: 1964–1980.* Washington, D.C.: USDA Forest Service, Dec. 1984.

USDA Forest Service and USDI Bureau of Land Management. *1985 Grazing Fee Review and Evaluation – Draft Report.* Washington, D.C.: GPO, 1985.

Schuster, Ervin G., and J. Greg Jones. "Below-Cost Timber Sales: Analysis of a Forest Policy Issue." General Technical Report INT-183. Ogden, Utah: USDA Forest Service, Intermountain Research Station, May 1985.

Alexander, Thomas G. *The Rise of Multiple Use Management in the Intermountain West: A History of Region 4 of the Forest Service.* FS-399. Washington, D.C.: Forest Service, May 1987.

USDA Forest Service, Pacific Northwest Research Station. *Forest Statistics of the United States, 1987.* Forest Service Resource Bulletin, PNW-168.

Roth, Dennis. *The Wilderness Movement and the National Forests: 1980–1984.* Washington, D.C.: USDA Forest Service, Aug. 1988.

Maser, Chris, R. F. Tarrant, J. M. Trappe, and J. F. Franklin. "From the Forest to the Sea, A Story of Fallen Trees." USDA Forest Service General Technical Report. Portland, Oreg.: Pacific Northwest Research Station, 1988.

Baker, Robert D., Robert S. Maxwell, Victor Treat, and Henry C. Dethloff. *Timeless Heritage: A History of the Forest Service in the Southwest.* FS-409. Washington, D.C.: USDA Forest Service, Aug. 1988.

USDA Forest Service. *RPA Assessment of the Forest and Rangeland Situation in the United States.* Washington, D.C., May 1989.

USDA Forest Service. *Resources Planning Act 1989 Assessment: Fact Kit,* FS-430. Washington, D.C.: GPO, May 1989.

USDA Forest Service. "Sunbird Proceedings": 2nd National Forest Supervisor's Conference, Tucson, Arizona: Nov. 13–16, 1989. (In author's possession; portions of the proceedings reprinted in *Inner Voice* 2 [Winter 1990]: 7, 11.)

USDA Forest Service. *Timber Sale Program Annual Report, Fiscal Year 1988 Test, National Summary.* Washington, D.C.: USDA Forest Service, 1989.

USDA Forest Service. *The Forest Service Program for Forest and Rangeland Resources.* Washington, D.C.: USDA Forest Service, May 1990.

USDA Forest Service. *An Analysis of the Timber Situation in the United States: 1989–2040.* General Technical Report RM-199. Fort Collins, Colo.: Rocky Mountain Forest and Range Experiment Station, December 1990.

Steen, Harold K. *The Beginning of the National Forest System.* USDA Forest Service, Washington, D.C.: GPO, 1991.

Williams, Gerald. "Forest Service Leadership: Credibility Problems Facing Current and Future Leaders." Unpublished essay. Umpqua and Willamette National Forests, Roseburg and Eugene, Oregon, Feb. 1992.

MISCELLANEOUS GOVERNMENT DOCUMENTS (ARRANGED BY DATE)

U.S. Department of Agriculture. *Soils and Men: 1938 Yearbook of Agriculture.* Washington, D.C.: GPO, 1938.

The President's Materials Policy Commission. *Resources for Freedom,* vol. 1, *Foundations for Growth and Security.* Washington, D.C.: GPO, June 1952.

White House Conference on Conservation: Official Proceedings. Washington, D.C.: GPO, 1963.

Report of the President's Advisory Panel on Timber and the Environment. Washington, D.C.: GPO, April 1973.

U.S. Department of the Interior and U.S. Department of Agriculture. *Study of Fees for Grazing Livestock on Federal Lands.* Washington, D.C.: GPO, Oct. 21, 1977.

Bean, Michael. *The Evolution of National Wildlife Law.* Report to the Council on Environmental Quality. Washington, D.C.: GPO, 1977.

U.S. General Accounting Office. *Need to Concentrate Intensive Timber Management on High Productive Lands.* Washington, D.C.: GPO, 1978.

Rangeland Policies for the Future, Proceedings of a Symposium, January 28–31, 1979, Tucson, Arizona. Washington, D.C.: GPO, Oct. 1979.

Council on Environmental Quality. *Global 2000 Report.* Washington, D.C.: GPO, 1980.

U.S. General Accounting Office. "Report to the Congress: Congress Needs Better Information on Forest Service's Below-Cost Timber Sales." GAO/RCED-84–96. Washington, D.C.: GPO, June 28, 1984.

Congressional Research Service. *State by State Estimate of Situations Where Timber Will Be Sold at a Loss or Profit: A Report to the Subcommittee on Interior Appropriations.* Washington, D.C.: Library of Congress, CRS, 1984.

U.S. General Accounting Office. "Some Riparian Areas Restored but Widespread Improvement Will Be Slow." GAO/RCED-88–105. Washington, D.C.: GPO, June 1988.

U.S. General Accounting Office. "Public Land Management: Attention to Wildlife Is Limited." GAO/RCED-91–64. Washington, D.C.: GPO, March 1991.

U.S. General Accounting Office. *Forest Service: The Flathead National Forest Cannot Meet Its Timber Goal.* GAO/RCED-91–124. Washington, D.C.: GPO, May 1991.

U.S. Office of Technology Assessment. *Forest Service Planning: Accommodating Uses, Producing Outputs, and Sustaining Ecosystems,* OTA-F-505. Washington, D.C.: GPO, Feb. 1992.

Index